Making and Managing Public Policy

Understanding how public policy is made and managed is a key component in studying the disciplines of public management and administration. Such are the complexities associated with this topic that a deeper understanding is vital to ensure practising public managers excel in their roles.

This textbook synthesizes the key theories, providing a contemporary understanding of public policy and how it relates to private and other sectors. It integrates this with the management and implementation of public policy, including outlines of organizations, practices and instruments used.

Pedagogical features include chapter synopses, learning objectives, boxed international cases and vignettes and further reading suggestions. This useful, concise textbook will be required reading for public management students and all those interested in public policy.

Karen Johnston Miller is Professor of Politics and Public Policy at Glasgow Caledonian University. She has worked in Africa, the USA and UK for public, non-governmental and academic institutions. Her research areas are: public policy, governance, political–administrative relations and representative bureaucracy. Professor Johnston Miller has published extensively in these areas. She is a board member of a number of learned societies and editorial boards, and is joint editor of the journal, *Public Policy and Administration*.

Duncan McTavish is Professor of Public Policy and Management at Glasgow Caledonian University. He has worked in a number of universities and has operated in the UK and internationally as an academic, teacher, researcher and consultant. He has authored a substantial number of articles, books and other publications. He has also project managed major research projects. Professor McTavish is joint editor of *Public Policy and Administration*.

ROUTLEDGE MASTERS IN PUBLIC MANAGEMENT

Edited by Stephen P. Osborne, Owen Hughes, Walter Kickert

Routledge Masters in Public Management series is an integrated set of texts. It is intended to form the backbone for the holistic study of the theory and practice of public management as part of:

*   a taught Masters, MBA or MPA course at a university or college;
*   a work-based, in-service programme of education and training; or
*   a programme of self-guided study.

Each volume stands alone in its treatment of its topic, whether it be strategic management, marketing or procurement and is co-authored by leading specialists in their field. However, all volumes in the series share both a common pedagogy and a common approach to the structure of the text. Key features of all volumes in the series include:

*   a critical approach to combining theory with practice which educates its reader, rather than solely teaching him/her a set of skills;
*   clear learning objectives for each chapter;
*   the use of figures, tables and boxes to highlight key ideas, concepts and skills;
*   an annotated bibliography, guiding students in their further reading; and
*   a dedicated case study in the topic of each volume, to serve as a focus for discussion and learning.

Managing Change and Innovation in Public Service Organizations
Stephen P. Osborne and Kerry Brown

Risk and Crisis Management in the Public Sector
Lynn T. Drennan and Allan McConnell

Contracting for Public Services
Carsten Greve

Performance Management in the Public Sector
Wouter van Dooren, Geert Bouckaert and John Halligan

Financial Management and Accounting in the Public Sector
Gary Bandy

Strategic Leadership in the Public Sector
Paul Joyce

Managing Local Governments: Designing Management Control Systems that Deliver Value
Emanuele Padovani and David W. Young

Marketing Management and Communications in the Public Sector
Martial Pasquier and Jean-Patrick Villeneuve

Ethics and Management in the Public Sector
Alan Lawton, Julie Rayner and Karin Lasthuizen

Making and Managing Public Policy
Karen Johnston Miller and Duncan McTavish

Making and Managing Public Policy

Karen Johnston Miller and
Duncan McTavish

Routledge
Taylor & Francis Group

LONDON AND NEW YORK

First published 2014
by Routledge
2 Park Square, Milton Park, Abingdon, Oxon OX14 4RN

and by Routledge
711 Third Avenue, New York, NY 10017

Routledge is an imprint of the Taylor & Francis Group, an informa business

British Library Cataloguing in Publication Data
A catalogue record for this book is available from the British Library

Library of Congress Cataloging in Publication Data
Miller, Karen Johnston.
    Making and managing public policy / Karen Johnston Miller
    and Duncan McTavish.
    pages cm
    Includes bibliographical references and index.
    1. Policy sciences. 2. Political planning. 3. Public
    administration. I. McTavish, Duncan. II. Title.
    H97.M54 2014
    320.6–dc23
    2013005049

ISBN: 978–0–415–67994–7(hbk)
ISBN: 978–0–415–67995–4(pbk)
ISBN: 978–0–203–75834–2(ebk)

Typeset in Bembo and Bell Gothic
by Florence Production Ltd, Stoodleigh, Devon, UK

MIX
Paper from
responsible sources
FSC
www.fsc.org   FSC® C013604

Printed and bound by CPI Group (UK) Ltd, Croydon, CR0 4YY

Contents

Illustrations

FIGURES

TABLES

BOXES

Acknowledgements

This book is dedicated to our families.

We are grateful to the team at Routledge. We would like to thank those who participated and supported the research for this book, especially those who devote their lives to public service.

Introduction

LEARNING OBJECTIVES

■ To be able to overview the key concepts of public policy and management as used throughout the book
■ To understand and appreciate the key attributes and definitions of public policy, and in particular the definition used by this book

KEY POINTS IN THIS CHAPTER

■ An explanation of definitions and concepts used in the study of public policy
■ An introduction to how power and authority are distinguishable
■ An explanation of the different disciplines contributing to the study of public policy
■ Why public policy is a vital subject to study

The conventional understanding of the policy process is that, within a liberal democratic state, the citizenry vote for politicians who most represent and articulate their interests, and in executive and legislative institutions, politicians formulate policies on behalf of the citizenry. These policies are then implemented by a public bureaucracy that is impartial, neutral and objective, and by extension represents the interests of the citizenry by implementing policies as mandated by political masters. A quote from the movie, *Crimson Tide* (1995) by the protagonist, Captain Ramsey: 'We're here to preserve democracy, not to practise it . . .' illustrates that even in popular culture there is a simplistic notion of the policy process – politicians formulate policy and civil and public servants merely implement policies. This linear conception of the policy process, within a democratic context of the will of the people being represented in policies, enacted by a political class and implemented through a public bureaucracy is somewhat of a simplistic notion; reality is far more complex. Often the policy process is discussed in terms of policy formulation, implementation and evaluation forming a cyclical pattern with a feedback loop from evaluation to formulation. The reality is that the public policy process rarely follows this orderly pattern.

The book will unravel for you the complex nuances of the public policy process, the context of the process and how policy is made. It will provide you with the realities of the policy process in a contemporary context. In order to provide the contemporary context of the public policy process, we first need to review models, theories and conceptualizations of public policy, the policy process and the changing definitions of public policy making. The book will demonstrate the complexity of the policy process in the modern context by exploring differentiated polities, policy communities, networks, governance including public governance and multi-level governance, varied configurations between the state, non-state, regulatory and other actors, etc. You are encouraged to engage in more contemporary perspectives of public policy, understand the role of state and non-state actors in policy making and critically reassess the linear, simplistic approach to public policy.

STRUCTURE OF THE BOOK

The book includes chapters that provide conceptual, theoretical and critical perspectives of the policy process. There are also case-study chapters, which are interspersed throughout to provide you with the opportunity to critically reflect and engage with issues raised in the preceding chapters.

Thus, this introductory chapter first defines public policy to provide a conceptual framework for later chapters of the book. Chapter 1 reviews models and theories of the public policy process and provides a critical and contemporary perspective of the process. Chapter 2 describes the location and domains of policy making and formulation with a discussion of mechanisms, institutions, and state and non-state actors involved in the process. Specifically, the chapter explores the public bureaucracy as an institution of the state. The chapter also explores the trajectories of public sector reforms with the move from more hierarchical systems to marketization and the involvement of state and non-state actors in the policy process. Chapter 2 also discusses perspectives of public bureaucracy, New Public Management (NPM), the public–private sector interface, governance and concludes with a discussion of new public governance. Chapter 3, entitled 'Public policy making', provides you with theoretical perspectives by exploring the political–administrative interface, the involvement of networks, communities and coalitions in the process of making public policy. The chapter concludes with a discussion on representation in public policy process. The first three chapters of the book review extant models and theories of the public policy process but explore more contemporary thinking and practice on the linkages and/or disjunctures between state and non-state policy actors. Chapter 4 is a case study to illustrate the real-world realities of contemporary public policy. The case study explores the influence and impact of feminist movements on public policy process within the context of networks and multi-level governance. The first four chapters of the book therefore provide you with approaches, normative and descriptive, of how government formulates and makes public policy. Although this section provides theoretical perspectives, you will be challenged to think of the relevance of these theories and approaches in the real world – a recurrent theme throughout the book. As such there are a number of vignettes (in box format) for you to reflect upon.

Chapter 5 examines the roles of individuals in policy capacity, focusing on what they do and the roles played by individuals and groups in the system's capacity. The chapter explores the relationship between policy capacity and the regulatory environment as an important aspect of the contemporary policy arena. Chapter 5 also analyzes the role of government institutions and its organizational ability in addressing policy capacity. The chapter explores policy capacity in the context of an interdependent world and concludes with the impact of the outsourced and extended state on policy capacity. Chapter 6, entitled 'Inter- and intra-organizational relationships', examines the key structural forms through which public policy is delivered – within and between organizations. The chapter focuses on the increasing presence of partnerships and the rationale behind partnership working with references to policy communities and networks. The chapter also includes a discussion of the management and leadership of partnerships. Chapter 7 provides a discussion of the professional-led model of service delivery and the influence of market mechanisms in public service delivery. Specifically, the chapter explores the trustee model of professional activity with the various notions and concepts of 'client', 'user', 'consumer' and 'customer' assessed. Chapter 7 focuses on the co-governance and co-production of public services. Chapter 8 provides the opportunity for critical reflection and discussion of the issues explored in Chapters 5 to 7 by providing a case study on partnerships and practices. Specifically, Chapter 8 provides the case study of Community Health Partnerships in Scotland's National Health Service.

Chapter 9 provides a conceptual discussion of accountability by exploring political and legislative controls; constituency relations; managerial processes; judicial and quasi-judicial reviews; and market accountability. The chapter will also discuss accountability when public policy is a success or failure. Chapter 9 concludes with a discussion of the role of government with arguments of accountability, public service ethos and good governance in society. Chapter 10 continues with the discussion of accountability by viewing performance management as a form of market accountability. The chapter introduces and defines a range of performance measurement concepts from inputs to outcomes and outlines the complexity involved at organizational, governmental and policy sector levels. The chapter then examines the three broad aims of performance management: research into what works; managerial control; accountability. Chapter 11 provides a context and reflection of the preceding chapters with a case study of the foot-and-mouth disease crisis in the UK during 2001 and 2002.

We conclude with some key reflections and arguments of the book such as the policy capacity of governments to address increasingly complex socio-economic problems; that is, wicked policy problems in a global era. Furthermore, we argue that NPM or market-orientated reforms of the public sector will at best introduce organizational change in terms of efficiencies and effectiveness of inputs and outputs at a micro level, but may not necessarily address more fundamental macro-level policy concerns. We argue that an increasingly interrelated global world requires good governance – effective intra- and inter-organizational working – to achieve positive and intended outcomes for society. Thus, the public policy process is an interrelated policy cycle and requires improved public policy making within a governance framework which is inclusive of a variety of state and non-state actors – particularly those affected by the policy or those socially excluded from the process.

WHY STUDY PUBLIC POLICY?

Public policy decisions emanate from government decision-making processes relevant to our everyday lives. From the moment of our birth, whether we are born in a private or publicly funded hospital or even at home, our birth is surrounded by government decision-making such as the regulation of the midwife or the hospital in order to provide safe patient and clinical care. Our identity is registered and regulated making us a citizen of a nation state. In some countries your caste, ethnicity or tribe may be registered at birth. For example, in apartheid South Africa your race would have been recorded at registration of your birth, which would have determined your life chances and opportunities. Government and public policy decisions surround us throughout our lives – from the obvious, such as taxation policies and our adherence to paying taxes, to the less obvious such as state security policies some of which we only learn about with the declassification of government documents at some future date. We can observe public policy decisions all around us and engage with them on a regular basis: conforming to traffic regulations, sending our children to school and expecting them to receive a quality education; when we work we are protected by employment laws, our use of money is regulated by monetary policy, our purchases are protected under consumer policies; and when we retire we expect some form of pension often regulated by pension policies, and towards the end of our lives we expect some protection and care, etc. There are public policies that are also complex and

4

seemingly insurmountable, wicked policy problems, but we expect government to address these societal challenges such as global warming, poverty, terrorism, etc. We are in a public policy era where governments in a globalized world face increasing challenges such as the financial crisis, large-scale national debts, currency declines, increasingly elderly populations with consequent demands for care and pensions, mass urbanization and integration, and so on.

Thus, we should study public policy first because the decisions and actions or inactions by government affect us all – not just as citizens of a nation state but as global citizens. There is a political and citizenship reason to understand public policy. What happens in our neighbourhood regarding refuse bin collections has implications for landfills and global warming. Informing our knowledge and improving our understanding of what government does empowers us as citizens. Within a democratic context, this knowledge allows us to hold government accountable for its actions.

Second, we should study public policy for the purposes of scientific enquiry. Thus, whether as a student of political science or public administration, studying public policy allows us to understand various factors which impact upon government decision-making. These enquiries help us understand the behaviour of political and policy actors. For example, what was the impact of pressure groups on the policy process? What does this say about policy making in a democracy? Were the pressure groups part of an elite group? Did they have technical expertise? Or did they articulate the broader interests of society? What were the outcomes of the policy, and how did it affect society? A fascinating case in point would be a group of women working in a motor factory plant in Dagenham in the UK who, in 1968, took industrial action calling for the right to equal pay. Their grassroots action resulted in UK government policies and law guaranteeing women equal pay rights and today this right is entrenched in many countries' national legislation. It is important in the study of public policy to understand the broader implications of public policy as an outcome for society in terms of its scale (from local, regional, national and international) and magnitude (whether the impact is confined to a small group of people or extended to a larger population). As with the example of the demands for equal pay for women, it started at a local level but rippled to national and international scale with a larger impact for women's rights. Another reason to study public policy, as part of scientific enquiry, is to understand the relationships, or even causality, of public policy decisions and how one decision may affect another societal issue. Public policies often have intended and unintended outcomes because human behaviour is never predictable. For example, government may introduce a drug rehabilitation programme in a particular area with the positive, intended outcome to reduce drug and substance abuse. Assuming that there is causality between crime rates and drug abuse, the local area experiences a reduction in crime. We could conclude that there were positive outcomes: one intended (reduction in drug abuse) and the other unintended (reduction in crime

5

rate) by government action. We could, of course, have the converse of negative outcomes of government action. For example, government decides to host a major sporting event such as the Olympic Games. The obvious intended positive outcomes will be a major event showcasing the country, an increase in tourism and consequent boost to the economy, the upgrade of transport infrastructure and national pride in the success of athletes. A positive unintended outcome would perhaps be inspiring youth to participate in sporting events and thereby increase the health benefits of the population for years to come. However, there could be negative outcomes such as the event becoming a focal point for a terrorist attack. Governments invariably attempt to prevent or ameliorate these negative outcomes. These could include unanticipated or unintended outcomes. In our example of the Olympic Games the local population may become resentful of an increase in overcrowded local areas with an influx of tourists, or worse may increase xenophobia. It is important to understand the dynamic factors that result in positive and negative outcomes of public policy to improve public policy decisions for society and prevent negative impacts.

This brings us to the third reason for studying public policy – the development of professional expertise. Governments need policy analysts, whether as part of the civil service or as experts contracted from academia, or private and voluntary sectors, to improve public policy processes. Governments search for ways to address societal concerns and need skilled public policy analysts to formulate policies which will have a positive intended outcome. Politicians may have some expertise in a specific policy area or portfolio, but for the most part they are reliant on a cadre of public policy experts to develop policies. For example, should a government cull or vaccinate badgers to prevent the spread of tuberculosis to cattle? This has an obvious impact for the farmers and the agricultural economy, but equally there are implications for wildlife and countryside tourism. Weighing the costs and benefits of public policy on this agriculture issue and the political, economic and social impact requires a high level of expertise. Politicians want to make the correct public policy decision with positive, intended outcomes and require an evidence base to inform their decision-making.

It is hoped that this book will assist students, policy professionals and practitioners, pressure groups, politicians and indeed individual citizens to better understand how public policy is made and managed. Whether the use of this book is for political, citizenship, scientific and professional purposes, we hope that you are better informed of public policy processes and how to increase positive outcomes for society.

PUBLIC POLICY: CONCEPT AND DEFINITIONS

Public policy is essentially decisions that are made by government, which has the authority and power to make and enact these decisions. As mentioned previously, public policy can vary in scale and magnitude but the effects, whether positive or negative, intended or unintended, have implications for society in terms of political, social and/or economic effects. Friedrich (1963: 79) in his seminal writing on public policy described it as a course of action of a person, group or government to reach a goal or realize an objective or a purpose. Other scholars such as Dye (1976) describe public policy as what governments do, and in the study of public policy why governments undertake certain actions and whether it makes a difference for society. Dye (2002) simply defined public policy as whatever government chooses to do or not to do. He argues that public policies regulate behaviour, organize bureaucracies, distribute benefits or extract taxes – or all of these things at once (Dye 2002: 1). Jenkins (1978) regarded public policy as a set of interrelated decisions taken by a political actor or group of actors concerning the selection of goals and the means of achieving them. Anderson (1997) conceptualizes public policy as a relatively stable, purposive course of action followed by an actor or set of actors in dealing with a problem or matter of concern. Anderson's statement focuses on what is decided instead of what is proposed, which he argues differentiates policy from a decision: that is essentially a choice among competing alternatives. Anderson also acknowledges that there are non-governmental actors such as pressure groups that influence policy, but argues that it is governmental bodies and officials who make policy.

Heclo (1972), foremost writer and scholar of public policy, conceptualized public policy through a review of various scholarly definitions and it is worth revisiting this review. First, in a debate as to whether public policy is a decision, Heclo states that the term public policy is usually considered to apply to something 'bigger' than particular decisions, but 'smaller' than general social movements. Heclo (1972) cites Richard Rose's (1969) definition of public policy as a long series of more-or-less related activities and their consequences rather than a discrete decision. Heclo (1972) then contrasts this definition with that of Amitai Etzioni's (1968) view, which considers policy as a form of more generalized decision-making 'in which whole sets of decisions are considered and the contexts for decisions reviewed'. Heclo (1972) then discusses Braybrooke and Lindblom's use of the term public policy. They argue that public policy encompasses both conscious decisions and the course that policies take as a result of interrelations among decisions including certain political processes (Braybrooke and Lindblom 1963, as cited in Heclo 1972). Rosenau (1968), Heclo argues, considers decisions too limited by their non-sequential and non-dynamic nature. Rosenau considers public policy as an undertaking and refers to goals and the action taken to realize and maintain them (Rosenau 1968 as cited in Heclo 1972). Heclo (1972) concludes that public policy is, in terms of level of analysis, a concept placed roughly in the middle range in that it is not a discrete decision but much larger in achieving a goal towards some societal end. Hogwood and Gunn (1984) agree that public policy is larger than a decision as it involves a series of specific decisions and while one decision may be crucial in a 'moment of choice' when an option is preferred above others, it is only then that it becomes a policy. Thus, the process of public policy involves decisions and decision-making, but it is when an authoritative policy maker – usually government – decides on a preferred option that it becomes a public policy towards achieving some social end or public good. Public policy is therefore a means to achieving an end that is intended to benefit society.

Heclo (1972: 84) in his review questions whether public policy is purposive and argues that indeed public policy is 'a course of action intended to accomplish some end'. This issue has been an enduring debate in policy studies: whether policy is intended action or not (see discussion below under Birkland 2005). Heclo (1972) concludes that public policy is purposive, but a statement of purpose (for example, a speech by a politician) does not itself constitute the sum of a policy. A converse view is that an intention produces a policy regardless of whatever actually occurs (ibid). Thus, while the purpose of a policy maker is certainly one of the factors creating a policy, his or her intention may very often not coincide with the policy as it operates in the external world (ibid). Heclo (1972) argues that public policy needs to be able to embrace both what is intended and what occurs as a result of the intention. Heclo (1972) therefore states that public policy should be operationally identified, not by its goals, but by the actual behaviour attempting to affect the goals. He concludes that public policy is a 'course of action or inaction rather than specific decisions or actions . . . pursued under the authority of governments . . .' Heclo (1972: 86).

Similarly, contemporary writers such as Howlett and Ramesh (2003) provide a useful review of the conceptualization of public policy by various seminal scholars. First, they agree that the agent of public policy is indeed government and they too acknowledge that private sector organizations, charitable bodies, interest groups, social organizations and even individual citizens may influence public policy but are not the authoritative decision makers. For example, in Western countries there is an increasing concern over obesity. While medical professionals possess the nutritional knowledge and clinical commitment to reduce obesity, charitable and social organizations (e.g. British Heart Foundation) equally may have interests in reducing ill health associated with obesity; individual citizens such as celebrities highlighting the problems of obesity (e.g. Oprah Winfrey) and private sector organizations, such as food manufacturers and retailers, may want to reduce government regulation – these groups influence but do not make policy. They do not have the authority to make and enact public policy which will affect society in scale and magnitude. Peters (1999) therefore argues that public policy is the sum of government activities, whether acting directly or through agents, as it has an influence on the life of citizens.

Howlett and Ramesh (2003) discuss a further aspect of public policy that has also been an enduring debate in public policy scholarship (see Parson 1995): whether public policy involves a fundamental choice on the part of governments to do something or to do nothing. This is what Clemons and McBeth (2001) term a Hobson's choice between competing values, with government making that choice. Similarly, Cochran *et al.* (1999) describe public policy as the outcome of the struggle in government over who gets what. Thus, public policy is a choice made by government to undertake a course of action given competing value choices. The contentious issue is the 'non-decision': that is government's decision or choice to do nothing and maintain the status quo (Howlett and Ramesh 2003). Arguably, if government decides to introduce a ban on smoking in public places – or not, we would regard this as a public policy decision. The former public policy decision would regulate people's smoking behaviour, while the latter gives tacit approval for individuals to continue smoking unabated; the decision or non-decision has health implications for smokers and non-smokers. A further aspect of the conceptualization of public policy is whether it is an outcome or output (Cairney 2012; Colebatch 2005). So in the case of our smoking ban example: whether the decision as an output is to reduce smoking or as an outcome the decision is to improve the health of the population. Arguably, the decision is the output as a product of a choice between competing values and the outcome is the desired, intended impact. Anderson (1997) differentiates between policy outputs and outcomes. He provides a number of examples of policy outputs such as amount of taxes collected, miles of highways built, welfare benefits paid, restraints of trade eliminated, foreign-aid projects undertaken, etc. whereas policy outcomes are described as those which have 'societal consequences' (Anderson 1997: 11).

We summarize Birkland's (2005) attributes of public policy listed below with our additional comments as sub-points:

1   Public policy is made in the public's name.
    The intention of the public policy process is to have some desired societal outcome which has a beneficial or benevolent value for the greater good of society.
2   Public policy is made by government.
    Government is the authoritative body that has been given a mandate through a democratic process to make policy and enact laws that impact upon society as a whole in scale and magnitude. Government therefore has the monopoly in decision-making upon weighing up competing interests in society (Hobson's choice).
3   Public policy is interpreted and implemented by public and private actors.
    Although government is the authoritative decision maker, and in making public policy is influenced by state and non-state actors, it is the implementation of public policy that can be undertaken by various actors and groups in society. This is increasingly the case given the context of governance (discussed Chapters 2, 6 and 7).

9

4   Public policy is what government intends to do.
    This issue is somewhat debatable as intention is not necessarily action. Political
    parties may advocate certain policy positions and stances on particular issues
    in election manifestos and speeches, but when elected as a government, they
    may not necessarily act upon it. The converse is true as well where issues not
    articulated in election manifestos are acted upon. A case in point would be the
    UK Liberal Democrats' emphatic electoral promise that they would not raise
    university tuition fees, but once part of a coalition government they enacted
    an increase in tuition fees. Thus we argue, as do the scholars cited above, that
    public policy involves what government chooses to do. We agree with
    Anderson (1997: 11): the policy involves 'what governments actually do, not
    just what they intend to do or what they say they are going to do'.
5   Public policy is what government chooses not to do.
    Our view is that government, in choosing not to do anything – that is maintain
    the status quo – in itself has made a choice and the inaction is indeed action
    or what we term passive public policy as opposed to active public policy. In
    our policy example of a smoking ban, the enactment of a smoking ban
    constitutes an active policy while the decision not introduce a smoking ban is
    a tacit approval of smoking and therefore a passive policy.

CRITICAL REFLECTIONS OF PUBLIC POLICY

When considering the concepts and definitions of public policy it is worthwhile to
reflect upon the dimensions of power and authority, the multi- and inter-
disciplinarity of public policy and the study vis-à-vis the practice of public policy.

■   Political systems:
    Many of the scholarly definitions of public policy are derived from observations
    of Anglo-Saxon or Western political systems. These systems are often liberal
    democracies which allow for the influence of non-state actors in the policy
    process and an adherence to other democratic principles such as accountability
    of government decisions. One cannot study public policy in a vacuum – it
    takes place within a political system. As we have discussed above, government
    is an authoritative decision maker, but what happens if government does not
    have authority, but power? In other words, government does not have the
    legitimate use of power and does not have the mandate, through a democratic
    electoral process, to make decisions that impact upon society. In these non-
    democratic regimes would our definitions of public policy hold true? We
    therefore argue that public policy definitions should include dimensions of
    power and authority.
        Power is the ability to enforce one's will on another, while authority is
    legitimate use of power (Weber 1968). Power may be exercised through

force or coercion, but the right to exercise power is given by virtue of tradition, charisma or a legal–constitutional authority (see Chapter 2 for the Weberian explanation of power and authority). In authoritarian regimes, devoid of democratic practices such as voting by the general populace, the decisions made by the government would be regarded as public policy, for example Syria's violent repression of its citizens. But do these authoritarian governments have the authority to make public policy or do they have the power? Even within liberal democracies governments use power as well as authority to make public policy. For example, the public opposition to the UK's invasion of Iraq did not have a political mandate; the public policy decision was regarded by the British public as the government not having the authority to do so nor was the public policy decision regarded as legitimate (hence the UK government's desire to seek a legal basis for invading Iraq). Thus, would the war in Iraq and the deployment of British troops be regarded as an act of power or authority? Was it an authoritative decision or one made from a source of power?

■ The study of public policy:

Public policy is multidisciplinary in practice but interdisciplinary as a field of study. Indeed, Heclo (1972) in his review of public policy argues that public policy studies integrate various part of the 'multidiscipline' into a coherent 'inter-discipline'. It is worthwhile discussing this distinction as many scholars often use these terms synonymously. Public policy draws upon multiple disciplines in order to understand a problem and develop solutions beyond an extant paradigm. Policy makers in practice do so, for example, if they are attempting to develop a policy solution to crime: they may draw upon sociology, psychology, criminology, etc. in an effort to address a public policy concern. Policy studies are interdisciplinary in that they cross traditional disciplinary and methodological boundaries to develop a discipline with continuous freshness of insight and approach. Public policy as a discipline is probably unique in this respect. Although principally a field of study that draws upon political science since its focus is on political institutions (e.g. legislatures), political actors (e.g. politicians, pressure groups), political systems, political processes (e.g. elections) (see Anderson 1997), public policy nevertheless draws upon other disciplines. The disciplines each and collectively add value to the field of study and equally provide tools for analyses. Birkland (2005: 6) provides a useful table of analyses of how the various disciplines have contributed to the field of study. For example, economic studies, whose focus is on the allocation of resources in communities, have contributed to the discipline of public policy through studies on employment and productivity patterns, economic growth, etc. and they have even provided public policy with theories and tools of analysis such as public choice theory, cost–benefit analysis and rational choice theory, in an attempt to understand why some

11

policies succeed while others do not, in a descriptive sense, and, in a normative sense, which policies should be adopted and which should not. Sociology has also made its contribution to the study of public policy where sociology concerns the social life, social change and social causes and consequences of human behaviour (ibid). Public policy benefits from sociology in that it provides theories of how groups within society will react to public policy or how they form to make demands upon government. The field of psychology too has its uses for those studying public policy as it helps policy makers understand individual human behaviour and how individuals are likely to react as recipients or beneficiaries of public policy or as state actors involved in the policy process – will individuals behave in a self-interested manner or act in the interest of society? Management and organizational studies also contribute to the study of public policy particularly in the observations of public or government agencies. Other disciplines such as history provide a context as to why public policy decisions were taken, and even contemporary fields of study such as media provide us with the tools to understand the increasing impact of the media on public policy decisions (see 'Celebritization of Public Policy', Chapter 3).

■ The study and practice of public policy:

The practice of public policy is what government does or chooses not to do. The process of observing, researching and collecting evidence is policy analysis. Policy analysis can inform the practice of public policy through an evidence base of what is the better course of action among competing alternatives. Those involved in policy analysis can include state actors such as civil servants or government officials employed in a public agency, or scholars studying the public policy process as non-state actors – the latter being more engaged in academic and scientific enquiry and the former in the process of public policy. In reality, scientific enquiry often informs the practice of public policy and these are sometimes interrelated activities. An example of this is the European Commission's large-scale funding of research often undertaken by academics to assist the Commission in public policy making through the provision of evidence. The study of public policy can be descriptive (how government makes policy) and normative (how government ought to make policy). Although there is a debate as to whether public policy as a field of study is a science, we would agree with Birkland (2005) that it is an applied science because in public policy the line between theory and practice is often blurred. Indeed as discussed in the preceding paragraph, it is the multi-disciplinary nature of public policy that it is not a 'pure science' rather it draws upon various disciplines to gather evidence in a robust manner to seek to address societal problems, challenges and issues. The study of public policy is a 'science' in a sense that there is an attempt to gather evidence in an empirical and objective manner to better inform policy practitioners and government. In a previous example, we mentioned the case of badger culling or vaccinations.

Here a number of scientists (whether civil servants or commissioned academic experts), farmers and wildlife organizations would provide evidence and attempt to influence the policy process. Government would employ the empirical evidence from the scientists and consider the interests of other actors to make an informed public policy decision. In other words they would apply the knowledge to make some informed decision or governments may disregard the evidence. In so doing public policy becomes an 'applied science' because it informs practice through the collection and analysis of data which is robust, reliable and valid, which has some utility for society in a practical sense (Birkland 2005). While to a large extent the use of robust empirical evidence is true to making public policy, there are circumstances where government chooses to ignore the empirical data and chooses interests above evidence. This often occurs in reality when the evidence is not considered politically palatable and government chooses a populist or other policy option. A case in point would be the evidence base provided to the UK government in the formulation of drugs policy. Often the evidence is ignored in a highly politicized environment where decisions relating to drugs policy are a contentious and controversial matter (see Monaghan 2011).

Thus drawing upon a review of the literature of public policy, as a concept we define public policy, for the purpose of this book, as:

An intended course of action made by government, which has power and/or authority to make a decision among competing interests, with the purpose of achieving an outcome beneficial for society.

REFERENCES

Anderson, J. (1997) *Public Policy Making*, New York: Houghton Mifflin.

Birkland, T. (2005) *An Introduction to the Policy Process: theories, concepts, and models of public policy making*, New York: M.E. Sharpe.

Braybrooke, D. and Lindblom, C.E. (1963) *A Strategy of Decision: policy evaluation as a social science*, New York: Free Press of Glencoe.

Cairney, P. (2012) *Understanding Public Policy*, London: Palgrave Macmillan.

Clemons, R.S. and McBeth, M.K. (2001) *Public Policy Praxis. Theory and Pragmatism: a case approach*, Upper Saddle River, NJ: Prentice Hall.

Cochran, C.E., Lawrence Mayer, T.R., Carr, T.R. and Cayer, N.J. (1999) *American Public Policy: an introduction*, New York: St. Martin's Press.

Colebatch, H.K. (2005) *Policy*, Maidenhead: Open University Press.

Dye, T. (2002) *Understanding Public Policy*, 10th edition, Upper Saddle River, NJ: Prentice Hall.

Dye, T.R. (1976) *Policy Analysis: what governments do, why they do it, and what difference it makes,* Tuscaloosa: University of Alabama Press.

Etzioni, A. (1968) *The Active Society: a theory of societal and political processes,* New York: Free Press.

Friedrich, C.J. (1963) *Man and His Government,* New York: McGraw-Hill Book Company.

Heclo, H. (1972) 'Review article: policy analysis', *British Journal of Political Science,* 2, 1: 83–108.

Hogwood, B.W. and Gunn, L.A. (1984) *Policy Analysis for the Real World,* Oxford: Oxford University Press.

Howlett, M. and Ramesh, M. (2003) *Studying Public Policy, Don Mills,* Ontario: Oxford University Press.

Jenkins, W.I. (1978) *Policy Analysis: a political and organisational perspective,* London: Martin Robertson.

Monaghan, M. (2011) *Evidence versus Politics: exploiting research in UK drug policy making?* Bristol: The Policy Press.

Parsons, W. (1995) *Public Policy: an introduction to the theory and practice of policy analysis.* Cheltenham: Edward Elgar.

Peters, G. (1999) *American Public Policy: promise and performance,* Chappaqua, New York: Chatham House/Seven Rivers.

Rose, R. (ed.) (1969) *Policy Making in Great Britain,* London: Palgrave Macmillan.

Rosenau, J. (1968) 'Moral fervor, systematic analysis and scientific consciousness in foreign policy research' in Austin Ranney (ed.) *Political Science and Public Policy,* Chicago, IL: Markham Publishing.

Weber, M. (1968) *Economy and Society. An Outline of Interpretative Sociology.* Translated by Günther Roth and Claus Wittich (eds), New York: Bedminster Press.

Chapter 1

The policy process

INTRODUCTION

On a warm summer's day in 1994 in Hamilton, New Jersey in the US, a seven-year-old girl, Megan Kanka, was coaxed by a neighbour to play with a puppy. The neighbour was Jesse Timmendequas, a twice-convicted paedophile. On that day, 29 July 1994, he raped, murdered and then dumped Megan's body in a park.

Megan's family began a campaign to ensure notification of paedophiles living within a community. There was public outrage and anger that a convicted paedophile was allowed to live in proximity to children without notification to the local population. The public outcry was articulated into New Jersey state legislation and then enacted by Congress in 1996 as US federal legislation. The Crimes Against Children and Sexually Violent Offender Registration Act, commonly known as Megan's Law, allows US states discretion in establishing criteria to disclose information about registered sex offenders. It was deemed that the public notification of registered sex offenders would assist law enforcement investigations, would deter sex offenders from committing new offences and offer citizens information to protect children from victimization. Although, there was public sympathy and support for such a law, the passage of the law was not without opposition. Many argued that it violated the rights of sex offenders, such as a right to privacy, that offenders would be victimized and once they had served their conviction they should be not be convicted again by society. Various other countries around the world, through a form of policy transfer, introduced similar legislation.

There have been mixed results in the US with states implementing the law in different ways. Opponents of the law argue that sex offenders are victimized and consequently 'go underground', moving to different locations, making it difficult for law enforcement to trace them – a negative, unintended outcome. Proponents of the law argue that in some states in the US there has been a decline in sexual offences against children, although opponents of the law argue that this is perhaps due to some sex offenders moving to another jurisdiction. This tragic story is a policy process story: how there is a concern or issue in the environment, external to government; how it becomes a demand for government action; how there are various support or contestations of the policy; how a government decision-making process becomes a public policy or a law; its implementation in society; and how perhaps the effectiveness of the public policy is evaluated and debated with a view of its outcome for society.

Most books will explain the public policy process as policy formulation (the process of making public policy), policy implementation (the application of the public policy in society) and policy evaluation (reviewing, measuring, assessing and/or investigating the effectiveness of public policy). For example, see Clemons and McBeth's work (2001), where the structure of the book is based on public policy as stages: problem or issue awareness (stage 1), policy determination (stage 2) and policy implementation (stage 3). As discussed in the introductory section of this book, this process is described in a linear manner or at best as a cycle. It is often simplistic in description, but policy in the real world is more complex. Thus, this chapter provides an overview of concepts, models and theories of the policy process. The overview is offered to aid the understanding and conceptualization of the complexities of public policy. The chapter also explores the roles of key actors in the process although this will be dealt with in greater detail in Chapter 3.

16

The conventionally accepted theories such as rationalism and incrementalism are discussed and more recent perspectives of public policy will also be explored. Thus, while this chapter provides a discussion of extant theories to provide a context of the policy process, you are encouraged to critically reflect upon its real world applicability. As such, we provide some critical discussion of the theories towards the development of a more contemporary perspective of the public policy process. Before we proceed to discuss policy cycles, we first need to discuss types of public policies in order to understand the policy process.

TYPES OF PUBLIC POLICIES

Regulation is perhaps the most obvious of government policies as it seeks to exert some form of control over society or individual citizens to achieve a societal outcome. However, policies can be more than merely regulatory, policies can be classified as distributive, constituent, and redistributive as well (Lowi 1972). Lowi (1972) developed a taxonomy of policies along the dimensions of likelihood and applicability of coercion. Although Lowi (1972) does not explicitly define coercion, he argues (1972: 299) that the 'most significant political fact about government is that government coerces'. We assume he is referring to power and authority of government to act (see discussion in the introductory chapter of this book). He argues that the likelihood of government to coerce can be immediate or remote: it can be remote if sanctions are absent, or if there is a subsidy where the coercive element is displaced, it encourages certain behaviours, and coercion can be immediate if the policy directly affects behaviours (ibid). Lowi's (1972) classification of types of policies is illustrated in Figure 1.1 overleaf.

The classification by Lowi draws upon the US political system and the evidence for his research is based upon US Presidential and Congressional historical records. Nonetheless, without holding his classification up to a robust standard of external validity, there is relevancy to the taxonomy of policies. Governments can enact policies that have a direct or immediate bearing on our lives such as eliminating substandard goods, which would require individuals or private sector businesses at a decentralized level to remove the goods from sale or being produced. This would take place at a decentralized level and act in a group's (e.g. consumers') interests. This we would regard as regulation. Thus regulative policies impose restrictions or place limits on behaviour of individuals or groups of individuals and reduce the freedom to act (Anderson 1997). An example of this would be banking regulation in order to reduce high-risk behaviour, which may have implications for the economy – there has been an increased call for more banking regulation since the 2008 banking and consequent financial crisis. Other examples include pollution control, property rights, censorship, reproductive rights, etc. Individuals or groups will always resist regulation or attempt to reduce its impact, but governments have to make a choice or balance the interests between those of society and individuals

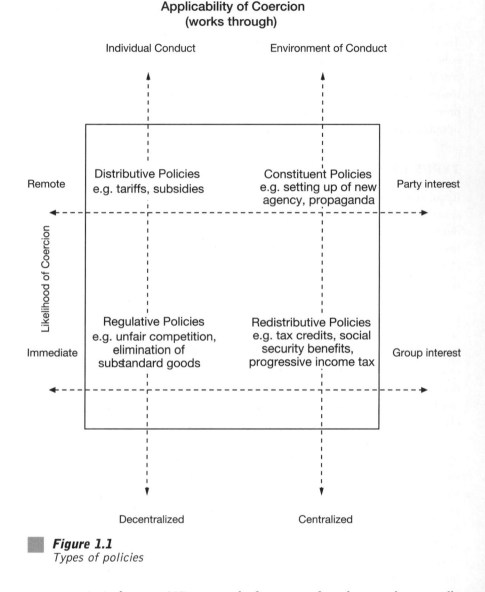

**Applicability of Coercion
(works through)**

Individual Conduct   Environment of Conduct

Remote

Distributive Policies
e.g. tariffs, subsidies

Constituent Policies
e.g. setting up of new
agency, propaganda

Party interest

Likelihood of Coercion

Regulative Policies
e.g. unfair competition,
elimination of
substandard goods

Redistributive Policies
e.g. tax credits, social
security benefits,
progressive income tax

Immediate

Group interest

Decentralized   Centralized

Figure 1.1
Types of policies

or groups. As Anderson (1997) argues, the formation of regulatory policies usually features conflict between two groups or coalitions of groups, with one side seeking to impose some sort of control (e.g. banning pornography), and the other side, which customarily resists regulation, arguing that control is either unnecessary or that the wrong kind of control is being proposed (e.g. pornography constitutes a freedom of expression or resistance to imposed age restrictions).

Government can also enact policies that operate at a more centralized level that benefit a group (e.g. those living below the poverty line) and that have an immediate and broader effect. Lowi (1972) classifies these as redistributive policies such as welfare benefits. Thus, redistributive policies involve deliberate efforts by government to shift or reallocate wealth, income, property or rights among broader groups in the population (Anderson 1997). Typically in Western liberal democracies redistributive policies are social and welfare benefits for the poor or elderly. Redistribution can also take place on a global scale such as foreign aid being provided to impoverished communities or countries e.g. food aid to Somalia. Redistributive policies attempt to address an imbalance or achieve a level of equality and fairness in society. But as Anderson (1997) notes, redistributive policies are difficult to enact because they involve the reallocation of resources and those who possess wealth and power, sometimes the political class, rarely yield the resources willingly and possess ample means to resist their diminution.

Then there are policies that have a remote or indirect effect. This may be on an individualized and decentralized basis, such as subsidies to farmers, but are in a party political interest to do so – these are distributive policies (ibid). Finally, Lowi (1972) refers to constituency policies which are also in the party interest to enact a policy, such as setting up an agency to deal with particular constituency concerns. Thus, distributive policies involve allocation of services or benefits to particular individuals in the population with some benefits being accrued to individual citizens or a few beneficiaries (Anderson 1997). Distributive policies typically involve using public funds to assist particular individuals or groups such as flood barriers to protect those living in high-risk areas (ibid), while constituent policies benefit a potential voting bloc or support base for the political party as an incumbent government.

Anderson (1997) provides other categories of public policies. He argues that policies can be substantive or procedural. Substantive policies involve government action that directly distributes to the population advantages and disadvantages, benefits and costs (ibid). Anderson (1997) provides the example of constructing a highway, which is substantive and tangible with obvious economic benefits of creating transport infrastructure, but also incurs costs such as taxes to pay for the highway and levels of pollution. Procedural policies in contrast are policies that concern the process: how something is going to be done or who is going to take the action (ibid). The procedural policies relate to, for example, creating a public agency, determining matters over jurisdiction, specifying the process and techniques employed and allowing for procedures of accountability (ibid). Most public organizations involved in protective and care services, such as law enforcement or social care agencies, have a number of procedural policies to adhere to and are held accountable in their compliance with these procedures. Procedural policies also apply on a macro and global scale such as procedural policies negotiated through G8 and Euro Group summits.

Policies can also be categorized as material and symbolic depending on the benefit they allocate (Anderson 1997). Material policies provide tangible resources or substantive benefit to individuals or groups, or impose real disadvantages on those who are adversely affected by the policy (ibid). Minimum wage policies are an example of a material policy where one group benefits (e.g. employees with increased wages) and the other loses (e.g. employers with increased labour costs) (ibid). Symbolic policies by contrast have little real material impact and allocate no tangible advantages or disadvantages (ibid). These policies appeal to people's values such as their sense of patriotism, peace or social justice (ibid). Anderson (1997: 19) uses the example of the Kellogg–Briand Pact of 1928 in the US, which outlawed war. The US involvement in a number of wars since 1928 provides sufficient evidence that the policy was ineffective. In other countries, the monarch or chief has evolved to be symbolic with no real constitutional authority other than playing a role as figure head for a nation in ceremonies, receiving foreign dignitaries and providing the nation with a sense of patriotism, history and nationalism.

Public policies whether distributive, redistributive, regulatory, symbolic, etc. are made through a series of complex decision-making processes emanating from and developed within environments involving an array of state and non-state actors. The next section of this chapter explores the policy process through a theoretical lens of models and cycles.

THE POLICY PROCESS: MODELS AND CYCLES

David Easton (1965) is often cited in reference to explaining the policy process. He developed a simple yet elegant model, illustrated in Figure 1.2: The Political System, to explain the various inputs and outputs of political systems. Although simplistic in describing the policy process, it is useful to explain the process, policy making and the impact of the external environment.

Easton (1965) stated that a political system receives inputs from the broader external environment. These inputs are information flows from the external environment in the form of demands and supports (ibid). The inputs are mediated through various channels such as political parties, interest groups and/or media (ibid). The inputs are then filtered through a 'black box' of government – a policy-making process. The demands and supports through this 'black box' are converted into outputs in the form of government decisions (ibid) – public policy. The outputs then become inputs again through a feedback loop and a cycle of a policy making develops.

If we apply the Eastonian model to Megan's Law, the process would be described as:

■ External environmental factors – Megan's family campaigns for government action after the tragic and violent death of their seven-year-old daughter by a convicted paedophile. The campaign, facilitated by the media, gains broader public support.

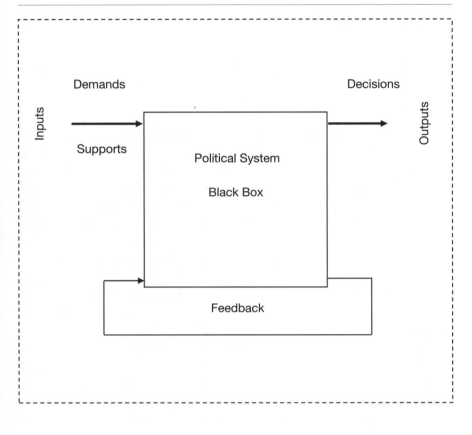

Figure 1.2
The political system

- Demands — Megan's family, media, interest groups, sympathetic politicians, etc. make demands on government to enact a law to prevent the victimization of children by sex offenders. There are those who support the introduction of such a law and there are opponents who demand that such a law is not introduced.
- Black Box — there are discussions, deliberations, consultation and decision-making within the New Jersey state government and then latterly in the US Congress, which result in a decision.
- Output — New Jersey introduces a state law and the US federal government follows with a course of action as well, introducing the Crimes Against Children and Sexually Violent Offender Registration Act in 1996. Subsequently, most states adopt the law. In terms of a type of public policy the output was a regulatory policy.

■ Feedback – the decision to introduce the law is fed back and the decision may be supported or extra demands are made to government. In the case of Megan's law, her family and proponents of the law supported government's policy, while others saw the output as potentially ineffective or problematic, and therefore made further demands.

Public policy scholars developed cyclical models to explain the policy process (see Parsons 1995). Often in textbooks the policy process is synonymous with the term policy cycle (see Hudson and Lowe 2004). According to Howlett and Ramesh (2003) a popular method of studying public policy has been to disaggregate the process into a series of discrete stages and sub-stages with the resulting sequence of stages referred to as a 'policy cycle'. Indeed, although many authors of public policy textbooks acknowledge that the public policy process is in reality complex, they nonetheless use the stagist and cyclical approach to explain the process. For example, Parsons (1995: 80) in his book on public policy states that, 'This book adheres to the stagist approach because, given the sheer range of frameworks and models which are available as analytical tools, we need some way in which this complexity can be reduced to a more manageable form.'

Foremost among scholars in developing a cyclical model of the policy process was Harold Lasswell (1956), who described the policy process as first gathering intelligence about a problem, then promoting the issue, developing prescriptions of what ought to be done, invoking some government action, applying the policy into action, terminating the policy when there is a resolution to the problem and finally appraising the policy to provide lessons for resolving future problems (Lasswell 1956; see also Parsons 1995; Hudson and Lowe 2004). Similarly, Jones (1970) describes the policy process as defining a problem, setting government agenda, formulating proposals to address the problem, the proposals in some coherent form are legitimated by the legislature, a budget is then assigned, and then policy is implemented and evaluated. The typical stages of the policy process can be summarized and illustrated as in Figure 1.3 on the following page.

THE POLICY PROCESS: A NORMATIVE APPROACH

Hogwood and Gunn (1984) in their book, *Policy Analysis for the Real World*, adopt a stagist approach to explaining the public policy process as well and devote a chapter to each stage of the process. Their book is somewhat normative in approach by prescribing how policy as a process ought to be undertaken. Although they provide various descriptive examples of the policy process in each chapter, the book is focused on prescriptive ways to improve the policy process. We summarize Hogwood and Gunn's (1984) approach to the public policy process as stages 1 to 9 in the next section.

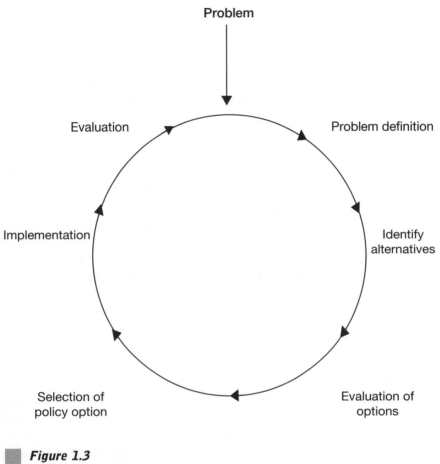

Problem

Evaluation

Implementation

Selection of
policy option

Problem definition

Identify
alternatives

Evaluation of
options

Figure 1.3
Policy process as a cycle

1 Deciding to decide (issue search or agenda setting)

This stage involves the identification and anticipation of problems or opportunities which require a course of action. Some issues come on to the policy agenda while others do not. Issues from the external environment move on to the policy agenda, in general, if one or more of the following factors apply: the issue may have reached crisis proportions; the issue may have achieved particularity, such as air pollution; there is an emotive issue that resonates with the broader public, such as the case of Megan's law described above; the issue has wide impact, such as regressive taxation; the issue is about power and legitimacy, such as introducing regulations to restrict government to act; and/or the issue is fashionable, such as addressing concerns over street crime. Some of the issues are similar to Kingdon's (1984)

23

mechanisms of how problems come on to the policy agenda (e.g. events and crisis), but Hogwood and Gunn's description is perhaps narrower in classification.

2   Deciding how to decide (or issue filtration)

Once a problem or opportunity is identified and government action is deemed to be necessary, the question then arises as to how the policy should be made. How policy is made is a focus and theme of this chapter and will be dealt with in greater detail in later sections.

3   Issue definition

Once a problem is identified it requires definition or clarification. Often the problems consist of a number of strands and may be highly politically subjective. There are often attempts to understand the causes, but the definition of the problem affects later stages of the policy process to apply analyses to solve the problem. When the then Prime Minister Tony Blair announced that he was going to be tough on crime and the causes of crime, his announcement was politically palatable to both the centre-left and right of the political spectrum, but it was a rather vacuous statement as the causes of crime were not defined. Hogwood and Gunn (1984: 8) argue for more 'objective analysis' in defining the problem and, where possible, problems (and opportunities) should be measured and identified as there are 'advantages to quantification'.

4   Forecasting

Hogwood and Gunn (1984) state that it is necessary to forecast how a situation will develop with an appreciation of the theoretical and practical advantages and limitations of a wide variety of techniques from modelling to subjective judgement. In other words, as a stage, forecasting provides information of potential consequences, thinking through the positive and negative, intended and unintended outcomes of a policy (ibid).

5   Setting objectives and priorities

When deciding on policies it would be important to consider priorities given limited resources and competing objectives. Hogwood and Gunn (1984) suggest that an analytical approach is required to answer two questions: what are we trying to do, and how will we know when we have done it? Thus, since there is a gap between desired and expected outcomes, it is important to consider constraints and limiting factors. For example, government may want to reduce the incidence of childhood obesity and therefore introduce a nutritional programme for students in an attempt to introduce positive health outcomes. Government may consider introducing a programme of free school meals for every child under the age of five, but there may be financial (e.g. cost of the programme) and practical (e.g. food distribution) limitations of introducing such a programme. The programme may be considered too costly in view of other government priorities such as cutting a budget deficit.

6   Option analysis

There may be several ways of achieving policy objectives and government may have to consider a broad range of options. In our example of addressing the policy problem of childhood obesity, other options to government may be to introduce a sports programme in schools, regulating food manufacturers and retailers or undertaking a public awareness campaign through the media. Option analysis requires analytical tools such as cost–benefit analysis, decision analysis and programme analysis and review (PAR), etc.

7   Policy implementation, monitoring and control

Hogwood and Gunn (1984) continue with the stagist view of the public policy process that once the 'preferred' option emerges from the preceding stage, the preferred policy option is then communicated with resultant associated programmes designed and implemented. Thus, implementation is part of the policy process since effective policy implementation aims to address the problem identified in the preceding stages. Hogwood and Gunn (1984) therefore argue that during the implementation stage, the policy should be monitored to check if actual performance is meeting desired outputs or if control and remedial action is necessary.

8   Evaluation and review

A policy may require a fundamental review to assess whether the policy has been successful in achieving desirable outcomes. Evaluation depends on whether there was prior specification of desired outcomes, analytical frameworks and capacity or even desire to conduct an evaluation. A policy which has been deemed to have poor or negative outcomes is often a political liability for government as governments do not like to admit failure for political (e.g. it becomes an electoral liability), legal and/or financial reasons (e.g. government opens itself up to litigation and costly compensation claims).

9   Policy maintenance, succession and termination

The results of an evaluation may result in the policy being maintained, assuming it is successful in outputs and outcomes, or the policy may be succeeded or even terminated. Here too are limitations, often political, organizational, financial and legal, in the succession and termination of a policy. Arguably, politicians and governments do not want to admit failure of a policy which requires the termination of a policy.

Similarly, Bardach (2008) proposes an eight-stage path to more effective problem solving and policy making:

1 Define the problem

Bardach (2008) encourages a policy maker to think of a deficit or excess (e.g. the levels of public expenditure are too high) and provides a number of tips to this regard. He argues that often the way the problem is semantically defined is done through the political environment or emanates from the media. Bardach asks the policy maker to consider whether the problem is really a problem and whether the policy maker should seek evidence to define the problem. He argues that the policy maker should evaluate whether the problem is a market failure, a social issue or ideological, and attempt to quantify the problem (e.g. what is the magnitude of the problem) (ibid).

2 Assemble the evidence

In this stage Bardach (2008) states that the policy maker should conduct a cost–benefit analysis, use experience and expertise, access available literature and research, conduct surveys, consider analogies (e.g. similarities in other countries or sectors), gather the evidence in a timely manner, broker a consensus among credible stakeholders and consult broadly beyond the usual informants.

3 Construct alternatives

The policy maker has to consider all the policy options, start comprehensively and then narrow in focus, model alternatives, simplify a list of alternatives and then design alternatives (Bardach 2008).

4 Select criteria

Bardach (2008) states that policy makers should establish criteria to evaluate projected policy outcomes including criteria such as efficiency, equality, equity, fairness, justice, freedom, community, transparency, etc. – which are cues from the political environment – criteria weighting, consideration of practical criteria such as legality, political acceptability, robustness in implementation, etc.

5 Project outcomes

The policy maker should then think of future possibilities of the policy achieving its objectives and analyze evidence of the likelihood of success and failure. Here Bardach (2008) acknowledges that there are cognitive limitations of policy makers (see Simon 1965), political expedience and bureau-shaping behaviour (see Chapter 2) which may affect this decision-making process.

6 Confront trade-offs

Bardach (2008) suggests that in this stage the policy maker should focus on projected outcomes and explain the trade-offs between various alternatives. Thus, almost like scenario planning, the policy maker should explain if a particular policy is chosen, then what likely outcomes may occur.

7 Decide

The decision maker, usually an authoritative political decision maker (e.g. in the UK political system the policy is usually decided upon through a collective Cabinet decision-making process), a policy option is decided upon.

8 Tell your story

Bardach (2008) acknowledges the political and media intensive environments which policy makers operate in and as such includes a final stage to policy making where the policy maker has to present the policy to an audience, which Bardach acknowledges may precede stage 7.

Both the Hogwood and Gunn (1984) and the Bardach (2008) models of policy making include a series of sequential stages, broadly consistent with a rational approach which starts with identifying a problem; then gathering information, evidence, intelligence, etc.; making a decision after considering various policy options or alternatives according to various criteria; and then finally implementing the policy.

THE POLICY PROCESS: OTHER APPROACHES

There are various approaches, normative and descriptive, and explanations of the policy process. Wayne Parsons (1995: 78–79) in his book summarizes the scholarly explanations of the policy process and we repeat it here, in Box 1.1, to illustrate that most explanations of the policy process have a number of commonalities:

1   The starting point is some recognition of a problem and a need for government action in the form of a public policy. This 'awareness-raising' stage emanates from the external (e.g. media) and/or internal (e.g. public agency) environment to government.
2   There is an active effort to seek and gather information about the problem. This is 'intelligence gathering' usually directed by government.
3   Government may consider to take action or not, and will consider various options in addressing the problem. This may involve various analytical tools such as cost–benefit analysis, scenario planning and forecasting.
4   A decision is made to adopt or not, a particular public policy to address the problem.
5   The public policy is formulated, implemented and may be evaluated.

BOX 1.1   PUBLIC POLICY PROCESS – AN OVERVIEW AND FURTHER READING

Simon (1945) Administrative Behaviour
Intelligence
Design
Choice

Lasswell (1956)
Intelligence
Promotion
Prescription
Invocation
Application
Termination
Appraisal

Mack (1971) Planning and Uncertainty
Deciding to decide: problem recognition
Formulating alternatives and criteria
Decision Proper
Effectuation
Correction and Supplementation

Rose (1973) Comparing Public Policy
Public recognition of a need for a policy to exist
How issues are placed on the agenda of public controversy
How demands are advanced
The form of government involved in policy making
Resources and constraints
Policy decisions
What determines government choice
Choice in its context
Implementation
Outputs
Policy Evaluation
Feedback

Jenkins (1978) Policy Analysis: A Political and Organisational Perspective
Initiation
Information
Consideration
Decision
Implementation
Evaluation
Termination

Source: Parsons (1995: 78–79)

Thus, the public policy process involves: the identification of a problem that may exist in society as defined by various policy actors (e.g. government, media, interest groups, etc.); a transfer of knowledge to inform policy makers of the nature, scale and scope of the policy; government as the authoritative policy actor considers various options to address the problem; government may decide to formulate and adopt a policy to address the problem with intended outputs and outcomes; the policy is implemented; and depending on the political and organizational dynamics, the policy may or may not be evaluated.

The stagist approach to the public policy process (useful in pedagogy and textbook explanations to provide students of public policy with a step-by-step explanation and for practitioners a normative, practical guide how policy ought to be made) is nonetheless a construct of reality. The public policy process and making public policy is far more complicated in reality (see Nakamura 1987; Parsons 1995; Howlett and Ramesh 2003). Although the starting point in the policy process is invariably the identification of a problem or issue which may exist in society, the policy process does not enter into neat and sequential stages. Government may have already decided to implement a policy before all the information is gathered. This may be due to political calendars, reactivity to media pressure, crisis requiring immediate action, etc. Indeed government may even evaluate a policy, as implemented in another country or jurisdiction, and decide to implement the policy within its national jurisdiction – a policy transfer. An example of this would be the introduction of a smoking ban in public places where various countries, given the initial success of the policy, implemented the policy within their respective countries. There is limited empirical evidence that policy is made through a sequential process (Smith 1993; John 1998). The policy process through a stagist approach is 'top down' and ignores the realities of multiple levels of government (e.g. policy may be developed from the bottom up) and policy networks operating at various levels and intervals of the policy process (ibid). Parsons (1995: 80), for example, provides similar criticisms of the stagist approach to public policy but adopts the approach given that it reduces the complexity of public policy process into a manageable explanatory form. Although this section of Chapter 1 provides an overview of the policy process in its stagist form, having reviewed the literature, this book departs from the convention and seeks to explain public policy in reality and increasingly within the context of governance arguing that it is complicated, messy and muddled. How then can we make sense of, or seek to understand public policy? Theories provide a framework to understand reality, but are contestable – empirical evidence from reality may refute or substantiate extant theories – and theories are validated or new theories emerge. The study of public policy is no different from other social sciences with the interface between theory and practice continuously contributing towards our understanding and knowledge base of public policy processes. The following sections of the chapter provide some theoretical perspectives of public policy.

29

THEORIES OF PUBLIC POLICY

> If I had a world of my own, everything would be nonsense. Nothing would be what it is because everything would be what it isn't. And contrary-wise; what it is it wouldn't be, and what it wouldn't be, it would. You see?
>
> (Lewis Caroll, *Alice's Adventures in Wonderland*, Kindle Edition 2010)

> Reports that say that something hasn't happened are always interesting to me, because as we know, there are known knowns; there are things we know we know. We also know there are known unknowns; that is to say we know there are some things we do not know. But there are also unknown unknowns . . . the ones we don't know we don't know
>
> (Donald Rumsfeld, US Secretary of Defence, 2002)

We start this section of the chapter with the quotes from the book *Alice's Adventures in Wonderland* and Donald Rumsfeld; although somewhat amusing and confusing, the quotes provide a more sublime lesson of public policy in practice and theory. First, theory is an abstraction of reality and the practice of public policy is often muddled. For example, we would hope that government gathers as much information as possible to formulate policy and be fully informed of options, but it is not always possible given resource, time and cognitive limitations, and consequently there will always be 'unknowns' or unintended policy outcomes. Second, theory can provide explanations but not necessarily predictions. For example, although governments seek to address a societal problem to achieve an intended outcome, what may occur is contrary to the intention or in Alice's words 'contrary-wise'. The explanatory power of a theory increases if evidence gathered from reality substantiates the theory and adds to its internal and external validity. Thus, theory attempts to provide us with a lens of reality or of the 'muddle', and through empiricism capture reality or make sense of the world. We therefore strive to understand the 'unknowns' or the 'nonsense'. The following section provides us with theories which help us understand how policy is made (descriptive theory) and ought to be made (normative theory). Nevertheless, it is worthwhile to consider that in reality, no matter how well the policy is made with the intention to achieve some positive, desired outcome for society, there will always be 'unknown knowns' and 'what it is, it wouldn't be'. Human behaviour is never predictable and public policy as a human endeavour involving decision-making by actors in the process is equally unpredictable.

Normative theory of public policy: rationalism

Herbert Simon's most significant contribution was his book *Administrative Behaviour*, first published in 1945. The focus of the book was on decision-making in organizations, but has been adopted very often as a text to discuss how policy ought to be made. Most writings on public policy making, such as Hogwood and Gunn (1984) or Bardach (2008), have elements of Simon's rational-comprehensive theory. Indeed most textbooks on public policy use Simon's work as a starting point in contrast to other theories.

The rational-comprehensive theoretical approach to policy making centres on maximising social gain. In other words, policy makers should choose the policy option which has the maximum benefit for society over expected costs. It follows an economic logic of maximum utility. Simon, who was awarded a Nobel Prize for Economics in 1978, often contrasted economic and psychological rationalities (Simon 1986). He argued that:

> The assumption that actors maximize subjective expected utility (economic rationality) supplies only a small part of the premises in economic reasoning, and that often not the essential part. The remainder of the premises are auxiliary empirical assumptions about actors' utilities, beliefs, expectations, and the like. Making these assumptions correctly requires an empirically founded theory of choice that specifies what information decision makers use and how they actually process it. This behavioural empirical base is largely lacking in contemporary economic analysis, and supplying it is essential for enhancing the explanatory and predictive power of economics.
>
> (Simon 1986: 209)

Simon recognized that, in decision-making and reasoning, elements of public policy making – expected utility, rationality and economic logic – are important to the process, but that there are other rationalities or subjectivities which influence decision-making. Simon (1965) in his explanation of rational decision-making provides a cost–benefit logarithm, as applied in a private sector organization, as:

1   The total cost (C), incurred by the firm during the month is a function of the quantity of product (X), and of a variable (a), that sums up the effects of supply conditions – wage rates, costs of materials, and so on.
2   The price (P) at which the product is sold is a function of the quantity (X) and of a variable (β) that sums up the effects of demand conditions, e.g. consumer incomes.
3   Total revenue for the month is defined as price (P) times quantity (X), and profit (rr) is defined as the difference between total revenue (PX) and total cost (C).
4   The positive theory is completed by the assumption that X*, the quantity actually produced, equals XM, the quantity that maximizes profit. On the other hand, the normative theory is completed by the injunction: choose the production quantity X* that will maximize profit! To avoid irrelevant detail

31

the assumption is that there is some unique, finite, positive production quantity for which profit assumes an absolute maximum. Then, the positive economist could derive from (4) and (3) the familiar theorem: marginal cost (change of cost per unit increase in quantity) equals marginal revenue (change in total revenue per unit increase in quantity) when production is set at the level that maximizes profit.

Simon (1959; 1965) purported an 'economic' rationality to decision-making to maximize benefits over costs from a normative perspective: decision makers ought to make decisions which have maximum gain. Yet he acknowledged that there are psychological limitations of decision makers because of values and beliefs, and that 'environmental parameters' are not known with certainty by the decision maker (Simon 1965; see Rumsfeld 2002). Thus, profit maximization or rationality in an economic logic is revised with variables of uncertainty entering into the equation (Simon 1965). Simon (1965) distinguished between economic rationality of profitability and utility which took cognizance of variables of uncertainty. Simon (1965: 176) argued that:

> unlike profits, utilities are not directly observable, but instead, it is postulated that the consumer exhibits a certain consistency in his choices; if we observe him in a sequence of choices which bundles he prefers to which others, as his alternatives change we can infer what his utility function is, and what his probability estimates are of outcomes, from his choice behaviour.

Thus, in decision-making a decision maker is confronted with a number of choices and ought to behave in a rational sense to maximize utility. In this decision-making process there are common constraints which are not 'objects of rational calculation' and are: the number of set alternatives open to choice; the relationships that determine the pay-offs (the relationships between costs and benefits) as a function of the alternative which is chosen; and how preferences are ordered (Simon 1955: 100–101).

In sum the rational-comprehensive theory is a normative approach, cognizant of environmental and human variables which create uncertainty, of how decisions ought to be made to ensure maximum attainment of goals and in a public policy context – maximum social gain (Dye 2002). Thus, the policy maker should strive to choose the alternative which has the best possible benefit for society. The rational-comprehensive theory involves a number of key elements:

- A decision maker is confronted with a problem which is discernible from other problems.
- The goals, values and/or objectives are known and can be clarified and ranked according to importance.

■ Various alternatives to address the problem are examined.

■ The consequences of each alternative option are investigated using techniques such as cost–benefit analyses.

■ Each alternative and respective consequences are then compared with each alternative.

■ The decision maker should choose the alternative which maximizes the attainment of goals and objectives (Simon 1945; Anderson 1997; Hill 1997; Dye 2002; Wu *et al.* 2010).

As with most theories, the rational-comprehensive theory was not without critics, with the empirical basis for the theory being contested. These criticisms are summarized as:

■ Policy makers are not confronted with clearly defined problems and various policy actors may have different explanations of the problems. For example, what are the causes of crime in society?

■ There is always incomplete information and data when it comes to decision-making. Indeed there may be barriers to collecting all the information required to make informed decisions about which alternative is the best option. For example, time, human capacity and funding may restrict the ability to conduct a comprehensive analysis.

■ The consequences of each alternative may never be known.

■ There are cognitive limitations on behalf of decision makers such as intelligence, learning, memory, attention spans, psychological subjectivities such as biases, etc.

■ There are environmental limits, such as the political and organizational environment of a public agency, which may shape the processes or choice and indeed the criterion for the selection of alternatives.

■ The rational-comprehensive theory also assumes a sequential process of decision-making which may not necessarily be possible in reality.

■ There may be value conflicts among policy actors which the decision maker has to navigate.

■ Previous decisions may limit the ability for a decision maker to adopt a rational-comprehensive approach. For example, there may be 'sunk costs' where previous policies involving commitments, investments, public monies, etc. may restrict the capacity to undertake a rational-comprehensive analysis (see Parsons 1995; Anderson 1997; Dye 2002; Howlett and Ramesh 2003).

The rational-comprehensive theory is illustrated in Figure 1.4 overleaf.

Simon's (1957; 1986) later writings acknowledge the criticisms of rational-comprehensive theory, but he added that the decision maker within an organization is bounded by environmental and psychological factors. Simon (1957: xxv) assumes

Input

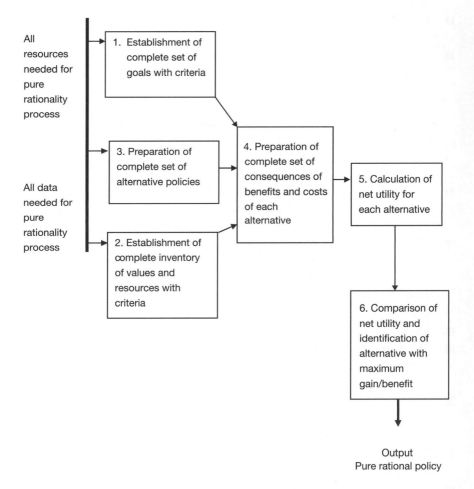

Figure 1.4
Rational-comprehensive theory

a 'bounded rationality' in that the decision maker '. . . makes his choice using a simple picture of the situation that takes into account just a few of the factors that he regards as most relevant and crucial.' In other words the decision maker faced with overwhelming complexity and environmental variables, ought to adopt a rational-comprehensive approach to make sense of the reality, but does not given limited cognitive capacities and as such does not necessarily choose the alternative that has maximum gain (Parsons 1995; Howlett and Ramesh 2003). Rather the decision maker chooses the alternative which satisfies a narrow set of criteria given the 'bounded rationality' and the decision is not based on maximising utility, but satisficing (ibid).

Descriptive theory of public policy: incrementalism

Charles Lindblom in his paper entitled 'The Science of Muddling Through', published in 1959, outlined much of the criticism of the rational-comprehensive theory discussed above. Lindblom based his paper on observations of the public policy-making environment – that there is often bargaining, consensus seeking and agreements within a political context rather than a comprehensive analysis to seek the policy alternative with the maximum benefit (Lindblom 1959; Parsons 1995; Anderson 1997). The policy maker 'muddles through' this environment to find solutions to problems which are workable, agreeable and satisfy most policy actors' interests (ibid). The process is not irrational but 'scientific' in the sense that the inquiry of policy alternatives is based on rational strategies that are politically and organizationally feasible (Howlett and Ramesh 2003). Lindblom (1979) argued that policy makers face a number of limitations in terms of analysis and focus on a few familiar policy alternatives some of which differ marginally from previous, extant policies. The analysis of policy goals, values and problems are interrelated and not distinguishable (ibid). There is an emphasis by policy makers on remedial action rather than a comprehensive analysis to achieve maximum policy outcomes (ibid). Thus, the analysis is limited to a few policy alternatives and only some consequences are considered in terms of trial and error (ibid). Policy makers also analyze policy alternatives cognizant of partisan policy and political environment (ibid).

Lindblom argued that policy makers make policies from a narrow set of comparisons with the process 'continually building out from the current situation, step-by-step and by small degrees' (Lindblom 1959: 81). Policy is thus derived from marginally differentiated alternatives, but usually based on preceding or existing policies (Howlett and Ramesh 2003; Cairney 2012). Lindblom argued that the reason for the narrow selection of policies is twofold: (1) bargaining in the political environment requires distribution of narrow resources among various actors and therefore it is easier to continue with existing patterns of distribution rather than impute values from radically different, new policy options and thereby difficult to gain consensus; and (2) standard operating procedures are embedded in public bureaucracies which tend to promote the continuation of existing practices (Howlett and Ramesh 2003). The separation of ends and means was seen as unworkable in practice, and policy makers therefore adopted an incrementalist approach to policy making because of constraints of time, information, cognitive limitations and the environment, particularly the political and public bureau context

35

of policy making (Parsons 1995; Howlett and Ramesh 2003; Cairney 2012). According to Dye (2002) the incremental description of policy making gained traction as it was empirically observable that:

- Policy makers do not have the time, information and funding to investigate all the alternatives of policy options. The cost of collecting the data to make informed choices is great and the consequences of each alternative cannot be realistically known. It is not possible to calculate the costs and benefits of each alternative policy particularly in the face of many diverse political, social, economic and cultural values.
- Policy makers accept the legitimacy of previous policies because of the uncertainty associated with new or different policies.
- Policy makers accept the investments of time and human and financial resources (the 'sunk costs') of previous policies and therefore choose policies which have little physical, economic, financial, organizational, political and administrative dislocation.
- Policies which are not radically at variance with previous policies, and are politically expedient with agreement among political and policy actors are easier to reach. Conflict is therefore heightened if there are major policy shifts and there is an attempt to retain the status quo, maintaining stability and preserving the political and administrative system.

Thus, incrementalism assumes that policy makers do not maximize benefits but are pragmatic and search for solutions that satisfy the various and diverse interests and values of policy actors. Incrementalism has often been criticized as being conservative as the policies are incremental revisions to existing policies. Incrementalism, it is argued, only appears to be relevant in environments of stability and does not explain dramatic changes to policy, responses to crisis or problems that do require radical departure from existing policies (Howlett and Ramesh 2003). Thus, some argue that incrementalism is a barrier and cannot explain innovative policies (Anderson 1997).

Lindblom in his later writings saw the need for innovative policies to deal with increasingly complex global changes rather than incremental modifications to existing policies (see Parsons 1995: 292–293 for a discussion on the contradictions in Lindblom's collection of papers). Nonetheless, despite Lindblom's revision of the incrementalist approach to public policy, he held that the policy-making process moved slowly in marginal steps, but acknowledged that there was a need for improvement. Thus Lindblom's theory is descriptive but his revisionist ideas became more normative. Lindblom (1979: 519) made the case for disjointed incrementalism as 'a norm would improve the analytical efforts of many analysts, for the several now familiar reasons given in the article 20 years ago'. Disjointed incrementalism is an analytical method in that it is neither the 'seat-of-pants', haphazard incrementalist approach, nor the formal completeness associated with rationalism, but rather a way to simplify problems (Lindblom 1979). Disjointed incrementalism involves:

- a limited analysis of a few policy alternatives;
- an interrelated analysis of policy goals and values;
- a focus on the remedies for problems rather than a goal;
- a trial-and-error learning;
- an analysis of a limited number of alternatives and its consequences; and
- fragmented analysis given the many partisan policy actors involved in the policy process (Lindblom 1979; Parsons 1995).

We have discussed two classic theories of public policy making – rationalism and incrementalism – and often in textbooks these two theories are explored in a dichotomous manner. According to John (1998: 33) textbooks often outline this 'false debate' between rationalism and incrementalism. He argues that public policy writers hope the contrast between the two models will help students understand how policy is made even though it is accepted the dichotomous debate obscures reality (ibid). While we largely agree with John's (1998) comments, and hence our discussion of policy making in the real world, nevertheless it would be remiss not to include the discussion of rational and incremental theory of public policy as it provides a discussion of seminal theories of public policy and it does provide insights into public policy making whether normative or descriptive.

Other theories of policy making

The debate of rationalism and incrementalism continued in academia and there were various alternative perspectives of public policy making. Dror (1964) criticized the incremental approach as being anti-innovation and pro-inertia, but also accepted that the rational approach to policy making was unrealistic. He therefore proposed a normative optimum model to combine realism and idealism (Dror 1964). Dror viewed incrementalism as only applicable in circumstances when there was stability and certainty, but that policy making may require radical adjustments in another context (Parsons 1995; Hill 1997). Thus, the normative optimum model involved an attempt to increase both rationalism and an acceptance of subjectivities in the environment of public policy making (ibid). Dror (1964) referred to these subjectivities as 'extra-rational' which involved judgements, values, creativity and innovations.

Etzioni (1967) proposed a third approach (neither 'rational' nor 'incremental') to public policy making: 'mixed scanning'. Etzioni (1967) was critical of both the rational and incremental approach and used the analogy of weather forecasting to illustrate his theory. World weather observation uses a system of satellites and if the rational approach was employed then there would be an exhaustive, costly search of scanning the environment involving a detailed analysis of problem areas (Etzioni 1967: 389). He argues that this would produce an avalanche of data which would be difficult to analyze, costly and time-consuming (ibid). The incremental approach would focus on similar weather patterns in the recent past or in other regions and would thus ignore formations which deserve attention if they arose in unexpected areas (ibid). Thus the mixed scanning approach includes elements of both rationalism and incrementalism (ibid). In Etzioni's (1967: 389–390) words, there would be two cameras: one providing a broad sweep of the sky and another focusing in on problem areas which would require in-depth analysis. How does this apply to public policy making? Mixed scanning essentially involves a policy maker making a broad review of the problem without engaging initially in too much detailed examination, but when there are problems which require a fundamental review of policy alternatives, a more in-depth analysis is conducted as suggested by the rational approach (Hill 1997).

Of course the mixed scanning theory was not without its critics, with much of the criticism questioning the validity of analogous explanation of weather observation vis-à-vis public policy making. The debate moved beyond rationalism and incrementalism with scholars attempting to capture the complexity of public policy making. Cohen et al. (1972) argued, based on their observations of organizational choices, that decision-making is 'organised anarchy' due to problematic preferences, unclear technologies and fluid participation by actors in the decision-making process. Cohen et al. (1972) argue that in organizations there are inconsistent goals, with the decision maker in situations of goal ambiguity, which are common in complex organizations. Furthermore, members of the organization are activated in occasional manner with attention directed towards, or away from, a decision (ibid). According to Cohen et al. (1972) it is important to understand the attention patterns within an organization, since not everyone is attending to everything all of the time. Decisions, they argue, act as stimuli within organizations, and within organizations a set of procedures are provided through which 'participants arrive at an interpretation of what they are doing and what they have done while in the process of doing it' (Cohen et al. 1972: 2). Cohen et al. (1972) go on to argue that, to understand processes within organizations, one should view decision-making as a garbage can into which various kinds of problems and solutions are dumped by participants as they are generated. The mix of garbage in a single can depends on the mix of cans available, on the labels attached to the alternative cans, on what garbage is currently being produced and on the speed with which garbage is collected and removed from the scene (ibid). In the garbage can process there are exogenous, time-dependent choice opportunities, problems, solutions and decision makers in a milieu (Cyert and March 1992). The garbage-can theory described decision-making not as sequential or hierarchical, but rather that there is a simultaneous linkage between the problems and solutions (ibid). The garbage-can theory illustrates that decision-making within organizations is messy; its untidy mode of identification by policy makers will depend on the time, availability of resources and organizational processes (Parsons 1995). The theory therefore acknowledges that values are complex, knowledge uncertain and that organizational rules and processes are complex (ibid). The garbage-can theory provides useful insights into public policy making as it identifies four variables or factors that characterize and consistently appear in public policy processes, whether as a theoretical discussion or based on empirical analysis. These variables Cohen *et al.* (1972: 3–4) refer to as streams:

- A stream of choices
  Some fixed number of choices is assumed. Each choice is characterized by: (a) an entry time at which that choice is activated for decision; and (b) a decision structure involving participants eligible to participate in making that choice.
- A stream of problems
  Some number of problems is assumed. Each problem is characterized by: (a) an entry time at which the problem becomes visible; (b) an energy requirement to resolve a choice to which the problem is attached (if the solution stream is as high as possible); and (c) an access structure with a list of choices to which the problem has access.
- A rate of flow of solutions
  The theory assumes a stream of solutions and a matching of specific solutions with specific problems and choices. A simpler set of assumptions is made and focus is on the rate at which solutions are flowing into the system. It is assumed that, either because of variations in the stream of solutions or because of variations in the efficiency of search procedures within the organization, different energies are required to solve the same problem at different times. It is further assumed that these variations are consistent for different problems.
- A stream of energy from participants
  It is assumed that there is some number of participants. Each participant is characterized by a time series of energy available for organizational decision-making. Thus, in each time period, each participant can provide some specified amount of potential energy.

This review of theories of public policy reveals that there are a number of common variables in the process. First, there is a problem as identified by policy actors. Second, there is an attempt to find a solution. Various aforementioned theories argue how this is or ought to be achieved within organizations. Third, there are participants in the policy-making process and, as we shall see in Chapters 2 and 3, there is an increasing number of participants/policy actors involved in the policy process. Finally, there is an issue of resources (time, human and financial) and organizational processes that shape the policy process. Human cognitive abilities, funding, infrastructure, technology and time (e.g. crisis requires speed to make a decision because of media and/or political pressure) all impact upon the policy-making process.

Heuristic theories of public policy centre on learning to solve a problem through experimentation, experientialism or trial and error. Heuristic approaches to public policy are not haphazard but involve evaluation and feedback through experiential learning; they are fundamentally about discovering ways to solve problems. Unlike incrementalism, which consists of marginal modifications to existing policies, heuristic approaches encourage learning from the past to develop new and innovative solutions to problems. Most of the heuristic theories of public policy focus on the cognitive capacity of decision makers. Once again Herbert Simon wrote seminal papers in this area where he viewed decision-making as a problem-solving activity. He described heuristic approaches to decision-making thus: when consideration is frequently given to accomplish the desired goal, but where there is failure to accomplish the goal, something else should be tried (Simon 1965: 183). Thus, heuristics is a process of selective trial and error, using rules derived from previous experience, that is sometimes successful in discovering means that are more or less efficacious in attaining some end (Simon 1965: 186). Simon identified a number of ways to facilitate effective problem solving: (1) well-organised and stored information; (2) long-term commitment to the problem; (3) a high level of motivation to solve the problem; (4) originality in abandoning earlier constructions of the problem; (5) use of long term memory to incubate the problem; and (6) the use of tools, techniques and technology to aid analysis (e.g. computers) (Parsons 1995: 355). The basis of most heuristic approaches to public policy is learning: gaining knowledge and information to solve a problem. This involves cognitive and psychological perspectives of decision-making.

BOX 1.2 REFLECTION – PUBLIC POLICY IN DEVELOPING COUNTRIES

Many of the theories and models of public policy have developed from observations of US and European public policy processes and political context. How relevant are these to developing countries? Saasa's (1985) article on public policy making in developing countries offers some insights into the utility of some of the theories discussed in this section of the book. Saasa (1985) argues that public policy is the conscious, goal-setting process undertaken by actors in a decision-making system and it includes the identification of the means to achieve a goal. Saasa (1985) goes on to argue that the rational theory is the least applicable to developing countries due to the costly, time-consuming nature of comprehensive data and information collection of all policy alternatives and consequences. Furthermore, the cognitive limitations of decision makers limit the implementation of rational approaches to policy making (ibid). While Saasa (1985: 316) acknowledges these limitations to be true of any society, he argues that the application of the rational approach is worse in developing countries because of a lack of skilled and experienced policy analysts. Moreover, given the lack of adequate and reliable data, policy makers in developing countries lack the capacity to successfully analyze alternatives and consequences in a highly unpredictable environment (ibid). Saasa (1985) argues that developing countries experience rapid societal transformations which make for an uncertain environment and as a result goals, values and problems are dynamic and fast paced.

Saasa (1985: 317) proceeds to criticize the applicability of the incremental approach. He argues that incrementalism is particularly 'distasteful' in developing countries where the inheritance is colonialism and associated decision-making. In developing countries there is a need for radical, innovative solutions to complex problems in countries which require societal transformation (ibid). Thus, continuity of existing policies could not address resource scarcities that exist in many developing countries (ibid). Furthermore, the incremental approach as Lindblom himself argued is applicable to stable environments, but in developing countries the politico-economic environment can be uncertain (ibid). Saasa (1985: 318) argues that rational and incremental approaches to policy making are limited in applicability due to inherent limitations within developing countries:

- low levels of formal education among citizens;
- primordial attachments along traditional class, ethnic and/or tribal lines;
- relative absence of well-organized interest groups;
- weaknesses in administrative and organizational infrastructure;
- low levels of political consciousness; and
- vulnerabilities to external pressures and influences such as donor agencies.

The limitations are reinforced by political–bureaucratic elites which ensure that policy making is centralized and restricted to a few (ibid). Given that Saasa wrote his paper in 1985, is his analysis still relevant? Are the limitations described above still evident in developing countries?

PUBLIC POLICY MAKING IN THE REAL WORLD

The synthesis of the above theories and models of the public policy process and how policy is made is relevant given that many are based on empirical observations, albeit on Anglo-Saxon political and policy-making systems, and are not to be dismissed as they do provide scholars with insights. Yet, we argue that public policy making has increased in complexity given globalization, multi-levels of governance and 'wicked' public policies. We therefore suggest a revisionist theory of the public policy process. The policy process is not one cycle, in a stagist, linear model, but rather we argue that policy is made in interrelated cycles (see Wu *et al.* 2010). We base our theory on the review of extant, contemporary research; empirical and ethnographic observations of the public policy process in various countries; and upon reflection on delivering policy skills training to civil servants and public officials.

First, as most theories of the public policy process have identified, there is a problem that emerges from the internal (i.e. within the government machinery, the 'black box' process) and/or from the external environments (e.g. media). For example, a problem identified from the external environment could be a campaign to improve nutrition for children through school meals and from the internal environment civil servants, public officials or policy makers providing an evidence base of a problem requiring a policy intervention. There are also instances when actors from the internal and external environment interact through a network and identify a problem. An example of this would be the identification of 'colony collapse disorder', a disease affecting honey bees, which has severe financial implications for the honey industry and rural economies. The industry and public agency epidemiologists worked collectively to raise awareness of the problem and bring it on to the policy agenda. We acknowledge that policy actors from the internal and external environments interact in various ways to ensure that the identified problem arrives on the policy agenda (this is discussed in greater detail in Chapter 3). Thus, in our interrelated cycles (see Figure 1.5) the internal and external environments interact with permeability between the environments and cycles, but central to the theory is the identification of a problem.

Most of the literature that describes the policy process and cycle starts with a 'problem'. How does a problem become recognized as a problem which government feels requires action? There are an infinite number of problems in society, but what makes one problem come on to the agenda above others? Kingdon (1984) observed, after studying the policy process by conducting primary research, that there are three mechanisms which facilitate a problem coming on to a policy agenda. The first is indicators that serve as measures to assess the scale and change in problems, such as government performance reports that play a role in shaping government attitude about a problem (ibid). Examples of this would be cancer rates, performance of students in tests, terrorism risks, congestion on transport services, immigration, etc. Indeed, in the UK the Labour government (1997–2010) was attuned to performance reports when it came to making policy (see Power 1997). The second mechanism is events that may dramatically focus government's attention on a problem such as a crisis or disaster (ibid). Chapter 11 provides a case study of a crisis, the foot-and-mouth crisis, to illustrate an event that required government action. The final mechanism is feedback, which provides government with information on performance of a policy and whether remedial action is required (ibid). A key concept of Kingdon (1984) is policy streams, which serve to determine the profile of a problem on the policy agenda. These policy streams include national mood (e.g. public opinion), organized political forces (e.g. political parties, pressure or interest groups), government (e.g. a change in functionality or jurisdiction) and consensus-building (e.g. bargaining between pressure or interest groups and government) (ibid). These streams may operate in the external environment independently but may on occasion come together so that a problem is recognized and a change takes place (ibid). Kingdon (1984) uses the metaphor of a window: the streams merge to create a window of opportunity for a policy change to take place. Thus, a policy window opens because of a problem, solution or proposal, and political receptivity is aligned thereby creating a higher probability of the problem reaching the policy agenda (ibid). A criticism of Kingdon's model suggests it is fatalistic and far too dependent on random probabilities (see Parsons 1995). Baumgartner and Jones (1993) explain how problems come on to the policy agenda through what they termed a punctuated equilibrium. They argue that the policy process has relatively long periods of stability accounting for the incrementally conservative nature of political systems, but on occasion there is a need for rapid change (ibid). Thus, there is equilibrium but this is interspersed with periods of instability or policy change (ibid). Baumgartner and Jones (1993) argue that problems come on to the policy agenda through two principle and interacting forces: (1) the policy image, i.e. how an issue is portrayed; and (2) institutional policy venues, i.e. the institutional context of the policy.

Increasingly in a globalized world there are complex, interrelated policy problems. The recent banking crisis with its economic consequences – complex and global in scale and scope – is a typical example of the type of policy problems governments face. In this increasingly inter-connected world there are policy problems which do not have an easy, readily defined solution. Indeed, even identifying and structuring the problem may prove difficult. For example, terrorism has proven difficult for many governments around the world to address. Some have defined terrorism in defence policy (e.g. 'War on Terrorism'), others in social policy terms (e.g. addressing poverty and social exclusion on a global scale), and others in criminal justice terms (e.g. a crime requiring law enforcement policies) or even all of the above. In the field of public policy, these problems are defined as wicked policy problems. The concept refers to problematic social situations where: (1) there is no obvious solution; (2) many individuals and organizations are necessarily involved; (3) there is disagreement among stakeholders; and (4) desired behaviour changes are part of the solution (Rittel and Webber 1973; see Head 2010; Ferlie *et al.* 2011). The problems, for example, include inter alia policy areas such as poverty, social exclusion, inequalities, climate change, pollution, terrorism, etc. Often, attempting to address the problem as identified may lead to unintended outcomes. Dunn (1994) argues that policy problems are invariably interdependent, i.e. policy problems in one area frequently affect policy problems in another. He argues that policy problems are parts of whole systems of problems best described as 'messes', that is, systems of external conditions that produce dissatisfaction among different segments of society (Dunn 1994: 141). Thus, we too argue that public policy problems cannot be thought of in isolation, but are part of many interrelated systems.

Once a problem has been identified, a decision to take a purposive course of action is made. Still the policy actors from the external and internal environments will interact in the decision-making process, with internal policy makers often consulting external policy makers for advice, evidence and data to inform the process and ensure the acceptance of the decision, principally to avoid contentious decisions that may result in conflict. However, not all external policy actors will be satisfied with the decision. For example, a decision to regulate junk food will not be welcomed by the food industry, but in making the policy there will be compromises until the policy satisfies most policy actors. This form of consensual policy making is evident in policy-making systems where there is a high level of governance and network arrangements. The problem and decision are interrelated as well, with perhaps the problem being redefined once a decision is made. For example, in many countries in Europe there is a high level of teenage pregnancy, which is identified as a socio-health problem. In various countries the decision has been to introduce a sexual health educational programme in schools, therefore identifying the issue as one of 'health' policy. In other countries the problem has been redefined as a social problem with some governments introducing broad policies to combat poverty, social exclusion and welfare-benefit dependency. Thus, policy makers are making various assumptions to embark upon a purposive course of action in defining or redefining the problem.

So, a problem may be identified, defined and redefined, and a decision, whether in a passive (do nothing) or active (decision to take action) sense, is made to undertake a purposive course of action. Various options are considered when defining the problem and deciding to act or not, and are therefore interrelated with the problem and decision cycle. This cycle involves various types of decision-making by policy makers:

- Political: policy makers are keenly aware of whether an option will be politically and/or ideologically feasible for the government of the day.

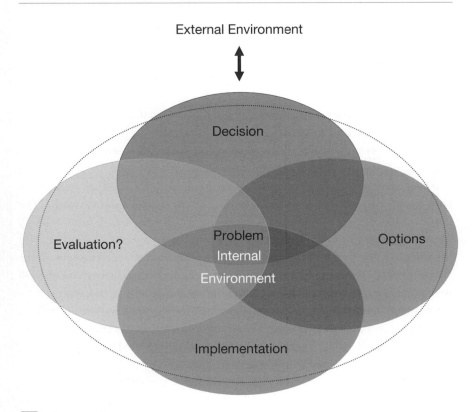

External Environment

Figure 1.5
Interrelated policy cycles

- Legal: consideration of regulatory frameworks and feasibility of options (e.g. Human Rights, European Union (EU) directives, UN obligations, etc.).
- Technocratic: cost–benefit ratios; financial, economic, budgetary, etc. considerations.
- Practical: policy makers will consider whether there is administrative and technological infrastructure as well as time to deliver the policy.

This is not an exhaustive list of decision-making criteria involved in considering various options. The criteria – and which of these loom larger – very much depend on the current economic, political and/or social climate. For example, within this period of austerity many governments are placing the emphasis on reducing public expenditure as a criterion when considering various policy options. Policy makers may spend a considerable period of time in contemplating policy options or may, given time pressures, give a cursory analysis. The option cycle also interacts with other cycles: the options may be too costly, for example, and this may become a problem in itself with the authoritative decision maker – government – deciding to do nothing and thereby redefining the problem as a non-problem. For many years the problem of global warming was defined as a non-problem until the cost implications outweighed the benefits of non-action and so a decision was made by governments to address global warming, hence the Kyoto Protocol (1997) as a global policy.

The problem, decision and options all interact in a cyclical manner with inputs from the internal and external environments, as well as interfacing with the implementation cycle. Particularly, in an era of governance and co-governance, policy actors are involved in the implementation of policies. In the internal and external environments policy actors deliver on policies whether delivery is outsourced, co-produced or undertaken through partnerships and networks. The implementation cycle interacts with the problem, decision and option cycles by identifying problems in implementation that may not have been considered. This is particularly the case when there are unintended outcomes. For example, in the US the Personal Responsibility and Work Opportunity Reconciliation Act of 1996 was introduced to reduce the number of welfare dependents and enable their employment. However, there were unintended outcomes: most welfare dependents were single-parent families, mostly headed by women in low-wage employment, consequently caught in a cycle of low wages and paying for child care support, resulting in the feminization of poverty.

A further cycle, that may or may not take place, is evaluation. Evaluation, depending on resourcing and the administrative and political palatability to undertake an evaluation of a policy, may take place within the internal environment. The evaluation may be made public or embargoed, but many countries have various rights guarantees for citizens to gain access to information (e.g. UK Freedom of Information Act). A policy which does not meet with success may result in a problem being identified and so the policy becomes cyclical. The policy may also be evaluated independently in the external environment by academic experts, interest groups, private sector companies affected by a particularly policy, the media, or even individual citizens (particularly if there are negative outcomes, these actors may illuminate the policy failures in order to lobby government to revise or redefine the policy). Within the internal environment there is a host of public agencies as independent evaluators or actors within the responsible implementing public agency involved in evaluation. For example, in the UK there are audit offices, review boards and inspection agencies. The internal and external environments may also interact with evaluation studies being commissioned by government and outsourced to independent experts. But often governments do not want to know about 'unknown' outcomes of a policy and there are some outcomes they prefer not to know about, distancing themselves from any liabilities. Hence our question mark about evaluation in Figure 1.5.

CONCLUSION

To conclude, the book views policy making as taking place within cycles, which are interrelated and embedded within dynamic internal and external environments. These interrelated cycles involve problem identification, decision-making, options analyses according to various criteria, implementation and possible evaluation – all impacting upon each other. The book to some extent follows these cycles in various parts of the book, but you should be cognizant of underlying themes: globalization; governance; political architectures or systems; internal and external policy actors or stakeholders; organizational dynamics or institutional policy venues – all forming the context in which policy is made. Chapter 2 describes and discusses the domains of public policy within the context of hierarchies, markets and governance. Chapter 3 explores policy making among the various policy actors and stakeholders involved and marginalized in the process. Thereafter, a detailed analysis of the key elements in the policy process is provided: the capacity of the policy system (Chapter 5); the structure and organizational forms through which policy is delivered (Chapter 6); the role of professions, markets and consumers (Chapter 7); accountability and performance (Chapters 9 and 10). Thus, we define the policy process as:

> An interrelated number of cycles involving problem definition and redefinition; decision-making; option analyses according to various criteria emanating from the political, economic, legal, socio-cultural, technocratic and practical contexts; which result in a policy that is implemented and may or may not be evaluated. These interrelated cycles, involving state and non-state actors, take place within the context of internal and external environments continually interacting with problem, decision, option, implementation and evaluation cycles.

REFERENCES

Anderson, J. (1997) *Public Policy Making*, New York: Houghton Mifflin.

Bardach, E. (2008) *A Practical Guide for Policy Analysis: the eightfold path to more effective problem solving*, Washington, DC: CQ Press.

Baumgartner, F. and Jones, B. (1993) *Agendas and Instability in American Politics*, Chicago, IL: University of Chicago.

Cairney, P. (2012) *Understanding Public Policy*, London: Palgrave Macmillan.

Caroll, L. (2010) *Alice's Adventures in Wonderland*, Kindle Edition www.gutenberg.org. (Accessed 5 February 2013.)

Clemons, R.S. and McBeth, M.K. (2001) *Public Policy Praxis. Theory and Pragmatism: a case approach*, Upper Saddle River, NJ: Prentice Hall.

Cohen, M., March, J. and Olsen J. (1972) 'A garbage can model of organisational choice', *Administrative Science Quarterly*, 17, 1: 1–25.

Cyert, R. and March. J. (1992) *Behavioural Theory of the Firm*, Oxford: Basil Blackwell.

Dror, Y. (1964) 'Muddling through – "science" or inertia?' *Public Administration Review*, 24, 3: 153–157.

Dunn, W.N. (1994) *Public Policy Analysis: an introduction*, 2nd edition, Upper Saddle River, NJ: Prentice Hall.

Dye, T. (2002) *Understanding Public Policy*, 10th edition, Upper Saddle River, NJ: Prentice Hall.

Easton, D. (1965) *A Framework for Political Analysis*, Englewood Cliffs, NJ: Prentice Hall.

Etzioni, A. (1967) 'Mixed scanning: a "third" approach to decision-making', *Public Administration Review*, 27, 5: 385–392.

Ferlie, E., Fitzgerald, L., McGivern, G., Dopson, S. and Bennett, C. (2011) 'Public policy networks and "wicked problems": a nascent solution?' *Public Administration*, 89, 2: 307–324.

Head, B.W. (2010) 'Public management research: towards relevance', *Public Management Review*, 12, 5: 571–585.

Hill, M. (1997) *The Policy Process in the Modern State*, Harlow: Pearson.

Hogwood, B.W. and Gunn, L.A. (1984) *Policy Analysis for the Real World*, Oxford: Oxford University Press.

Howlett, M. and Ramesh, M. (2003) *Studying Public Policy*, Don Mills, Ontario: Oxford University Press.

Hudson, J. and Lowe, S. (2004) *Understanding the Policy Process: analysing welfare policy and practice*, Bristol: The Policy Press.

Jenkins, W.I. (1978) *Policy Analysis: a politics and organisational perspective*, London: Martin Robertson.

John, P. (1998) *Analysing Public Policy*, London: Continuum.

Jones, C.O. (1970) *An Introduction to the Study of Public Policy*, Belmont, CA: Wadsworth.

Kingdon, J.W. (1984) *Agendas, Alternatives and Public Policies*, Boston, MA: Little Brown.

Lasswell, H.D. (1956) *The Decision Process: seven categories of functional analysis*, College Park, MD: University of Maryland.

Lindblom, C. (1959) 'The science of muddling through', *Public Administration Review*, 19, 2: 78–88.

Lindblom, C. (1979) 'Still muddling, not yet through', *Public Administration Review*, 39, 6: 517–525.

Lowi, T.J. (1972) 'Four systems of policy politics and choice', *Public Administration Review*, 32, 4: 298–310.

Mack, R. (1971) *Planning and Uncertainty*, New York: John Wiley.

Nakamura, R. (1987) 'The textbook policy process and implementation research', *Policy Studies*, 7, 1: 142–154.

Parsons, W. (1995) *Public Policy: an introduction to the theory and practice of policy analysis*, Cheltenham: Edward Elgar.

Power, M. (1997) *The Audit Society: rituals of verification*, Oxford: Open University Press.

Rittel, H.W.J. and Webber, M.M. (1973) 'Dilemmas in a general theory of planning', *Policy Sciences*, 4: 155–169.

Rose, R. (1973) 'Comparing public policy: an overview', *European Journal of Political Research*, 1, 1: 67–94.

Rumsfeld, D. (2002) Press Conference speech at the NATO Headquarters, www.nato.int/docu/speech/2002/s020606g.htm. (Accessed 12 February 2012.)

Saasa, O. (1985) 'Public policy making in developing countries: the utility of contemporary decision-making models', *Public Administration and Development*, 5, 4: 309–321.

Simon, H. (1945) *Administrative Behaviour*, New York: Free Press.

Simon, H. (1955) 'A behavioral model of rational choice', *The Quarterly Journal of Economics*, 69, 1: 99–118.

Simon, H. (1957) *Administrative Behaviour*, 3rd edition, New York: Free Press.

Simon, H. (1959) 'Theories of decision-making in economics and behavioral science', *The American Economic Review*, 49, 3: 253–283.

Simon, H. (1965) 'The logic of rational decision', *The British Journal for the Philosophy of Science*, 16, 63: 169–186.

Simon, H. (1986) 'Rationality in Psychology and Economics', *Journal of Business*, 59, 4: 209–224.

Smith, M. (1993) *Pressure, Power and Policy: state autonomy and policy networks in Britain and the United States*, Hemel Hempstead: Harvester Wheatsheaf.

Wu, X., Ramesh, M., Howlett, M. and Fritzen, S. (2010) *The Public Policy Primer: managing the policy process*, London: Routledge.

49

Chapter 2

Public policy domains

LEARNING OBJECTIVES

■ To develop a specific and precise appreciation of state and non-state actors involved in public policy making and management
■ To recognize the changing, yet nonetheless pre-eminent, role of government in the diverse and enlarged environment of public policy

KEY POINTS IN THIS CHAPTER

■ How government bureaucracies are positioned as a public policy domain
■ The way in which markets, managerial and reform initiatives have become significant drivers in public policy
■ An outline and explanation of governance: why and how the organization of nation states, institutions beyond and above the nation state, civil society organizations have become part of governance
■ The way in which two schools of thought explain and define governance
■ How new public governance has emerged as an explanatory paradigm for understanding public policy

INTRODUCTION

In 1995 three former private sector managers founded New Century Financial Corporation in California, US. The company was a mortgage lender and within ten years had an estimated net income of almost $500 million. New Century Financial, like most mortgage lenders, was capitalising on the property boom in

■ **50**

the US at the time. New Century Financial became the second largest mortgage lender in the US. And in time many other financial institutions began to loan credit to high-risk borrowers (people with poor credit histories or who probably could not afford to repay the mortgage given their low incomes). This credit for high-risk mortgages became known as sub-prime mortgages. Unregulated financial services then bundled these loans or assets into portfolios known as Collateralized Debt Obligations (CDOs) and sold them on to investors globally. From 2004 US interest rates started to increase resulting in those high-risk mortgage lenders defaulting. In April 2007 New Century Financial Corporation filed for bankruptcy with many more lenders to follow. The collapse of the sub-prime mortgage market rippled across the global financial and banking sector. Major losses began to emerge. Banks collapsed. And so began the financial crisis. Governments around the world responded with various policies to stem the crisis such as bail-outs (e.g. US) and nationalization of banks (e.g. UK), deposit guarantees (e.g. Germany), extra government funding (e.g. Russia), lower interest rates (e.g. Australia) and sometimes all of the above (BBC 2009).

The domains of public policy are seldom discrete and localized, rather in an increasing globalized context, public policy takes place in various and often inter-connected domains. This chapter outlines the domains or venues of public policy. As discussed in the preceding chapters, public policy is made by government as an authoritative decision maker. As such, this chapter discusses public bureaucracy as one of the main domains of public policy making. Yet, as the chapter will discuss, public policy is not the sole domain of government. There are increasingly a number of other actors involved in the policy process. The chapter therefore discusses governance as a domain of public policy. Public policy takes place among public, private and voluntary sectors at an international, national, sub-national and local level. The story of the banking crisis demonstrates that in a globalized policy domain what happens at a local level within a private sector context resonates far beyond the boundaries of sectors and nation states. This chapter will outline the complexities surrounding the location of policy making. It will look at government and governance structures and arrangements at supra-national, national and sub-national levels: multi-level governance. But first there is a discussion of public policy as made within government, within top-down bureaucratic structures, then broadening out towards markets and finally governance structures. The chapter is devoted to where policy is made within interrelated cycles.

Public policy is generally formulated within the institutional machinery of government – the public bureaucracy, but it is also formulated within the interface between state and non-state actors – within the context of governance. We start with an explanation and discussion of public bureaucracy as a domain of public policy making and then proceed with an outline of public sector reforms: the move away from bureaucratic hierarchies towards marketization and private sector managerialism. This section of the chapter discusses NPM as the scholarly

51

interpretation of the simulacrum allocation of public resources by competitive markets, the privatization of public services and utilities, and the integration of private sector managerialism into the public sector (Lynn 2007). Thus, the interface between the public and private sector is discussed as a domain of public policy. But, there are other non-state actors also involved in the policy process, often including civil society organizations such as the voluntary sector. The chapter concludes with a discussion of governance. It is here that you are introduced to concepts of governance, such as networks of state and non-state actors in the policy process, and multi-level governance as locations and venues of public policy. Finally, within the context of governance there is a discussion of trajectories of public policy domains under New Public Governance (NPG) and some critical reflection. First though, we discuss government, in particular public bureaucracy, as a domain of public policy given its authoritative role in the policy process.

GOVERNMENT: PUBLIC BUREAUCRACY

The public policy domain of government requires an exploration of the Eastonian 'black box'. This often involves the core executive of government and although we acknowledge policy making within the core executive involves both politicians and civil or public servants (see Chapter 3), the focus of this section is on public bureaucracies as a venue for the formulation and implementation of public policy. Although variant political architectures and systems of countries may see diverse civil and public service systems, there are commonalities in structure of public bureaucracies. It is beyond the scope of this volume to provide a comprehensive comparative analysis of civil and public service systems, but we encourage you to refer to the text *International Handbook on Civil Service Systems* edited by Massey (2011). Nevertheless, most public service systems follow a Weberian-style bureaucracy (Barberis 2011) with an integration of NPM type reforms (Pollitt and Bouchaert 2000). The conventional understanding of bureaucracy is rule-bound, the adherence to standardized procedures inflexible, impervious to change and thereby slow, inefficient and wasteful (Meier and Hill 2007; Barberis 2011). To understand public bureaucracy as a domain of public policy, we have to return to the seminal writing on bureaucracy by Max Weber.

Max Weber's idea of bureaucracy is within the context of power, legitimacy and rationality. Weber explained bureaucracy through the lens of power ('Macht') and domination/authority ('Herrschaft') (Weber 1968; Mommsen 1974; Miller 2012). According to Weber (1968) power is when one actor in a social relationship is in a position to carry out his/her will despite resistance. Domination or authority is when a command with specific content will be obeyed by a given group of persons (Weber 1968). The concepts underpin the idea of legitimacy, which according to Weber (1968) is the motivation that induces persons to obey given commands regardless of whether these commands are addressed to them personally or in the language of rules, laws and regulations. So, the extent to which people are likely to obey a command depends on whether they believe the system of commands to be legitimate. Weber believed that legitimacy was imperative to the stability of political systems for, if the governed did not believe in the legitimacy of a political system, it would be bound to be unstable and eventually collapse (Mommsen 1974). Weber was an advocate of democracy since he believed that every stable government enjoyed the consent of the governed (ibid). He viewed the formal enactment of laws as established legitimacy and was the most rational form of authority (Mommsen 1974; Blau and Meyer 1987, Miller 2012). Weber constructed the 'pure type of legal domination', as counterparts to other forms of domination (charismatic and traditional), with laws administered through a bureaucracy (ibid). Weber therefore constructed an 'ideal type' of administrative organization – a bureaucracy that represented the average of all existing organizational structures, abstracting the most common characteristics to develop an organizational type that maximized rationality and legitimacy (Blau and Meyer 1987; Du Gay 2000; Thompson and Miller 2003, Miller 2012). The main characteristics of Weberian bureaucracy include:

- Regular activities required for the purposes of the organization are distributed in a fixed manner as official duties (Weber 1946). In modern organizations these regular activities and distribution are manifest in the division of labour and specialization (Blau and Meyer 1987; Du Gay 2000; Meier and Hill; 2007; Miller 2012).
- The organization follows a principle of hierarchy with each lower office supervised by an office higher in the organization (Weber 1947). Thus, every official is accountable to a superior in the organization with the superior having authority over subordinates (Blau and Meyer 1987; Du Gay 2000; Meier and Hill; 2007).
- The administration of the governed is through a consistent system of abstract rules and the application of these rules to particular cases (Weber 1947). Thus there are standards to ensure the consistent application of the uniformity of rules with explicit rules defining the responsibility of members of the organization and their relationship with others within and outwith the organization (Blau and Meyer 1987; Du Gay 2000; Meier and Hill 2007, Miller 2012).
- The ideal official conducts the office in the spirit of formalistic impersonality without hatred or passion (Weber 1947). This characteristic of the organization is a form of rational detachment from official duties and a separation of the personal from the professional (Blau and Meyer 1987; Du Gay 2000; Meier and Hill; 2007, Miller 2012). Weber believed that, in order for officials to rationally implement legitimate laws, personal detachment and objectivity was required especially when dealing with clients of the organization (ibid).

53

■ Employment is based on technical qualification with members of the organization protected by rules to avoid arbitrary dismissal (Weber 1947). Weber envisaged a career system of selection based on competence and meritorious promotion, which would encourage an esprit de corps with members of the organization motivated by the acknowledgement of performance, a development of loyalty and permanence of service (Blau and Meyer 1987, Miller 2012).

■ Weber (1947) believed that 'experience tends universally to show that the purely bureaucratic type of administrative organization . . . is, from a purely technical point of view, capable of attaining the highest degree of efficiency'. Thus the longevity of the membership of an organization by virtue of meritorious promotion coupled with qualifications ensured experience was not lost to the organization and thereby maximized efficient application of laws and duties of the office (Blau and Meyer 1987; Du Gay 2000; Meier and Hill 2007, Miller 2012).

The characteristics of a Weberian bureaucracy are firmly embedded in modern government. The fixed and official jurisdictional area ordered by laws and rules, the persistence of hierarchy, officialdom, occupations based on careers and promotion, etc. are all pervasive aspects of government (Meier and Hill 2007; Barberis 2011). For a more detailed conceptual discussion of bureaucracy and the public sector a good text is *The Public Sector: concepts, models and approaches* by Jan-Erik Lane (2000).

Bureaucracy as the machinery of government plays a pivotal role in the policy process. First, bureaucracy is involved in the policy process by virtue of its expertise, information and knowledge (Peters 2001; Page and Jenkins 2005). This resource is concentrated in bureaucracies with the technical expertise to inform the policy process, and this monopoly of information is translated in a number of ways (Peters 2001). The Weberian bureaucracy's emphasis on qualified officials with the appropriate skills, experience and longevity of office provides bureaucrats with the argument that they have more intimate knowledge of the policy area, should be in control of making the policy and be principal advisers to politicians on the policy (ibid). This Peters (2001) argues means that bureaucracy is in a situation in which it can at least implicitly trade information for influence over policy. A second role of the bureaucracy is its linkage between interest groups, non-state actors and policy stakeholders with the political arena (ibid). Bureaucrats are the interface between the politicians, particularly those within the executive branch of government (e.g. Cabinet), and various organizations and even individual citizens who wish to influence the policy process. They articulate to ministers, secretaries of state, prime ministers, presidents, etc. the interests of various societal groups and/or citizens and become a channel of information. A further way in which bureaucrats impact upon the policy process is through their neutrality and apolitical roles (Peters 2001). These are features of Weberian bureaucracy. Bureaucrats serve the government of the day and remain isolated from partisan politics to ensure the policy advice they provide is objective and based on technical expertise (ibid). Politicians, particularly those within the executive, are highly dependent upon bureaucrats who work to fashion policies that they believe may be politically palatable to their political masters (Page and Jenkins 2005). Another way in which the bureaucracy impacts upon the policy process is its permanence and stability (ibid). This feature of the Weberian bureaucracy enables bureaucrats to gain expertise, knowledge and information about a policy area over a long period of time (ibid). Additionally, it allows for continuity in times of political uncertainty, i.e. an electoral outcome may result in no outright winner or a 'hung' legislature (e.g. the 2000 US Presidential elections, the 2010 UK general election) and the bureaucracy plays a role in the continuity of policy implementation. Thus, an important role of the bureaucracy is its expertise in informing policy formulation as well as its role in the implementation of policy and public service delivery.

According to Page and Jenkins (2005) bureaucrats are involved in the process of making policy in three ways:

- Production – the production policy process produces drafts, statements and documents such as statutory instruments and legislation. This process invariably involves interest groups, individuals and stakeholders outside of government.
- Maintenance – this entails tending to particular sets of arrangements governing particular policies. While various bureaucrats may be involved in the production of a policy, others may be involved in the implementation of the policy.
- Service – the service role involves offering knowledge, skills and advice in the production of policy. The offering of advice to political executives is a clear example of service policy work.

There have been various critics and proponents of Weberian bureaucracy (for example see Blau 1963; Downs 1967; Goodsell 1983; Blau and Meyer 1987; Clegg 1990; Du Gay 2000; Peters 2001; Stokes and Clegg 2002; Thompson and Miller 2003; Olsen 2006; 2008; Meier and Hill 2007). The neo-liberal reforms of the public sector saw a revisionist view of bureaucracy, i.e. rather than a rational and efficient administrative organization it became synonymous with inefficiency through rule-bound, monopolistic behaviour (see Thompson and Miller 2003). Particular criticism of bureaucratic behaviour is principally from 'Public Choice' theorists.

Anthony Downs' (1967) book *Inside Bureaucracy* explored the behaviour of bureaucrats and three 'laws'. First, Downs (1967) argued that there is limited span of control in the supervision of others in large organizations such as multi-level hierarchical bureaucracies. At each stage in a hierarchy, he argued that bureaucrats filter information that they pass upwards through the hierarchy; he called this the 'law of imperfect control' (Downs 1967: 143). Second, he argued that there is a 'law of diminishing control', which he referred to as an organizational increase in scale that results in more distance between those at the apex of the hierarchy and those at the bottom of the hierarchy. As such, senior bureaucrats devise means to control policy implementation but these efforts consume resources (Dunleavy 1991). Thus, the 'law of counter-control' holds that the 'greater the effort made by a top official to control the behaviour of subordinate officials, the greater the efforts made by these subordinates to evade or counteract such control' (Downs 1967: 147). The final 'law' described by Downs was that of the 'law of decreasing coordination'. Downs argued that top-ranked officials become overloaded with information from lower-ranked officials as decisions are invariably pushed up the hierarchy in search of an authoritative decision maker. The consequence of overloaded top officials is a lack of coordination and strategic direction (Dunleavy 1991).

In addition to Downs' laws, he described bureaucratic behaviours:

- bureaucrats who were 'climbers' who maximized their power, income and prestige by securing promotion or acquiring additional responsibilities;
- those who maximized their job security by defending their existing responsibilities known as the 'conservers';
- 'zealots' who were committed to particular policy areas and promoted their expansion; and
- the 'statesman' who was committed to the public interest (Downs 1967: 88–111).

William Niskanen argued in his book, *Bureaucracy and Representative Government* (1971), that bureaucrats shaped bureaus on the basis of self-interest. Niskanen based his argument on economic theory: humans make rational choices of maximising benefits over costs. Thus, in the private sector the interest is profit maximization, but by definition the public sector is not a profit-maximising sector. Niskanen therefore argued that bureaucrats maximize the budget of their bureau in order to gain power, income, prestige and job security (Hindmoor 2006). Niskanen (1971) referred to this as budget-maximizing and bureau-shaping behaviour. Budget maximization and bureau-shaping behaviour, it is argued, explain the growth of bureaucracies and public expenditure (Niskanen 1971; Dunleavy 1991; Peters 2001). The similarities with Downs' writings and the characteristic of Public Choice theory is that public bureaucrats behave in a manner to maximize their own interests and that bureaucracies, like all social entities, involve individual actors who behave in a rational economic manner (Lane 2000). Public Choice theorists argue that the bureau-shaping and budget maximization explain the inefficiencies of public bureaucracies.

PUBLIC SECTOR REFORM: FROM HIERARCHIES TO MARKETS

The 1970s saw a global economic crisis and many governments, particularly in Europe, sought to reduce public expenditure and stimulate economic growth. The complex challenges of the European welfare state required a revisionist view of the role of the state. There were criticisms that the state was too large in scale and scope with the delivery of public services neither efficient nor effective. Similarly, in the US there were calls to reduce the role of the state and encourage market forces (Lynn 2007). These views were articulated by 'New Right' thinking and the 'Public Choice' school of US academia, which saw the public sector as restricting the benefits of individualism, market activity and private sector competition in stimulating economic growth (Massey and Pyper 2005). 'New Right' and 'Public Choice' proponents criticized the role of the state as over-regulatory and indeed viewed government intervention in the economy as distorting markets with adverse outcomes for economic growth. The public sector, with its hierarchical bureaucratic structures and observance of rules and regulations, was seen as anachronistic and unable to meet the dynamic economic and social challenges of an increasingly globalized world. These global changes of technological innovation, the development of supra-national institutions and rapid global economic advances saw increasing public pressure to redefine the role of the state with politicians answering the call to reform the public sector (Massey 1993; Hughes 2003).

The 'New Right' school of thought gained traction and by the late 1970s politicians, principally Margaret Thatcher in the UK, sought to reform the public sector. These reforms first centred on reducing public expenditure and introducing fiscal prudence thereby reducing the tax burden and the role of the state (Flynn 2007). For example, in the early 1980s Michael Heseltine as the then Conservative government's Secretary of State for the Environment introduced the Financial Management Initiative (FMI), which divided the department into cost centres and enabled Heseltine to compare actual with planned expenditure, conduct budget reviews and evaluate output (ibid). The initiative was borrowed from private sector accounting principles and gained Mrs Thatcher's support (ibid). By 1982 the Treasury and Civil Service Committee recommended that FMI be implemented throughout civil service (ibid). During the Thatcher premiership the belief in the superiority of the market with competitive forces being more efficient and effective in service delivery saw the public sector reformed along private sector management principles, accompanied by the large-scale privatization of public services and utilities (Massey and Pyper 2005; Flynn 2007). For example, Mrs Thatcher introduced Derek Raynor, then managing director of Marks and Spencer — a private sector retail company – to head an efficiency unit in the Cabinet Office and conduct scrutiny studies of the public sector in order to make efficiency savings (Flynn 2007).

From the 1980s onwards the UK under Thatcher's Conservative government began to scale back government by releasing public sector activity to the private sector, introducing markets in the public sector, embracing private sector practices with the notion of reducing public expenditure (and thereby the tax burden) and improving the public sector in terms of efficiency and effectiveness in the delivery of services. The reform of the public sector gained momentum, was transferred on a global scale by governments learning from the UK experience (Lynn 2007). Governments around the world embraced the idea of privatization of public services; the introduction of marketization and competition in the public sector, such as the tendering of public services to private sector providers; the adoption of private sector management practices; the decentralization and fragmentation of large public sector bureaucracies into single purpose agencies; the focus on the citizen as a 'customer' in an effort to improve responsiveness; an emphasis on choice and greater value to individual citizens rather than as a collective electorate; and exploring new structures of government and service delivery based on best practice in the private sector (Massey and Pyper 2005).

Collectively, the reform of the public sector with the integration of private sector managerialism and marketization, and a shift away from more bureaucratic, rule-bound public sector structures, become known as NPM (Hood 1991). The salient features of NPM include inter alia: an emphasis on management skills with a focus on greater efficiency, effectiveness and economy; a shift from bureaucratic reliance on rules to quantifiable output measures and performance targets; a preference for privatization and/or the integration of private sector management practices; separation of large hierarchical bureaucratic structures to more semi-autonomous agencies; and embracing the idea of responsiveness to the 'customer' as opposed to the citizen (Pollitt 1990; Kamensky 1996; Peters and Savoie 1998; Pollitt and Bouckaert 2000; Hughes 2003; Massey and Pyper 2005). This new form of management in the public sector saw an ideological shift from the idea of public administration concerns for social collectivism to market-based notions of self-sufficiency. Scholars began to analyze the impact of these reforms on the public sector with observations centring on the withering of the state; the de-bureaucratization of public services and the rise of marketization; the integration and often inappropriate application of private sector managerial practices to the public sector context; etc. (see Pollitt 1990; Ferlie et al. 1996; Peters and Savoie 1998; Pollitt and Bouckaert 2000; Hughes 2003;).

As the private sector ethos became embedded in the public sector, there was an elaboration of the market model such as the development of quasi-markets within the public sector (Ferlie et al. 1996). For example, in the UK the National Health Service, a public service, saw the integration of the market model resulting in the internal market and purchaser–provider split as a means of allocating resources more efficiently in an attempt to improve health care delivery (Ham 2009). The de-bureaucratization of the public sector went further with the fragmentation of public organizations into agencies to increase responsiveness and efficiency gains (Massey and Pyper 2005; Flynn 2007;). This fragmentation or agencification of public sector organization was in some ways consistent with the purchaser–provider or principal–agent split in the delivery of services. The relationship between principal–agent or purchaser–provider was maintained through contractual agreements, often increasing transactional and administrative costs. By the late 1980s contracting out of non-strategic functions became the norm with the consequent downsizing of government activity and staff (Ferlie *et al.* 1996). A new generation of managerialist practices arose with an emphasis on partnership working, innovative methods of management, flexibility and collaborative efforts to problem solving (ibid).

Similarly in the 1990s in the US, the Clinton administration was influenced by the ideas of Osborne and Gaebler (1992) with the publication of their book *Reinventing Government*. Osborne and Gaebler (1992) called for an entrepreneurial government, one that promotes competition between providers, empowers citizens to push control of bureaucracy into the community and focuses on the performance measurement of government activity. These ideas were similar to those of the UK Conservative government: that government could provide services where markets failed, but that government was not necessarily the most efficient means to provide these services (Hughes 2003). Public sector reforms became much more focused on results, in addition to efficiency savings, consistent with political objectives of responsiveness and public sector accountability. For example, in the UK the then Prime Minister John Major championed the Citizen's Charter which was a manifest for the public sector to be more performance and results orientated with an emphasis on responsiveness to the public (Flynn 2007). The public sector was by now emulating private sector management practices such as integrating continuous quality improvement, strategic management, performance management and entre-preneurial leadership. The common features of Anglo-Saxon public sector reforms can be summarized as:

- a focus on financial control and savings with consequent efficiency savings and privatization;
- an emphasis on managerialism with a command-control mode of practice in order to ensure performance targets were being achieved;
- an emphasis on performance management and target-driven mode of practice with consequent financial and performance audits and benchmarking;
- the integration of markets and competition to ensure a customer orientation;
- deregulation of the labour market with the introduction of pay–performance contracts, fixed term contracts and staff turnover;

- a shift from the professional public servant to a general manager;
- the de-bureaucratization of public sector organizations in terms of less bureaucratic processes and more entrepreneurial management; and
- new forms of governance such as the marginalization of trade unions and the integration of new partners in public service delivery, i.e. the private sector (see Ferlie *et al.* 1996; Pollitt and Bouckaert 2000; Greenwood *et al.* 2002; Hughes 2003; Massey and Pyper 2005; Flynn 2007).

NPM sought to reduce the role of government, and thereby bureaucracy, by moving many public service functions to the private sector (Meier and Hill 2007). Government became contract administrators rather than delivery agents, the quest guided by the notion that the private sector was more efficient than public bureaucracies (ibid). A further aspect of NPM was to reduce rules and regulations, to liberate public officials from red tape and be more innovative and entrepreneurial in order to deliver public services more effectively (ibid). Thus, there was a rejection of the Weberian bureaucracy (Hughes 2003). Yet despite the reform of the public sector, the Weberian characteristics of public bureaucracies still resonate within modern public departments (Barberis 2011). For example, NPM challenge to bureaucracy is to replace bureaucracy with the liberated contract manager, but private bureaucracies substituted public ones, and the rules and regulations of accountability took on a new form of contract process and performance management regime with its myriad of metrics (Meier and Hill 2007; Power 1997). The outcomes of NPM reforms include inter alia:

- fragmented and uncohesive government with the proliferation of semi-autonomous public bodies, which has resulted in difficulties vis-à-vis policy coordination and coherence;
- the separation of policy and public service delivery with the consequential fragmentation and 'distance' between policy designers and those tasked with delivering upon the policy;
- accountability and audit processes that have become complex with new modes and instruments of delivery often fragmenting accountability, yet government is still held accountable for the public service delivery necessitating the development of new modes of accountability;
- failure to deliver a learning culture in government with learning across organizational boundaries more difficult to achieve given fragmentation of services; and
- impoverished understanding of the public ethos, the role of the citizen and how governments should engage with citizens as active partners in public services (see Pollitt and Bouchaert 2004; Lodge and Kalitowski 2007; Power 1997).

Globally, the reforms of public services along NPM lines have left a legacy. There is greater use of markets with an emphasis on entrepreneurialism and the accountability of public servants to individual service users or 'customers' rather than collective publics (Greener 2009). There are of course contradictions that emerge from the privatization and marketization of public services. The extent to which the private sector could ever deliver services without government involvement, oversight, accountability or hindrance is questionable (ibid). But this section of the book explains the shift of the public policy domain from the public bureaucracies to more market or private sector venues. Public bureaucracies originally had a monopoly of the public policy domain; public sector reforms gradually eroded public bureaucracies' dominance and increasingly the involvement of non-state actors in public policy became the norm.

GOVERNANCE

Over the past few decades there has been the adoption of NPM reforms on a global scale in an attempt to improve the capacity of administrative systems to effectively and efficiently deliver upon policies and public services. Many NPM reforms and trends involve decentralization, results-orientation, marketization, systems to increase workforce productivity and efficiencies and evolving accountability regimes (Torres 2004; Commission on 2020 Public Services 2009; Pollitt and Bouchaert 2011). The result of these reforms was the delivery of public services through various state and non-state actors, for example the contracting out of services to the private sector, the inclusion of various 'partners' such as the voluntary sector in the planning and delivery of services. This has been conceptualized as governance, which refers to the changing nature of the policy process and service delivery over recent decades. Rhodes (2012: 33), on governance describes it thus: 'Governance signifies a change in the meaning of government, referring to new processes of governing; or changed conditions of ordered rule; or new methods by which society is governed.'

The term is often used in conjunction with the ever-increasing variety of domains (e.g. supra-national, national and sub-national) and actors (e.g. from the political, public, private, civil society and community realms) involved in the policy process (Rhodes 1997; 2006; Richards and Smith 2002). Governance is often used within the context of replacing government as a hierarchical mode of service delivery as part of the public services reform movement (NPM and reinventing government) toward the integration of public service delivery through non-state actors (Fairholm 2010). Lynn (2010: 671) defines governance as the 'action or manner of governing – that is, of directing, guiding, or regulating individuals, organizations, or nations in conduct or actions'. This somewhat broad and all-encompassing definition illustrates that government is no longer directly involved in governing, but is steering others in the policy process. Governance is

61

often discussed within the context of aforementioned neo-liberal public sector reforms. Klijn (2012: 209), for example, provides a useful comparison of NPM vis-à-vis governance and can be illustrated in Table 2.1.

The debates recognize that there are networks consisting of a multiplicity of actors involved in public policy processes, from policy making to implementation, through multiple levels of government often in partnership with non-state actors. This conceptualization is often referred to as network governance. Network governance is associated with the changing role and nature of the state with a shift from hierarchical bureaucracy toward greater use of markets and non-state actors in the delivery of public services (Rhodes 2011). According to Rhodes (2011) the effects of neo-liberal type public sector reforms (NPM) were intensified by global changes such as transnational economic activity and the rise of regional institutions (e.g. the EU) with resultant complexity and fragmentation of the state increasingly relying on other organizations to secure its policy intentions and service delivery objectives. Rhodes (1994) argued that there is a differentiated polity with governments' authority being 'hollowed-out'. Governance was a product of this 'hollowing-out' process with the erosion of state authority from above through, for example, international interdependencies; from below by marketization

Table 2.1 New public management and governance

	New Public Management	Governance
Focus	Organizational and institutional changes and adaptations within the public sector (intra-organizational)	Changes and adaptations in the relations between governments and other actors (inter-organizational)
Objectives	Improving effectiveness and efficiency of public service delivery and public organizations	Improving inter-organizational coordination and quality of decision-making
Core ideas/ management techniques	Using business instruments (e.g. market mechanisms, performance indicators) to improve service delivery	Using network management: activating actors, organizing research gathering, arranging interactions, etc.
Politics	Elected officials set goals and implementation is achieved by independent agencies or market mechanisms on the basis of clear performance indicators	Goals are developed during interaction and decision-making processes, elected officeholders are part of the process or are meta-governors
Complexity	Modern society is complex but there is a need for clear goals and flexible implementation	Modern society is complex and requires interdependence and interacting with actors in society is unavoidable and/or necessary to reach satisfactory outcomes

Source: Klijn (2012)

and networks; and horizontally through agencies (Rhodes 1994; 1997; 2011). Rhodes (2000) characterizes governance as interactions between actors within governing networks. He (2000; 2011 [the latter citation is a review of his scholarly writings over the twenty-five years]) defined governance as self-organizing, inter-organizational networks with the following characteristics:

- Interdependence between organizations. Governance is broader than government, covering non-state actors. Changing the boundaries of the state meant that boundaries between public, private and voluntary sectors became shifting and opaque.
- Continuing interactions between network members, caused by the need to exchange resources and negotiate shared purposes.
- Game-like interactions, rooted in trust and regulated by rules of the game negotiated and agreed by network participants.
- A significant degree of autonomy from the state. Networks are not accountable to the state; they are self-organising. Although the state does not occupy a privileged, sovereign position, it can indirectly and imperfectly steer networks.

Governance is characterized by decision and policy systems in which territorial and functional differentiation disaggregates effective problem solving capacity into a collection of sub-systems of actors (Hanf and O'Toole 1992). The result is functional interdependence between public, private and civil society actors in policy formulation and implementation, as governments become increasingly dependent and interdependent on the cooperation and joint resource mobilization of policy actors outside traditional hierarchical governmental institutions (Börzel and Heard-Lauréote 2009). Key to the concept of governance is networks, which have resulted in new forms of structural relationships, interdependencies and dynamics between actors for the mobilization of resources between actors where resources are widely dispersed (see Kooiman 1993). Thus, governance is a much broader term than government, with public resources and services provided by any permutation of government and private and civil society organizations such as the voluntary sector (Rhodes 2006; Pierre and Peters 2000).

The increasing use of the term governance as a conceptual frame for research on the determinants of public sector performance has produced valuable insights into the relationships between policy processes, public management, service delivery and citizen/stakeholder involvement in public policy (Robichau and Lynn 2009). For example, the EU is widely considered as a unique system of multi-level governance and its multi-level structure and processes have been widely conceptualized as a system of network governance in which the authoritative allocation of values is negotiated between state and non-state actors (Puchala 1972; Meier *et al.* 2004; Kohler-Koch and Rittberger 2006; Rhodes 2006). For example, the White Paper on Governance (European Commission 2001) reflected

63

a search for more 'modern forms of governance' based on networks, which are considered most appropriate in managing the policy and service delivery challenges of the EU. In fact many EU treaties, directives and structural funding prescribe the involvement of social and civil society partners in the policy processes and delivery of services (Börzel and Heard-Lauréote 2009). The reality is that increasingly public services are being decentralized within the context of new forms of governance arrangements, with the trend towards co-governance and co-production of services, i.e. where public services are designed and/or delivered between state bodies and individuals or communities (Johnson and Osborne 2003; Kooiman 2003).

Tenbensel (2005) argues that there are multiple modes of governance with the nexus of interactions based on knowledge and power. The first mode Tenbensel describes is hierarchical with the legal-rational authority residing in state agencies and is derived from a constitutional basis in liberal democracies. The hierarchical mode is evident when those charged with tasks of spending, administering and managing publicly funded programmes are subject to formal mechanisms of accountability. Within this mode of governance, government 'steers' the network through various performance accountabilities (ibid). The second mode is based on markets where consumers are viewed as sovereign and their power is manifest when decisions regarding the allocation of public resources are the product of decisions of purchasers and/or consumers (ibid). This mode of governance is consistent with the NPM doctrine. The third mode of governance is that of networks involving state and non-state actors (ibid). Finally, Tenbensel (2005) refers to an ideal type of governance based on the collective values of communities. This mode of governance manifests in populist movements and grass-roots community activism consistent with pluralism (ibid). Lowndes and Skelcher (2011) are also of the view that there are several modes of governance involving markets, hierarchy and networks.

There appears to be a general consensus that governance involves:

- a set of institutions and actors drawn upon beyond the boundaries of government;
- a blurring of boundaries and responsibilities for tackling socio-economic issues;
- a power dependence involved in the relationships between institutions involved in collective action;
- autonomous self-governing networks of actors; and
- recognition of the capacity to achieve policy objectives that do not necessarily depend on government to command or use its authority (Stoker 1998; Koliba et al. 2010).

Governance can therefore be understood within the context of state and non-state actors within networks acting collectively to achieve public policy objectives.

Indeed, Bovaird and Löffler (2003: 316) describe public governance as 'the ways in which stakeholders interact with each other in order to influence the outcomes of public policies'. There are two schools of thought about governance: governance with government and governance without government (Lynn 2012) as outlined below in the various viewpoints.

Viewpoint 1

Some scholars argue that governance with government is government acting in conjunction with non-state actors as partners in a process of collectivity with regard to public policy (Lynn 2012). This conceptualization of governance is government as part of a network, with an emphasis on horizontal relationships between government, private and civil society actors, although the relationship may not necessarily be equitable (Klijn 2008; Lynn 2012). According to Klijn (2008) governance is not traditional bureaucratic government or NPM and neither is it a process of operating outside of government influence. Governance is non-state actors becoming part of government through mechanisms which confer authority on their inputs to a policy process (Lynn 2012).

Viewpoint 2

The second school of thought: governance without government describes actors operating with a significant degree of autonomy (Lynn 2012; Rhodes 1997). This conceptualization of governance is of actors functioning beyond the influence of governance with governing mechanisms that do not rely on the authority and sanction of government (Lynn 2012; Stoker 1998). Governance without government is the functioning of government centred in civil society (Lynn 2012). This would be consistent with the idea of the 'Big Society' in the UK. Rhodes' (1997) contention is that networks are autonomous from government. Similarly Jessop (2004) argues for meta-governance which involves a complex plurality of modes of coordination. He argues that governments play a role in meta-governance by being involved in the redesigning of markets, in constitutional change and the juridical re-regulation of organizational objectives, and in organizing the conditions of self-organization (Jessop 2004: 70). Meta-governance involves negotiated decision-making to coordinate markets, hierarchies and heterarchies but the 'state is no longer sovereign authority . . . It becomes just one participant among pluralistic guidance system' (Jessop 2004: 71). Sørensen and Torfing (2007) argue that meta-governance is concerned with how the state steers organizations within networks rather than directly providing services through bureaucracy. Meta-governance refers to the role of the state in securing coordination in governance and its use of negotiation and informal modes of steering a network to deliver services (Rhodes 2011).

65

Critical reflection of viewpoints

We disagree with the conceptualization of governance as without government in terms of public policy (see Fenwick *et al.* 2012). There are, of course, non-state actors involved in the delivery of services that are for public and social benefit and hence their activities can be described as a public service function. Examples of these would be: voluntary sector organizations providing social care for the elderly, palliative care for patients; support to vulnerable people in society; philanthropic organizations involved in disease prevention, educational advancement opportunities, establishment of research and development organization; private sector organizations involved in social enterprises; all of which constitute various types of service delivery activities for the benefit of society. This type of governance may or may not involve government. The non-state actors may act as a separate entity from government, but they are not autonomous and without government. These actors do encounter government in some form or another whether it is working in partnership or adhering to regulation with regard to the service, or being funded by government to provide a service. Klijn (2008) argues government within a network is usually working in some form of 'partnership' with non-state actors, but the relationship is never equitable as government has the regulatory authority and financial resources to play a dominant role in the network. Davies (2011) too challenges governance theory and argues that asymmetries exist within networks with a hegemonic role played by government in order to achieve its objectives. Bell and Hindmoor (2009: 150) also 'reject the notion that governments have lost their capacity to govern and argue instead that governance is about government seeking to govern better rather than seeking to govern less'.

Robichau (2011) argues that in defining governance, often an elusive concept, the use of words such as networks, rules, steering, order, control, good, governing and authority is involved. Robichau's review of the governance literature demonstrates that there is conceptual ambiguity and much debate on the concept of governance. He argues that this debate stems from scholarly definitions on state-centric and society-centric approaches to studying governance (Robichau 2011). The state-centric perspective maintains that the state retains its power and authority as chief policy actor and centre of society, while society-centric position contends that the state is being 'hollowed out', decentred, and thus is progressively relying on non-state actors to fulfil its duties (ibid). This is similar to the debate of governance without or with government. As Robichau's (2011) literature review shows, there is much debate on governance with a vast volume of literature on the matter, most scholars agreeing that in a post-NPM era, there are observable networks between state and non-state actors. While there is empirical evidence for network governance, we agree with scholars that there has been no real retraction of the state and its authority to govern, and its ability and authority to make policy decisions still remain pre-eminent (Pierre and Peters 2005; Bell and Hindmoor 2009; Lynn 2012).

As discussed in the Introduction and Chapter 1, public policy is the authoritative allocation of resources and courses of action undertaken by government. Thus, courses of action taken outwith government's authority, we argue, cannot be conceptualized in relation to public policy. Indeed, Lynn's (2012) review of the empirical evidence of governance demonstrates that in the policy process government has still maintained its authoritative and regulatory function. Similarly, Stivers (2008) argues that governance is statecraft, an art of governing with the exercise of distinctly governmental responsibilities by actors adhering to a state's rules and constitutional arrangements. Furthermore, Stivers (2008) argues and indeed calls for state and non-state actors in the exercise of governmental responsibilities to act in the public interest and to embody democratic and public service principles in their interpersonal interactions to find creative solutions to policy problems. Stivers is essentially acknowledging the move from hierarchical modes of government towards governance with other actors, but calls for good governance in the exercise of governmental responsibilities and the accountability of actors in serving the public.

It is also the case that state and non-state actors are involved in service delivery for social and public benefit. This is referred to as co-governance. Yet even in this relationship the authors' empirical research of partnerships between state and non-state in the UK revealed that state actors still play a pivotal and dominant role in the network, with government using various regulatory frameworks to steer the network (Fenwick *et al.* 2012; see also Bell and Hindmoor 2009; Davies 2011). In making public policy, government invariably has the monopoly of power and authority and the regulatory capacity to ensure the enforcement and implementation of the policy. When non-state actors are involved in making public policy this mode of governance is with government and takes place within public governance arrangements, policy networks and policy communities (see Chapter 3). In managing public policy and public service delivery, state and non-state actors are involved in several modes of governance (see Lowndes and Skelcher 2011) with government in a network and/or partnership. It is nevertheless important to bear in mind that government, in making policy, works within a governance framework to formulate (e.g. through policy networks) and implement (e.g. co-governance) policy objectives. It is therefore argued that governance is more state-centric, but where it enters the realms of society-centric practices caution should be exercised that decentred government responsibilities do not lose sight of good governance and that the public interest is preserved. We started this chapter with a brief overview of the events which led to the global banking and financial crisis. This illustrates our view, and perhaps that of Stivers (2008), that too much de-centred government – in this case government through deregulation provided banks with the opportunity to undertake high-risk ventures – results in bad governance. Government is central to society in order to maintain the public interest and should not renege on its legal–constitutional role of serving the public interest. Thus, although policy in a global era is increasingly being made within the domain of governance, we nonetheless argue that policy should be the authority of government.

MULTI-LEVEL GOVERNANCE

Public policy making takes place within networks as well as across jurisdictional domains. Marks (1993) defines multi-level governance as a system of continuous negotiation among nested governments at several territorial tiers (local, national and global) with power distributed across and within these different tiers. Thus, power is shared by various actors and institutions across a spectrum rather than principally located within states at the 'centre' (ibid). The combination of horizontal interaction between state and non-state actors within networks, and the vertical interaction across sub-national, national and supra-national levels is referred to as multi-level governance. Hooghe and Marks (2003) argued for a twofold typology of multi-level governance. Type I multi-level governance depicts the distribution of authority across jurisdictions with a limited number of levels (ibid). The jurisdictional boundaries are clearly defined and there is non-intersecting membership of levels (ibid). In this context multi-level governance is system-wide governing arrangements in which authority is restricted to a limited number of clearly defined, non-overlapping jurisdictions at a limited number of territorial levels, each of which has responsibility for a bundle of functions (Hooghe and Marks 2003; Marks and Hooghe 2004; Bevir 2009; Bache 2012). Type I is consistent with the federalist political architecture of the state subdivided into territorial layers and authority restricted to each respective level. The USA and Germany are examples of federal states, with other countries such as Canada and South Africa having central-provincial government arrangements. The Type II multi-level governance involves more fluidity in that there are no set jurisdictional boundaries (Hooghe and Marks 2003). The governing arrangements are such that authority is task or policy specific with jurisdictions operating at and across numerous overlapping levels (ibid). Thus the boundaries expand and contract as the policy requires. The membership of Type II multi-level governance is intersecting with state and non-state actors involved in a policy process across jurisdictional boundaries. Most scholars refer to the EU in this context with membership empowering sub-state and non-state actors across member states to implement policy (Bevir 2009; Bache 2012). Keating (2008) and Hooghe and Marks (1996) argue that territorial authority within the EU has been transformed with sub-national or regional governments becoming empowered to deliver upon various policy objectives, particularly in the management of EU development funds. Type II multi-level governance also includes the notion of networks where state and non-state actors across jurisdictional boundaries are working in partnerships to deliver upon policy-specific objectives.

The conceptualization and typology of multi-level governance is not without academic debate. First, the debate centres on whether the authority of the state is being eroded by supra-national bodies and sub-national entities. While some argue that the empowerment of sub-national levels of government (vertical dimensions) and non-state actors (horizontal dimensions) combined with the increasing authority of supra-national bodies such as the EU point to a 'hollowing out' of states, others argue that authority is not finite (see Bache and Flinders 2004; Bevir 2009). The authority of the state is therefore not diminishing but extending (ibid). Second, scholars argue that the horizontal networks between state and non-state actors with the vertical dimension of various levels of government involved in the policy process lead to better policy formulation and implementation (ibid). Proponents of multi-level governance argue that this pluralism leads to a better policy process as well as enhancing democracy. Yet, various scholars have also shown that the multiplicity of actors and layers involved in multi-level governance leads to fragmentation and complexities in accountability (ibid). The third debate is more of an academic one. It concerns multi-level governance as a concept to describe observable relationships between various actors within an era of increasing globalization and likewise the ebb and flow of the state and non-state actors' roles in the policy process. Many would argue that Type I is principally intergovernmental relations with the emphasis on government, and Type II multi-level governance is network governance (Bache 2012). Within this academic debate, as well, is the view that a typology over-simplifies the complexity of interactions between state and non-state actors across jurisdictions and political structures. Skelcher (2005), for example, argues that there are four types of relationships between Type I and Type II multi-level governance: parallel (the body is an alternative to existing governmental organizations); complementary (the body is independent but undertakes activities that add to those carried out by government); incorporated (the body is a formal extension of government); and oppositional (the body challenges government and advocates for particular interests). Bache (2012: 631), using Skelcher's (2005) description of multi-level governance relationships, provides examples of these various relations within an EU context:

- parallel – regional partnership bodies involved in implementing EU development policy;
- complementary – member states reporting directly and formally to an EU institution, for example, the European Central Bank;
- incorporated – member states are accountable to an EU institution, for example, the European Aviation Safety Agency; and
- oppositional – these are corporatist relations with advocates representing particular interests, for example, the European Trade Confederation.

Beyond the conceptual debate about multi-level governance, what is apparent is that the policy process is no longer restricted to state-centric systems within a unitary political structure; rather policy is being made within the context of various jurisdictional boundaries, vertical and horizontal dimensions, state and non-state actors and entities with consequent extension of authority and implications for policy implementation and outcomes. Multi-level governance has become a domain in which policy is made across horizontal and vertical linkages and networks.

BOX 2.1   INSIDE THE BLACK BOX OF THE EU – WHO DOES WHAT AND HOW?

The EU and its myriad of institutions are sometimes an enigma to the lay person. Yet, the complexity of the EU offers valuable insights into the policy process within an era of global governance. In order to demystify the EU policy process we will first outline who does what and then discuss the outputs and outcomes of policy.

European Parliament

The European Parliament (EP) is a directly elected legislative body consisting of 751 members with approximately a minimum of 6 and maximum of 96 seats per member state, according to the size of the member state. In contrast to national parliaments, the EP cannot directly initiate legislation and its budgetary powers only cover spending. The EP's authority lies within the following roles: legislative, budgetary, scrutiny of the European Commission and key appointments. It plays a powerful role in electing the President of the Commission and in co-deciding nearly all EU legislation.

The Council of Ministers

The Council is the EU's primary decision-making body and it consists of a representative, at ministerial level, from each member state. The Council together with the EP exercises legislative and budgetary responsibilities and conducts policy making and coordinating functions. Its function is twofold: it acts as a legislative chamber and is a forum where member states resolve and coordinate EU policy issues. There are approximately ten different configurations that co-determinate with policy areas (i.e. if there is a policy issue relating to agriculture then all the ministers with the agricultural responsibilities meet) and then there is also the General Affairs Council, which has responsibility for policies that affect more than one policy area such as the EU's budget. The Council is supported by a Secretariat comprising of approximately 2500 officials.

The European Council (heads of state)

The European Council consists of the heads of member states that provide the EU with general direction and priorities. It plays a powerful agenda-setting role such as enlargement decisions, climate change strategy, treaty reforms, etc. There are usually four 'summits' per year and policy problems that cannot necessarily be resolved at the Council of Ministers level is elevated to the European Council. The European Council, under the Lisbon Treaty, is now headed (previously on a rotational basis) by a President who acts as a chairperson or facilitator.

European Commission

The European Commission (EC) is probably one of the most powerful international administrations. It has authority in a number of areas: to propose policy; leadership in international trade negotiations; its role in competition policy; and ensuring compliance with European law. The EC performs a number of roles within the EU: it represents the general interest of the EU; acts as a guardian of treaties; ensures the application of EU legislation; and manages and negotiates international trade agreements. Its most powerful role is as the designer and manager of EU policy. The EC comprises of two separate bodies: the College of Commissioners and the Commission. The Commission undertakes administrative roles and is akin to a civil service. The Commission recruits its own civil servants through competitive recruitment and selection procedures and is not dependent on national member states to provide appointees. This is, however, different for the College. The College consists of twenty-seven members – one from each member state – nominated by the president or prime minister of respective countries. The College Commissioners are like ministers of national governments, and although not directly elected, are the political arm of the Commission. The Commission is headed by a President who is elected by the EP on proposal from the European Council, which is obliged to take into account the EP election results. The President distributes policy responsibilities (e.g. agriculture) to individual Commissioners. The Vice President of the Commission, however, is the EU's high representative for foreign policy and is chosen by the European Council with the agreement of the Commission President.

European Court of Justice

The Court consists of twenty-seven judges (one appointed from each member state) and eight Advocate Generals who draft opinions for the judges. The Court's role is to ensure that the interpretation and application of treaties are observed. The authority of the Court lies in its role as final arbiter in legal disputes. The Court ensures national compliance with treaties and legislation that EU institutions do not go beyond their legal remit and individual rights are upheld. This allows domestic courts to seek the Court's ruling on European law of the case. The Court's ruling is then used by domestic courts in judging cases. Some argue that the Court adopts a policy-making role within member states and has shaped national policies such as health provision, abortion services, equal pay, etc.

The policy outputs are: regulations, which are binding and directly applicable to member states; directives, which are binding on member states but provide discretion in achieving the policy objective such as introducing national legislation; and decisions, which are only binding on specific individuals or entities to which the decision is addressed.

The EU presents an interesting case of vertical and horizontal multi-level governance. Policy is made across EU institutions and in conjunction with member states which make up the EU. There is interdependence of member states within the EU and in the formulation of policy they have to co-operate to reach a consensus. The EU through its various institutions formulates policy across a broad range of state and non-state actors. For example, the Commission may be lobbied by active policy networks which represent organized interests. There is also a downloading and uploading of policy, with member states through various institutions developing policy; once regulations, directives and decisions are made, laws enacted and treaties adopted, these are implemented within member countries.

Sources and further reading:
Jørgensen et al. (2007)
Versluis et al. (2010)
Bomberg et al. (2011)

NEW PUBLIC GOVERNANCE

New Public Governance is seen as a post-bureaucratic and post-NPM paradigm of statecraft. Osborne (2009) argues that public administration and the bureaucratic, hierarchical manner of public service delivery have at their core a concern with the unitary state and where public policy making and implementation was vertically integrated within a closed system of government. NPM by comparison was borne out of neo-liberal classical economic and rational choice theories, where the state was disaggregated and where public policy making and implementation was through a collection of independent service units, often in competition with each other (ibid). In contrast to public administration and NPM, NPG is based on governance and network theory with a pluralist state informed by multiple processes in public policy making and implementation (ibid). Thus, there are multiple interdependent state and non-state actors contributing to public policy making and implementation (ibid). Osborne (2009) draws upon 'open natural systems theory' to argue that there are institutional and external environmental pressures and factors which enable and constrain public policy making and implementation. The focus therefore is on co-production, inter-organizational relationships and governance processes in order to achieve effective public policy outcomes (ibid). The resource allocation and interactions are inter-organizational networks with power and accountability being negotiated within these networks (ibid). Osborne acknowledges that the networks are rarely an alliance of equals but that within the networks power inequalities are negotiated to ensure effectiveness of process and policy outcomes. Osborne (2009) argues that NPG offers a useful framework for the study and practice of public administration and management. Furthermore, it combines the strengths of studying public administration and NPM, by recognizing the legitimacy and interrelatedness of both the policy making and the implementation or service delivery (ibid). Thus, in a post-bureaucratic and pluralist system of networks and governance, NPG offers a coherent conceptual framework for the study of the governance of public policy processes, the management of inter-organizational relationships and the governance of networks. NPG offers a framework to understand post-bureaucratic public policy making and relationships within network governance as distinctive from past perceptions of government, i.e. public administration (Robichau 2011). Yet, some scholars are not convinced by NPG as a new theory or paradigm of public policy making and implementation. There is evidence to suggest that a post-bureaucratic paradigm is overstated and that the state, through its authority and centrality of public policy making and implementation, still remains a dominant feature in the governance landscape (see Meuleman 2006; Budd 2007; Bell and Hindmoor 2009; Goldfinch and Wallis 2010; Robichau 2011). Nevertheless, the domains of public policy making and service delivery have been extended beyond the state and now involve state and non-state actors interacting within networks. Thus in an increasingly complex, globalized world with equally complex policy problems, with state and non-state actors interacting in policy processes, NPG could offer a framework of analysis in understanding the increasingly pluralist nature of the state, inter-organizational governance and interdependencies of actors and institutions.

CONCLUSION

To conclude, this chapter outlined the domains of public policy. As Chapter 1 discussed, there are state and non-state actors in the internal and external environments which interact and influence interrelated cycles of public policy. The internal and external environments interact, in an ever-increasingly globalized world, through various interdependent domains. As illustrated at the beginning of this chapter, the banking crisis highlights the interrelated nature of policy domains, actors, sectors and institutions. As such, this chapter sought to explain the domain of government, through a discussion of public bureaucracy as a venue for public policy making. The reform of public bureaucracies along neo-liberal doctrines saw the integration of private and civil society sectors in government policy process. There has been much debate as to whether this was an erosion or extension of the state. Nonetheless, the observable network of state and non-state actors involved in contemporary public policy processes demonstrates that governance is a domain of public policy. We acknowledge, as others have, that the power relationships in governance networks are unequal, with government still maintaining a key role in the policy process as the authoritative decision maker. Multi-level governance also describes the domain of public policy through horizontal and vertical dimensions across policy actors and jurisdictions. Finally, we acknowledge NPG may offer a useful framework of analysis in understanding public policy within the domain of the increasingly pluralist nature of the state with inter-organizational interdependencies and modes of governance between state and non-state actors. Yet, in public policy contexts and domains, government remains the pre-eminent policy actor that makes a decision, mediates competing interests among other policy actors and draws upon its power and/or authority to follow an intended course of action. Chapter 3 explores these interdependencies and relationships between the policy actors.

REFERENCES

Bache, I. (2012) 'Multi-level Governance in the European Union', in D. Levi-Faur (ed.), *The Oxford Handbook of Governance*, Oxford: Oxford University Press: 628–641.

Bache, I. and Flinders. M. (2004) *Multi-Level Governance*, Oxford: Oxford University Press.

Barberis, P. (2011) 'The Weberian Legacy', in A. Massey, *International Handbook on Civil Service Systems*, Cheltenham: Edward Elgar: 13–30.

BBC (2009) 'Timeline: credit crunch to downturn', http: //news.bbc.co.uk/1/hi/7521250. stm. (Accessed 26 March 2012.)

Bell, S. and Hindmoor, A. (2009) 'The governance of public affairs', *Journal of Public Affairs*, 9: 149–159.

Bevir, M. (2009) *Key Concepts in Governance*, London: Sage Publications.

Blau, P. (1963) *The Dynamics of Bureaucracy*, Chicago, IL: University of Chicago Press.

Blau, P. and Meyer. M. (1987) *Bureaucracy in Modern Society*, New York: McGraw-Hill.

Bomberg, E., Peterson. J. and Corbett. R. (2011) *The European Union. How does it work?* Oxford: Oxford University Press.

Börzel, T.A. and Heard-Lauréote, K. (2009) 'Networks in EU multi-level governance: concepts and contributions', *Journal of Public Policy*, 29, 2: 135–152.

Bovaird, T. and Löffler, E. (2003) 'Evaluating the quality of public governance: indicators, models and methodologies', *International Review of Administrative Sciences*, 69, 3: 313–328.

Budd, L. (2007) 'Post-bureaucracy and re-animating public governance: a discourse and practice of continuity', *International Journal of Public Sector Management*, 20, 6: 531–547.

Clegg, S. (1990) *Modern Organisations: organisation studies in the postmodern world*, London: Sage Publishing.

Commission on 2020 Public Services Trust (2009) *A Brief History of Public Service Reform*, London: 2020 Public Services Trust.

Davies, J. (2011) *Challenging Governance Theory: from networks to hegemony*, Bristol: Policy Press.

Downs, A. (1967) *Inside Bureaucracy*, Boston, MA: Little Brown.

Du Gay, P. (2000) *In Praise of Bureaucracy: Weber. Organisation. Ethics*, London: Sage Publishing.

Dunleavy, P. (1991) *Democracy, Bureaucracy and Public Choice: economic explanations in political science*, Harlow: Prentice Hall.

European Commission (2001) *European Governance – A White Paper*, COM(2001)428, Brussels: Commission of the European Communities.

Fairholm, M.R. (2010) 'Why a rational move towards "governance" may destroy the soul of public administration: or why governance isn't concerned with government anymore', in T. Brandsen and M. Holzer (eds) *The Future of Governance*, Newark, NJ: National Centre for Public Performance, EGPA/IIAS and American Society for Public Administration: 3–17.

Fenwick, J., Miller, K. Johnston and McTavish, D. (2012) 'Co-governance or meta-bureaucracy: perspectives of local governance "partnerships" in England and Scotland', *Policy and Politics*, 40, 3: 405–422.

Ferlie, E., Ashburner, L., Fitzgerald, L. and Pettigrew, A. (1996) *The New Public Management in Action*, Oxford: Oxford University Press.

Flynn, N. (2007) *Public Sector Management*, London: Sage Publishing.

Goldfinch, S. and Wallis. J. (2010) 'Two myths of convergence in public management reform', *Public Administration*, 88, 4: 1099–1115.

Goodsell, C. (1983) *The Case for Bureaucracy*, Chatham, NJ: Chatham House Publishers.

Greener, I. (2009) *Public Management: a critical text*. Basingstoke: Palgrave Macmillan.

Greenwood, J., Pyper, R. and Wilson. D. (2002) *New Public Administration in Britain*, London: Routledge.

75

Ham, C. (2009) *Health Policy in Britain*, Basingstoke: Palgrave Macmillan.

Hanf, K.I. and O'Toole, L.J. (1992), 'Revisiting old friends: networks, implementation structures and the management of inter-organizational relations', *European Journal of Political Research*, 20, 1–2: 163–180.

Hindmoor, A. (2006) *Rational Choice*, Basingstoke: Palgrave Macmillan.

Hood, C. (1991) 'A public management for all seasons', *Public Administration*, 69, Spring: 3–19.

Hooghe, L. and Marks. G. (1996) ' "Europe with regions": channels of regional representation in the European Union', *Publius: The Journal of Federalism*, 26, 1: 73–91.

Hooghe, L. and Marks G. (2003) 'Unravelling the central state, but how? Types of multi-level governance', *American Political Science Review*, 97, 2: 233–243.

Hughes, O. (2003) *Public Management and Administration: an introduction*, Basingstoke: Palgrave Macmillan.

Jessop, B. (2004) 'Multi-level Governance and Multi-level Meta-Governance', in I. Bache and M. Flinders (eds) *Multi-Level Governance*, Oxford: Oxford University Press: 49–74.

Johnson, C. and Osborne, S.P. (2003) 'Local strategic partnerships, neighbourhood renewal, and the limits to co-governance', *Public Money & Management*, 23, 3: 147–154.

Jørgensen, K.K.E., Pollack. M.A. and Rosamond. B. (2007) *Handbook of European Politics*, London: Sage Publications.

Kamensky, J. (1996) 'Role of the "reinventing government" movement in federal management reform', *Public Administration Review*, 56, 3: 247–255.

Keating, M. (2008) 'A quarter century of the Europe of the regions', *Regional and Federal Studies*, 18, 5: 629–635.

Klijn, E. (2008) 'Governance and governance networks in Europe: An assessment of ten years of research on the theme', *Public Management Review*, 10, 4: 505–525.

Klijn, E. (2012) 'New Public Management and Governance: a comparison', in D. Levi-Faur (ed.) *The Oxford Handbook of Governance,* Oxford: Oxford University Press: 201–214.

Kohler-Koch, B. and Rittberger, B. (2006) 'The "governance turn" in EU studies', *Journal of Common Market Studies*, 44, 1: 27–49.

Koliba, C., Meek, J. and Zia, A. (2010) 'Gordian Knot or Integrated Theory? Critical Conceptual Considerations for Governance Network Analysis', in T. Brandsen and M. Holzer (eds) *The Future of Governance*, Newark: National Centre for Public Performance, EGPA/IIAS and American Society for Public Administration: 277–300.

Kooiman, J. (1993) *Modern Governance: New Government-Society Interactions*, London: Sage Publications.

Kooiman, J. (2003) *Governing as Governance*, London: Sage Publishing.

Lane, J. (2000) *The Public Sector: concepts, models and approaches*, London: Sage Publications.

Lodge, G. and Kalitowski, S. (2007) *Innovation in Government: international perspectives on civil service reform*, London: Institute for Public Policy Research.

Lowndes, V. and Skelcher. C. (2011) 'The Dynamics of Multi-organisational Partnerships: an analysis of changing modes of governance', in R.A.W. Rhodes (ed.) *Public Administration: 25 years of analysis and debate*, Chichester: John Wiley & Sons: 59–75.

Lynn, L.J. (2007) 'Public Management: a concise history of the field', in E. Ferlie, L.J. Lynn and C. Pollitt (eds) *The Oxford Handbook of Public Management*, Oxford: Oxford University Press: 27–71.

Lynn, L.J. (2010) 'Has Governance Eclipsed Government?', in R. Durant (ed.) *The Oxford Handbook of Governance*, Oxford: Oxford University Press: 669–690.

Lynn, L.J. (2012) 'The Many Faces of Governance: Adaption? Transformation? Both? Neither?', in D. Levi-Faur (ed.) *The Oxford Handbook of Governance*, Oxford: Oxford University Press: 49–64.

Marks, G. (1993) 'Structural Policy and Multi-level Governance in the EC', in *The State of the Euopean Community: the Maastricht debate and beyond*, Boulder, CO: Lynne Rienner: 391–411.

Marks, G. and. Hooghe. L. (2004) 'Contrasting Visions of Multi-Level Governance', in *Multi-Level Governance*, Oxford: Oxford University Press: 15–30.

Massey, A. (1993) *Managing the Public Sector*, Aldershot: Edward Elgar.

Massey, A. (2011) *International Handbook on Civil Service Systems.* Cheltenham: Edward Elgar.

Massey, A. and Pyper R. (2005) *Public Management and Modernisation in Britain*, Basingstoke: Palgrave Macmillan.

Meier, K. and Hill. G. (2007) 'Bureaucracy in the Twenty-First Century', in *The Oxford Handbook of Public Management*, Oxford: Oxford University Press: 51–71.

Meier, K.J., O'Toole, L.J. and Nicholson-Crotty, S. (2004) 'Multilevel governance and organizational performance: investigating the political–bureaucratic labyrinth', *Journal of Policy Analysis and Management*, 23, 1: 31–47.

Meuleman, L. (2006) *Internal Meta-Governance as a New Challenge for Management Development in Public Administration*, Aix-en-Provence: EFMD.

Miller, K. Johnston (2012) 'Representative bureaucracy and multi-level governance in the EU', *Geopolitics, History and International Relations*, 4, 1: 50–75.

Mommsen, W. (1974) *The Age of Bureaucracy: Perspectives on the Political Sociology of Max Weber*, Oxford: Basil Blackwell.

Niskanen, W.A. (1971) *Bureaucracy and Representative Government*, Chicago, IL: Aldine-Atherton.

Olsen, J. (2006) 'Maybe it is time to rediscover bureaucracy', *Journal of Public Administration Research and Theory*, 16, 1: 1–24.

77

Olsen, J. (2008) 'The ups and downs of bureaucratic organisation', *Annual Review of Political Science*, 11: 13–37.

Osborne, D. and Gaebler, T. (1992) *Reinventing Government: how entrepreneurial spirit is transforming the public sector*, Reading, MA: Addison Wesley.

Osborne, S. (2006) 'The new public governance?' *Public Management Review*, 8, 3: 377–387.

Osborne, S. (2009) 'Delivering public services: are we asking the right questions?', *Public Money & Management*, 29, 1: 5–7.

Page, E. and Jenkins, B. (2005) *Policy Bureaucracy: government with a cast of thousands*, Oxford: Oxford University Press.

Peters, B. (2001) *The Politics of Bureaucracy*, London: Routledge.

Peters, B. and Savoie, D. (1998) *Taking Stock: assessing public sector reforms*, Montreal: McGill-Queen's University Press.

Pierre, J. and Peters, B.G. (2000) *Governance, Politics and the State*, Basingstoke: Macmillan.

Pierre, J. and Peters, B.G. (2005) 'Governance: a garbage can perspective', in J. Pierre and B.G. Peters (eds) *Governing Complex Societies: Trajectories and Scenarios*, Basingstoke: Palgrave Macmillan: 49–63.

Pollitt, C. (1990) *Managerialism and the Public Services: the Anglo-American experience*, Oxford: Basil Blackwell.

Pollitt, C. and Bouchaert, G. (2000) *Public Management Reform: a comparative analysis*, Oxford: Oxford University Press.

Pollitt, C. and Bouchaert, G. (2004) *Public Management Reform: a comparative analysis*, Oxford: Oxford University Press.

Pollitt, C. and Bouchaert, G. (2011) *Public Management Reform: a comparative analysis*, Oxford: Oxford University Press.

Power, M. (1997) *The Audit Society: rituals of verification*, Oxford: Oxford University Press.

Puchala, D. (1972) 'Of blind men, elephants and international integration', *Journal of Common Market Studies*, 10, 3: 267–84

Rhodes, R.A.W. (1994) 'The hollowing out of the state: the changing nature of the public service in Britain', *Political Quarterly*, 65, 2: 138–151.

Rhodes, R.A.W. (1997) *Understanding Governance: policy networks, governance, reflexivity and accountability*, Buckingham: Open University Press.

Rhodes, R.A.W. (2000) 'Governance in Public Administration', in J. Pierre (ed.) *Debating Governance: Authority, Steering and Democracy*, Oxford: Oxford University Press, pp. 54–90.

Rhodes, R.A.W (2006) 'Policy Network Analysis', in M. Moran, M. Rein and R.E. Goodin (eds) *The Oxford Handbook of Public Policy*, Oxford: Oxford University Press: 425–447.

Rhodes, R.A.W. (ed.) (2011) *Public Administration: 25 years of analysis and debate*, Chichester: Wiley-Blackwell.

Rhodes, R.A.W. (2012) 'Waves of Governance', in D. Levi-Faur (ed.) *The Oxford Handbook of Governance*, Oxford: Oxford University Press: 33–48.

Richards, D. and Smith, M. (2002) *Governance and Public Policy in the United Kingdom*, Oxford: Oxford University Press.

Robichau, R. (2011) 'The mosaic of governance: creating a picture with definitions, theories and debates', *Policy Studies Journal*, 39, 1: 113–131.

Robichau, R.W. and Lynn, L.E. (2009) 'The implementation of public policy: still the missing link', *Policy Studies Journal*, 37, 1: 21–36.

Skelcher, C. (2005) 'Jurisdictional integrity, polycentrism, and the design of democratic governance', *Governance*, 18, 1: 89–110.

Sørensen, E. and Torfing, J. (2007) 'Theoretical Approaches to Metagovernance', in E. Sørensen and J. Torfing (eds) *Theories of Democratic Network Governance*, Basingstoke: Palgrave Macmillan: 169–182.

Stivers, C. (2008) *Governance in Dark Times: practical philosophy for public service*, Washington, DC: Georgetown University Press.

Stoker, G. (1998) 'Governance as a theory: five propositions', *International Social Science Journal*, 50, 155: 17–28.

Stokes, J. and Clegg, S. (2002) 'Once upon a time in the bureaucracy: power and public sector management', *Organization*, 9, 2: 225–247.

Tenbensel, T. (2005) 'Multiple modes of governance', *Public Management Review*, 7, 2: 267–288.

Thompson, F. and Miller, H. (2003) 'New public management and bureaucracy versus business values and bureaucracy', *Review of Public Personnel Administration*, 23, 4: 328–343.

Torres, L. (2004) 'Trajectories in public administration reforms in European continental countries', *Australian Journal of Public Administration*, 63, 3: 99–112.

Versluis, E., van. Keulen, M. and Stephenson, P. (2010) *Analysing the European Union Policy Process*, Basingstoke: Palgrave Macmillan.

Weber, M. (1946) *From Max Weber: Essays in Sociology.* Translated H.H. Gerth and C. Wright Mills (eds), Oxford: Oxford University Press.

Weber, M. (1947) *The Theory of Social and Economic Organisation.* Translated A.M. Henderson and T. Parson (eds), Oxford: Oxford University Press.

Weber, M. (1968) *Economy and Society. An Outline of Interpretative Sociology.* Translated Günther Roth and Claus Wittich (eds), New York: Bedminster Press.

Chapter 3

Public policy making

LEARNING OBJECTIVES

■ To have a critical understanding of the political–administrative interface and to be able to appreciate the various roles and interests of politicians and administrators
■ To understand the part played by policy communities and networks in public policy
■ To develop an awareness of who is included and excluded from policy making and management processes

KEY POINTS IN THIS CHAPTER

■ How the traditional explanations of politicians' and administrators' roles are over simplistic
■ How we distinguish policy communities and issue networks
■ The part played by pressure groups in public policy (and how pressure groups differ)
■ How key groups in society have their interests (under-)represented and how this affects policy

INTRODUCTION

Administration lies outside the proper sphere of politics. Administrative questions are not political questions. Although politics sets the task for administration, it should not be suffered to manipulate its offices . . . Public administration is the detailed and systematic execution of public law. Every particular application of general law is an act of administration. The assessment and raising of taxes, for instance, the hanging of a criminal, the transportation and delivery of the mails, the equipment and recruitment of the army and navy, etc., are all obviously acts of administration, but the general laws which direct these things to be done are as obviously outside of and above administration. The broad plans of governmental action are not administrative; the detailed execution of such plans is administrative.

(Wilson, 1887)

The quote is by the twenty-eighth President of the United States, Woodrow Wilson, one of the foremost thinkers of public policy and public administration. Wilson created a distinction between the roles of politicians and public servants. The quote illustrates the dichotomous roles within political and public service spheres of government: politicians formulate policy and public servants implement policy. As discussed in the Introduction, this dichotomous and simplistic understanding of the roles of policy actors is a myth. The focus of this chapter is: who is involved in public policy making and how does it occur? The preceding chapters provided a theoretical discussion of the concept of public policy, policy cycles and process and the domains of public policy making. Chapter 3 will delve further into the Eastonian 'black box' and explore by whom and how policy is made. The chapter will start with a discussion of how policy is made by exploring the relationship between politicians and bureaucrats as key policy actors. Thus, we begin with a theoretical discussion of the political–administrative interface. Scholarly attention has always focused on the role of politicians and senior bureaucrats at the apex of a hierarchical, public administrative structure. We review scholarly writings, but acknowledge that policy is not necessarily the exclusive domain of bureaucrats and politicians in the executive of government. We have argued in the preceding chapters, public policy making involves other actors – beyond the key policy actors of politicians and bureaucrats. Public policy is increasingly being formulated and implemented within a governance domain. The chapter will therefore also include a discussion of policy communities, policy networks and advocacy coalitions which involve various actors in the policy process. Chapter 3 sets out to analyze the diverse range of relationships and interactions of different policy actors involved in the policy process. Thus, attention is given to the roles of various societal sectors and their relationship with more traditional actors in the policy process. The chapter will encourage you to think critically about who is involved in public policy making and how change is affected. The concluding section of this chapter explores the issue of who is represented in the policy process and interrelated cycles, questioning who and who is not involved in policy making.

POLITICAL–ADMINISTRATION INTERFACE

We start our discussion with the relationship between key policy actors: politicians (ministers, secretaries of state, prime ministers and/or presidents) and bureaucrats (civil servants, policy advisers, directors general, permanent secretaries, directors, etc.). It is the conventional understanding that in most liberal democracies those policy actors involved in the administration of public policy and its implementation do so as an instrument of the political masters within an executive branch of government. Thus, through a hierarchical structure of policy, actors within the administration (bureaucrats, civil and public servants) report to politicians, with policies being formulated by politicians and then implemented down through the hierarchy. The public bureaucracy, consisting of civil and public servants, would serve the government of the day – the elected politicians. The convention is consistent with Weber's ideal type bureaucracy of politically neutral, impartial and professionally objective bureaucrats serving politicians in a hierarchical structure of authority. Neutrality, as political, non-partisanship, is considered a cornerstone of good governance to ensure that citizens, regardless of their political orientation are treated fairly and in an equitable manner (Matheson *et al.* 2007). This requires bureaucrats to behave in a professional manner ensured through a selection process based on merit and competence. Bureaucrats have to be accountable to the government of the day to ensure effective delivery of policies, and responsiveness of bureaucrats to the government of the day within the law and constitution is key to effective implementation of policies (ibid). This balance is often described as a bargain or game where politicians seek to ensure responsiveness of bureaucracy and effective implementation of policies, while the bureaucracy seeks to maintain its neutrality and autonomy, and to act free from political interference. It is within this relationship or 'bargain' that scholars explore how policy is made.

In a parliamentary system the theory of bureaucracy and democracy is seemingly straightforward: democratic control would be exerted through a line running from ministers, as politicians within the government of the day, to all those who exercise power and authority in the name of the government – the bureaucracy (Savoie 2003). The bureaucracy would have no constitutional personality or responsibility distinct from the government of the day (ibid). The government of the day and its ministers are not permanent officials but transient political actors in the policy-making process. Nevertheless, ministers are the political masters in the government and as such have the final say in the policy-making process because they are ultimately accountable to the people – the electorate – through a legislative body such as a parliament (ibid). The minister is responsible for everything in a government department within his or her respective policy portfolio and as such is held up to public scrutiny (ibid). Thus, for example, in a Westminster system the lines of accountability would be clear: it would run from bureaucrat to minister, to cabinet, to parliament and to the people (ibid). Colebatch (2005) explains the political–administrative interface within this paradigm with the politician in the executive arm of government being the authoritative decision maker and the bureaucracy within a government department implementing the policy. He does, however, acknowledge that there are other influences on the policy-making process such as those outside of government (e.g. media), policy actors within the multi-level governance or other levels of government context (e.g. local government), other agencies within the public sector, and international policy actors (e.g. World Health Organization) (ibid). Colebatch (2005: 24) configured the interface between policy actors along horizontal and vertical dimensions, and this is illustrated in Figure 3.1. Although he has included these dimensions to explain the relationships between various actors in the policy process, he nonetheless argues that the relationship across organizational boundaries takes place within a hierarchical context with the political master at the apex of the hierarchical authority structure and the bureaucracy together with other policy actors informing and implementing public policy (i.e. governance) (Colebatch 2005: 22–27).

The relationship between elected politicians within the executive of a government (e.g. cabinet) and bureaucrats has been to contextualise as a public service bargain. This bargain is a mutually beneficial relationship between politicians and bureaucrats with an understanding over their respective roles and responsibilities (Savoie 2003). Hood and Lodge (2006) describe the bargain as bureaucrats sacrificing a political life, given that they have to be impartial and neutral, in return for permanent employment. This permanence provides for the bureaucrat the benefits of job security, pension to compensate for relatively modest salaries, anonymity, trusted and loyal service (ibid). For politicians, the permanence of the bureaucracy offers longevity of service with bureaucratic experience, knowledge and expertise (ibid). Politicians on the other hand, sacrifice the right to blame and dismiss bureaucrats in exchange for loyal service with the required expertise and professional policy advice (ibid). The foundation of the public service bargain is impartial advice, expertise and experience, which bureaucrats provide in the formulation of policy (ibid). Thus, in making policy politicians expect impartial, objective and neutral policy advice based on professional expertise and experience with politicians making policy decisions based on the advice (Savoie 2003; Hood and Lodge 2006). Politicians would be ultimately responsible for the policy and would be accountable as such (Savoie 2003). Bureaucrats would receive remuneration and employment benefits for their years of loyal, impartial and professional service (Savoie 2003; Hood and Lodge 2006). The roles and responsibilities of politicians and bureaucrats were therefore distinct with the assumption that bureaucrats were neutral policy advisers and implementers.

Aberbach et al. (1981) in their study of politicians and bureaucrats in Western Europe found that bureaucrats have substantial responsibilities for managing the administrative machinery of government and that politicians spend their energies on electoral, party political and constituency affairs, but there is a 'contested

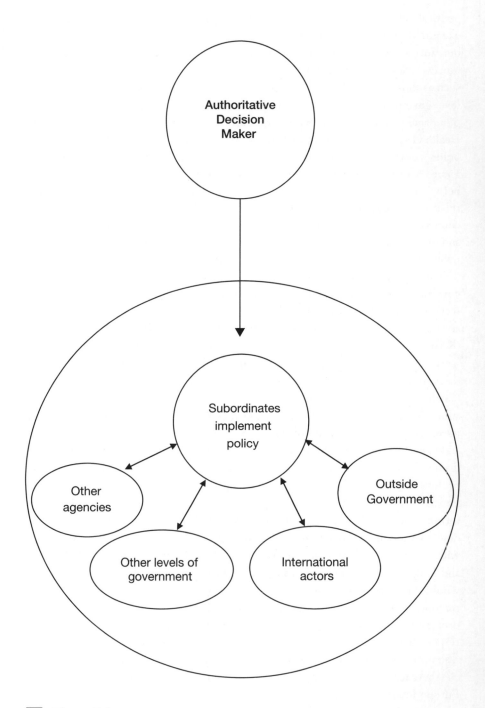

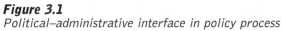
Figure 3.1
Political–administrative interface in policy process

territory' in the political–administrative interface: public policy. They explained the relationship between politicians and administrators/bureaucrats and their respective roles within a taxonomy of four 'images' (ibid). The first image of the policy–administrative dichotomy describes the nature of the relationship between politicians and senior bureaucrats in dichotomous terms, in the Wilsonian tradition of a separation of roles where politicians formulate policy and bureaucrats merely implement the policies as decided by their political masters within the executive branch of government (Aberbach et al. 1981: 4–6). The second image is that of facts–interests. This image describes the political–administrative interface as politicians and bureaucrats both participating in policy formulation, but bureaucrats bring technocratic knowledge and expertise in making policy (Aberbach et al. 1981: 6–7). In other words, based on the Weberian ideation of bureaucracy, bureaucrats by virtue of their expertise and experience based on their qualifications and longevity of service, bring facts, knowledge and technical expertise to the policy-making process (Aberbach et al. 1981). Politicians on the other hand, in the facts–interest image, represent the values, interests and constituency concerns within the process. Thus, bureaucrats would emphasise the technical efficacy of policy while politicians emphasize responsiveness to relevant constituencies (ibid). Aberbach et al. (1981) provide empirical evidence for this image, but also argue that there is evidence to suggest that there are increasing educational standards and professionalization within the political–administrative interface (ibid). Bureaucrats, they argue, may not necessarily have the monopoly of expertise since professional politicians reduce the plausibility of this image by increasingly bringing their own technical expertise to the policy-making table (ibid).

Aberbach et al. (1981) also found evidence in their research for an energy–equilibrium image. This third image describes the political–administrative interface as bureaucrats and politicians both involved in policy formulation (ibid). Collectively, bureaucrats and politicians are concerned with politics and the political environment (ibid). Yet, there is still a distinction: politicians in the policy-making process articulate broad, diffuse interests of unorganised individuals (Aberbach et al. 1981: 9–16). Bureaucrats have an understanding of these political interests and mediate narrow, focused interests of organised individuals (ibid). There is an element of bureaucratic political sensitivity in the formulation of policy in order to mediate pressure group interests or departmental clientele (ibid). In the energy–equilibrium image bureaucrats are concerned with aggregating the interests of a narrow group of extra-departmental stakeholders or societal actors involved in the policy-making process (Aberbach 1981: 9–10). The politicians in this image are more concerned with the broad partisan and ideological interests (ibid). Therefore, the politicians represent party and ideological interests while the bureaucrats articulate the interests of external pressure/interest groups in society.

The final image described by Aberbach et al. (1981: 16–23) is the pure hybrid. Here the policy-making roles between politicians and bureaucrats converge.

Aberbach *et al.* argued that the policy-making roles between politicians and bureaucrats become blurred with the bureaucratization of politics and the politicization of the bureaucracy. The politicization of the bureaucracy could take the form of political influence in appointments of bureaucrats (ibid). In countries, particularly those that follow the Westminster system such as the UK and many Commonwealth countries, where the independence of the bureaucracy is sacrosanct, the politicization of the bureaucracy is viewed as a concern (see Box 3.1 of the UK Civil Service Code). Yet in other countries such as the US, the President is involved in the appointments of senior officials of federal agencies; in France there is an interchange between political and administrative careers; and in countries such as South Africa the President has some say in the appointment and dismissal of senior bureaucrats. Aberbach *et al.* (1981) found evidence for the bureaucratization of politicians, with politicians becoming increasingly involved in administrative affairs. The latter point they argued was more inclined to the 'American exception' where politicians within congressional committees and sub-committees could influence administrative matters through their scrutiny role and where they were accustomed to legislative detail which influences administrative matters (ibid). Thus, the hybrid image required bureaucrats to combine substantive expertise with political commitment, and politicians with increasing levels of accountability look inwards to administrators to ensure implementation and look outwards as political leaders (ibid). Aberbach *et al.* argued that the pure hybrid image has seen over the decades the virtual disappearance of the political–administrative dichotomy and the overlap of roles between politicians and bureaucrats. Arguably, the introduction of public sector reforms (as described in Chapter 2) saw an increase in performance management systems, with politicians holding bureaucrats accountable for the implementation of policies, meeting performance management targets and becoming involved in administrative matters. For example, in the UK the Chief Advisor on Delivery, Michael Barber, reported directly to the Prime Minister, Tony Blair, on the performance of government departments in the implementation of the policy priority areas and became increasingly involved in the administrative detail of government departments' performance.

The political-administrative dichotomy is largely a myth. Bureaucrats are involved in policy making and are not merely implementers of policies. The extent to which they are involved in policy making and their involvement in the political environment very much depend on the political system and constitutional framework of a country.

Aberbach *et al.* (1981) acknowledge that bureaucrats are intimately involved in policy making and shape decisions which are inherently political and therefore, depending on the political system, cannot help but be political and policy actors. The 'political game' is different for politicians and bureaucrats in the formulation of policy. The involvement of interest groups and societal actors in the policy-making process requires bureaucrats to be political in a sense that they have to mediate, bargain and broker conflicting interests into specific terms in order to develop coherent and workable policy (ibid). The politics of bureaucrats are the politics which juggle carefully the interests of key groups and together with their technocratic expertise make policy. Aberbach *et al.*'s (1981: 84–114) study showed that the most common and top ranked traits of bureaucrats involved organisational and managerial skills, intellectual capacity, policy making, and technical expertise. The most common and top-ranked traits for politicians were policy making, intellectual capacity, representation and responsiveness and ideological and advocacy issues (ibid). Bureaucrats are concerned with technical and administrative feasibility of policies, whereas politicians are more concerned with political advantage and policies made out of political and/or ideological principle (ibid). In the policy-making process politicians are inspired by broad ideological and political goals and the advancement of interests to ensure constituency and electoral support, whereas bureaucrats consider more sobering possibilities of the policy in a more pragmatic sense (ibid).

According to Aberbach *et al.* (1981: 113) politicians are more concerned with 'Whom will this benefit?', while bureaucrats are concerned with 'What is an efficient outcome?' Politicians are therefore concerned with the distribution and redistribution of benefits; bureaucrats on the other hand are sensitized to issues involving collective goods (ibid). In Chapter 2 we describe that bureaucrats are involved in public policy through: the production policy process by developing drafts, statements and documents such as statutory instruments and legislation; by maintaining particular sets of governing arrangements of policies; and offering a service of knowledge, skills and advice in the production of policy (Page and Jenkins 2005). This pragmatic, technocratic expertise is a consistent theme of how bureaucrats formulate policy.

It would be erroneous to assume that bureaucrats are value-free, devoid of subjectivities – bureaucrats are human with various cognitive limitations and psychological rationalities (see Simon 1965) – in their policy-making role. Bureaucrats are not policy eunuchs, but influence how policy is made. Although, for the most part in liberal democracies bureaucrats may adhere to constitutional and legal frameworks, they nonetheless operate within a public policy environment, which is a political process. Bureaucrats and politicians are involved in a public service bargain but also a 'political game' with various ploys to ensure a 'check and balance' of respective roles. This game was caricatured in a BBC satirical television series, *Yes Minister*, with the main bureaucratic protagonist, the fictitious Permanent Secretary, Sir Humphrey Appleby, comically running rings around the Minister.

Bureaucrats influence the policy-making process through a number of resources. First, bureaucrats have information and expertise concentrated within public organizations and this relative monopoly is a source of power over the policy process (Peters 2001). According to Peters, this source of power manifests in a blatant argument that since bureaucrats know more about the policy they should

BOX 3.1   UK CIVIL SERVICE CODE

The British system of government, commonly known as the Westminster model, upholds the ideation of the Weberian bureaucracy with an impartial, politically neutral and professional civil service. Most countries, particularly Commonwealth countries, through colonialism, adopted this model. The model can be traced to the recommendations of the Northcote–Trevelyan and Carltona doctrine, which sought to establish a qualified cadre of bureaucrats who would loyally serve the elected government and adhere to a public service ethos (see O'Toole 2006). The Civil Service Code was first published in 1996 and then enacted, providing a statutory basis, in the Constitutional Reform and Governance Act of 2010. The Code includes standards of behaviour and values, instructing bureaucrats to conduct themselves with integrity, honesty, objectivity and impartiality:

Integrity

- Fulfil duties and obligations responsibly.
- Always act in a way that is professional and that deserves and retains the confidence of all those with whom you have dealings.
- Carry out fiduciary obligations responsibly (that is make sure public money and other resources are used properly and efficiently).
- Deal with the public and their affairs fairly, efficiently, promptly, effectively and sensitively, to the best of one's ability.
- Keep accurate official records and handle information as openly as possible within the legal framework.
- Comply with the law and uphold the administration of justice.
- Officials must not misuse their official position, for example, by using information acquired in the course of official duties to further private interests or those of others; accept gifts or hospitality or receive other benefits from anyone which might reasonably be seen to compromise personal judgement or integrity; or disclose official information without authority (this duty continues to apply after you leave the Civil Service).

Honesty

- Set out the facts and relevant issues truthfully, and correct any errors as soon as possible.
- Use resources only for the authorised public purposes for which they are provided.
- Officials must not deceive or knowingly mislead Ministers, Parliament or others; or be influenced by improper pressures from others or the prospect of personal gain.

Objectivity

- Provide information and advice, including advice to Ministers, on the basis of the evidence, and accurately present the options and facts.
- Take decisions on the merits of the case.
- Take due account of expert and professional advice.
- Officials must not ignore inconvenient facts or relevant considerations when providing advice or making decisions; or frustrate the implementation of policies once decisions are taken by declining to take, or abstaining from, action which flows from those decisions.

Impartiality

- Carry out responsibilities in a way that is fair, just and equitable and reflects the Civil Service commitment to equality and diversity.
- Officials must not act in a way that unjustifiably favours or discriminates against particular individuals or interests.

Political impartiality

- Serve the Government, whatever its political persuasion, to the best of one's ability in a way which maintains political impartiality and is in line with the requirements of this Code, no matter what your own political beliefs are.
- Act in a way which deserves and retains the confidence of Ministers, while at the same time ensuring the ability to establish the same relationship with those whom you may be required to serve in some future Government.
- Comply with any restrictions that have been laid down on political activities.
- Officials must not act in a way that is determined by party political considerations, or use official resources for party political purposes; or allow personal political views to determine any advice you give or your actions.

Source: Civil Service Code of the Constitutional Reform and Governance Act (2010)

be given control. Consequently, the bureaucrats within an agency exert control over a policy area, creating silos and monopolies over information. They trade this information to exert influence over policy (ibid). This argument is consistent with the notion of bureau-shaping behaviour. Second, bureaucrats have the power of decision with standard operating procedures which allow for systematic decision-making process devoid of politicking (ibid). Although, in Chapter 2, we discussed how rules and regulations create red-tape inefficiencies, the decision-making process within a hierarchy allows for relative efficiencies compared to the protracted political process. For example, during negotiations to establish a coalition government (e.g. UK in 2010), the bureaucracy just gets on with the job and follows standard operating procedures and extant legal frameworks. Third, the bureaucratic interface with interest and pressure groups allows bureaucrats to articulate these interests to their advantage. For example, bureaucrats may mobilize interest and pressure groups to amplify a problem to accrue more funding for their agency (Peters 2001). Fourth, bureaucrats claim that their impartiality and political neutrality provides them with 'superior' expertise as their policy advice is based on technical grounds above the subjectivities of politicking (ibid). For example, their permanence provides stability in the policy-making process and allows for longer-term planning, which it is argued lends to better decision-making than the arbitrary and value-laden nature of politics (ibid). A final source of power for bureaucrats is related to their permanence: ministers rarely have expertise in a policy area and do not have time to learn about the government department within their policy portfolio while bureaucrats have the expertise and institutional knowledge of departments based on their years of experience (ibid). Ministers as elected politicians invariably face the political calendar of election cycles and look to the bureaucracy to provide policy solutions. Politicians in a liberal democracy come and go through a turnstile of elections, but bureaucrats remain and therein lies their power over policy making.

Politicians within the public service bargain do, however, have their own sources of power over the bureaucracy. Ministers through the electoral process have legitimacy and as such have claimed to be political masters. This legitimacy enables them to legislate on policy matters, and have the power to create a bureaucratic agency responsible for the policy or make an agency defunct (Peters 2001). Thus, ministers transfer authority to bureaucratic agencies and provide them with legitimization (ibid). Ministers also have the power of the purse (ibid). Through a budgetary process bureaucratic agencies are accorded financial resources. The budget enables the agency's survival and government departments are wholly dependent on disbursements from a Treasury. Politicians may also restrict the autonomy of bureaucracies through rules and regulations, modes of accountability and scrutiny (ibid). The game within the public service bargain depends on the political system and legal–constitutional basis of a country and the degree to which the bureaucracy and politicians can exert control over policy.

Scholars have explored the relationship between politicians and bureaucrats in making policy (see Smith 1984; Page and Wright 1999; Peters *et al.* 2000; Page and Jenkins 2005) and have revealed that bureaucrats have a number of common roles. These roles and skills include: political, in order to operate within a political environment; policy making, providing technical advice; and representing a government institution. Bureaucrats in conducting these roles have to contend with two rationales: (1) professionalism, hierarchy, due process, jurisdictional and input–output logistics; and (2) efficiency, democracy, responsibility, leadership and accountability (Peters *et al.* 2000: 14). There are generally three types of bureaucrats: administrative generalists; technical experts; and personal or political appointments by the political executive (Smith 1984; Page and Wright 1999; Peters *et al.* 2000). The capacity of bureaucrats to influence policy is dependent on the constitutional and political opportunity to influence political leadership, administrative structures and institutional opportunity structure (Peters *et al.* 2000: 18–21). Although the principles of neutrality in the sense of non-partisanship are espoused by most liberal democratic countries, this does not necessarily equate to the absence of political involvement in the bureaucracy (Matheson *et al.* 2007). The 'political game' is to increase bureaucratic responsiveness and to ensure effective policy implementation by the bureaucracy (ibid). According to Matheson *et al.* (2007: 6) politicians have a distinctive incentive for politicization and it gives them a stronger handle on an otherwise unresponsive bureaucracy, but there are negative effects of political involvement damaging for good governance. They argue that in countries with weaker governance systems, politicization of the bureaucracy presents risks and exposes the system to associated problems of senior officials lacking the competence to undertake their roles, functions and responsibilities (Matheson *et al.* 2007). The degree of autonomy and professional independence bureaucrats enjoy in the dispensing of policy advice very much depends on the legal and constitutional arrangements within countries. Obviously, the less professional autonomy that can be exercised by bureaucrats, the more there tends to be political involvement in the policy process. The 'checks and balances' within the public service bargain therefore fail. In Sweden the Constitution requires that all appointments in public administration are made on objective grounds even though they may be made by politicians. In the US most senior positions in federal government are 'at the pleasure of the President' who plays an important role in the appointment and dismissal of public officials. Similarly in Mexico senior bureaucrats are also political appointees. In Belgium there is a hybrid system where senior bureaucrats are appointed through an administrative selection process based on merit and experience, yet the final decision to appoint is made by politicians. In the UK positions throughout the bureaucracy are filled through an administrative process premised on merit-based selection. There are of course special advisers who are political appointees. Special advisers often provide the political actors with policy advice with a keen eye for the political implications of policy decisions. They can act as a counterweight to politically neutral bureaucracy. However, there are often legal parameters concerning the appointment, role and delineation of special advisers in the policy process. In countries such as the US, Italy, Mexico, Belgium and Sweden political appointments of special advisers can be found. In South Africa during the transition from apartheid to democracy, the African National Congress (ANC) as part of the government of national unity, made a number of political appointments of special advisers to include more progressive policy advisers given the inheritance of an apartheid bureaucracy. We summarize the relationship and extent of political involvement of politicians in the bureaucracy in Box 3.2. We encourage you to read further by referring to Larson and Coe (1999); Rhodes and Weller (2001); Peters and Pierre (2004); Hondeghem (2011); and Rhodes (2011).

Politicians and bureaucrats are the key policy actors within government, which is the authoritative decision maker in the policy process. Each actor, in the political–administrative game, attempts to influence the policy process and exert control over it. Yet, there are more actors involved in policy making.

POLICY COMMUNITIES AND ISSUE NETWORKS

Richardson and Jordon (1979) in their study of British government argued that policy is made within a community, by a limited number of policy actors who

BOX 3.2 EXTENT OF POLITICAL INVOLVEMENT IN BUREAUCRACIES

Country	Degree of ministerial involvement in senior civil service management responsibility	Degree of political involvement in administrative matters with changes of government
Belgium	Frequently to rarely	Never
Denmark	Frequently	Never
France	Rarely	Never
Italy	Frequently to rarely	Never
Mexico	Rarely	Always
New Zealand	Never	Never
Poland	Frequently	Always
Sweden	Rarely	Never
United Kingdom	Rarely	Never
United States	Frequently to rarely	Always

Source: adapted from Matheson et al. (2007)

interact frequently and share some common values. Furthermore, they argued that policy making is not restricted to politicians and bureaucrats, but with an increasingly fragmented society, policy was being made by a growing number of interest groups. Interest groups are a collection of people or organizations which unite in an attempt to influence the policy-making process so that the outputs and/or outcomes of the policy satisfy their own desired agenda and they advance their constituent interests. Thus, government as the authoritative decision maker is lobbied and campaigned by interest groups in order to influence policy making or change a policy in an interest group's favour.

The observation is frequently made in reference to the US political system, which, as many scholars argue, is a pluralist system of bureaucrats, legislators and interest groups interacting and negotiating in making policy (see Rhodes 2008). Heclo (1978) for example, described an 'iron triangle' of mutually reinforcing relationships between regulated interests, congressional committees and the public bureaucracy charged with regulating interest. The relationship within the triangle is relatively closed with few 'outsider' interests involved and the relationship remains stable (Heclo 1978; Birkland 2005). The idea of interest groups being 'inside' and 'outside' of public policy-making process relates to their ability to influence or lobby the government (Birkland 2005; Dorey 2005). 'Insider' interest groups generally enjoy a close relationship with government, while 'outsider' interest groups normally are obliged to influence government through indirect means such as campaigning (ibid). Interest groups can take a number of forms: voluntary, charitable or third sector organizations (e.g. Oxfam, World Wide Fund for Nature); professional organizations (e.g. British Medical Association, Chartered Institutes); and social movements (e.g. Occupy Wall Street, Suffragettes).

Marsh and Rhodes (1992) added to the literature by identifying a continuum of government and interest group interaction to conceptualize policy communities and issue networks. A policy community, at one end of the continuum, is described as a closed, stable and often consensual relationship between government and a small number of interest groups (ibid). At the other end of the continuum are issue networks, which involve a wide and less consensual and stable network of a broad variety of interest groups (ibid). A policy community is small, with many excluded from its membership; government frequently consults with the community and there is a level of consensus where actors share the same understanding of the policy problems (Marsh and Rhodes 1992; Hill 1997; Dorey 2005; Cairney 2012). Issue networks are large with less restrictive entry requirements; the interaction with government is variable depending on the policy issue, and there is often a degree of conflict, although a measure of agreement may be reached between government and opposing interest groups (ibid). In policy communities there appears to be a relative balance of power within the policy-making process, but in networks the relationship is unequal (Marsh and Rhodes 1992; Hill 1997). Policy communities and issue networks can be characterized in Table 3.1 as follows:

93

Table 3.1 Continuum of policy communities and issue networks

Dimension	Policy Community	Issue Network
Membership		
Participants	Limited	Many
Interest	Professional, narrow/economic	Wide ranging
Interaction		
Frequency	Frequent and high quality	Constant fluctuation
Continuity	Membership and values stable	Fluctuating access
Consensus	Shared basic values	Varied
Resources		
Distribution within network	All actors exchange resources	Few resources
Distribution within participating organisations	Hierarchical	Varied
Power		
Nature of power	Relatively equal	Unequal

Sources: Marsh and Rhodes (1992); Richards and Smith (2002); Cairney (2012)

'Insider' interest groups or policy communities are regularly consulted by government in the formulation of a particular policy. For example, in the UK prior to the introduction of the smoking ban in public places, the government consulted the British Medical Association, voluntary sector organizations such as Action on Smoking and Health (ASH) and the British Heart Foundation, as well as the tobacco industry, all of whom attempted to influence the policy and regulation in their favour. 'Outsider' interest groups or issue networks may not necessarily be consulted in the formulation of a particular policy, but campaign government to undertake a course of action or to place an issue on the policy agenda. The 'Make Poverty History' campaign, for example, has broad aims and lobbies government to introduce fairer trade policies, to cancel unpayable poor-country debts and to provide more and better aid.

There are a number of reasons for including interest groups in the policy-making process. First, 'insider' interest groups have professional and technical expertise that the political–administrative actors require in order to formulate policy (Dorey 2005). For example, if government sought to introduce a policy on improving education standards it would usually involve 'insider' interest groups and policy communities involved in the education sector such as the representatives of teachers' trade unions. Second, the co-operation and acquiescence of 'insider' interest groups is important to the successful implementation of the policy (ibid). Thus, in the example of a new curriculum to improve education standards, the implementation of the policy would be dependent on teachers. Third, the involvement of a policy community adds legitimacy to the policy; in other words the interest group or

94

community is 'representative' of constituents affected by the policy (ibid). By contrast 'outsider' interest groups or issue networks rarely have such access to the policy-making process. There are a number of reasons for this: their interests are considered 'unreasonable'; the policy being canvassed is considered ideologically incompatible with government's agenda; their campaigns and tactics are viewed as 'extreme'; their demands are not considered as salient; and the aims may be considered too broad and wide ranging (ibid). 'Outsider' interest groups and issue networks attempt to influence the policy-making process by lobbying legislators; through demonstrations, marches and rallies; petitions; legal action; and raising awareness through media (ibid). Media has become an important platform for 'outsider' interest groups, issue networks and social movements to raise public awareness and increase the salience of the policy issue. Social media has become a useful tool to publicize issues, extend membership and place concerns on the policy agenda. Media plays an important role in the policy-making process and can be considered as a policy actor, although outside of government. Politicians, bureaucrats

BOX 3.3   INDIVIDUAL POLICY ACTORS – THE CELEBRITIZATION OF PROBLEMS IN PUBLIC POLICY

In the UK Jamie Oliver, a celebrity chef, began a campaign in 2005 to improve catering standards in schools. The campaign began with a television series entitled *Jamie's School Dinners*. The series highlighted the poor standards of nutrition, the inadequate training of catering staff and the low level of public expenditure on school meals. The campaign sought to improve nutrition, diet and health outcomes (e.g. reducing obesity) for children. He successfully lobbied government, which resulted in a change of policy. The success was partly due to media, teachers' and parents' support; his ability to link nutrition with better health outcomes; and the salient policy area of children's well-being. Although the output of the campaign was effective with a policy change and a number of schools nationwide adopting Oliver's programme, there were intended and unintended outcomes. As intended, there were improvements in school-children's nutrition and health as Oliver's follow-up programme, *Jamie's Return to School Dinners*, demonstrated. However, not everyone was enthusiastic about the healthier school meals. There were reports that parents were providing their children with the desired junk food at school gates during lunch breaks. Children were also foregoing the healthier school meal and accessing neighbouring fast food outlets. The unintended outcome was that children's nutrition and health did not necessarily improve.

and interest groups are keenly aware of how the media will portray and interpret policy decisions. The Lord Leveson Inquiry in the UK investigated the relationship between the media, politicians and public officials. The televised broadcast of the Inquiry revealed an 'iron triangle' of policy actors seeking to influence each other in making policy. The newspaper, *News of the World*, which became defunct after revelations of unethical practices, played on occasion a pivotal role in policy areas by bringing issues on to the agenda. For example, the newspaper campaigned for government to adopt Megan's Law in the UK (see Chapter 1). The media also provides a platform for celebrities to raise the profile of a policy issue (and of course the profile of the celebrity as well). The policy issue may be of personal salience to the celebrity (e.g. George Clooney's 'Not on Our Watch' campaign), or as a representative of an 'outsider' interest group (e.g. Bill Nighy's support for the 'Robin Hood' tax on certain types of financial transactions). The issue creates media reactivity in the policy-making process where the political and bureaucratic actors feel obliged to deal with a problem and place it on the policy agenda.

POLICY CHANGE

For many scholars of public policy the focus of study is on the behaviour and relationships of policy actors and how they influence change or set the agenda in the policy process. Paul Sabatier developed the Advocacy Coalition Framework (ACF) to understand how policy changes occur and the relationship among various policy actors. Sabatier (1988) viewed the policy process as more permeable than the 'iron triangle' with various policy actors such as politicians, bureaucrats, interest groups, researchers, journalists, etc. interacting to influence change in the policy process. Thus he viewed policy making not as a narrow political–administrative relationship within a hierarchical framework, but rather as a bottom-up process involving various policy actors (ibid). The policy process was seen as consisting of policy subsystems, rather than policy restricted to a government agency, with actors from a variety of public and private organizations concerned about a particular policy problem, organized in policy communities within a policy domain (Sabatier 1987; Birkland 2005). Within the subsystems, Sabatier (1987; 1988) argued that policy actors are aggregated into a number of advocacy coalitions composed of people from various organizations who share a set of common normative and causal beliefs and who act in concert to affect policy. When there is conflict within the subsystem, it is mediated by a third group of actors termed 'policy brokers' whose principal concern is to find a reasonable compromise and maintain the coalitions (ibid). The brokers are more likely to succeed if the compromise does not threaten the coalitions' core beliefs and values (Birkland 2005). According to Sabatier (1987; 1988) in most policy subsystems the number of politically significant advocacy coalitions are small, consisting of two to four important coalitions often involving 'elites' (ibid).

Sabatier (1987; 1988) argued that any political system and its policy subsystems are constrained by a variety of social, legal and resource features of society. Thus, there are external factors which impact upon the policy subsystems (ibid). These external factors consist of 'relatively stable' systems with coalitions sharing common beliefs and values, but there are also 'dynamic system events' (Sabatier 1987; 1988; Birkland 2005). The interaction between the relatively stable system parameters and the dynamic system events can enable or inhibit public policy making (ibid). The stable parameters include the problem, the distribution of resources, fundamental cultural values and social structure, and the legal structure (ibid). The dynamic system events include socio-economic changes, technological innovations, public opinion, changes in government and policy decisions from other subsystems (ibid). For example the global financial crisis within the ACF could be explained as: a coalition between the political class and financial institutions; the stable parameters of shared cultural and social values; the distribution of profits to the banks and taxation of profits to the state and the legal structure which enabled the deregulation of banks. The dynamic events would be the crisis, change in public opinion against financial institutions, technological innovations such as social media which enabled scrutiny and critical public opinion, and policy decisions emanating from other countries.

Coalitions within the policy subsystems seek to translate their beliefs into policy or some type of government action (Sabatier 1987; 1988). The ability to translate these beliefs into policy depends on available resources such as money, expertise, number of supporters and legal authority (ibid). Policy change within a subsystem can be understood as a result of four processes:

- A shift in core policy beliefs of the subsystem due to external events. These external events or shocks include broad changes in socio-economic conditions, public opinion, etc. that foster change in a subsystem by shifting and augmenting resources, tipping power coalitions and changing beliefs.
- In a subsystem policy learning takes place where relatively enduring alternations of thought or behavioural intensions that result from experience and/or new information and are concerned with the revision of policy objectives.
- Internal subsystem events occur, which highlight failure in the status quo and require a revision of the policy.
- Cross-coalition learning where professional forums provide an institutional setting that allows coalitions to safely negotiate, agree and implement agreements. There are nine conditions that allow for cross-coalition learning, which include an inhibiting stalemate, effective leadership, consensus-based decisions, diverse funding, duration of process and commitment of members, focus on empirical evidence, trust, and a lack of alternative venues (Weible *et al.* 2009).

The appeal of ACF is that it captures the variety of policy actors involved in the policy-making process, encompasses multi-level governance, recognizes external and internal dynamics which impact upon the policy process, deviates from the linear notions of policy making and cycles, and attempts to explain the behaviour and interaction of policy actors and how they influence the policy process. ACF also attempts to explain the influence of core beliefs of policy actors and consequent relative stability of subsystems, but recognizes the impact of dynamic events which can result in policy change.

A similar theory that attempts to explain policy change and the dynamic processes that affect the relative stability of policy systems is punctuated equilibrium. Punctuated equilibrium theory was purported by Baumgartner and Jones (1991; 1993) who argued that the balance of power between policy actors and groups remains relatively stable over long periods of time, punctuated by shifts in the understanding of problems and the balance of power between groups seeking to ensure their interests. According to Baumgartner and Jones (1991; 1993) there are policy monopolies that are closed, concentrated systems of important policy actors. Policy monopolies are akin to policy subsystems or policy communities (Birkland 2005; Cairney 2012). The policy actors within policy monopolies are interested in keeping an insular system because it ensures a measure of control and benefits accruing to the policy actors within the monopoly (Baumgartner and Jones 1991; 1993). The policy monopoly is influenced by two factors: policy image, which is the way in which policy issues are portrayed; and institutional policy venues, which are the institutional context of the policy issue (ibid). Policy change occurs when an issue emerges, unsettles the policy image and the institutional venue; the policy monopoly is then challenged, reconstructed or destroyed (ibid). This instability creates an opportunity for agenda setting where the policy monopoly is challenged by the media, courts, public opinion, other policy monopolies, etc. (ibid). Policy change is therefore not incremental and in a state of flux, but policy remains relatively stable, followed by a period of change and then stability with a new policy image (Baumgartner and Jones 1991; 1993; Parsons 1995; Birkland 2005; Cairney 2012).

REPRESENTATION IN PUBLIC POLICY

We have discussed the key policy actors; 'insider' and 'outsider' groups as policy actors; the interaction between these actors; how they make policy; and how they affect change in the policy process. A further issue that deserves exploration is representation: who is represented in policy making; who is excluded; and how does this affect how policy is made?

Representation is fundamental to democratic principles of who is included within the governance of a country. Representation involves standing for and acting for others (Pitkin 1967). Thus, the notion of representation is concerned with policy actors acting in the interests of others, with the assumption that the representative has the authority to act for others (Pitkin 1967). This assumption raises the issue of accountability of the representative, particularly where there is discretion to make a judgment on behalf of others' interests (Pitkin 1967). In many liberal democracies, institutional, constitutional and legislative arrangements exist to ensure that the representative acts in the interests of others, and to prevent a conflict of interest or a disjuncture between the interests of those who are represented and those who act on their behalf. Thus the 'political game' is to ensure that interests of constituents are represented, with political actors ensuring responsiveness to these interests, while also ensuring that no person or group is disadvantaged, excluded or treated unfairly. Bureaucrats in this 'game' ensure objectively the equal application of the law of the government of the day. But how and who is represented in the game?

In terms of who is represented, it is those actors who have given another the mandate and authority to act on their behalf. In our common understanding of representation in a democratic political context, the 'who' is usually citizens that elect an actor to represent their interests in a formal institutional setting thereby becoming the electorate or constituents (Miller 2012). The representative is therefore legally empowered to act for another (Pitkin 1967; McBride and Mazur 2010). The notion of who is represented is complex particularly when we explore the 'how' of representation (Miller 2012). According to Pitkin (1967) representation as 'standing for' rather than 'acting for' is descriptive representation. In other words, making present something by resemblance or reflection that was previously absent (Pitkin 1967). According to Mansbridge (1999) descriptive representation involves persons who are in some sense typical of a larger class of persons and make representation of the larger class. In other words the representative emanates from a collective group of actors. So, descriptive representation involves a notion of a proportion of the population which is represented (Lovenduski 2005). Indeed many scholars argue that, in terms of the quality of how people are represented, there is a requirement that the representatives are proportionate to the population which they represent (Miller 2012). Descriptive representation involves representatives who stand for a group by virtue of sharing similar characteristics such as race, gender, ethnicity or residence (Wise 2003; McBride and Mazur 2010). Descriptive representation in the literature is often referred to as passive representation (Kelly and Newman 2001; Weldon 2002; Wilkins and Keiser 2004). According to Mosher (1982) passive representation is concerned with representatives, as a proportion of the population, having the same demographic origins (gender, race, income, class, religion, etc.) as the population they serve. The representatives reflect (Pitkin 1967) the 'who' that they represent.

When representatives act for those whom they represent, this is referred to as substantive representation (Pitkin 1967). The representative seeks to advance the component group's interests and preferences (McBride and Mazur 2010). In the

99 ◼

literature, substantive representation is referred to as active presentation (Kelly and Newman 2001; Weldon 2002; Wilkins and Keiser 2004). In terms of active representation, representatives actively advance the interests of a group (Mosher 1982). There is much debate on whether active representation assumes the existence of passive representation. For example, Mansbridge (1999) argues that in terms of passive representation, descriptive characteristics often act as a proxy for identifying shared experiences, which results in active representation when a person is in fact most similar to his or her constituents and substantively acts in their interests. Much of this debate on descriptive/passive representation and substantive/active representation has been within the field of political science, particularly in the context of the under-representation of groups or minorities (e.g. gender, race, ethnicity, disability, etc.) in political life (Miller 2012). There is a large volume of literature examining the determinants and consequences of representation for women and minorities in political life, which tend to conceptualize and operationalize representation as the presence and behaviour of individual minorities (see Grofman et al. 1992; Weldon 2002; Lovenduski 2005; Childs 2006; Kittilson 2006; Karp and Banducci 2008; Celis 2009). Typical research in this area is examining the voting behaviour and opinions of individual minority legislators and whether these have favourable outcomes for a minority group. Many would argue that the marginalization of minorities undermines the principles of representation, indeed democracy, since marginalized groups have a distinctive perspective that is unlikely to be articulated effectively by persons representing another group or where that group's representation is absent (Weldon 2002).

There is a body of research that explores representation within bureaucracies with the view that bureaucrats will be more responsive to the citizens if the bureaucrats reflect the demographic characteristics of the public they serve (Meier 1975; Saltzstein 1979; Krislov and Rosenbloom 1981). Kingsley (1944) conducted a study of the British Civil Service in the 1940s and argued that senior bureaucrats did not represent the dominant social class but rather the upper, elite social class. Consequently he argued that the British Civil Service did not represent the larger society and could not be considered as a legitimate representative institution (ibid). Similarly, other studies by Levitan (1946), Long (1952), Krislov (1974), and Krislov and Rosenbloom (1981), with research on the race, gender and ethnicity of bureaucrats, argued that the bureaucracy that did not include the demographic profile of the population could not be considered representative and thus legitimate. Much of the early research on representative bureaucracy focused on passive representation, but increasingly representative bureaucracy theorists are concerned not merely about the demographic composition of bureaucracies, but the implications that representation has for public policy and service delivery (Meier 1975; Cayer and Siegleman 1980; Mosher 1982; Saltzstein 1983; 1986; Dometrius 1984; Rehfuss 1986; Riccucci 1987; Hindera 1993; Riccucci and Saidel 1997; Hindera and Young 1998; Selden et al. 1998; Brudney et al. 2000; Dolan 2000;

Keiser *et al.* 2002; Weldon 2002; Wise 2003; Wilkins and Keiser 2004; Meier and Nicolson-Crotty 2006; Wilkins 2006). Representative bureaucracy theory 'assumes that shared experiences and values, which may not be shared across gender or race divisions, fundamentally affect the decisions made by and the actions taken by bureaucrats' (Meier and Nicolson-Crotty 2006). Research in this area has shown that there is a relationship between passive and active representation, and indeed the theory of representative bureaucracy holds that the gender and/or race of the bureaucrats affect the relationship that bureaucrats have with citizens or recipients of a public agency's service and how policy is made and implemented (Riccucci and Saidel 1997; Thielemann and Stewart 1996; Keiser *et al.* 2002; Weldon 2002; Meier and Nicolson-Crotty 2006; Wilkins and Keiser 2004).

For example, representative bureaucracy scholars have investigated the representation of female bureaucrats and how it affects the policy outcomes that benefit women as a group (Dolan 2001). A review by Wilkins and Keiser (2004) of extant empirical research on the theory of representative bureaucracy found mixed results. There are a range of studies which provide evidence of active representation in terms of favourable policy outcomes for particular groups (see Meier and Stewart 1992; Meier 1993; Keiser *et al.* 2002; Meier and Nicolson-Crotty 2006; Meier and O'Toole 2006; Wilkins 2006; Wilkins and Keier 2006). Research also shows a range of bureaucratic and organizational intervening factors: individual bureaucratic discretion can lead to higher active representation (see Meier and Bohte 2001; Dolan and Rosenbloom 2003); salience both in terms of individual bureaucrat demographic identity (see Keiser *et al.* 2002) and in terms of symmetry between bureau organizational goals and specific policy arenas (Kelly and Newman 2001; Lovenduski 2005); inter-sectionality of several identities and characteristics – this can be difficult for research to disentangle (e.g. in the US Equal Employment Opportunity Commission (EEOC) research has not found a link between active and passive representation for gender but has for race and it is hypothesized that this may be due to difficulties of sorting out multiple identities where many EEOC female bureaucrats are also African Americans [see Meier *et al.* 2005]); and position in organization hierarchy with some research showing greater dynamic for active representation at higher levels (see Pitts 2005), some showing more effects at lower levels (see Meier 1993) and some showing effects only at the highest levels (e.g. Dolan 2001).

The translation of passive to active representation in public policy occurs under certain conditions. First, the policy area must be one where bureaucrats have discretion in the policy process (Mosher 1982; Keiser *et al.* 2002; Sowa and Selden 2003; Wilkins and Keiser 2004). Discretion is a necessary condition because it provides bureaucrats with the opportunity to shape outputs and rewards for a particular group (Mosher 1993; Sowa and Selden 2003; Wilkins and Keiser 2004). Second, the policy area must be salient for the demographic characteristics in question – the implementation of the policy must benefit a group (Mosher 1982;

101

Keiser *et al.* 2002; Wise 2003; Wilkins and Keiser 2004). Sowa and Selden (2003) and Keiser *et al.* (2002) argue that if an organization's goals are inconsistent with acting on behalf of clients, it is less likely that representative bureaucracy will occur. Third, when minorities are represented at senior echelons of bureaucracies they should have the authority to represent marginalized groups more actively (see Dolan 2000; 2001).

It is argued that within the 'iron triangle' or the political–administrative relationship there are elites – those disproportionally drawn from society who act to 'represent' the interests of society. Publications from Kingsley's (1944) *Representative Bureaucracy*, to Barberis' (1996) book entitled *The Elite of Elite: Permanent Secretaries in the British Higher Civil Service* and Page and Wright's (1999) book *Bureaucratic Elites in Western European States* highlight a political and bureaucratic class from similar socio-economic backgrounds, education systems, institutions and qualifications, and values. Arguably, this does not provide for representation of broader societal interests in public policy. Others would argue that it is exactly policy communities and issue networks which provide for a more representative and pluralist perspective in the making of policy. Yet the key policy actors, the politicians and bureaucrats, are the gatekeepers to the policy process. It is government that is the authoritative decision maker and that allocates resources and values in the policy process. It is government that decides who to consult, include and listen to in the making of policy. It can be lobbied, cajoled and even pressurized by the media and social movements, but ultimately government decides what to do and what not to do. In countries such as the UK and the US, the continued lack of representation of women, ethnic minorities, people with disabilities and other marginalized populations in the policy-making process is an issue of concern, since the lack of passive representation leads to a lack of active representation and legitimacy of the policy-making process.

CONCLUSION

To conclude we have considered the various policy actors involved in the policy-making process. There are key policy actors, politicians and bureaucrats, with a relationship which impacts upon how policy is made. It is within this relationship, the political–administrative interface, that bureaucrats bring technical and pragmatic expertise based on skills, experience and professional practice of objectivity and impartiality to policy making; politicians articulate ideological and constituency interests to policy making with a tendency towards responsiveness to the electorate. This relationship has often been described as a 'bargain' or a 'game' with each mediating various interests. It is the assumption that this 'bargain' or 'game' is done in the public interest, although public choice theorists may differ with this view. This relationship differs within each country depending on the legal–constitutional framework or political architecture. The political architecture of a country may also allow for the extent to which other policy actors influence policy making. The US, for example, has a long history of pluralist influences on the policy-making process – for example, with lobbyists often embedded in the system as a matter of course. In other countries too there is a wide variety of policy actors, from interest and pressure groups, to social movements, to the media, which all impact upon policy to a larger or lesser degree depending on whether they form part of a policy community or network, or whether they are 'insiders' or 'outsiders'. Yet even within contemporary liberal democracies there are questions about who are 'insiders' and 'outsiders' in policy making, who is included, represented, and who is excluded. The policy-making process and who is represented has implications for how policy is made, the quality of policy decisions, the legitimization of the policy and the acceptance of the policy by actors during implementation.

REFERENCES

Aberbach, J.D., Putnam, R.D. and Rockman, B.A. (1981) *Bureaucrats and Politicians in Western Democracies*, Cambridge, MA: Harvard University Press.

Barberis, P. (1996) *The Elite of The Elite*, Aldershot: Dartmouth.

Baumgartner, F.R. and Jones, B.D. (1991) 'Agenda dynamics and policy subsystems', *Journal of Politics*, 53, 4: 1044–1074.

Baumgartner, F.R. and Jones, B.D. (1993) *Agendas and Instability in American Politics*, Chicago, IL: University of Chicago.

Birkland, T. (2005) *An Introduction to the Policy Process: Theories, Concepts, and Models of Public Policy Making*, New York: M.E. Sharpe.

Brudney, J.J., Herbert, F.T. and Wright, D.S. (2000) 'From organizational values to organizational roles: examining representative bureaucracy in state administration', *Journal of Public Administration Research and Theory*, 10, 3: 491–521.

Cairney, P. (2012) *Understanding Public Policy: theories and issues*, Basingstoke: Palgrave Macmillan.

Cayer, N.J. and Sigelman, L. (1980) 'Minorities and women in state and local government: 1973–1975', *Public Administration Review*, 40, 5: 443–450.

Celis, K. (2009) 'Substantive representation of women (and improving it): what it is and should be about?', *Comparative European Politics*, 7, 1: 95–113.

Childs, S. (2006) 'The complicated relationship between sex, gender and the substantive representation of women', *European Journal of Women's Studies*, 13, 7: 7–21.

Civil Service Code of the Constitutional Reform and Governance Act (2010), http://civilservicecommission.independent.gov.uk/wp-content/uploads/2012/03/Constitutional%20Reform%20Governance%20Act.pdf. (Accessed 16 May 2012.)

Colebatch, H. (2005) *Policy*, Maidenhead: Open University Press.

Darcy, R., Welch, S. and Clark, J. (eds) (1994) *Women, Elections and Representation*, 2nd edition, Lincoln, NB: University of Nebraska Press.

Dolan, J. (2000) 'The senior executive service: gender, attitudes, and representative bureaucracy', *Journal of Public Administration Research and Theory*, 10, 3: 513–529.

Dolan, J. (2001) 'Women in the executive branch: a review essay of their political impact and career opportunities', *Women and Politics*, 22, 4: 89–104.

Dolan, J. and Rosenbloom, D.H. (eds) (2003) *Representative Bureaucracy: Classic Readings and Continuing Controversies*, Armonk, NY: M.E. Sharpe.

Dometrius, N.C. (1984) 'Minorities and women among state agency leaders', *Social Science Quarterly*, 65, 1: 127–137.

Dorey, P. (2005) *Policy Making in Britain*, London: Sage Publishing.

Grofman, B., Handley, L. and Niemi, R. (1992) *Minority Representation and the Quest for Voting Equality*, Cambridge: Cambridge University Press.

Heclo, H. (1978) 'Issue Networks and the Executive Establishment', in A. King (ed.) *The New American Political System*, Washington, DC: American Enterprise Institute, pp. 87–124.

Hill, M. (1997) *The Policy Process in the Modern State*, Harlow: Pearson.

Hindera, J.J. (1993) 'Representative bureaucracy: further evidence of active representation in the EEOC district offices', *Journal of Public Administration Research and Theory*, 3, October: 415–430.

Hindera, J.J. and Young, C.D. (1998) 'Representative bureaucracy: the theoretical implications of statistical interaction', *Political Research Quarterly*, 51, 3: 655–671.

Hondeghem, A. (ed.) (2011) 'Changing public service bargains for top officials' special issue of the journal, *Public Policy and Administration*, 26, 2: 159–165.

Hood, C. and Lodge, M. (2006) *The Politics of Public Service Bargains: reward, competency, loyalty and blame*, Oxford: Oxford University Press.

Karp, J.A. and Banducci, S.A. (2008) 'When politics is not just a man's game: women's representation and political engagement', *Electoral Studies*, 27: 105–115.

Keiser, L.R., Wilkins, V.M., Meier, K.J. and Holland, C. (2002) 'Lipstick and logarithms: gender, institutional context, and representative bureaucracy', *American Political Science Review*, 96, 3: 553–564.

Kelly, R.M. and Newman, M. (2001) 'The gendered bureaucracy: agency mission, equality of opportunity, and representative bureaucracies', *Women and Politics*, 22, 3: 1–33.

Kingsley, J.D. (1944) *Representative Bureaucracy*, Yellow Springs, OH: Antioch Press.

Kittilson, M.C. (2006) *Challenging Parties and Changing Parliaments: women and elected office in contemporary western Europe*, Columbus, OH: Ohio State University.

Krislov, S. (1974) *Representative Bureaucracy*, Englewood Cliffs, NJ: Prentice Hall.

Krislov, S. and Rosenbloom, D.H. (1981) *Representative Bureaucracy and the American Political System*, New York: Praeger.

Larson, P.E. and Coe, A. (1999) *The Evolving Role of Top Public Servants*, London: Commonwealth Secretariat.

Levitan, D.M. (1946) 'The responsibility of administrative officials in a democratic society', *Political Science Quarterly*, 61, 4: 562–98.

Long, N.E. (1952) 'Bureaucracy and constitutionalism', *American Political Science Review*, 46, September: 808–18.

Lovenduski, J. (2005) *Feminizing Politics*, Cambridge: Polity Press.

McBride, D. and Mazur, A.G. (2010) *The Politics of State Feminism*, Philadelphia, PA: Temple University Press.

Mansbridge, J. (1999) 'Should blacks represent blacks and women represent women? A contingent "Yes"', *Journal of Politics*, 61, 3: 628–657.

Marsh, D. and Rhodes, R.A.W. (1992) *Policy Networks in British Government*, Oxford: Oxford University Press.

Matheson, A., Weber, B., Manning, N. and Arnould, E. (2007) 'Study on the political involvement in senior staffing and on the delineation of responsibilities between ministers and senior civil servants', *OECD Working Papers on Public Governance*, 2007/6, OECD Publishing.

Meier, K.J. (1975) 'Representative bureaucracy: an empirical analysis', *The American Political Science Review*, 69, 2: 526–542.

Meier, K.J. (1993) 'Latinos and representative bureaucracy: testing the Thompson and Henderson hypotheses', *Journal of Public Administration Research and Theory*, 3, 4: 393–414.

Meier, K.J. and Bohte, J. (2001) 'Structure and discretion: missing links in representative bureaucracy', *Journal of Public Administration Research and Theory*, 11, 4: 455–470.

Meier, K.J. and Nicholson-Crotty, J. (2006) 'Gender, representative bureaucracy, and law enforcement: the case of sexual assault', *Public Administration Review*, 66, 6: 850–860.

Meier, K.J. and O'Toole, L.J., Jr (2006) *Bureaucracy in a Democratic State*, Baltimore, MD: John Hopkins University Press.

Meier, K.J. and Stewart, J., Jr (1992) 'The impact of representative bureaucracies: educational systems and public policies', *American Review of Public Administration*, 22, 3: 157–71.

Meier, K.J., Pennington, M.S. and Elder, W.S. (2005) 'Race sex and Clarence Thomas: representation change in the EEOC', *Public Administration Review*, 65, 2: 171–179.

Miller, K. Johnston (2012) 'Representative bureaucracy and multi-level governance in the EU', *Geopolitics, History and International Relations*, 4, 1: 50–75.

Mosher, F. (1982) *Democracy and the public service* 2nd edition, New York: Oxford University Press.

O'Toole, B. (2006) *The Ideal of Public Service: reflections on the higher civil service in Britain*, London: Routledge.

105

Page, E. and Jenkins, B. (2005) *Policy Bureaucracy: government with a cast of thousands*, Oxford: Oxford University Press.

Page, E. and Wright, V. (1999) *Bureaucratic Elites in Western European States: a comparative analysis of top officials*, Oxford: Oxford University Press.

Parsons, W. (1995) *Public Policy: an introduction to the theory and practice of policy analysis*, Cheltenham: Edward Elgar.

Peters, B.G. (2001) *The Politics of Bureaucracy*, London: Routledge.

Peters, B.G. and Pierre, J. (eds) (2004) *Politicization of the Civil Service in Comparative Perspective: the quest for control*, London: Routledge.

Peters, B.G. Rhodes, R.A.W. and Wright, V. (2000) *Administering the Summit: administration of the core executive in developed countries*, Basingstoke: Palgrave Macmillan.

Pitkin, H.F. (1967) *The Concept of Representation*, Berkeley, CA: University of California Press.

Pitts, D.W. (2005) 'Diversity representation and performance: evidence about race and ethnicity in public organizations', *Journal of Public Administration Research and Theory*, 15, 4: 615–631.

Rehfuss, J.A. (1986) 'A representative bureaucracy? Women and minority executives in California career service', *Public Administration Review*, 46, 5: 454–460.

Rhodes, R.A.W. (2008) *Understanding Governance*, Maidenhead: Open University Press.

Rhodes, R.A.W. (2011) *Everyday Life in British Government*, Oxford: Oxford University Press.

Rhodes, R.A.W. and Weller, P. (eds) (2001) *The Changing World of Top Officials*, Buckingham: Open University Press.

Riccucci, N.M. (1987) 'Black employment in municipal workforces', *Public Administration Quarterly*, 11, 1: 76–89.

Riccucci, N.M. and Saidel, J.R. (1997) 'The representativeness of state-level bureaucratic leaders: a missing piece of the representative bureaucracy puzzle', *Public Administration Review*, 57, 5: 423–430.

Richards, D. and Smith, M.J. (2002) *Governance and Public Policy in the UK*, Oxford: Oxford University Press.

Richardson, J.J. and Jordan, A.G. (1979) *Governing Under Pressure: the policy process in a post-parliamentary democracy*, Oxford: Martin Robertson.

Sabatier, P.A. (1987) 'Knowledge, policy-orientated learning and policy change', *Knowledge: Creation, Diffusion, Utilization*, 8, 4: 649–692.

Sabatier, P.A. (1988) 'An advocacy coalition framework of policy change and the role of policy-oriented learning therein', *Policy Sciences*, 21, 2–3: 129–168.

Saltzstein, G.H. (1979) 'Representative bureaucracy and bureaucratic responsibility: problems and prospects', *Administration and Society*, 10, 4: 464–75.

Saltzstein, G.H. (1983) 'Personnel directors and female employment representation: a new addition to models of equal opportunity policy?' *Social Science Quarterly*, 64, 4: 734–746.

Saltzstein, G.H. (1986) 'Female mayors and women in municipal jobs', *American Journal of Political Science*, 30, 1: 140–164.

Savoie, D. (2003) *Breaking the Bargain, Public Servants, Minsters, and Parliament*, Toronto: University of Toronto Press.

Selden, S.C., Brudney, J.L. and Kellough, J.E. (1998) 'Bureaucracy as a representative institution: toward a reconciliation of bureaucratic government and democratic theory', *American Journal of Political Science*, 42, 3: 717–744.

Simon, H. (1965) 'The logic of rational decision', *The British Journal for the Philosophy of Science*, 16, 63: 169–186.

Smith, B. (1984) The *Higher Civil Service in Europe and Canada: lessons for the United States*, Washington, DC: The Brookings Institution.

Sowa, J.E. and Selden, S.C. (2003) 'Administrative discretion and active representation: an expansion of the theory of representative bureaucracy', *Public Administration Review*, 63, 6: 700–710.

Thielemann, G.S. and Stewart, J. (1996) 'A demand-side perspective on the importance of representative bureaucracy: AIDS, ethnicity, gender, and sexual orientation', *Public Administration Review*, 56, 2: 168–173.

Weible, C., Sabatier, P. and McQueen, K. (2009) 'Themes and variations: taking stock of the advocacy coalition framework', *Policy Studies Journal*, 37, 1: 121–140.

Weldon, S.L. (2002) 'Beyond bodies: institutional sources of representation for women in democratic policymaking', *The Journal of Politics*, 64, 4: 1153–1174.

Wilkins, V.M. (2006) 'Exploring the causal story: gender, active representation, and bureaucratic priorities', *Journal of Public Administration Research and Theory*, 17, January: 77–94.

Wilkins, V.M. and Keiser, L.R. (2004) 'Linking passive and active representation by gender: the case of child support agencies', *Journal of Public Administration Research and Theory*, 16, 1: 87–102.

Wilson, W. (1887) 'The study of administration', *American Political Science Quarterly*, 2, 2: 197–222.

Wise, L.R. (2003) 'Representative Bureaucracy', in B.G. Peters and J. Pierre (2003) *Handbook of Public Administration*, Thousand Oaks, CA: Sage Publishing: 343–353.

Chapter 4

Case study: women in public policy?[1]

LEARNING OBJECTIVES

The case study integrates many of the concepts outlined in Chapters 1 to 3. After reading and discussing the case, you should be able to:

- understand the policy process and interrelated policy cycles of the case;
- outline the interests and roles of key actors in the policy debates set out in the case;
- critically evaluate the role of policy communities;
- assess the positioning of active and passive representation in the case;
- critically reflect upon the lack of representation of women in public policy.

INTRODUCTION

In 1992 Bhanwari Devi, a social worker (a saathin) in the State of Rajasthan, India, was protecting an infant girl against a forced marriage. This was, as a public servant employed by the State of Rajasthan, part of her responsibility to protect the welfare of children. Her intervention in attempting to prevent the marriage was resented by the infant girl's father, Ramkaran Gujjar, and a number of villagers. Bhanwari Devi was intervening in the face of inherent conservative, patriarchal and traditional culture, customs and values.

The marriage, despite Devi's efforts, proceeded. In September 1992 Devi was violently gang raped, in front of her husband, by Ramkaran Gujjar and other male villagers. Worse was to follow. She suffered physically and psychologically like any rape victim and was subject to further humiliation and victimization: the only doctor in the nearest primary care health centre, a male doctor, refused to provide her with medical care; the doctor who finally agreed to examine her at Jaipur hospital did not make any reference to the rape or her injuries in the medical report; at the police station Devi was taunted by the police and in the early hours of the morning was asked to leave the police station where she had sought refuge; before being forced to leave the police station Devi was asked to remove her lehenga (dress) and leave it with the police as evidence; Devi left the police station wearing only her husband's blood-stained dhoti (traditional Indian male garment); she begged for protection but was forced out into the night.

At the trial the men who gang raped Devi were acquitted. She wanted justice and took a very courageous step to seek redress through the High Court. Devi inspired many women to support her cause and speak out against rape – a social taboo in many societies. In December 1993, the High Court ruled that Devi had been gang raped. As a protest campaign, women's groups throughout India filed a petition in the Supreme Court of India under the case name of Vishaka vs. State of Rajasthan regarding sexual harassment of working women. Devi had been a public servant working for the State and was sexually victimized in conducting her duties of employment. On 13 August 1997, the Supreme Court decreed guidelines and norms to be observed to prevent sexual harassment of working women (for the full ruling see Vishaka and Others vs State of Rajasthan and Others [JT 1997 (7) SC 384]). It was a victory for Devi and for all women in India.

In many societies today the victimization, harassment and discrimination of women continues. There have been many public policy initiatives over the decades to ensure women's human rights and equality of treatment. Yet the status of women in society remains low; women and their dependent children are often trapped in poverty; women are more likely to experience sexual violence; they are often enslaved and trafficked; they are under-represented in politics and business; they face occupational discrimination, unequal pay, etc. This chapter discusses the role of women and their representation in the policy process. The chapter first outlines the under-representation of women in public policy and the poor policy outcomes for women. This discussion includes an account of policy initiatives to improve the representation of women but which had limited effect. The chapter then outlines how women influence the policy process and finally provides a real-world case study of the passive and active representation of women in public policy. The case involves the criminalization of purchasers of sexual services (prostitution) in Sweden. The case study describes the policy problem, the framing of the policy problem, the decision-making process, options that were considered, the policy actors and their interaction, advocacy coalitions, domains and the policy output and outcome. This chapter concludes with a series of questions based on the case to encourage you to reflect on the interrelated issues in public policy.

109

THE REPRESENTATION OF WOMEN?

The United Nations (UN) has through various platforms, declarations, programmes and policies attempted to address gender inequality and discrimination, empower women and improve their quality of life. Most famously, the UN held the Fourth World Conference of Women in 1995, where an action plan and global framework was developed to improve the status and lives of women and girls. Fifteen years later a review by the UN Entity for Gender Equality and the Empowerment of Women acknowledged that not much had been achieved in empowering women (see www.unwomen.org/ accessed 29 April 2013).

A case in point would be Europe; arguably consisting of many liberal democracies with progressive policies, yet women are over-represented among the most vulnerable population groups in the EU. The number of women living in poverty is disproportionate in relation to men with 17 per cent of women in EU27 countries classified as living in poverty (EC 2008). For example, in sixteen member countries the risk of extreme poverty for women greatly exceeds poverty among men (ibid). Women are at greater risk of poverty – especially single mothers and women aged over 65 (ibid). Although women constitute 59 per cent on average of the workforce, many women remain in low paid work with gender segregation resulting in disadvantaged pay and career outcomes for women (ibid). Eurostat data reveals that in 2009 the unadjusted gender pay gap for EU27 countries was 17 per cent. There are also broader economic and social outcomes for women: the feminization of poverty and the social exclusion of women and their dependents, mostly children. In Europe, 35 per cent of households consist of single parents with the majority being women (ibid). There is a higher incidence of poverty among women often bearing the burden of poverty, being at risk of poverty, on low incomes and vulnerable to social exclusion (Miller 2012). Female poverty is a consequence of various factors such as stereotyping, gender pay gaps and barriers caused by the lack of reconciliation between work and family life, longer life expectancy of women and various types of gender discrimination and victimization (ibid).

In September 2010, the EC introduced its fourth road map as a five-year plan to improve gender equality. The five-year plan is integral to the EU 2020 strategy to achieve broader social inclusion goals, including the goal to increase the representation of women in politics and key decision-making roles. However, the representation of women in politics, public policy and key decision-making roles remains low (EC 2008; 2010a). Currently, in the European Parliament women's representation is 31 per cent (ibid). Women in senior positions within the national public administrations of the EU27 countries are on average 26 per cent (ibid). There is also evidence of occupational gender segregation in the European Civil Service which provides administrative (policy and legislative decision-making support) and assistant (secretarial, clerical and support work) functions to the EC, EP, Council of the EU, European Court of Justice and the European Court of

Auditors. In terms of vertical segregation, men dominate the most senior positions within the Service with representation at approximately 70 per cent, and within administrative and assistant grades, 81 per cent and 76 per cent respectively (EC 2010a; 2010b). Furthermore, there is a high proportion of female employment in assistant (service) compared to administrative (decision-making and advice) functions (ibid). Although, women account for the majority of those employed as assistants (65 per cent), there is a high proportion of men at senior levels of assistant grades (ibid). Much has been written about the under-representation and paucity of women in senior positions within the EU policy-making arenas (see Kantola 2010). Occupational gender segregation in the labour market, discrimination and a lack of representation of women in policy, political and key decision-making roles have implications for women in policy outcomes. A report by the EC (2008) provides an egregious account of gender inequality and the policy outcomes for women: women are more likely to live in poverty; women are concentrated in a relatively small number of sectors and in lower paid jobs; women are less likely to hold managerial or decision-making positions; more women than men are employed on fixed-term contracts of employment etc. – all of which impact upon the economic and social status, quality of life and opportunities of women and their dependents.

The EU has introduced a number of directives and policies that have been transposed for the most part to member countries, but there remains a policy implementation gap (see Kantola 2010). The EU has enacted a number of laws and policies that, explicitly and implicitly, seek to promote gender equality. For example: Council Directive 75/117/EEC of 10 February 1975 relates to the principle of equal pay for men and women; Council Directive 76/207/EEC of 9 February 1976 established the principle of equal treatment for men and women with regard to access to employment, vocational training and promotion and working conditions; Council Directive 2000/78/EC of 27 November 2000 established a general framework for equal treatment in employment and occupation, consistent with the Treaty on the EU (specifically, Articles 3(2) and 6); and Council Directive 2006/54/EC of 5 July 2006 regards the implementation of the principle of equal opportunities and equal treatment of men and women in matters of employment and occupation. However, successive directives have not sufficiently addressed gender inequality within member countries despite the transposition of the directives (Kantola 2010). A document published by the EC (2009) reveals that laws and directives relating to gender equality represent the highest number of infringement proceedings within the sector of employment, social affairs and equal opportunities. The EC (2009: 75) concluded with a concern over the number of infringements related to gender equality directives. A report authored by Burri and Prechal (2009) on the transposition of the Recast Directive 2006/54/EC, commissioned by the EC, reveals that there is a lack of, or partial transposition of, the directive into national law in some of the member countries. The EU has

111

attempted to address gender inequality in policy processes. Indeed the implementation gap has seen the policy prioritization of gender equality and reducing inequalities in the workplace as emphasized in the European Social and Equality Agenda for 2011–2015 (Miller 2012). The EC has also adopted gender mainstreaming, which is the '(re)organization, improvement, development and evaluation of policy processes, so that a gender equality perspective is incorporated in all policies at all levels and at all stages, by actors normally involved in policymaking' (Council of Europe 1998: 15).

Yet, various studies have revealed superficial compliance (Weaver 2008; Hafner-Burton and Pollack 2009; Kantola 2010), the co-option of gender mainstreaming to favour other policy priorities (Stratigaki 2004; European Women's Lobby 2007; Hafner-Burton and Pollack 2009), and/or the disappearance of gender equality from the policy agenda once transposition takes place (Verloo 2001; Woodward 2003; Miller 2009). In some countries in the EU where gender mainstreaming has been adopted, women policy units within national administrations, for example, became defunct (Miller 2012). The view is often held that if gender equality is being mainstreamed in public policy, then a separate public agency ensuring gender equality would not be necessary. Stratigaki's (2004: 50) study of the implementation of gender mainstreaming in policy processes reveals that:

> The process of co-option of the gender equality concept . . . exemplifies how the outcome of conflicting policy frames in the EU is shaped, as well as how policy opportunities and barriers are evolving throughout the project of European integration . . . the policy goal of involving flexibility of the labour market eventually prevailed over gender equality objectives for framing reconciliation, resulting in the co-option of the concept. This co-option transformed and corrupted its meaning.

It has left many feminist scholars to argue that the implementation of gender mainstreaming across European national administration has to a large extent been limited (see Verloo 2001; Stratgaki 2004; 2005; Hafner-Burton and Pollack 2009; Kantola 2010).

WOMEN'S INFLUENCE IN THE POLICY PROCESS

Arguably, a lack of passive representation of women in political and public policy making has implications for active representation, legitimacy and good governance. Yet, there are ways in which women are represented in public policy processes: first, as women working within the state and government as legislators and public officials; and second, as actors within the domain of governance as part of networks, advocacy coalitions, interest groups and across multi-levels of governance.

According to Mazur (2002) there are generally four types of feminist analyses of how women influence the state and governance:

- A focus on public policy making and the way in which public policy makers promote women's status and address gender inequality. Feminist scholars study the actors, obstacles, content and the process. Here the analysis is of policy processes, the politics of the process and not necessarily the impact on society. It is not that these scholars ignore how policy impacts on women as a class, but they recognize the difficulty of uniquely attributing changes in gender relations in women's status to a set of specific policies. Nonetheless, there is a volume of published research in this area (see Mazur 2002).

- The study of feminist movements and its interface with the state and policy process. Feminist scholars observe how, why and whether women's or feminist movements' ideas and actions are translated into public policy. Here the focus is on examining the activities of women's movements and how these movements interact with the state through policy formulation and other state activities such as women's or equality policy offices. The main issue of concern is the success of women's movements in influencing the content of public policy or how these movements frame public policy in the interests of women as a class (see Mazur 2002).

- The study of state feminism considers whether state institutions and actors promote feminism. Here the focus is on female actors in state policy arenas, the gendered nature of state bureaucracies and structures that influence women's roles, and the activities of women in policy machineries. The focus of study is usually on women's policy offices and femocrats (see Mazur 2002; Lovenduski 2005; Kelly and Newman 2001; Chappell 2002). It is within this area of study that representative bureaucracy theory is usually located.

- The final analysis is whether the welfare state is an obstacle or promoter of gender discrimination and equality. Much of the scholarship explores the link between women's and men's roles in the public and private domains in relation to policies of the welfare state. Here the focus is on the impact of welfare policies on the status of women. The attention is often on how non-feminist policies affect women and increasingly the scholarship has examined policies related to male and female caring roles (see Mazur 2002).

Women can therefore influence the policy process as: (1) members of the political class, such as legislators, although in many societies their representation in parliaments and legislatures remains low (see Inter-Parliamentary Union 2012); (2) bureaucrats, civil servants and public officials involved in the formulation and implementation of policy by actively representing women, but as discussed women's passive representation in decision-making positions in government is often lacking; (3) communities, networks and social movements such as the feminist movement,

113

although their power to influence the policy process is dependent on their 'insider' and 'outsider' status and in most societies feminist movements tend to be outside the policy process; and (4) as individual citizens making representation to the political and/or judicial process such as in the case of Bhanwari Devi.

CASE STUDY: POLITICS, POLICY AND PROSTITUTION

We discuss the case study of the criminalization of the purchase of sexual services (CPSS) in Sweden to demonstrate the framing of the policy problem; the decision-making process; the options explored; the intersectionality of problems, advocacy coalitions and interactions of policy actors within various domains; and the influence of external factors towards the active representation of women in a policy process. The adoption of this policy in Sweden is a unique policy as it presents a departure from existing paradigms of addressing the issue of prostitution in society. Other countries such as Norway, Denmark, Finland and France have observed the policy lessons and outcomes from the Swedish case (see Bucken-Knapp and Karlsson 2008; St. Deny 2012), which represents a policy transfer and isomorphic process across multi-level governance within Europe. As argued in the first chapter of this book, we cannot neatly separate the various aspects of the policy-making process. Thus, we analyze the case using the interrelated policy cycle: discussing the problem, decision, options, policy actors, domains and networks and communities involved in the policy-making process.

The issue of prostitution and how to address it has long presented a problem for policy makers in many countries (Outshoorn 2005). Prostitution, whether the interaction is heterosexual or homosexual, is the commercialization of sex as a service and the commoditization of the 'seller' – usually women. Sex is therefore traded for money, but this is not purely an economic or commercial transaction; it is an egregious treatment of women. The commoditization of sex is often related to social, economic and cultural vulnerabilities of the women. Women within the patriarchal society face sexual exploitation, and prostitution represents the misogynist oppression of women and unequal power relationship between men (usually the purchaser) and women (usually the seller). It is often argued that women enter into prostitution voluntarily, yet there have been numerous studies that have proven that this is often not the case. Prostitution is linked to forced sexual exploitation, poverty, social exclusion, drug addiction and alcohol abuse, with women often faced with little choice but to engage in prostitution to sustain their lives and those of their dependents. Thus, prostitution is often viewed as women's oppression and a form of violence against women who are therefore the victim within the interaction (Outshoorn 2005). The issue of prostitution has gained prominence within various polities and forums such as the UN given the increase in prostitution-related migration and human trafficking – an outcome of increasing globalization (ibid).

114

The story of the Swedish policy of CPSS can be traced to 1976 with the appointment of a commission to investigate sexual offences (Svanström 2004). The commission was severely criticised by the women's movement for its suggestion of lower penalties for rape (ibid). Twelve different women's organizations galvanised to call for a new commission and a second commission to investigate prostitution (ibid). The women's movement received support in the media with extensive coverage on crime related to the sex industry and the abuse women and girls encounter in prostitution (ibid). The report of the second commission was equally controversial with many disagreements within the commission itself (ibid). The internal disagreement was between the chief investigator, Inger Lindquist, and the secretaries and external experts; it centred on the debate over the criminalization of prostitution with the view that criminalization would transfer the sex trade underground, place female prostitutes at risk, create enforcement difficulties, and that it may not necessarily be a deterrent (Gould 2001; Svanström 2004; Bucken-Knapp and Schaffer 2011). The report, presented to the Swedish Parliament, condemned prostitution as being a violation of women's rights and gender equality, but criminalization was not proposed (ibid).

During the 1980s the idea of gender equality and the rights of women gained resonance among the Swedish political class and non-state actors (Svanström 2004; Bucken-Knapp and Schaffer 2011). The success of the women's movement in Sweden in bringing issues on to the policy agenda was to define goals in terms of equality and democracy (Bucken-Knapp and Schaffer 2011). According to Bucken-Knapp and Schaffer, by defining women's rights within a broader discourse of gender (men and women) equality, it provided a rallying call for women's movement goals, regardless of political affiliation, and also facilitated the inclusion of men who supported equality. Thus, from the 1980s there is an increase: in gender equality references in bills presented to the Swedish Parliament; in the number of investigative commissions on women's rights; and in efforts to increase the political representation of women (ibid).

In 1992 the Liberal Minister of Gender Equality, Bengt Westerberg, announced an investigative committee on the extent of prostitution-related activity with the idea of criminalising the purchase of sex within the remit of investigation (Gould 2001; Svanström 2004; Bucken-Knapp and Schaffer 2011). The committee had as its chief investigator a former ombudsman for gender equality, Inga-Britt Törnell (ibid). The final report entrenched the idea that prostitution is the commercialization of sex and inconsistent with the democratic norms of equality, as the sex trade created physical and psychological harm with violence, substance abuse and mental health problems – all considered side effects of engaging in sex work (Ekberg 2004; Svanström 2004; Bucken-Knapp and Schaffer 2011; Jakobsson and Kotsadam 2011). Törnell argued for the criminalization of both the purchaser and the seller (Svanström 2004; Bucken-Knapp and Schaffer 2011). Once again the report was plagued with controversy and internal disagreements with some experts supporting

115

CPSS and others supporting the criminalization of both buyer and seller (ibid). Support for CPSS began to increase, with women's movements and political organizations, such as the Women's Association of the Centre Party, viewing CPSS as necessary to protect vulnerable women in an unequal power relationship of sexual exploitation (ibid).

In 1997 the ruling Social Democrat Party (SAP) held its annual party congress, where the issue of CPSS was to take centre stage on the policy agenda (Gould 2001; Svanström 2004; Bucken-Knapp and Schaffer 2011). Four party districts, including two from the major urban areas of Stockholm and Göteborg, had submitted motions calling for the party to adopt CPSS (Bucken-Knapp and Schaffer 2011). However, the party leadership rejected the idea with the party's central committee opposing any form of criminalization (ibid). The reasoning was that there were difficulties of implementing criminalization with the potential negative outcomes of driving the sex trade underground resulting in violence against prostitutes (ibid). The party leadership drew upon the law enforcement officials, as epistemic policy actors, to substantiate their views (ibid). Yet, as in most countries, the Swedish police are mostly male and homosocial with conservative working environments (Ekberg 2004). Women's movements and feminists within the SAP drew upon their own policy experts from academia and civil society (Svanström 2004). There was a heated debate, with the proponents of CPSS eventually winning the vote and the chairwoman of the Swedish Social Democratic Women's Federation, Inger Segelström, stating that the SAP as 'the world's most gender equal party in the world's most gender equal society . . . can no longer accept that men can use money to buy women' (Bucken-Knapp and Schaffer 2011). In February 1998, the SAP government introduced a bill that sought to address violence against women and prostitution (Ekberg 2004; Svanström 2004; Bucken-Knapp and Schaffer 2011). Any reservations about the criminalization of sexual services (e.g. driving prostitution underground) were rejected, with proponents arguing that the criminality and inequality associated with prostitution outweighed concerns (Bucken-Knapp and Schaffer 2011). By May 1998 a cross-party consensus emerged with the SAP, the Left Party, the Greens and the Centre Party supporting CPSS, while the Moderates and Liberals opposed any form of criminalization (Bucken-Knapp and Schaffer 2011). Segelström, in response to concerns over CPSS, supported by policy actors such as academics and the political leadership of Sweden's largest cities (Stockholm, Göteborg and Malmö), argued that:

> We cannot accept that roughly half of these women are drug addicts . . . they're not prostitutes in order to buy food, pay their rent or to live a life of luxury, rather they do so in order to finance their heroin abuse . . .
>
> (Bucken-Knapp and Schaffer 2011)

Throughout the debate of CPSS the policy was framed around issues of gender equality, the criminality and drug abuse associated with prostitution, and the often tragic and violent lives of female sex workers (Gould 2001; Ekberg 2004; Svanström 2004; Bucken-Knapp and Schaffer 2011). On 1 January 1999, Sweden passed a law that prohibited the purchase of sexual services and recognized that is it the man who buys women (or men) for sexual purposes and who should therefore be criminalised, and not the woman (Ekberg 2004). Sweden therefore recognized that human beings should never be a commodity that could be bought. Since CPSS was introduced there has been a dramatic decrease in prostitution in Sweden, with positive outcomes for women (ibid).

QUESTIONS

1   How was the problem of prostitution framed in Sweden so that it gained traction on the policy agenda?
2   Internationally, what are the policy options to address prostitution?
3   Who were the main policy actors and what were their roles in supporting or opposing CPSS in Sweden?
4   Discuss the role policy communities and issue networks played in formulation of the CPSS policy.
5   Discuss the link between passive and active representation in the adoption of CPSS.
6   In your opinion, why has there not been more of a policy transfer of CPSS to other countries?
7   Use the interrelated policy cycles, explained in Figure 1.5, to discuss the policy process of CPSS.

NOTES

1   The case study is based on research as published: Miller, K. Johnston (2012) 'Representative Bureaucracy and Multi-level Governance in the EU', *Geopolitics, History and International Relations*, 4, 1: 50–75.

REFERENCES

Bucken-Knapp, G. and Karlsson, J. (2008) 'Prostitution policy reforms and the causal role of ideas: a comparative study of policy making in Nordic countries', *Statsvetenskaplig tidskrift*, 110, 1: 59–65.

Bucken-Knapp, G. and Schaffer, J.K. (2011) 'The same policy, but different ideas: the ideational underpinnings of the Norwegian and Swedish bans on the purchase of sexual services', Budapest, Hungary, *2nd European Conference on Gender & Politics*, Central European University.

Burri, S. and Prechal, S. (2009) *The Transposition of Recast Directive* 2006/54/EC, Brussels: EC.

Chappell, L. (2002) 'The "Femocrat" strategy: expanding the repertoire of feminist activities', *Parliamentary Affairs*, 55: 85–98.

Council of Europe (1998) *Gender Mainstreaming: Conceptual Framework, Methodology and Presentation of Good Practices*. Strasbourg: Council of Europe, EG-S-MS (98) 2.

Ekberg, G. (2004) 'The Swedish law that prohibits the purchase of sexual services: best practices for prevention of prostitution and trafficking in human beings', *Violence Against Women*, 10, 10: 1187–1218.

European Commission (2008) *The Life of Women and Men in Europe: a statistical portrait*, Luxembourg: Eurostat.

European Commission (2009) *26th Annual Report on Monitoring the Application of Community Law* (2008), Brussels: EC.

European Commission (2010a) *More Women in Senior Positions: key to economic stability and growth*, Brussels: European Commission, Directorate-General for Employment, Social Affairs and Equal Opportunities.

European Commission (2010b) 'New strategy on gender quality', http://ec.europa.eu/social/main.jsp?langId=enandcatId=89andnewsId=890andfurtherNews=yes. (Accessed December 2010.)

European Women's Lobby (2007) 'Evaluation of the Implementation of the European Commission's Roadmap for Equality Between Women and Men 2006–2010 – Year One', www.womenlobby.org/site/abstract/asp? Doc ID=2040andV.11D. (Accessed December 2010.)

Eurostat (2011) http: //epp.eurostat.ec.europa.eu/portal/page/portal/statistics/search_database. (Accessed March to May 2011.)

Gould, A. (2001) 'The criminalisation of buying sex: the politics of prostitution in Sweden', *Journal of Social Policy*, 30, 3: 437–456.

Hafner-Burton, E.M. and Pollack, M.A. (2009) 'Mainstreaming gender in the European Union: getting the incentives right', *Comparative European Politics*, 7, 1: 114–138.

Inter-Parliamentary Union (2012) www.ipu.org/wmn-e/classif.htm. (Accessed 30 May 2012.)

Jakobsson, N. and Kotsadam, A. (2011) 'Gender equity and prostitution: an investigation of attitudes in Norway and Sweden', *Feminist Economics*, 17, 1: 31–58.

Kantola, J. (2010) *Gender and the European Union*, Basingstoke: Palgrave Macmillan.

Kelly, R.M. and Newman, M. (2001) 'The gendered bureaucracy: agency mission, equality of opportunity, and representative bureaucracies', *Women and Politics*, 22, 3: 1–33.

Lovenduski, J. (2005) *Feminizing Politics*, Cambridge: Polity Press.

Mazur, A.G. (2002) *Theorizing Feminist Policy*, Oxford: Oxford University Press.

Miller, K. (2009) 'Public policy dilemma – gender equality mainstreaming in UK policy formulation', *Public Money & Management*, 29, 1: 43–50.

Miller, K. Johnston (2012) 'Representative bureaucracy and multi-level governance in the EU: a research agenda', *Geo-Politics, History and International Relations*, 4, 1: 50–75.

Outshoorn, J. (2005) 'The political debates on prostitution and trafficking of women', *Social Politics*, 12, 1: 141–155.

St. Deny, E. (2012) 'Next stop Stockholm? The role of ideas in shaping French prostitution policy since 2002', Belfast, Political Studies Association Annual Conference.

Stratigaki, M. (2004) 'The cooptation of gender concepts in EU Policies: the case of "reconciliation of work and family"', *Social Politics*, 11, 1: 30–56.

Stratigaki, M. (2005) 'Gender mainstreaming vs positive action: an ongoing conflict in EU equality policy', *European Journal of Women's Studies*, 12, 2: 165–186.

Svanström, Y. (2004) 'Criminalising the John – A Swedish Gender Model?' in J. Outshoorn (ed.) *The Politics of Prostitution: Women's Movements, Democratic States and the Gloablisation of Sex Commerce*, Cambridge: Cambridge University Press: 225–244.

Verloo, M. (2001) *Another Velvet Revolution? Gender Mainstreaming and the Politics of Implementation*, IWM Working Paper, No. 5/2001, IWM Publications, Vienna.

Weaver, C. (2008) *The Strategic Construction of the World Bank's Gender and Development Agenda*, paper presented at the International Studies Association Annual Meeting 25 March, San Francisco.

Woodward, A. (2003) 'European gender mainstreaming: promises and pitfalls of transformative policy', *The Review of Policy Research*, 20, 1: 65–88.

Chapter 5

Policy capacity

LEARNING OBJECTIVES

- To understand the range of factors affecting the ability of governments to make and manage public policy
- To appreciate the range of tensions facing governments when trying to maintain and enhance their policy making and managerial capacity
- To situate competence and ability in policy capacity in the international, interdependent, regulatory and outsourced environments

KEY POINTS IN THIS CHAPTER

- How we describe and define policy capacity
- An account of the way in which capacity improvement reform and modernization has been conducted
- How policy capacity is articulated and actioned in multi-level governance environments

INTRODUCTION

There are various definitions of policy capacity. It has been described as the ability to gather intelligence, make informed policy decisions and develop programmes and resources to implement policy and then to evaluate (Honadle 1981). It has also been seen in terms of the state's capacity to respond to change, underpinned by its intellectual and organizational resources (Cummings and Norgaard 2004). Others focus on knowledge management and learning (Parsons 2004). Other definitions have a somewhat narrower focus: they address 'intelligent' decision-making ability (Davis 2000); focus on the capabilities of individuals (Aucoin and Bakvis 2005); stress the importance of coordination across government (Parsons 2004); accentuate the importance of making choices that involve deviation from the status quo (Peters 1996).

The approach adopted in this chapter examines first the policy capacity of government within a modern, contemporary era and how this is fundamentally grounded in a range of tensions; second, the relationship between policy capacity and the regulatory environment, which is an important aspect of the contemporary policy arena; third, the part played by the institutions of government; fourth, the organizational ability of government in addressing policy capacity; fifth, an analysis of policy capacity in the context of an interdependent, globalised world; finally, the impact on policy capacity of the outsourced and extended state.

POLICY CAPACITY

The first question to be asked is what is involved in policy capacity, and thereafter how this is enhanced. From the 1990s there have been a number of initiatives to enhance policy-making capacity across a range of political systems. For instance, it is perceived to be the case that a lack of policy professionalization has hindered the development of capacities in central and eastern European countries (Brans and Vancoppenolle 2005). Although in different countries, the responses have differed somewhat, there is a range of common themes addressed to improve policy capacity in countries such as Canada, UK, New Zealand and Australia, such as 'joining up' and 'thinking across' government departments, environmental scanning and the need to be outward looking, modernization, enhanced research to improve evidence based policy making, benchmarking of good practice, more effective use of information and the need to be more strategic (e.g. UK Government 1999; Organisation for Economic Co-operation and Development (OECD) 1999; Office of the Auditor General of Canada 2001; Australian Public Services Commission 2004). These initiatives are coupled with NPM-type reforms.

The impact of such initiatives on policy capacity must always be qualified and viewed in a nuanced way for three broad reasons. First, it is notoriously difficult to link policy capacity and policy outcomes. Even in discrete policy areas (let alone policies that are interwoven and cross cutting in nature) many other variables impact on policy outcomes; policy development can take a long time and practical outcomes may not be traceable to a particular period of development. However, aspects of policy can be evaluated if delineated in a specific way, for example as activities like information provision, participative policy process or as a set of methods and tools (Thissen and Twaalfhoven 2001).

Second, many of the aforementioned initiatives to improve capacity are somewhat misguided and miss the point. As indicated in a recent study in the UK

121

by the Institute for Government (Institute for Government 2011), 'official' government approaches to policy making have ignored the reality of politics, have not addressed the short-term nature of civil service institutional memory (hardly surprising when the thrust of NPM and modernization initiatives has been to attempt disjuncture from the past) and have not factored in the ability of powerful departments and agencies of government to frustrate policy initiatives, thereby compromising capacity to deliver.

Third, the above initiatives have all addressed key 'soft' individually based skills and competencies as an important dimension to policy capacity in knowledge, practical skills, creativity, intuition and judgement. While these skills and attributes may be generic across a range of public sector staff, any targeted capacity building begs questions about who the policy makers are and what they actually do. Research by Page and Jenkins for the UK and Fleischer for Germany has shown that policy making involves rather large numbers often at relatively junior levels who are often not technical specialists, receive little direction (and often have considerable discretion) and stay in the same job for relatively short periods of time (Page and Jenkins 2005; Fleischer 2009). Research has also shown similar practices in the Netherlands, Australia and New Zealand (Weller and Stevens 1998; Hoppe and Jeliazkova 2006).

There is also extant work linking policy capacity to level of government. In Canada, it has been indicated that policy (analytical) capacity is weaker at provincial, territorial and local levels (see Howlett 2009), but more recent work indicates capacity is more related to task than level of government (see Wellstead *et al.* 2011). Furthermore, the capacity of the policy system must clearly be linked to the individuals (and groups) who comprise that system. In Chapters 3 and 4 we explored the capacity of government to design and implement policies affecting groups which, traditionally, have been unequally represented in government, policy and top decisional environments.

TENSIONS IN POLICY CAPACITY

The capacity of government to make and manage public policy is affected by reforms and restructuring – often unabated – of government itself. As argued earlier, NPM and modernization reforms create tensions in government's capacity to formulate and implement policy. These tensions include:

Cost efficiencies and quality public services

A pervasive principle of NPM has been the reduction of public expenditure and lessening the tax burden, yet there is a need to balance cost efficiencies and savings with continued quality public services provision. Much of the mantra that has underpinned this NPM tension includes 'doing more with less' (Ferlie *et al.* 2007). This tension will become more acute in the current economic climate of fiscal constraints (Pollitt 2009). 'Quality' of public services is a consistent theme of public management and has been adopted in many countries in various forms (e.g. Total Quality Management (TQM) (ibid). The theme is contestable with debates including the appropriateness of quality approaches borrowed from the private sector and applied to the public sector; the limited cognizance of political and competing social values, the measurability of quality service; etc. (Massey and Pyper 2005; Ferlie *et al.* 2007; Flynn 2007; Pollitt 2009). The tension is persistent given the poor implementation by public organizations of strategies to reduce costs yet the necessity of the same organizations to provide quality services. Flynn (2007), for example, provides a number of case studies of poor implementation of strategies to reduce costs with effects on quality. He concludes that, 'Budget cutting may change volumes and quality but perhaps in ways which are never made explicit, other than by the number of complaints and mistakes which result' (Flynn 2007: 219). Thus, the current scholarly question remains: how can cost reductions (particularly within this era of austerity) and quality services be achieved; where is the balance between cost savings and quality provision; what are the appropriate implementation approaches; and what innovative services could achieve the balance? Governments will need to address this tension and where innovative public policies address both quality service provision and cost efficiencies thereof.

Cost efficiencies, citizen trust and social cohesion

An effort to continuously improve quality public services vis-à-vis cost efficiencies requires innovation and flexibility, which may impact on continuity and predictability of service provision for citizens (Pollitt and Bouckaert 2004). This presents a tension for public managers who have to balance divergent interests, perhaps disadvantaging communities while attempting to improve service delivery (ibid). It is the impression of Pollitt and Bouckaert (2004: 169) that literature on management reforms – either academic or professional – does not reflect this tension. Similarly, Greener (2009) argues that tensions concerning provision of services for the 'public' vis-à-vis the 'individual' are based on the assertion that what may be in the broader interest of the public may not necessarily be in the interest of the individual or community. For example, in health care systems public managers are often faced with the conundrum of whether to provide expensive individual life-saving treatment or to use the resources beneficially for the public as a whole (ibid). The perception that cost is prioritized over services for the public good or that there is an inequality in the provision of services erodes citizen trust. Moreover, the introduction of innovation in public services through market competition, productivity gains, 'customer choice' and cost savings may disadvantage certain communities and similarly erode social cohesion. Thus, there is a dichotomy between cost efficiencies and innovative service delivery, and the maintenance of the general public interest goals of service provision, which promotes social cohesion and safeguarding accessibility, equality, continuity, affordability, predictability and trust (Bergman 1998; Héritier 2001). Governments will have to develop efficient and innovative policies that are in the general public interest and that build citizen trust and social cohesion.

Change, innovation and staff

The introduction of change and reform of the public sector along NPM lines redefined the roles of public sector staff. Those employed in the public sector – from civil servants through to public officers at multi-levels of government, to professionals – had to redefine their roles in a more businesslike orientation. The changes staff experienced included the introduction of markets, the decentralization and contracting out of services, re-structuring, managerialist interventions and strategies, targetization, organizational cultural change, etc. These changes may have had positive outcomes, but there were also negative outcomes such as low staff morale, uncertainty, goal displacement, reform fatigue and an erosion of a public service ethos (Peters and Savoie 1998; Flynn 2007). Civil and public servants are now experiencing new forms of governance such as co-governance and co-production arrangements with private and community partners and stakeholders in the formulation and implementation of policies through to the actual delivery of services. Once again civil and public servants have to redefine their tasks and roles by externally engaging with other professionals, public officials and civil society representatives/community stakeholders – working beyond departmental silos and delivering services in a 'joined up' manner (Johnson and Osborne 2003; Brandsen and Pestoff 2006). The result is a tension for civil and public servants who, while externally engaging with other stakeholders in co-governance and co-production arrangements, have to mediate conflicting policy and organizational rationales (Leach and Lowndes 2007; Bode and Firbank 2009). This tension takes place intra- and inter-organizationally (the focus of Chapter 6) within a multi-level governance arrangement. Intra-organizational processes may, for example, involve clinical professionals and managers within a health care system mediating rationales for quality healthcare vis-à-vis the need for cost efficiencies. Inter-organizationally, the tension may manifest itself, for example, in the provision of care for the elderly with local/municipal government co-producing services with other public, private and third sector health care services (Bode and Firbank 2009). These tensions take place within the context of policy being made and managed at various levels of government and across sectors with requirements of various forms of accountabilities (Miller et al. 2009).

Governance, decentralization and accountabilities

NPM has resulted in the decentralization of public services and thereby resources such as budgets to the level of government closest to the users. However, this decentralization has taken place within a context of the need to maintain accountability for the performance of public organizations and public expenditure (Power 1997). According to Hammerschmid *et al.* (2007) there is an inherent tension in NPM reforms in that there are efforts towards decentralization of resource allocation so that service delivery is closer to the point of delivery and engages citizens, yet there is also a need for accountability of performance and policy implementation, which often requires centralization at a strategic level. Similarly, Pollitt and Bouckaert (2004) argue that a contradiction of NPM is that public managers require greater flexibility in the use of resources for improved and innovative public service delivery, yet their political masters require accountability for what has or has not been achieved. Amann (2006) calls this the innovative–accountability conundrum where civil and public servants' roles have become more complex with the demands for leadership, innovation and entrepreneurship within a political environment that necessitates accountability with consequent bureaucracy. The result is that civil and public servants are caught in a conundrum of the 'innovation narrative' (underpinned by efficiency, NPM and managerialism) and the 'accountability narrative' (underpinned by a traditional political–public notion of accountability) (ibid). Although Amann (2004) would argue that the innovative–accountability conundrum is a trade-off, Pollitt and Bouckaert (2004) would argue that power relations and thereby the need for accountability do not necessitate a zero-sum game. Nonetheless, there is need to account, particularly at a political and central level, for public sector performance and taxpayers' monies, which presents a pervasive challenge for public managers (Power 1997). They are often caught between the demands of various forms of accountabilities with consequent adherence to bureaucratic rules and regulations, compliance with accountability procedures and the transaction costs of bureaucratic accountability regimes resulting in reduced levels of flexibility and innovation in public service delivery (Amann 2004, Commission on 2020 Public Services Trust 2009). These issues will be explored in depth in Chapters 9 and 10.

Governance, decentralization and coordination

There is a tension between the centralization and decentralization of services within the context of the governance environment (Hood *et al.* 2004; Greener 2009). Increasingly, public services are being decentralized within governance arrangements focusing on co-governance and co-production of services (Johnson and Osborne 2003; Kooiman 2003). Co-governance refers to the arrangement of public, private and community organizations involved in the planning and/or delivery of services (Brandsen and Pestoff 2006: 497). Similarly, Bode (2006: 562) defines co-governance as consensual regulation shared by public, civic and professional actions in the delivery of public services. The aim often is to improve public service planning and delivery in a 'joined up' way, in conjunction with other aims of democratic and civil society involvement. However, the co-governance of

125

public services and partnership working has resulted in a pull between the differentiation and integration of public services that has not been resolved, with consequent impact on staff, skills, structure, management style and functioning (Brandsen and van Hout 2006) as well as accountability arrangements (Leach and Lowndes 2007; Miller *et al.* 2010). The multiplicity of partnerships, with different rationales and service priorities in the co-governance and co-production of public services, creates a tension of coordination. The outcome is often fragmentation and uncohesive government in policy formulation, implementation and service delivery (Lodge and Kalitowski 2007). Another tension of coordination is when we have implementation of policy across multi-levels of governance from supra-national (e.g. EU), to national (e.g. central governments), to sub-national (e.g. regional, federal, devolved and local/municipal) levels of government. The coordination of policy and ultimately the frameworks/directives for public services reveal problems or transposition deficits (Haverland and Romeijn 2007). For example, Haverland and Romeijn's (2007) study of EU countries revealed that transposition delays in EU policies and directives are associated with administrative inefficiencies and poor coordination. Thus, a state's capacity at policy implementation is partly explained by the extent to which the public sector is efficient and effective and the availability of fiscal resources (see Haverland and Romeijn 2007). For example, studies (see Pridham 1994; Knill 1998) on the capacity of European countries to implement policies revealed that public sector administrative procedures, competence, structure, efficiency and effectiveness were a variable in the effective implementation and transposition of policies.

POLICY CAPACITY AND REGULATION

In all policy environments there is a privileged position given to law and legal regulation that ultimately derives from the power and authority of the state and legitimate organizations and instruments of government. In particular, in parliamentary democracies there is the concept of parliamentary sovereignty whereby parliament can pass laws and claim to have the ultimate right to govern and therefore have the capacity to enact policies for the public good.

There are, however, three important nuances to be recognized. There are environments where policy is not enforced through the legal system and other instruments of government. The case of Greece is striking. The well-documented tax evasion has had profound impacts on Greek politics and society, contributing to high government deficits, crises in the country's financial infrastructure with serious impact on its relationship with the EU and membership of the European single currency. Tax evasion had other impacts running counter to the policy drive of the socialist government (in power until 2011) led by George Papandreou: a modelling exercise of tax evasion in Greece has shown income under-reporting at 10 per cent, resulting in a 26 per cent shortfall in tax receipts, the overall effect being significantly higher income inequality and poverty and reduced progressivity of the income tax system (Matsaganis and Flevotomou 2010). The short case below in Box 5.1 illustrates the lack of capacity to implement basic tax policy.

Another nuance is where there are competing policy perspectives – in the broadest rather than legislative sense – of how the law stands in the policy/political interface. As illustrated in Box 5.2 overleaf, the issue of a referendum on Scottish independence illustrates why it may be difficult to see a clear relationship between law and policy

A third nuance is to be found in an inversion of the system where the law and courts can be used for policy purposes. Such use is seen, for example, historically in the US where much social policy (racial discrimination, women's rights, criminal justice) was addressed initially through legal action. However this can be inverted when the legal process appears to be setting the terms of government policy capacity rather than the other way about. This is indicated in Box 5.3.

BOX 5.1   TAX EVASION IN GREECE

There is a backlog of over 160,000 pending tax cases, some of more than ten years' standing; this seriously questions the overall tax administration's efficiency. The Greeks have transferred vast amounts of money to Switzerland, and Greece faces the difficulty of cracking down on international tax evasion. The difference between what Greek taxpayers owed in 2010 and what they paid was over 30 per cent of total tax revenue, about the size of the country's budget deficit. The 'shadow economy' is larger in Greece than in almost any other European country, estimated at 27.5 per cent of GDP.

Greece has struggled with the first rule of a healthy, credible and legitimate tax system, i.e. enforce the law. There was little political pressure for tougher enforcement. Studies have shown that the enforcement of tax laws loosened in the month leading up to elections. When the system did track down evaders, it was virtually impossible to get them to pay up since tax courts took between seven and ten months to resolve a case.

Many Greeks have what is called low 'tax morale'. People pay taxes not just because of the fear of being caught, but because they feel a responsibility to contribute to the common good. That sense is based, however, on the belief that fellow citizens are doing the same. Many Greeks see fraud and corruption as endemic in business and the tax system. So inevitably if a significant number of the population is not paying taxes, then those who do feel they are being abused.

Source: adapted from Surowiecki (2011)

BOX 5.2   SCOTTISH INDEPENDENCE?

It's a matter for UK lawmakers:

Just as the Scottish people are not sovereign, neither is the Scottish Parliament. The Westminster Parliament has set legally enforceable limits on the power of the Scottish Parliament by providing in section 29 of the Scotland Act that any act of the Scottish Parliament which relates to the union between Scotland and England or the constitutional position of the crown or the UK parliament will simply not be law because any such act would be outside the legislative competence of the Scottish Parliament to pass . . .

Or maybe not:

Section 30 (2) of the Scotland Act allows the UK government to allocate powers reserved to it to be given to Holyrood, the Scottish Parliament. This is achieved by MPs passing a statutory instrument. In this way the Scottish Parliament can be given authority to run a referendum.

A Scottish Parliament perspective?

If the issue of the lawfulness of any independence referendum measure will ultimately have to be determined by the UK Supreme Court, then both First Minister and Scottish Cabinet Secretary for Justice have 'form'. The latter has said that, 'we're undermined routinely by a court that sits in another country and is presided over by a majority of judges who have no knowledge of Scots law, never mind Scotland . . . a court in London that is made up of a majority of judges who do not know Scots law . . . you need a succession of incidences of things that are happening before the extent of the encroachment and the vulnerability of the Scottish Parliament really hits home . . . if we are to be scrutinised in terms of the overall scrutiny then let it be by the European Court of Human Rights that scrutinises another 47 jurisdictions and not the Supreme Court in England.'

The political reality?

Professor Allan Page, constitutional law expert, dean of law at Dundee University and specialist adviser to Westminster and Holyrood committees stressed he did not envisage any insuperable legal problems . . . the thrust of legal challenge would instead be used as part of the negotiations between Westminster and Holyrood, 'by which I mean they could say unless we are happy with what you are proposing and that we are happy that this is going to be a free and fair referendum, we are going to do everything we can to make this difficult for you. It could slow things down. The real question now is over the terms of that referendum and the questions that are asked. My view is that it was effectively settled by the parliamentary election in May 2011. Once the SNP won an outright majority it was just accepted there would be a referendum as a political fact. That I think puts an end to the arguments – there is going to be one.'

Sources: adapted from O'Neil (2011); Maddox (2011)

BOX 5.3   THE JUDICIARY IN PUBLIC POLICY

Jonathan Sumpton QC, a member of the UK Supreme Court, has indicated that one of the most significant constitutional changes in the UK since the Second World War has been the rise in the political significance of the judiciary as a result of the exercise of judicial review. Part of the problem is that 'the judiciary's instincts are moulded by individual cases many of which have involved profound human tragedies. By comparison, policy makers are primarily concerned with a problem viewed impersonally en masse'. This has been exacerbated by introducing the Human Rights Convention into English law, which has 'shifted the boundaries between political and legal decision-making in such contentious areas as immigration, security and policing, privacy and freedom of expression'. The dilemma is that the Strasbourg court's [i.e. the European Court of Human Rights] actions act as a safeguard against arbitrary and despotic exercises of state power. But according to Sumpton, the actions 'include many matters which are governed by no compelling moral considerations . . . the result of this approach has been to shrink the margin of apprecia-tion allowed to contracting states to interpret general principles in different national ways to almost nothing'. 'How far can judicial review go? Parliamentary scrutiny is for the purpose of protecting the public interest in the area of policy making. It is the only way of doing so that carries any democratic legitimacy.' Judges should not be too closely involved in making what should be political decisions.

Source: Bowcott (2011)

Somewhat different from the traditional legal–bureaucratic methods used by governments to enable and activate policy is the context of much regulatory activity. Previously self-regulated professionals are now subject to forms of governmental locus on regulation, either in the interests of the public (as tax payers or users of services) or to enable government to deliver on policy priorities. From the 1980s the thrust of NPM reforms saw a range of contracted-out bodies, agencification, linked to what has been described as a regulatory 'audit explosion' inside and outside government (Power 1997; Hood *et al.* 1999; Moran 2003). In this environment, the accepted view of regulation is that it gives the state the capacity to police the market and control professionals and other agents. Within this view there are various approaches to regulation which can be thought of in terms of a pyramid offering varying degrees of discretion to regulated bodies or agents, see Figure 5.1.

Conventional regulation ('command and control') is straightforward: no discretion is permitted to agents who are commanded by their principal. The other end of the pyramid is the complete opposite, that is, unrestricted freedom for agents to operate without hindrance (e.g. a pure form of the free market). Self-regulation can have two approaches: first, one that relies on the goodwill and co-operation of the individual for compliance (Sinclair 1997); and second, where standard-setting bodies operate independently of and parallel to government regulation, but government does not set and implement standards (Freeman 2000). Meta-regulation can be defined as the state's oversight of self-regulatory

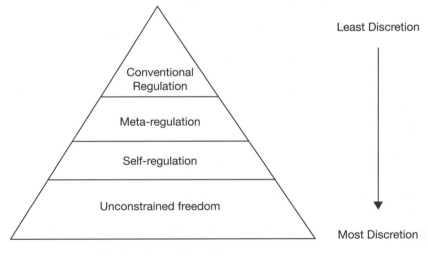

The Regulatory Pyramid

Figure 5.1
Regulatory pyramid

130

arrangements (Hutter 2006), 'regulating the regulators', where there are third-party gatekeepers in various combinations of horizontal and vertical influence (Parker 2002).

There are clearly some negative aspects of regulation/over-regulation for policy capacity. Top-down regulation and over regulation can lead to loophole chasing. Individuals or organizations may invent complex strategies to avoid regulation; if the rules are made precise then agents may think of actions not covered by the rules. This may frustrate policy makers developing the capacity to implement policy. Studies of environmental enforcement in the US have found that an over-precise or tough approach fails to develop the co-operative relationship required to implement policy intentions (see Bardach and Kagan 1982).

At a more fundamental level, the capacity of a public policy system may be compromised by the regulatory state. According to some perspectives the regulatory state is about diffusing public power to private or quasi-public organizations or agencies leading to 'the implantation of public power in private organizations' (Jayasuriya 2005: 30), or the privatization of public policy (McTavish 2003). In addition, the regulatory state – because it becomes dependent on the insider knowledge of the regulated groups – encourages strategic behaviour from these groups who seek advantage from the rules and regulations (Moran 2003). However, while there is the view that the regulatory state can compromise the capacity of the policy system, it is, somewhat ironically, also the case that attempts at deregulation may not conversely increase government's policy capacity with regard to its locus over the regulated interests or policy areas; rather, it increases the position of powerful interests vis-à-vis the government. For example, in the US the Bush administration's reforms to the regulatory process (positioned as anti-regulatory), introduced through the Information Quality Act (IQA) a requirement (among others) that agencies use peer reviews for critical information underlying regulations. Although driven by statute (the IQA) the reforms were issued via the executive (the Office of Management and Budget, OMB) who can control peer reviews – for instance by using pro- or anti-regulatory experts. If things do not move in the way desired by powerful regulated interests, there is then considerable scope for delay in the process, where Congress and the courts can step in if agency responses to complaints under the IQA are subject to judicial review. Studies of the IQA have shown that it is generally recognized the resulting delay will benefit powerful interests by increasing their capacity to halt the regulatory process (Shapiro 2007).

One approach to addressing this regulatory dilemma, but at the same time preventing dilution of policy capacity, is to have a responsive regulation, where regulation is an iterative process involving responsiveness to changing situations and encompassing several key tasks: detecting undesirable or non-compliant behaviour; responding to that behaviour by developing tools and strategies; enforcing these tools and strategies on the ground; assessing their success or failure;

131

modifying approaches accordingly (Black and Baldwin 2010). According to one authority this kind of regulation is increasingly popular among policy makers (John 2011). However, clearly this type of regulation requires constant attention and intervention, not episodic or failure-based interventions. Moreover, the political salience has to be maintained to hold policy makers' attention and this must be a cautionary factor. For example as indicated by John (2011):

> Dorbeck-Jung *et al.* (2010) study the problems in such a system to protect minors from exposure to harmful forms of media in Holland. In spite of the law, it was very easy for a minor to buy or rent a video or to buy a cinema ticket. Most of the stores were unclear about the legal rules and did not think the law was serious in its intent, thinking it was mainly there for information. Basically the Dutch government did not have an active interventionist approach to the problem. The observation that can be made about this case is that it is an example of where the government was not particularly interested in enforcement and so perhaps not a very good example of regulation – or perhaps it shows that legal regimes tend towards a lack of effectiveness if there is not the political will to enforce them . . . perhaps this is an example of where the difficulties of implementation feed back into the apathy of policy makers.
>
> (John 2011: 36)

POLICY CAPACITY AND POLITICAL INSTITUTIONS

The capacity of political institutions is fundamentally linked to their ability to enable policy makers to enact and implement policy. The literature has often viewed this around a debate regarding the extent to which centralist 'more unified' or pluralist 'more devolved' systems and institutions enable or inhibit this capacity.

In general, if there are more (or more opportunities for) veto players then the greater the challenges are on the system to work to capacity in enabling policy makers to enact and implement policy (Tsebelis 1995). Studies of particular sectors indicate how large numbers of veto players limit the ability of policy makers to pursue policy objectives (e.g. in health care, see Immergut 1992). Lijphart's (1999) framework (based on a number of variables including party system, variations in executive power sharing, unitary versus federal systems) claims that majoritarian systems perform less well than other types of (more consensually based) systems in terms of economic performance, though it has been claimed these arguments are founded on conceptually coupling 'consensus democracy' and 'corporatism' (Anderson 2001). Studies in other policy areas show a different picture. Research of seventeen OECD countries for instance found that corporatist institutions did help policy on environmental performance but consensus democracy certainly did not (Scraggs 1999; 2003; John 2011).

132

Outwith these relatively narrowly defined policy domains, Anderson and Guillory's (1997) research indicates that, on a scale of satisfaction with democracy/legitimacy of the political system, losers in consensual systems display higher levels of satisfaction than losers in more majoritarian systems, and conversely winners in majoritarian systems report higher levels of satisfaction than winners in consensual systems. Other studies have found that consensual decision-making has proved better at resolving longer term policy problems (Bovens *et al.* 2001).

For the last decade of the twentieth century and early years of the twenty-first, John (2011) has an interesting perspective on the relationship between strongly majoritarian governments and their ability to use this to implement radical labour market reforms, privatization and other policies to incur 'short-term pain' but achieve 'better economic growth rates, in the UK, New Zealand and Australia'. He does though point out the dangers of linking policy performance to majoritarian governmental institutions (ibid). For while in the 1990s more consensual democracies were performing less well, some of these economies (like Germany) started to grow early in the twenty-first century and it is difficult to say whether this resulted from policy transfer from the majoritarian countries, whether indigenous industries were more resilient or whether the financial crash in 2008 exposed certain types of economic–competitive systems more than others (see John 2011: 96).

An interesting dimension of analysis is the relationship between policy capacity and the degree of centralization or decentralization. One line of thinking may suggest centralization, with the attendant scale and scope, would be translated into increased professionalism with the reverse true for decentralization – that is, for example, lower 'quality' and calibre of politicians or bureaucrats at the more localized level (Smith 1985; De Vries 2000). However, counter-posing arguments favouring decentralization and greater sensitivity and responsiveness to local needs and how to address these with more localized and meaningful accountability etc., appear as more persuasive arguments favouring decentralization. A range of studies examining immunization and other aspects of health-care delivery and education show a positive link between decentralization and policy outputs (Khaleghian 2004, as cited in John 2011; Barankay and Lockwood 2007).

Finally, there is evidence that the link between political institutional arrangements and policy capacity can have a dynamic effect seen in the context of specific sets of arrangements arising at a specific point in time. This is especially so in the case of fractured societies. For example, Lijphart's (1968) work on consociational democracy was an attempt to enable divided societies to develop workable institutions on the assumption that this would give not only democratic legitimacy for society as a whole but provide a stable foundation for the implementation of government policies. The elements of such arrangements are large cabinets or policy centres (to include representatives of all the key voting blocs), mutual veto and other aspects of proportionality. Thought to be successful

133

first in the Netherlands in the late 1960s, it spectacularly failed in Cyprus and Lebanon in the 1970s. It appears to be successful in Northern Ireland, though the long-term success here is open to question: while it enables both loyalist and nationalist communities access to power and gives capacity to the Northern Ireland devolved government in a wide range of policy areas, it also solidifies pre-existing divisions which made consociational arrangements necessary in the first place.

POLICY CAPACITY AND THE ORGANIZATIONS OF GOVERNMENT

Structures, leadership and management

The classic Weberian organization of government departments and agencies is justified as giving capacity to the policy system through recruiting capable people (founded on merit-based careers, shielded from political partisanship and personal advantage) and giving the policy makers (that is, ultimately, elected representatives) effective means of dealing with control through a hierarchically ordered system. Research and practice since Weber has, of course, indicated variant forms of organizational bureaucratic arrangements – hardly surprising since Weber was writing in the nineteenth and early twentieth centuries. Nonetheless, organizational purpose remains the same in the broadest sense: to enable policy makers to have the capacity to manage and implement policy (see Perrow 1986).

What Weber would certainly have recognized is that structural weakness will be a critical barrier to policy capacity. Research on the Bush presidency's approach to 9/11 terrorist attacks in New York and the hurricane Katrina crisis that affected New Orleans illustrate one instance where the structural configuration around the policy area was benign and successful (9/11) and one where it was not (Katrina). In the former, appropriate expertise was in place, there was considerable organizational preparedness for this type of crisis and there was a significant degree of vertical and horizontal coordination. In the latter there was a lack of these factors within the support structures around the president; in fact there was uncertainty about the extent of federal powers and responsibilities in this emergency – the Department of Homeland Security had absorbed the Federal Emergency Management Agency 'leaving its top officials feeling de-based and cut out of the loop' ('t Hart *et al.* 2009).

Management and leadership of public organizations are linked to the policy capacity of government. Much indeed has been written on this with much of the writing focusing on: the need for leaders and managers to make the public sector a competitive employer; the knowledge-intensive economy's requirement for new types of leadership; the need to manage and lead organizational adaptation; and the requirement to address policy coherence, interconnected problems and shared power (OECD 2001). There is also an increasing body of writing that attempts to particularize public sector leadership (rather than rely on generic approaches to leadership – for a good account of the development and use of these approaches, see Jones 1988; Horner 1997; Yukl 2002; Storey 2004). Such writing focuses on the particular requirements in public sector organizations to build coalitions for action, to appreciate the wider group of stakeholders and the dual leadership requirements of, for example, co-production relationships, shared leadership between politicians and officials/managers (see Hartley 2011).

There is also an interesting trilateral framework outlining the key elements of impact, support and trustworthiness. Addressing each of these elements may have an effect on the public organization's ability to develop the overall system's policy capacity. Impact is about a realization of outcomes that can be attributed to the leader or manager and understanding that such individuals inhabit an environment where they are not the only people influencing events. Support is premised on the fundamental realization that (in a democracy) the ultimate authorizing body is the community, but leaders and managers have greater authority than citizens, leading to some tension and perhaps some principal–agent issues. Trustworthiness ensures there are institutions and mechanisms to keep leaders and managers in check, but capacity may of course be undermined if there is accountability overload or gridlock ('t Hart 2011).

There is a range of empirical research on the impact of management and leadership on organization capacity and performance in the public sector (for a good account of this, see John 2011). Research on the ability of managers to exploit opportunities and shape their environment tends to indicate more focused top-down approaches carry some success (Meier and O'Toole 2006). A range of studies using self-reported scoring (of subordinates and managers) tends to show that decentralised decision-making influences performance (Brewer and Seldon 2000; Moynihan and Pandey 2005). Other studies look at linkages between types of strategy followed (using specific strategic frameworks) and performance: these find that 'prospecting' strategies (i.e. pioneering–innovating) predict performance but that 'defending' (late adoption, defending the current position) is negatively associated with performance; however, the results thus found are not totally replicated in other settings that researchers studied (Andrews et al. 2006). Finally, research on the turnover of local authority chief executives found this was linked to measured performance (and by implication the local council's policy capacity). This only occurred where performance was poor (Boyne et al. 2008). However, when linked to a change in political control, this turnover led to improved performance, indicating a somewhat circuitous link between management and capacity (ibid.).

The political context of organizational capacity

The capacity of organizations to contribute to policy capacity cannot be viewed without cognizance of the political context. Cobb and Elder's (1983) 'systemic agenda' framework indicates that organizations may have the authority and credibility for capacity building and action in certain fields due to traditional areas of government locus, funding or other arrangements. For example, a UK government will have room for action in health care and higher education, but US governments will have less room in higher education (due to funding and governance arrangements) than in, for example, agriculture; French governments will legislate against public displays of religious symbols in a way that a US government would find difficult (Cobb and Elder 1983).

Some classic works in public administration and public policy show that policy capacity is fundamentally 'political', involving party politics, 'idea politics' and bureaucratic politics (Allison 1971; Lindblom 1979; Wildavsky 1979). Constitutional systems, public administrative styles and socio-economic regimes are among the politically contingent factors impacting on a system's capacity (Hill and Hupe 2009). One writer has indicated that policy is by definition the result of 'policy politics' (May 2002).

The fundamental political nature of policy leads to the issue of individual politicians. Policy capacity in a representative democracy is political control exercised by political executives and their authority to set strategic direction. The 'traditional' role of the political executive is complex. Executive politicians advance certain ideals (though not always) in certain policy areas; they add regulations when facing problems and crises; they prefer to solve short-term problems; they negotiate but normally more reactively than proactively or strategically (Aberbach and Rockman 2000). A 'modernist' and more managerial (NPM) view may be somewhat different, separating 'steering and 'rowing', leaving operational management to professional managers, this supposedly giving greater policy capacity. However, the reality is that many political executives are reluctant to trade off control of detail for an enhanced role over big strategic issues (Boston et al. 1996; Dunn 1997).

Political capacity can be strengthened at the political–administrative centre. Various mechanisms can be used to achieve this from hierarchy-type mechanisms to market-based approaches to networks. Each of these can be applied but contingent on a range of factors. For example, market-type mechanisms can only be applied where a market can be created and operates, and network arrangements implemented where there is some interdependency and trust among participating organizations (Verhoest and Bouckaert 2005). Other instruments for strengthening capacity range from initiatives for horizontal and/or vertical joining of departments and functions ('joined up government') to employing more people at the political–administrative centre, though the increase in the number and roles of partisan political staff has not enhanced policy competence – in most cases it has reduced policy capacity of government by sidelining public servants in the provision of advice to ministers (Campbell 2001; Aucoin and Bakvis 2005). Box 5.4 below indicates the difficulty and complexity of maintaining the political control and policy capacity nexus.

BOX 5.4   POLITICAL CONTROL AND CAPACITY

US presidents exert their authority over administrative agencies through budgetary agendas setting power, strategic selection of political executives and their comparative advantage over Congress, which is attributable to less severe coordination problems. These formal mechanisms of presidential control over executive administration rest solely on the application of expressed or implied constitutional powers.

But there are limitations: the size of the government and in particular the increasing size of the White House; the turnover of political executives with learning curve implications. There is also the need for horizontal coordination i.e. trade-off between 'committed' (i.e. politically appointed) and capable bureaucrats; there is also the need for vertical coordination (between president and agency heads). There is also the issue of 'credible commitment': stable agencies with lower turnover are likely to be more concerned with long-term bureaucratic reputation than the less stable with high turnover that are less politically insulated and therefore concerned with short-term electoral focus.

Source: adapted from Krause (2009)

Policy capacity and the interdependent world

Increasingly, there is a range of policies considered so complex that they cannot be addressed within existing policy domain capacities, wicked policy issues, which cross over policy, professional and service delivery boundaries (Rein 2006). A similar range of policies arises which are outwith the 'traditional' policy capacity of the nation state and which require some form of international response, for example, airline regulation, pandemic infection containment and control, security, matters pertaining to international markets, trading and finance. There are a number of ways in which this can be presented as a loss of policy capacity within a national domain. Capacity can be squeezed from above by a range of supra-state bodies such as the EU, intergovernmental bodies, trade regulatory organizations such as the World Trade Organization or parts of the global financial infrastructure and architecture such as the International Monetary Fund; but also from a complexity of private non-governmental bodies like credit-rating agencies whose rating of a country's creditworthiness can constrain policy action. Capacity can also be squeezed from below by devolved or sub-national governments and indeed powerful and/or well-organized interests, as Box 5.5 indicates.

BOX 5.5   PLAN TO REFORM ENGLISH FORESTS

Change of ownership will allow Forestry Commission to focus on its key role – but there will be opportunities created for community and civil society groups to buy or lease forests; commercially viable forests will be leased to commercial operators

(www.defra.gov.uk/news/2011/01/27/englands-forests (accessed 20 April 2012))

Public survey revealed that three-quarters of people are opposed to plans to sell off some of England's forests while leading figures have also called for the decision to be reversed – Campaigners, dignitaries such as the Archbishop of Canterbury are confident the government can be forced into a U-turn.

(Daily Telegraph, 23rd January 2011 www.telegraph.co.uk/agriculture/forestry/8275748/forest-sell-off (accessed 20 April 2012))

Establishment bodies like the National Trust and Woodland Trust were slow off the mark. But radical groups, most conspicuously the 38 degrees website, made effective use of social media – A YouGov poll found 84 per cent were against the sale, 'save our forests' petition achieved 533,138 signatures. The government dropped its plans.

(www.guardian.co.uk/environment/2011/feb/17/ forestry-sell-off-policy-u-turn (accessed 20 April 2012))

Generally, capacity may be diminished where there are more actors in a policy system, if it leads to more veto points through multiple decision nodes (see Pressman and Wildavsky 1974; Tsebelis 2003). It is also the case that a nation's policy capacity may be somewhat diminished if its policy management capacity at the supra-national level is somewhat patchy. Studies of Europeanized policy domains in various countries seem to show that knowledge, institutional capacity and effective coordination are often variable (Hanf and Soetendorp 1998; Kassim *et al.* 2000; Geuijen *et al.* 2008).

There are also areas that make it appear the policy capacity of the state has been eroded. For example in the EU although the functioning of the European single market does not compel member states on regulations to adopt (merely requesting them to make their own arrangements compatible with the functioning of the internal market) it does beg the question about capacity for independent action given that the major underlying premise is a liberal economic underpinning to policy. The dominance of the 'competition state', where globalization tends to encourage countries to adopt budget reductions, low inflation and deregulated labour market policies to attract and retain foreign capital inflows, restricts policy action and discretion; however, it can be argued this does not reduce policy capacity as such, it simply constrains the range of policies governments will adopt. In a similar vein, it may also be thought that the US sub-prime housing market collapse, which triggered near global financial meltdown, exposed a dangerously hollow capacity of the state in this policy area. However, the facts behind this indicate that a clear policy choice not to regulate was taken: until 2008, both Freddie Mac and Fanny Mae – the privately owned mortgage companies – were lightly regulated, abiding by minimal capital requirements lower than other financial institutions. The Bush administration and some members of Congress pushed for a tougher regulatory regime seeing the risks in the current system; others in Congress opposed this, believing that the delivery of home ownership was key. Both Freddie Mac and Fanny Mae were able to orchestrate lobbying to frustrate stronger regulation, driven it is claimed by campaign contributions leaving them 'free to borrow and lend recklessly'. Clearly this was not a lack of policy capacity, 'it was a choice of those who had authority to create a powerful state regulator and chose not to do so' (Thompson 2010: 140).

Similarly the 2010 and ongoing eurozone crisis has seen many thoughtful commentators analyze the situation in terms of policy failure, identifying an apparent inability or unwillingness of the European Central Bank to issue euro bonds or to act as lender of the last resort, the absence of an economic growth policy framework to grow the zone out of debt and avoid recession and the overwhelming lack of vision from Europe's political elites (see Sachs 2011). The crisis has the following key elements:

- The primacy of the nation state in matters of debt within the eurozone (notwithstanding attempts to institutionalize fiscal discipline in the future) has left the weakest members paying more than twice the level of interest on bonds they issue than the German government, increasing the risk that a eurozone member will default.
- Any default would hit all due to depreciation of the euro.
- If the eurozone were to issue common bonds this would raise the cost of borrowing of most creditworthy states. This could create bailout problems.
- At that point either the eurozone collapses, the nation state reasserts itself or an EU authority would be established to issue debt and raise taxes.
- Alternatively, (less likely to work) attempts would be made to use existing EU systems to impose tight fiscal and monetary controls on eurozone members.

(Adapted from Thompson 2010)

139

On the basis of the above, there is something of a trajectory towards transnational governance. This replaces individual state authority with the policy capacity shifted from the nation state 'but it would not repudiate the essentially political character of the state' (Thompson 2010: 144). In this perspective, the policy capacity of the state has been transferred to transnational level rather than a reduced capacity per se. Individual states will exert influence at transnational level.

Finally, policy capacity in an interdependent political environment – and it's in the EU where most of the research and literature is located – can perhaps be looked at differently from national state policy capacity. First, there are a number of policy issues that can only be addressed supra-nationally and in so doing can solve capacity problems at nation state level; so, for example, the development of EU air pollution legislation increases capacity to address problems caused by air pollution within the state; similarly, action on air passenger compensation for disruption caused by volcanic ash clouds in 2010 was settled at EU level thereby enabling national governments to enforce national airlines to implement compensation policies. Policies that can only be settled at supra-national level may make national policy capacity meaningful (like carbon emissions reduction, policies covering international travel regulations). Second, member states generally have a stronger say in the design of EU policies due to consensual decision-making (whether by qualified majority voting or not): consensus can be achieved by concessions and financial compensation packages (Knill 2005). Third, EU member states often use EU policy to strengthen their policy capacity at home. For example, it has been shown how European transport policy was used by the German government to liberalise road haulage, a policy the government was previously unable to carry out due to German hauliers' very close relations with the transport administration (Knill and Lehmkuhl 2002). Similar leverage enhancing policy capacity for specific policy ends has also been observed in Dutch and German railway systems (Knill 2005).

Outsourcing and extending the state: issues for policy capacity

Governments often wish to bring people into government from the outside, 'the real world' as it were, to increase the range of experience and expertise available in the broad area of policy: the underlying premise is to increase the capacity of the system. This is felt by some to be a particularly pressing concern due to the increasingly 'inbred' nature of political parties. From the former UK cabinet secretary, Lord Turnbull:

> There is a growing trend for people to come into politics more or less straight from university. They lick envelopes in central office, become a special adviser,

on and on it goes and by the time they are in their mid-30s they are cabinet ministers barely touching the sides of real life.

(House of Commons Public Administration Select Committee 2010)

In the same document he also argues:

[in the UK] you have no chance if you come in at 50 years old of getting anywhere in politics, so how can you develop in a senior position in local government, or in the trade unions or in business? You are so far behind in the climb up the greasy pole that you never catch up.

Although there may be some exaggeration here, it is a profile that matches that of the current (2013) UK Prime Minister, Leader of the Opposition, Chancellor and Shadow Chancellor. There is international comparative experience which, at first glance, appears to indicate a greater use of outsiders in the government and policy process than the above quote would suggest. France, Netherlands, Sweden and Germany allow the most senior levels of government (ministers) to be drawn from outside Parliament. Leading politicians in other countries have envied the apparent ability to capture 'the best brains in the country' (e.g. former Irish Taoiseach Jack Lynch, cited in O'Malley 2006). However, much of this capturing of external expertise is accounted for by the fact that, in some countries (e.g. France, Netherlands, Sweden), cabinet ministers are constitutionally prohibited from holding seats in the legislature and must resign their seats if appointed. It is clear that in these countries (especially the Netherlands) ministerial positions are opened to a wider pool beyond Parliament, but this pool can still be largely dominated by politics (albeit outwith the national legislature) and in particular, political parties. A study of France and the Netherlands has shown that the result is likely to be recruitment of ministers with hybrid skills from political and non-political worlds rather than the bringing-in of outsider technocratic expertise to government and policy making – and in the Dutch Parliament of 2011 all senior ministers were essentially politicians (Young and Hazell 2011).

Outwith the European context, the US system is thought to offer greater discretion for the co-option of extra-political outsiders to enhance government policy capacity. There is an attraction to this proposition – for instance there is considerable executive authority over the selection of cabinet secretaries who, not being part of the legislature, are nominated by the President (though must be confirmed by Senate). While experts or those with specialist offerings to enhance the capacity of the system may be appointed by the President to his cabinet in this way, there are those with business backgrounds who have found it difficult to acclimatise to the political environment (Young and Hazell 2011). And research shows it is the political role that is rather dominant in policy. The separation of

141

powers within the US system means there are checks and balances operating at several levels, not just between executive (President) and legislature (Congress) but also within the executive itself through core institutions such as the Executive Office of the President, the Council of Economic Advisers, National Security Council, Council on Environmental Quality, the Office of Administration, Office of Management and Budget, Office of National Drug Control Policy, Office of Science and Technology Policy, Office of the United States Trade Representative, Office of the Vice President and the Executive Residence (Young and Hazell 2011). Unsurprisingly, the research consensus is that the overwhelming requirement to sustain the system's capacity is political, navigating the separated powers within the US polity each with their checks and balances (Bennett 1996; Edwards 2001; Young and Hazell 2011). Not unexpectedly, the backgrounds of cabinet appointees have not been extra-political or technocratic but largely 'non-executive politics', that is, government administration: democratic presidents have tended to appoint those with a background in law (50 per cent); republican presidents have appointed 35 per cent with an experience in elective politics, democrats 24 per cent (Bennett 1996 as cited in Young and Hazell 2011). What is clear is that, in a range of countries, use of extra-political agents or expertise from outwith the system to enhance policy capacity is more apparent than real, or at least is more nuanced than it would at first appear. Very little is known with regard to the impact of external agents, 'outsiders' in governmental policy capacity, since this is an under-researched area with little published beyond subjective views or some individual cases. It is certainly the case that politics itself is a profession, and an understanding of the political complexities required to manage and implement policy is an extremely important dimension of any government's policy capacity.

There has been a trend for two to three decades now of the state sharing or outsourcing its capacity to deliver a range of activities or services in the US, Europe, Australia and elsewhere (also in developing countries) often under the drive of bodies such as the International Monetary Fund and World Bank. This has often been done via neo-liberal attempts to roll back the boundaries of the state – always ideologically present, but given a dynamic with economic crises from the 1970s. The result has led to the creation of arms-length bodies, hybridised public–private partnership arrangements often with complex lateral (network type) rather than (or in addition to) vertical and hierarchical relationships to the state (Ghobadian *et al.* 2004; Osei 2004; Pollitt and Talbot 2004; Hodge and Greve 2005).

The scope of this is extensive. In the UK in 2005 there were:

> 26 non-ministerial departments, 11 public corporations, 127 executive agencies, 17 national special health authorities, 439 advisory non-departmental public bodies (NDPBs) and 147 independent monitoring boards . . . in Britain the government has entered into more than 550 private finance initiative projects, 239 refurbished schools, 23 transport projects, 34 police and fire

stations, 13 prisons and secure training centres, 12 waste and water installations and a variety of other projects involving defence, leisure, tourism, culture, housing and IT.

(Flinders 2006: 227)

As indicated, the UK is not unique and according to OECD, it was not uncommon for more staff to be employed by such bodies than traditional departments of state (OECD 2002). There is an argument that this represents an attempt by governments to buy in strategic and policy capacity to deliver and improve public services in an increasingly competitive environment of constrained resources, outwith traditional state structures. There is evidence that a major driver of public private partnerships (PPPs) and the private finance initiative (PFI),

---

BOX 5.6 FRAGMENTATION AND LOSS OF POLICY CAPACITY – LEARNING LESSONS?

After the Bank of England took over interest-rate policy from the Treasury in 1997, its focus shifted away from bank regulation and financial markets. As part of the shake-up, the Bank lost its role as the manager of government debt, one that ensured regular contact with the City, and day-to-day supervision of banks, which went to a new regulator, the Financial Services Authority (FSA).

> the primacy of the bank's interest rate policy and the associated inflation target it was given by the government meant the bank's financial stability wing became a backwater . . . Ambitious youngsters sensed that getting on at the bank meant working on the inflation forecast and serving the monetary policy committee. Analysts who could articulate ideas in the technical language of economics were prized; the imprecise vernacular of financial markets was scorned. So when the financial crisis struck in the summer of 2007, bank staff with an understanding of the unfolding calamity were scarce. This helps explain why the bank's initial response was flat-footed. Legislation set out in 2011 will return the task of over-seeing banks to the Bank of England: a new prudential regulation authority, sitting inside the bank, will take over from the Financial Services Authority. Its remit will be to ensure that individual banks comply with capital adequacy rules. The new financial policy committee will advise the authority on actions needed to keep the whole banking system safe.

Source: adapted from Economist (2011)

143

for example, was to buy in (perceived or real) private sector expertise in major capital infrastructure construction projects and to transfer risks to the private sector (Jackson 2009). It has also been long recognized that, in some areas of urban development, without local community and business input, governments lack the strategic capacity to realize project aims (Fosier and Berger 1982).

There is, however, a sense in which the fragmentation thus represented by the removal of service delivery from large ministerial departments of state is seen as a decline of state capacity (Flinders 2006), or at best a lack of a coherent view from governments regarding the strategic capacity consequences (OECD 2002). It is also claimed that in certain fields there is a risk of undermining the intellectual or epistemic capacity of the state (Flinders 2006; Pollock *et al.* 2011).

There is a final irony in this area of strategic policy capacity. A range of attempts to increase or maintain capacity in the outsourced governance environment includes: the creation of additional layers of 'overseeing' or integrative bodies such as the Food Standards Agency, Office of the Communications Regulator etc. (Rosenau 2004; Flinders 2006); arrangements to share and/or pool budgets (though relatively few of the latter); and initiatives to join up services ('joined up government'), but so far there has been little evaluation of the impact on strategic policy capacity of the state. Moreover, of some concern in a democracy, the relationship between these structures and democratic accountability frameworks is increasingly opaque (Flinders 2006).

POLICY COMMUNITIES AS A SOURCE OF CAPACITY

As discussed in Chapter 3, policy communities and networks have long been known as a source of policy capacity, the argument being that the pluralistic underpinnings broaden involvement in the policy process (Richardson and Jordan 1979; Jordan and Richardson 1987) – an argument that has been seriously questioned by some in relation to the UK experience of the 1980s (e.g. Smith 2006). Epistemic communities (comprised of individuals or groups who have an authoritative claim to knowledge in a relevant policy area) can clearly be seen as an instrument to be used to increase policy capacity (Haas 1990). This can be observed in areas ranging from health care to climate change to financial regulation. Much of the empirical research into the effectiveness of policy communities indicates these are but one component explaining the policy process. Two key exponents of the importance of policy communities and networks in governance (Marsh and Rhodes 1992) have themselves indicated 'policy communities and networks are but one component of an exploration of policy change' (Marsh and Rhodes 1992: 260). The key concerns currently are about how policy capacity can be optimised in an environment where powerful (sometimes professional) interests and epistemic-type communities have significant influence in certain policy areas. For example, in financial services, self-regulation by the financial services community itself, internal risk management processes exemplified by the Basel II regime for banks or the self-regulation of complex markets (such as the 'over the counter' derivatives market) was sorely exposed during the 2008 financial crisis (Moloney 2010). These trends were further exemplified by the 'light touch' regulation adopted in the UK (as a result of the major study commissioned by the UK Financial Services Authority, concerned at the cost of regulation) and the establishment of the Risk and Regulation Advisory Council 'in order to encourage risk taking and the avoidance of propensities to overreact to risks by introducing new and excessive systems of regulation' (Risk and Regulation Advisory council 2008 as cited in Baldwin *et al.* 2010: 614). When allied to the close proximity of regulators and regulated ('an aping of private business practices . . . a revolving door operated between regulators and those in the financial industry' [Baldwin *et al.* 2010: 615]), this severely compromised the policy capacity of the banking and financial regulatory system. In other words, agents' interests rather than policy capacity were enhanced.

There is clearly a dilemma regarding ways in which policy capacity in such an environment can be maintained and sustained. The financial services community may be an extreme case, but many of the features outlined that have made policy capacity an issue are not unique: part of the sector forms what amounts to an epistemic community in the sense that it has a privileged position in access to knowledge; it is international in scope making coordinated inter-governmental or supra-national activity vital; different national interests drive policy in contrary directions. Other policy areas, for instance environmental policy addressing climate change, can lay claim to these features.

In such environments, it is argued that avenues to maintain and sustain policy capacity should focus on professional dialogue and 'responsive regulation'. For instance, studies of safety regulation in the mining industry have shown that co-operation (between owners and unions) allied to training and legal sanctions where co-operation fails have shown strong results in implementing safety policy (Braithwaite 1985).

The general importance of civil society and non-state actors in defining the policy capacity of governments has been long recognized. In Chapter 2 the role of global and supra-national bodies, as well as, within nation states, the function played by extra-state and near-state institutions and outsourced bodies, has been examined. The state often enables as much as it directs. In terms of civil society and policy capacity, the key issue is about the ability of the state to penetrate society and ensure its decisions are carried out. Studies on developing countries have attributed a lack of policy capacity to a range of factors including overwhelming influences of landowning classes, ethnic groupings and other structures often linked back to colonial pasts (Mann 1984; Migdal 1988). Studies have also shown that ethnic fragmentation can have an adverse impact on policy capacity, distorting policy making – research has shown this in such different environments as Canada, Zambia, Kenya, Mauritius, Trinidad and Tobago, Malawi (Barkan 1992;

Carroll and Joypaul 1993; Aucoin 1995; Andeweg 1997; Osei-Hwedie 1998; Brown 1999).

Civil society can, however, be seen as a means through which the state can enhance policy capacity. There is a linkage between the capacities of a society and the capacity of the state to govern (for a good discussion of this see Peters 2005). There is a range of governance configurations of state and non-state civil society organizations to reflect the degree of state influence, plurality and the extent of civil society influence, indicated in the typology below.

There is recognition too that at the most micro level, the individual and his/her relationship to the community may be a civil society source of capacity that impacts on the ability of governments to integrate and implement policies. This is addressed by the concept of social capital. Social capital is about connectedness among individuals and the resulting reciprocity and mutuality and the fact that these relational resources can be used to achieve desired outcomes (Putnam 2000). Intuitively, there is clearly a positive relationship between high levels of social capital, communal engagement and the desire to deliver policy outcomes. In the UK for example, governmental agenda for reform of public services includes a narrative of a 'Big Society', where individual social capital, exercised at neighbourhood and community level, is seen to be an important component of future delivery of key policy outcomes for public service delivery (see Open Public Services 2011).

However, it has been argued that emphasizing social capital as a wellspring for enhancing policy capacity de-emphasizes other explanatory frameworks (e.g. capital and class) that may be more powerful (Navario 2002; Fine 2010). Recent research has indicated conflicting evidence: on the one hand evidence of a strong relationship between indicators of high social capital and enhanced policy outcomes (e.g. parental involvement, electoral turnout and improved educational attainment); on

Table 5.1 Models of governance

Model	Characteristics
Etatiste	Dominant role for state institutions; limited involvement from society
Liberal	Involvement of limited number of social actors selected by state institutions; pluralist with government choosing legitimate actors
State-centric	State dominant, but societal actors have autonomous sources of legitimacy
'Dutch'	Networks are central participants but state retains capacity to make autonomous decisions and steer
Governance without government	Networks and markets are dominant; state legitimizes action of these societal actors

Source: adapted from Peters and Pierre (2006)

 146

the other, strong collective resistance from active communities to unwanted policy change (e.g. location of social housing in certain areas). It is also the case that much of the research on the impact of social capital has been in the US, and more cross-country comparative work is required (Andrews 2011).

CONCLUSION

This chapter built on Chapters 2 and 3 and analyzed some of the key aspects of policy capacity: factors that affect the ability to make policy decisions, develop, resource and implement such policy. The tensions within modern governments and capacity to make and manage policy within an increasingly globalised world were explored. The relationship between policy capacity and regulation, as a principal government activity, was examined. The conventional view of the law being used to put into effect policy was explored as were various degrees and types of legal, semi-legal and other types of regulation, as well as the way in which regulated interests may aid or hinder policy capacity. The role of political institutions, leadership and management structures and their political context were also analyzed. The complexities of assessing policy capacity in an interdependent world were explored, assessing the role played by supra-state institutions and environments 'above' the state, and bodies and organizations 'below' the state. The constraints or enablers in an increasingly internationalised and complex environment with a multiplicity of linkages and relationships within and outwith conventional nation state structures were discussed. Finally, there was an analysis of how policy capacity is affected by the increased use of external agents, partnerships and outsourcing arrangements, policy communities and non-state actors.

REFERENCES

Aberbach, J. and Rockman, B. (2000) *In the Web of Politics. Three Decades of the US Federal Executive*, Washington DC: Brookings Institution.

Allison, G.T. (1971) *Essence of Decision: explaining the Cuban missile crisis*, Boston, MA: Little, Brown and Company.

Amann, R. (2006) 'The circumlocution office: a snapshot of civil service reform,' *The Political Quarterly*, 77, 3: 334–359.

Anderson, C.J. and Guillory, C.A. (1997) 'Political institutions and satisfaction with democracy', *American Political Science Review*, 91, 1: 66–81.

Anderson, L. (2001) 'The implications of institutional design for macro-economic performance: re-assessing the claims of consensus democracy', *Comparative Political Studies*, 34, 4: 429–452.

Andeweg, R. (1997) 'Collegiality and Collectivity: cabinets, cabinet committees and cabinet ministers', in P. Weller, H. Bakvis and R.A.W Rhodes (eds) *The Hollow Crown: Countervailing Trends in Core Executives*, Basingstoke: MacMillan: 58–83.

Andrews, R. (2011) 'Social capital and public service performance: a review of the evidence', *Public Policy and Administration*, 27, 1: 49–67.

Andrews, R., Boyne, G. and Walker, R. (2006) 'Strategy content and organisational performance: an empirical analysis', *Public Administration Review*, 66, 1: 52–63.

Aucoin, P. (1995) *The New Public Management: Canada in Comparative Perspective*, Montreal: Institute for Research in Public Policy.

Aucoin, P. and Bakvis, H. (2005) 'Public Service Reform and Policy Capacity: Recruiting and Retaining the Brightest and the Best?' in M. Painter and J. Pierre (eds) *Challenges to State Policy Capacity: Global Trends and Comparative Perspectives*, Basingstoke: Palgrave Macmillan: 185–204.

Australian Public Services Commission (2004) *Connecting Government: Whole of Government Responses to Australia's Priority Challenges*, Canberra: Commonwealth of Australia.

Baldwin, R., Cave, M. and Lodge, M. (eds) (210) *The Oxford Handbook of Regulation*, Oxford: Oxford University Press.

Barankay, I. and Lockwood, B. (2007) 'Decentralisation and the productive efficiency of government: evidence from Swiss cantons', *Journal of Public Economics*, 91, 5–6: 1197–1218.

Bardach, E. and Kagan, R. (1982) *Going by the Book: the problem of regulatory unreasonableness*, Philadelphia, PA: Temple University Press.

Barkan, J.D. (1992) 'The Rise and Fall of a Governance Regime in Kenya', in G. Hyden and M. Bratton (eds) *Governance and Politics in Africa*, Boulder CD: Lynne Rienner.

Bennett, A.J. (1996) *The American President's Cabinet: from Kennedy to Bush*, Basingstoke: MacMillan.

Bergman, S-E. (1998) Swedish models of health care reform: a review and assessment, *International Journal of Health Planning and Management*, 13:2, 91–106

Black, J. and Baldwin, R. (2010) 'Really responsive risk based regulation', *Law and Policy* 32, 2: 181–213.

Bode, I. (2006) 'Co-governance within networks and the non-profit-for-profit divide: a cross-cultural perspective on the evolution of domiciliary elderly care', *Public Management Review*, 8, 4: 551–566.

Bode, I. and Firbank, O. (2009) 'Barriers to co-governance: examining the "chemistry" of home-care networks in Germany, England, and Quebec', *The Policy Studies Journal*, 37, 2: 325–351.

Boston, J., Martin, J., Pallot, J. and Walsh, P. (1996) *Public Management. The New Zealand Model*, Auckland: Oxford University Press.

Bovens, M., 't Hart, P. and Peters, B.G. (eds) (2001) *Success and Failure in Public Governance*, Cheltenham: Edward Elgar.

148

Bowcott, O. (2011) 'Judges too political', *Guardian*, 9 September 2011.

Boyne, G., James, O., John, P. and Petrovsky, N. (2008) 'Executive succession in English local government', *Public Money & Management*, 28, 5: 267–274.

Braithwaite, J. (1985) *To Punish or Persuade: enforcement of coal mine safety*, Albany, NY: State University of New York Press.

Brandsen, T. and Pestoff, V. (2006) 'Co-production the third sector and delivery of public services', *Public Management Review*, 8, 4: 493–501.

Brandsen, T. and van Hout, W. (2006) 'Co-management in public service networks', *Public Management Review*, 8, 4: 537–549.

Brans, M. and Vancoppenolle, D. (2005) 'Policy making reforms and civil service systems: an exploration of agendas and consequences', in M. Painter and J. Pierre (eds) *Challenges to State Policy Capacity: Global Trends and Comparative Perspectives*, Basingstoke: Palgrave Macmillan.

Brewer, G. and Selden, S. (2000) 'Why elephants gallop: assessing and predicting organisational performance in federal agencies', *Journal of Public Administration Research and Theory*, 10, 4: 685–712.

Brown, D.R. (1999) 'Managing diversity in the Trinidad and Tobago public service: challenges for human resource management', *Public Management*, 1, 2: 213–234.

Campbell, C. (2001) 'Juggling inputs, outputs and outcomes in the search for policy competence: recent experience in Australia', *Governance*, 14, 2: 253–282.

Carroll, B.W. and Juypaul, S.K. (1993) 'The Mauritian senior public service independence: some lessons for developing and developed nations', *International Review of Administrative Sciences*, 59, 3: 423–440.

Cobb, R.W. and Elder, C.D. (1983) *Participation in American Politics*, Baltimore, MD: John Hopkins University Press.

Coglianese, C. and Mendelson, E. (2010) 'Meta-Regulation and Self-Regulation', in R. Baldwin, M. Cave and M. Lodge (eds) *The Oxford Handbook of Regulation*, Oxford: Oxford University Press.

Commission on 2020 Public Services Trust (2009) *A Brief History of Public Service Reform*, London: 2020 Public Services Trust.

Cummings, S. and Norgaard, O. (2004) 'Conceptualising state capacity: comparing Kazakhstan and Kyrgyzstan', *Political Studies*, 52, 4: 685–708.

Davis, G. (2000) 'Conclusion. Policy Capacity and the Future of Governance', in G. Davis and M. Keating (eds) *The Future of Governance*, St Leonards, NSW: Allen and Unwin.

De Vries, M. (2000) 'The rise and fall of de-centralisation: a comparative analysis of arguments and practices in European countries', *European Journal of Political Research*, 38, 2: 193–224.

Dorbeck-Jung, B., Vrielink, M., Gosselt, J., van Hoof, J. and de Jong, M. (2010) 'Contested hybridisation of regulation: failure of the Dutch regulatory system to protect minors from harmful media', *Regulation and Governance*, 4: 154–174.

Dunn, D. (1997) *Politics and Administration at the Top. Lessons From Down Under*, Pittsburgh, PA: University of Pittsburgh Press.

Economist (2011) 'Bank regulation. Mervyn agonises', 25 June 2011: 33

Edwards, G. (2001) 'The Loyalty-Competency Trade-Off in Presidential Appointments', in G.C. MacKenzie (ed.) *Innocent Until Nominated: The Breakdown of the Presidential Appointments Process*, Washington DC: Brookings Institution.

Ferlie, E., Lynn, L.E. and Pollitt, C. (2007) *The Oxford Handbook of Public Management*, Oxford: Oxford University Press.

Fine, B. (2010) *Theories of Social Capital: researchers behaving badly*, London: Routledge.

Fleischer, J. (2009) 'Power resources of parliamentary executives: policy advice in the UK and Germany', *West European Politics*, 32, 1: 196–214.

Flinders, M. (2006) 'The Politics of Public–Private Partnerships in the United Kingdom', in C. Rouillard (ed.) Public–private Partnerships and the Reconfiguration of the State: *challenges and issues for democratic governance*, Ottawa: University of Ottawa Press.

Flinders, M. (2008) 'Public and Private: the boundaries of the state', in C. Hay, M. Lister and D. Marsh (eds) *The State. Theories and Issues*, London: Palgrave Macmillan.

Flynn, N. (2007) *Public Sector Management,* 5th edition, London: Harvester Wheatsheaf.

Fosier, R.S. and Berger, R.A. (eds) (1982) *Public Private Partnerships in American Cities: seven case studies*, Lexington, MA: Lexington Press.

Freeman, J. (2000) 'Private partners, public functions and the new administrative law', *Administrative Law Review*, 52: 813–858.

Geuijen, K., 't Hart, P., Princen, S. and Yesilkagit, K. (2008) *The New Eurocrats: national civil servants in EU policy making*, Amsterdam: Amsterdam University Press.

Ghobadian, A., O'Regan, N., Gallear, D. and Viney, H. (2004) *Public Private Partnership*, Basingstoke: Palgrave Macmillan.

Greener, I. (2009) *Public Management: a critical text.* Basingstoke: Palgrave Macmillan.

Haas, E. (1990) *When Knowledge is Power: three models of change in international organisations*, Berkeley, CA: University of California Press.

Hammerschmid, G., Meyer, K. and Demmke, C. (2007) 'Public administration modernization: common reforms trends or different paths and national understandings in the EU countries', *Research in Public Policy Analysis and Management*, 16: 145–169.

Hanf, K. and Soetendorp, B. (eds) (1998) *Adapting to European Integration: small states and the European Union*, London: Longman.

Hartley, J. (2011) 'Special issue on public leadership', *Public Money & Management*, 31, 5: 303–304.

150

Haverland, M. and Romeijn, M. (2007) 'Do member states make European policies work? Analysing the EU transposition deficit', *Public Administration*, 85, 3: 757–778.

Héritier, A. (2001) *Differential Europe: the European Union impact on national policy making*, Oxford: Rowman & Littlefield.

Hill, M.J. and Hupe, P. (2009) *Implementing Public Policy: an introduction to the study of operational governance*, London: Sage.

Hodge, G. and Greve, C. (2005) *The Challenge of Public Private Partnerships*, Cheltenham: Edward Elgar.

Honadle, B. (1981) 'A capacity building framework: a search for concept and purpose', *Public Administration Review*, 41, 5: 575–580.

Hood, C., James, O., Peters, B.G. and Scott, C. (2004) *Controlling Modern Government: variety, commonality and change*, London: Edward Elgar.

Hood, C., Scott, C., Jones, G. and Travers, T. (1999) *Waste Watchers, Quality Police and Sleaze-busters*, Oxford: Oxford University Press.

Hoppe, R. and Jeliazkova, M. (2006) 'How Policy Makers Define Their Jobs: A Netherlands Case Study', in H.K. Colebatch (ed.) *The Work of Policy: An International Survey*, Lanham, MD: Rowman & Littlefield.

Horner, M. (1997) 'Leadership theory. Past, present and future', *Team Performance Management*, 3, 4: 276–287.

House of Commons Public Administration Select Committee (2010) *Goats and Tsars: ministerial and other appointments from outside parliament*, HC 330, London: HMSO.

Howlett, M. (2009) 'Policy analytical capacity and evidence based policy making: lessons from Canada', *Canadian Public Administration*, 52, 2: 153–175.

Hutter, B.M. (2006) 'Risk, Regulation and Management', in P. Taylor-Gooby and J. Zinn (eds) *Risk in Social Sciences*, Oxford: Oxford University Press.

Immergut, E. (1992) 'The Rules of the Game: the logic of health policy making in France, Switzerland and Sweden', in S. Steinmo, K. Thelen and F. Longstreth, (eds) *Structuring Politics: Historical Institutionalism in Comparative Analysis*, Cambridge: Cambridge University Press.

Institute for Government (2011) *Policy Making in the Real World. Evidence and Analysis*, London: Institute for Government.

Jackson, M. (2009) 'The size and the scope of the public sector', in T. Bovaird and E. Loffler (eds) *Public Management and Governance*, London: Routledge.

Jayasuriya, K. (2005) 'Capacity beyond the boundaries: new regulatory state, fragmentation and relational capacity', in M. Painter and J. Pierre, (eds) *Challenges to State Policy Capacity: global trends and comparative perspectives*, Basingstoke: Palgrave Macmillan.

John, P. (2011) *Making Policy Work*, London: Routledge.

Johnson, C. and Osborne, S.P. (2003) 'Local strategic partnerships, neighbourhood renewal, and the limits to co-governance', *Public Money & Management*, 23, 3: 147–154.

Jones, G. (1988) 'The leadership of organisations', *RSA Journal*, 3, 4: 81–83.

Jordan, A.G. and Richardson, J.J. (1987) *British Politics and the Policy Process: an arena approach*, London: Allen and Unwin.

Kassim, H., Menon, A., Peters, B.G. and Wright, V. (eds) (2000) *The National Co-ordination of EU Policy: the domestic level*, Oxford: Oxford University Press.

Khaleghian, P. (2004) 'Decentralisation and public services: the case of immunisation', *Social Science and Medicine*, 59, 1: 163–183.

Knill, C. (1998) 'European Policies: The impact of national administrative traditions', *Journal of Public Policy*, 18, 1: 1–28.

Knill, C. (2005) 'The Europeanization of National Policy Capacities', in M. Painter and J. Pierre (eds) *Challenges to State Policy Capacity: global trends and comparative perspectives*, Basingstoke: Palgrave Macmillan.

Knill, C. and Lehmkuhl, D. (2002) 'The national impact of European Union regulatory policy: three Europeanization mechanisms', *European Journal of Political Research*, 41, 2: 255–280.

Kooiman, J. (2003) *Governing as Governance*, London: Sage Publishing.

Krause, G.A. (2009) 'Organisational complexity and co-ordination dilemmas in US executive politics', *Presidential Studies Quarterly*, 39, 1: 74–88.

Leach, S. and Lowndes, V. (2007) 'Of roles and rules: analysing the changing relationship between political leaders and chief executives in local government', *Public Policy and Administration*, 22, 2: 183–200.

Lijphart, A. (1968) *The Politics of Accommodation. Pluralism and Democracy in the Netherlands*, Berkeley, CA: University of California Press.

Lijphart, A. (1999) *Patterns of Democracy: government forms and performance in thirty six countries*, New Haven: Yale University Press.

Lindblom, C.E. (1979) 'Still muddling not yet through', *Public Administration Review*, 39, 6: 517–525.

Lodge, G. and Kalitowski, S. (2007) *Innovations in Government: international perspectives on civil service reform*, London: Institute for Public Policy Research.

McTavish, D. (2003) *Business and Public Management in the UK 1900–2003*, Aldershot: Ashgate.

Maddox, D. (2011) 'Westminster may hand over control of referendum', *Scotsman* 23 November 2011.

Mann, M. (1984) 'The autonomous power of the state: its origins mechanisms and results', *Archives Européennes de Sociologie*, 25, 2: 165–183.

Marsh, D. and Rhodes R.A.W. (eds) (1992) *Policy Networks in British Government*, Oxford: Clarendon Press.

Massey, A. and Pyper R. (2005) *Public Management and Modernisation in Britain*. Basingstoke: Palgrave Macmillan.

Matsaganis, M. and Flevotomou, M. (2010) 'Distributional implications of tax evasion in Greece', *Hellenic Observatory Papers on Greece and Southeast Europe*, London: London School of Economics.

May, P.J. (2002) 'Policy Design and Implementation', in B.G. Peters and J. Pierre, (eds) *Handbook of Public Administration*, London: Sage.

Meier, K.J. and O'Toole, L. (2006) *Bureaucracy in a Democratic State: a governance perspective*, Baltimore, MD: John Hopkins University Press.

Migdal, J.S. (1988) *Strong Societies and Weak States: state centred relations and state capabilities in the third world*, Princeton: Princeton University Press.

Miller, K. Johnston, McTavish, D. and Pyper, R. (2010) 'Changing Modes of Official Accountability in the UK', in T. Brandsen and M. Holzer (eds) *Future of Governance*, National Center for Public Performance, EGPA and ASPA, Newark, NJ.

Moloney, N. (2010) 'Financial Services and Markets', in R. Baldwin, M. Cave and M. Lodge (eds) *The Oxford Handbook of Regulation*, Oxford: Oxford University Press.

Moran, M. (2003) *The Regulatory State in Britain: high modernism and hyper innovation*, Oxford: Oxford University Press.

Moynihan, D. and Pandey, S. (2005) 'Testing how management matters in an era of government by performance', *Journal of Public Administration Research and Theory*, 15: 3, 421–439.

Navario, V. (2002) 'A critique of social capital', *International Journal of Health Services*, 32: 423–432.

O'Malley, E. (2006) 'Ministerial selection in Ireland: limited choice in a political village', *Irish Political Studies*, 21, 3: 319–336.

O'Neil, A. (2011) 'We need to talk about the referendum. Scotland's membership of the UK in focus', www.thecourier.co.uk/news/politcs/article/18415/constitutional-law-expert; www.legalweek.com/legal-week/blog-post2123838/talk-referendum. (Accessed 15 May 2012.)

OECD (1999) *Synthesis of Reform Experiences in Nine OECD Countries: government roles and functions and public management: government of the future: getting from here to there*, Paris.

OECD (2001) *Public Sector Leadership for the Twenty First Century*, Paris.

OECD (2002) *Distributed Public Governance: agencies authorities and other autonomous bodies*, London

Office of the Auditor General of Canada (2001) *Public Service Management Reform: progress setbacks and challenges*, Ottawa.

Open Public Services White Paper 2011, Cmnd. 8145

Osei, P. (2004) 'Public Private Partnerships in Service Delivery in Developing Countries', in A. Ghobadian, N. O'Regan, D. Gallear and H. Viney (eds) *Public Private Partnership*, Basingstoke: Palgrave Macmillan.

Osei-Hwedie, B. (1998) 'The role of ethnicity in multi-party politics in Malawi and Zambia', *Journal of Contemporary African Studies*, 16, 2: 227–247.

Page, E.C. and Jenkins, B. (2005) *Policy Bureaucracy: governing with a cast of thousands*, Oxford: Oxford University Press.

153

Parker, C. (2002) *The Open Corporation: effective self-regulation and democracy*, Cambridge: Cambridge University Press.

Parsons, W. (2004) 'Not just steering but weaving: relevant knowledge and the craft of building policy capacity and coherence', *Australian Journal of Public Administration*, 63, 1: 43–57.

Perrow, C. (1986) *Complex Organisations: a critical essay*, New York: McGraw-Hill.

Peters, B.G. (1996) The policy capacity of government, *Research Paper No. 18, Canadian Centre for Management Development*.

Peters, B.G. (2005) 'Policy Instruments and Policy Capacity', in M. Painter and J. Pierre (eds) *Challenges to State Policy Capacity: global trends and comparative perspectives*, Basingstoke: Palgrave Macmillan.

Peters, B.G. and Pierre, J. (2006) 'Governance, Government and the State', in C. Hay, M. Lister and D. Marsh (eds) *The State: theories and issues*, New York: Palgrave Macmillan.

Peters, B.J. and Savoie, D.J. (1998) *Taking Stock: assessing public sector reform*, Montreal: McGill/Queens University Press.

Pollitt, C. (2009) 'Structural change and public service performance: international lessons?' *Public Money & Management*, 29, 5: 285–291.

Pollitt, C. and. Bouchaert. G. (2004) *Public Management Reform: a comparative analysis*. Oxford: Oxford University Press.

Pollitt, C. and Talbot, C. (2004) *Unbundled Government: a critical analysis of the global trend to agencies, quangos and contractualisation*, London: Routledge.

Pollock, A., Shaoul, J., Rowland, D. and Player, S. (2011) *Public Services and the Private Sector*, London: Catalyst.

Power, M. (1997) *The Audit Society: rituals of verification*, Oxford: Oxford University Press.

Pressman, J.L. and Wildavsky, A. (1974) *Implementation*, Berkeley, CA: University of California Press.

Pridham, G. (1994) 'National environmental policy_making in the European framework: Spain, Greece and Italy in comparison', *Regional Politics and Policy*, 4, 1: 80–101.

Putnam, R. (2000) *Bowling Alone: the collapse and revival of American community*, New York: Simon and Schuster.

Rein, M. (2006) 'Reframing Problematic Policies', in M. Moran, M. Rein and R.E. Godwin (eds) *The Oxford Handbook of Public Policy*, Oxford: Oxford University Press.

Richardson, J. and Jordan, A. (1979) *Governing Under Pressure*, Oxford: Martin Robertson.

Rosenau, J. (2004) 'Huge Demand, Over Supply: Governance in an Emerging Epoch', in I. Bache and M. Flinders (eds) *Multi-Level Governance*, Oxford: Oxford University Press.

Sachs, J. (2011) 'Our leadership is dire, but we mustn't despise government', *Guardian*,
17 December 2011

Scraggs, L. (1999) 'Institutions and environmental performance in seventeen western
democracies', *British Journal of Political Science*, 29: 1–31.

Scraggs, L. (2003) *Sustaining Abundance: environmental performance in industrial
democracies*, Cambridge: Cambridge University Press.

Shapiro, S. (2007) 'An evaluation of the Bush administrative reforms to the regulatory
process', *Presidential Studies Quarterly*, 37, 2: 270–289.

Sinclair, D. (1997) 'Self-regulation versus command and control? Beyond false
dichotomies', *Law and Policy*, 19, 4: 529–559.

Smith, B. (1985) *Decentralisation: The Territorial Dimensions of the State*, London:
Unwin.

Smith, M. (2006) 'Pluralism', in C. Hay, M. Lister and D. Marsh (eds) *The State.
Theories and Issues*, London: Palgrave Macmillan.

State Services Commission (1999) *Essential Ingredients: Improving the Quality of
Policy Advice*. Occasional Paper No. 9, Wellington.

Storey, J. (2004) *Leadership in organisations – Current Issues and Key Trends*, London:
Routledge.

Surowiecki, J. (2011) 'Dodger mania', *The New Yorker*.

't Hart, P. (2011) 'Evaluating public leadership: towards an assessment framework',
Public Money & Management, 31, 5: 323–330

't Hart, P., Tindall, K. and Brown, C. (2009) 'Crisis leadership of the Bush presidency:
advisory capacity and presidential performance in the acute stages of the 9/11 and
Katrina crises', *Presidential Studies Quarterly*, 39, 3: 473–492.

Thissen, W.A.H. and Twaalfhoven, P.G.H. (2001) 'Towards a conceptual structure for
evaluating policy analytic activities', *European Journal of Operational Research*,
219, 3: 627–649.

Thompson, H. (2010) 'The Character of the State', in C. Hay (ed.) *New Directions in
Political Science. Responding to the Challenges of an Interdependent World*,
Basingstoke: Palgrave Macmillan.

Tsebelis, G. (1995) 'Decision-making in political systems: veto players in presidentialism,
multi-cameralism and multi-partyism', *British Journal of Political Science*, 25:
289–325.

Tsebelis, G. (2003) *Veto Players*, Princeton, NJ: Princeton University Press.

UK Government (1999) *Modernising Government*, London.

Verhoest, K. and Bouckaert, G. (2005) 'Machinery of Government and Policy Capacity:
the effects of specialisation and co-ordination', in M. Painter and J. Pierre (eds)
Challenges to State Policy Capacity: global trends and comparative perspectives,
Basingstoke: Palgrave Macmillan.

Weller, P. and Stevens, B. (1998) 'Evaluating policy advice: the Australian experience',
Public Administration, 76, 3: 579–589.

Wellstead, A.M., Stedman, R.C. and Howlett, M. (2011) 'Policy analytical capacity in changing governance contexts: a structural equation model (SEM)', *Public Policy and Administration*, 26, 3: 353–373.

Wildavsky, A. (1979) *Speaking Truth to Power: the art and craft of policy analysis*, Boston, MA: Little, Brown.

Young, B. and Hazell, R. (2011) *Putting Goats Amongst the Wolves. Appointing Minsters From Outside Parliament*, UCL Constitution Unit.

Yukl, G.A. (2002) *Leadership in Organisations*, Englewood Cliffs, NJ: Prentice Hall.

Chapter 6

Inter- and intra-organizational relationships

LEARNING OBJECTIVES

■ To reflect on the traditional organizational approaches to the management of public policy and criticism thereof
■ To form an understanding of the context of inter-organizational activity
■ To identify the elements and components of effective management of partnerships

---

KEY POINTS IN THIS CHAPTER

■ How traditional conceptions of organizational bureaucracy explain leadership in public organizations
■ Why partnerships, policy communities and networks have developed a major presence in public policy and management
■ How a partnership management model is applied in a real political and policy context
■ The roles played by individuals in the quest for effective partnership working

---

INTRODUCTION

This chapter will examine the key structural forms through which public policy is delivered, within and between organizations. As discussed in Chapter 2, there is a declining reliance on single (Weberian-styled) bureaucracies and more of a focus towards governance with the increasing presence of co-governance and co-production arrangements. The chapter analyzes the rationale behind co-governance and co-production such as partnership working. This discussion is linked to the preceding analyses of policy communities and networks in Chapter 3. Chapter 6 provides a critical perspective of co-governance and co-production by exploring some of the successes and limitations of partnership working. But first we explore aspects of management and leadership in the implementation and delivery of public services, within and between state and non-state organizations.

MANAGEMENT AND IMPLEMENTATION WITHIN ORGANIZATIONS

The conventionally accepted approach is that the public sector is founded on bureaucracies, the organizational means or machinery through which policies are managed and implemented; bureaucracies are apolitical in the sense that they are staffed by professionally skilled and qualified people, subject to rational and laid-out rules and merit-based career structures. Based on the principles of efficiency and technical knowledge bureaucracies are the means of administering public organizations.

From the last two decades of the twentieth century, this conception of bureaucracy as a normative approach to the running of organizations (public and private) has been subjected to much criticism; the emphasis rather has been to depart from bureaucratic norms in the pursuit of innovation, risk taking, personal empowerment and so forth (Armbruster 2005; Du Gay 2005). The focus on implementation and management of policies through public organizations has focused more on leadership than bureaucratic structures and processes. The OECD, for example, has suggested that the public sector environment requires leadership due to:

- the growing need to address inter-connected problems in a public policy context of shared power which demands leaders pay more attention to policy coherence;
- leadership being a key component required to make the public sector a competitive employer;
- a knowledge-intensive economy and public sector, calling for a new type of leadership that inspires others to create and share knowledge;
- a continuing need for public sector organizations to adapt, which requires leadership not just among senior managers but among all public officials.

(OECD 2001)

The focus on the role of leadership in the modernization of public services has been noted in a large number of policy documents, guidance statements and institutional practices throughout government (Hartley and Allison 2000).

There are instances where this emphasis on leadership has been positioned against the traditional bureaucratic processes. In this light Weberian bureaucracy can be viewed as a barrier to delivery. From the former head of the UK Prime Minister's public service delivery unit:

> Most of all, there is the danger of underestimating the extraordinary dead-weight of institutional inertia. Senior civil servants generally recognised the need for change, but found it hard to bring about – the deadweight of the culture held them back . . . bold sustained leadership is a pre-requisite for transformation, professions left to themselves, rarely advocate more than incremental change . . .
>
> (Barber 2008 as cited in Du Gay 2011)

The tension between the political wish to implement policy and the bureaucratic organization is illustrated in Box 6.1.

There is a growing research and literature base which seeks to move beyond the traditional conception of management and implementation of policy as occurring through Weberian-style, process-driven bureaucracies and the perceived or real inadequacies of such; this in turn has led to emphasizing the leadership required to address these inadequacies in order to transform, innovate and change. Such conceptions recognize there is often a context where delivery and implementation of policy requires processes, responsibilities and accountabilities that are shared through co-production relationships and through shared contributions between politicians, officials and managers (Hartley and Allison 2000; Shoop 2004; Morrell

---

BOX 6.1 POLITICAL–BUREAUCRATIC TENSIONS

The tensions began almost as soon as Labour got into power. Some permanent secretaries departed at the earliest possible moment. Senior press officers went even more quickly. The clashes seemed to subside but in reality they just faded from public view. If anything, ministerial frustration has increased. 'We've got to kill off the idea that the civil service is some kind of Rolls Royce machine that we've been fortunate to inherit,' confides a minister who has served in two departments. The complaint is that in Whitehall everything happens slowly. 'Most civil servants,' said another minister, 'are not interested in delivery. They like to be involved in policy making, but delivery and measuring the success of the policies are seen to be lower grade activities'.

Source: Richards (2000: 21–22)

and Hartley 2006; Hartley 2011). One such approach by 't Hart (2011) suggests that a framework for analyzing how policies are implemented and managed must look at:

■ the impact – that is the value of outcomes attributed to individuals or units of responsibility, recognizing that the environment within which much public policy is managed and implemented is where there may be multiple actors influencing events and where the nature of problems may be collective;

■ the nature of support that comes from the authorising environment – which may be those in a superior position or ultimately (in a democracy) the community or members of a network. Public organizations may be in a chain of principal–agent relationships where money, resource and direction is passed down a chain;

■ trustworthiness – which is about an understanding (and respect for) the boundaries of responsibility between different groups and individuals in the policy implementation and management environment, including the limitation of action. The checks and balances which are put in place to ensure the observance of these boundaries can sometimes slow down, compromise or even gridlock implementation and management of policy.

('t Hart 2011)

MANAGEMENT AND IMPLEMENTATION THROUGH INTER-ORGANIZATIONAL PARTNERSHIP WORKING

Environment of partnership working

Governments have long been involved in inter-organizational and partnership working to manage and implement policy. In the US, from the late 1930s, housing in urban areas was provided to stimulate market activity: 'within the US, public–private co-operation has always formed the touchstone for urban development policy' (Fainstain 1994: 115). Similar partnership working between government and private companies in urban regeneration has taken place in Europe with port redevelopment in Bristol, Liverpool and Barcelona particularly notable in the scale of work undertaken (Bovaird and Tizard 2009).

However, despite this historical trajectory, the environment for partnership working intensified from the 1980s, with the 'hollowing out of the state' symbolizing a transition from state-centric government (Rhodes 1997). This thesis suggests that the unitary nation state has lost functions to supra-national bodies (i.e. bodies above the state level such as the EU), downward to strong regions (or indeed community-based or civil-society organizations) and sideways to executive agencies, arm's length bodies etc. This has been mirrored by a relative decline in unified, vertically structured bureaucratic organizations (Jessop 1994). Such fragmentation (and therefore the necessity of inter-organizational or partnership working) has been intensified by globalization and information technology developments, both of which can make remote working, independent of physical space and location, possible (Castells 1997). Consequently, the forms of public sector organizations have expanded significantly since the 1980s with appointed boards (e.g. quangos and non-departmental government bodies), multi-organizational partnerships alongside 'traditional' public sector organizations like central government departments, local authorities etc., sometimes in hybridized forms. There are arm's-length executive agencies (Pollitt *et al.* 2001; Sullivan and Skelcher 2002; Skelcher 2005), quasi-governmental hybrids (Koppell 2003). In fact, it is not exaggerating to say that partnerships have become embedded in the public sector organizational environment. Public Private Partnerships (PPPs) are written into urban policy legislation in the UK and USA, industrial policy in France, economic development policies in Italy, Netherlands and the UK, as well as in all EU structural funds programmes – in the latter case partnership being broadly defined to include public and private organizations but also social partners (Bovaird and Tizard 2009).

Policy communities and networks

Policy communities and policy networks have a longer tradition in politics and political science than partnerships and inter-organizational working as concepts and phenomena for research and study (see Chapter 3), but there are conceptual similarities and parallel concerns, since identified policy communities or networks are often involved in the implementation and management of policy. Some of the literature in this area has focused on definitional distinctions with policy communities often considered a stronger variant than networks with more coherence and permanence (Jordan and Richardson 1987; Smith 1993; Koppenjan and Klijn 2004). There is a wide variety of such networks and the typology used by Rhodes (1997) remains a useful summary of the range of networks found.

Although communities, networks and partnerships are clearly part of the public sector infrastructure, these have a negative image with a belief held that these instruments of policy and implementation carried a responsibility for failure due to the (in some cases) somewhat opaque and non-transparent nature and the dominance of strong or vested interests represented, thereby preventing policy innovations and efficient and effective delivery of public policy (Kickert *et al.* 1997).

However, such communities or inter-organizational relationships and partnerships can be seen to have many positive aspects. Such arrangements can in fact facilitate a more consultative style of government it is claimed; they can reduce policy conflict and depoliticize issues. Also, communities and partnerships can lead to a stronger continuity between policy formation and policy making on the one hand and implementation and management on the other than a top-down approach

161 ■

Table 6.1 *Typology of policy networks*

Type of network	Characteristics
Policy community/ territorial community	stability; restricted membership, usually with strong political links; vertical interdependence; limited horizontal articulation
Professional network	stability; restricted membership, vertical interdependence and limited horizontal articulation; serves profession's interests
Intergovernmental network	limited membership, usually political representation; extensive horizontal articulation, limited vertical interdependence
Producer network	fluctuating membership; limited vertical interdependence; serves producer interests
Issue network	unstable; large number of members including political representatives; limited vertical interdependence

Sources: Rhodes (1997); Loffler (2009)

that centralizes and implements policy through mono-organizational government bureaucracies and departments – there is evidence of such in areas like health and agriculture (Hill and Hupe 2009). Partnerships and inter-organizational relationships are considered appropriate in tackling 'wicked problems'. For example, with the demographics of an increasingly elderly population in Europe, care for older people will often require inter-organizational working between primary health care providers, hospitals, local authority social services departments and perhaps the voluntary or third sector (Clarke and Stewart 1997). There is also a category of wicked problems that has consequences so large that it can impact on many aspects of society and therefore demands systems working between agencies, departments, organizations and indeed individuals, for example, security threats or epidemics being the most obvious (Moran 2010).

Success and limitations of inter-organizational and partnership working

It has been claimed that partnerships and networks have an impact on the outcome and implementation of policy (Marsh and Rhodes 1992); much of this work has been criticized on the grounds that networks or partnerships may not have such an impact at all, rather the key determinant is the resource power base determined outwith the network (Dowding 1995). Empirical studies have found some link between the centralization (that is, the degree of central coordination) found in networks and partnerships and performance effectiveness, thereby claiming a relationship between centralization and effectiveness (Provan and Milward 1995).

Another range of empirical studies (many of them related to US school education) explores some factors influencing managerial choice to invest in networks and partnerships which can improve effectiveness and performance. First, in the interdependent environment both globally and within the nation state, networks and partnerships may be a means to retain some form of control over this environment. It may also enable greater decentralization in certain parts of the organization, or can lead to innovation and knowledge transfer throughout the network (Meier and O'Toole 2001; O'Toole and Meier 2003). There is also evidence, however, that partnerships and networks may benefit the most advantaged, in that agents in networks will respond to the most powerful interests (Selznick 1949; O'Toole and Meier 2004).

Any assessment of the success of inter-organizational working must be aware of institutional and other contexts. Studies of inter-organizational work between local authorities in Europe have outlined the scope and motivation for this in that it increases policy capacity across single local authority boundaries (Hulst and van Montfort 2007). Yet the actual pattern of co-operation and partnership working between authorities is relatively light in England due to their relatively large size but small policy domain, along with the concept of ultra vires, implying local government cannot easily increase its domain; conversely in a number of European countries, local authorities can take up a wide range of tasks and services but are relatively small in size and therefore are required to co-operate. For example, France, Spain and Italy have basic local authority units much smaller than the UK (Hulst and van Montfort 2012). Also, recent studies of the NHS in England indicate that despite the mandating of a managerial drive towards network and partnership forms, the actual performance of some very high-performing clinical units was rooted not in the virtues of cross boundary network operation per se but in the professional protection of organizational memory and learning shaped over a long time period (Ferlie *et al.* 2011).

It is important to assess the 'democratic performance' (i.e. accountability, answerability or sensitivity to public or citizen representation) of these inter-organizational collaborations. There are a number of studies that have attempted to do this. These have found that the levels of democratic performance are variable but usually lower than elected bodies — with multi-organizational collaborations showing widest variation (Weir and Hall 1994; Walti *et al.* 2004; Skelcher *et al.* 2005). There is a broader debate about the extent to which networks and partnerships enhance or inhibit input to policy implementation and management. First, it is argued that there is inherent tension — even incompatibility — with representative bureaucracy. This view states that the terrain becomes interactions between various stakeholders rather than accountability to the electorate or public, and that public administration becomes over-focused on managing and coordinating these networks (Sørensen 2002). Similarly, it is contended that policy management and implementation by specialists and technocrats appointed to partnership bodies is at the expense of politicians: this can be seen in some policy areas of Europe such as transport and defence (Klijn and Skelcher 2007). Second, there is a contrasting view that partnerships and networks actually enhance democratic engagement, opening up decision-making and implementation to a group wider than the narrowly defined government–institutional players (Klijn and Koppenjan 2000); this can re-engage citizens with the democratic process, and much of the co-governance and co-production discourse is couched in these terms. Third, there is a body of research indicating that in the governance, networks and partnership environments, far from these partnerships being self-governing, the hand of formal government is at play in providing policy implementation frameworks and shaping network and partnership activity – but with the democratic nexus to the citizen somewhat obscured and seen at a distance in the fog of the network (Bache 2000; Skelcher *et al.* 2005; Fenwick *et al.* 2012).

KEY ISSUES IN INTER-ORGANIZATIONAL AND PARTNERSHIP WORKING

The first issue is that partnerships may be the means by which powerful actors or stakeholders increase their influence over the policy and implementation process. Powerful (usually governmental) bodies can increase their capacity through regulating partnership activities; this power can actually be used to block action, keep items off the agenda or withhold resources (Klijn and Skelcher 2007). Second, research has shown that within partnership organizations concerned with the implementation and management of policy, the collaborative arrangements are often overlaid on existing hierarchical boundaries rather than replacing them. This can be observed in the UK (Wilson 2004); research there also shows that in some important partnerships, accountability and budget-holding responsibilities remain with the 'parent' bodies not the partnerships (e.g. McTavish and Mackie 2003). In the USA, a review of a range of federal and state statutes indicated a lack of authorization to collaborate in networks with others – as a result these agencies retained their own authority under law (Bingham 2008; McGuire and Agranoff 2011). In addition to this of course, key actors can achieve many of their goals without the formal instrument of partnership, for example, by use of grants, contractual agreements, etc.

The third issue is that perhaps more attention should be paid to the softer aspects of partnerships as vehicles for inter-organizational working to implement and manage policy. Networks and partnerships are seen by some as part of the process of non-hierarchical management, which, it is argued, is required in responding to environmental uncertainty (Koppenjan and Klijn 2004). There are also a number of authors who accentuate the intrinsic value of process: it is argued that if people believe in the intrinsic value of the collaboration process, then this gives resilience in the wake of financial and other shocks from the environment

(Rodriguez *et al.* 2007). Studies of rural and economic development in the USA (Radin *et al.* 1996; Agranoff 2005) suggest that the role network members play,

> sharing information, capturing knowledge and building partner capacities as well as programming and making policy/programme adjustments are not only less threatening to agency domain [than the attempt to change policy or seek additional funds which could easily be perceived as encroaching on the turf of these agencies] but also push the boundaries in a much gentler fashion.
>
> (McGuire and Agranoff 2011: 278)

MANAGEMENT AND LEADERSHIP OF PARTNERSHIP

Given the importance of partnerships in policy implementation, increased attention is given to their management and leadership. It is almost common sense and intuitive to state that a key premise of effective leadership and management of partnerships and collaborative activities is some minimum requirement for effective working: a broad agreement between parties on leadership; governance and accountability requirements; agreement on planning and resourcing even if not shared resourcing. Yet there are many instances of ineffective management and leadership such as the case study explored in Chapter 8.

Beyond these basics, there are two important aspects of leadership and management to be considered. First is the management of the relationships between partners. Second is supra-member management, that is, managing the environment to enable the partnership to work effectively. These elements can be respectively labelled 'game management' and 'institutional arrangements' (or 'network constitution') (see Klijn and Teismann 1997). In this perspective, the different partners' perceptions require to be aligned, areas where goals converge or diverge identified ('covenanting') and subsequent goals and actions determined ('game management'). Supra-member management involves longer-term strategies: re-constitution of a partnership may be necessary if partners cannot work together to change perceptions or activities of some partners; some partners – or excluded actors – may wish for greater involvement than current arrangements allow, so the 'rules of the game' may require modification, more/different partners involved, some given greater prominence (i.e. network constitution). This is diagrammatically illustrated in Table 6.2.

This model can also apply to the management and leadership of policy when undertaken through a variety of partners, where these actors and partners are predominantly political. This is illustrated through an analysis of the Northern Ireland peace process. Box 6.2 outlines: (a) a summary historical context statement; (b) a list of key actors; (c) a chronology of the Northern Ireland peace process; and (d) an application of the above model.

165

Table 6.2 *Key partnership management strategies*

	Perceptions	Actors	Institutional arrangements
Game management	Covenanting	Selective (de)activation	Creating/implementing the rules of the game
Network constitution (supra-member management)	Reframing perceptions	Formation of new networks	Changing the rules of the game

Sources: adapted from Klijn and Tiesman (1997); Loffler (2009)

BOX 6.2   NORTHERN IRELAND PEACE PROCESS

(a) Summary historical context

The island of Ireland from the seventeenth century was under British control. Much of the north (six of the nine counties forming what was traditionally called Ulster) was largely settled by Scottish and English Protestants. The south (twenty-six counties), though predominantly Catholic, had large areas of land owned by Anglican Protestants. In the south, which was predominantly agricultural, the issue of land ownership, tenants' rights, poverty and hardship resulting from harvest failure, lack of religious equality for Catholics formed different but interlocking strands of a struggle for home rule and (eventually) a weakening of the ties of British rule. The north, relatively prosperous, had more of an industrial and manufacturing base, with land and religious equality having less political salience there in the nineteenth and early twentieth centuries.

Various violent campaigns, increased radicalization and failed attempts to pass home rule legislation culminated in the Easter Rising in Dublin in 1916 against British rule; this lasted one week and the leaders were executed. Majority Catholic opinion in Ireland favoured independence from Britain though Protestant opinion in the north was polarized against living in a Catholic-dominated country. The 1920 Government of Ireland Act divided Ireland into two separate entities, each with some self-government; this was accepted by Ulster Protestants but rejected in favour of an independent united Ireland by the majority Catholic population, mainly in the south. There followed a period of violent war between the Irish Republican Army (IRA) and British forces leading to legislation in 1921 creating the Irish Free State (twenty-three southern counties and three in the north, which later became a completely independent country, the Irish

Republic, in 1949) and the remaining six counties in the north east continuing as part of the United Kingdom.

Northern Ireland had its own governing assembly (Stormont). The majority of the population was Protestant and the unionist party dominated; however, there was a sizeable minority of Catholics, nationalist rather than unionist in terms of political support (around 30 per cent). From the middle of the twentieth century, conflict in Ireland has been focused in Northern Ireland. From the late 1960s there was a civil rights movement which coalesced around discriminatory housing and labour market practices, either perpetuated or not addressed by the Stormont government. From the late 1960s this movement – in its organization of demonstrations and other protests – clashed with the Northern Ireland police force, the Royal Ulster Constabulary (RUC), leading to serious civil unrest, which gave the IRA some locus of attention in the nationalist Catholic communities. British troops were deployed and initially welcomed by the Catholic population; but in a fairly short period of time the British army was drawn to support the RUC against the activities of the IRA. The ensuing period has been termed 'the troubles'.

The period 1971–1975 saw a policy of internment without trial (targeted in the main at IRA members and sympathisers), which radicalized and polarized opinion in many communities; in 1972 'Bloody Sunday' saw British troops open fire on demonstrators in Londonderry, thirteen of whom were shot dead. Political responses at conflict resolution were largely unsuccessful. In 1972 the Stormont Parliament was suspended and direct rule from Westminster introduced; in 1973 a power-sharing executive, the Northern Ireland Assembly, was established. Also in 1973 the Sunningdale Agreement proposed a Council of Ireland to coordinate shared concerns between Northern Ireland and the Republic. In opposition to the agreement the Ulster Army Council – an umbrella for loyalist paramilitary groups – was formed to resist the establishment of the Council of Ireland, an act which itself was condemned by the Northern Ireland Assembly. This led to the loyalist Ulster Workers' Council strike which brought down the power-sharing assembly.

The next phase came in the early 1980s with IRA prisoner protests and hunger strikes. Bobby Sands, leader of the IRA in the Maze prison, began a hunger strike to protest against the ending of special category status (these prisoners saw themselves as prisoners of war and therefore resisted being treated as criminals). Sands died and the hunger strikers generated sympathy and cohesion within the Catholic community. At around the same time the political wing of the IRA (Sinn Fein) became more politically visible with Gerry Adams as president. There started a range of contacts, secret at first, then evolving into talks between the British government and Sinn Fein–IRA and at various times other parties. This has eventually led to a peace process, a relatively peaceful Northern Ireland (though not without its tensions) and a functioning democratically elected devolved assembly within the UK.

(b) Some key actors

The Democratic Unionist Party (DUP) initially opposed to the Good Friday Agreement and the establishment of a power-sharing, devolved assembly and executive, led by the Rev. Ian Paisley. At the first election to the Northern Ireland Assembly in 1998 the DUP came third after the Ulster Unionists (UUP) and the nationalist Social Democratic Labour Party (SDLP). By 2007 the DUP emerged as biggest party and formed a power-sharing executive with the second biggest party Sinn Fein.

The Irish Government held the view that the Irish constitution traditionally laid claim to sovereignty of all thirty-two counties of Ireland. But in 1992, the UUP opened talks for the first time with the Irish Government and in 1993 Irish (Albert Reynolds) and UK (John Major) leaders made the Downing Street Declaration, including the possibility of a united Ireland if all people, north and south wish it. In a simultaneous north– south referendum on the Good Friday Agreement in 1998, the Irish Government gave up its constitutional claim on all thirty-two counties. Irish leader Bertie Ahern was a key figure in talks preceding the Good Friday Agreement.

The Irish Republican Army (IRA) consisted of paramilitary groups in support of a united Ireland and an end to British rule in the north and was responsible for terrorist activities in Northern Ireland and mainland UK. Loyalist paramilitaries consisted of fragmented groups, with terrorist activities often targeted at Catholics and/or suspected members or sympa-thisers of the IRA, in reprisal for IRA activities. The main groups included the Ulster Volunteer Force (UVF) and Ulster Freedom Fighters (UFF).

The Patten Commission was led by Chris Patten, an ex-UK cabinet minister and the last Governor of Hong Kong; he recommended a change in the organization and functioning of policing in Northern Ireland.

The Social Democratic Labour Party (SDLP) was a traditionally moderate or 'constitutional nationalist' party, led by John Hume. The second largest party in the first elected assembly after the Good Friday agreement, by 2007 it was in fourth place behind DUP, Sinn Fein (SF) and UUP.

Sinn Fein (SF) was the political wing of the IRA and, with the emergence of leaders like Gerry Adams (president) and other leading IRA figures (e.g. Martin McGuiness) realising a violent campaign against the UK state was unwinnable, this led to the development of a political strategy complementing/eventually replacing violence.

The UK government's view was that Northern Ireland was a major security issue for UK government, involving military deployment in the 1970s and 1980s, lessening somewhat in the 1990s. Peter Brookes, the Northern Ireland secretary, initiated peace talks with Sinn Fein in 1990. On-and-off ceasefires in the 1990s, talks between UK and Irish governments under John Major and acceleration of agreement and consensus building under Tony Blair and his Irish counterpart Bertie Ahern post 1997 provided the backdrop for a meaningful peace process.

(c) Chronology of the Northern Ireland Peace Process

i   11 Jan 1988: SDLP leader John Hume meets Sinn Fein's Gerry Adams for the first time. Hume believed discussions with Adams could draw IRA towards putting down its arms, creating opportunity for talks and a peace process. Hume's strategy was to tie Adams into accepting self-determination for all including rights of unionist community.

ii 5 March 1989: Gerry Adams says he wants 'non-armed political movement to work for self-determination'.

iii 3 Nov 1989: NI Secretary Peter Brooke says IRA cannot be entirely defeated militarily and talks could follow an end to violence.

iv 9 Nov 1990: Peter Brooke's 'no selfish strategic interest' speech. Peter Brooke said Britain had no 'selfish strategic or economic interest' in Northern Ireland and would accept unification if the people wished it. 'It is not the aspiration to a sovereign, united Ireland against which we set our face, but its violent expression.'

v   14 March 1991: First round table talks, excluding Sinn Fein, begin. Although they appeared to achieve little, the Brooke/Mahew (later NI Secretary) talks were the first to have three strands: the relationships within Northern Ireland, between Northern Ireland and the republic, and between London and Dublin.

vi 1 July 1992: Ulster Unionists agree for the first time to talks with the Irish Government.

vii 28 November 1993: Secret communications between London and IRA revealed. Despite protestations to the contrary from John Major, secret contacts via intermediaries and MI5 had begun shortly after

Peter Brooke's key speeches 1989–90. London insisted the IRA had acknowledged the conflict was over but it needed help in bringing it to a close, something republicans have always denied.

viii 15 December 1993: John Major and Albert Reynolds make Downing Street Declaration. The document accepts the principle of self-determination on the basis of consensus for all the people of Ireland. Includes the possibility of a united Ireland, but Dublin accepts that unionists have a right to object – this was a key concession eventually leading to the republic removing its constitutional claim to Northern Ireland.

ix 13 October 1994: Combined Loyalist Military Command announces a ceasefire. Gusty Spence, a veteran loyalist paramilitary reads a statement: 'We are on the threshold of a new and exciting beginning, with our battles in future being political battles ... decency and democracy against the negativity of mistrust and malevolence ...'

x February 1996: The Mitchell Report sets out proposals for how to tackle decommissioning amid political talks. The International Body on Arms chaired by US senator George Mitchell concludes paramilitaries would not disarm before talks. It recommends disarmament alongside talks and confidence-building measures to help this happen.

xi September 1997: Unionists including Ian Paisley's DUP boycott talks because Sinn Fein has been admitted.

xii Northern Ireland's parties sign up to the Good Friday Agreement. DUP opposes the deal. The agreement, the first of its kind in Northern Ireland's history, establishes a power-sharing, devolved assembly and executive, new links across the Irish border and a change in relationships between London and Dublin. It also paves the way for military scale-down and police reform.

xiii 10 September 1998: Gerry Adams and UUP's David Trimble meet for the first talks between unionists and republicans in 75 years.

xiv February 1999: Disagreement between parties over arms decommissioning continues to prevent start of power sharing.

xv 9 September 1999: Patten report recommends wholesale reform on Northern Ireland policing. Patten Commission made 175 recommendations including name change, its oath, badges and symbols. Recommends complete organizational change including creation of controversial community-led policing boards. Force to be answerable to a board carefully balanced between both communities. Also demands 50–50 recruiting of Protestants and Catholics.

xvi November 1999: IRA announces it will talk to the international arms decommissioning chief. IRA announces it will start talks about arms decommissioning, provided the power-sharing executive takes office. Unionists back the deal paving the way for devolution.

xvii 29 November 1999: Assembly meets and nominates executive ministers as power sharing begins. UUP leader David Trimble becomes first minister, Seamus Mallon of SDLP his depute. SF's Martin McGuiness becomes education minister. DUP remains opposed to the deal. This all occurs on 2 December, the same day Dublin drops its claim to the northern six counties, new north–south and British–Irish bodies created.

xviii 7 June 2001: Sinn Fein and Democratic Unionists gain at general election. Throughout the political process, David Trimble finds it difficult to keep the UUP on board, the result being divisions within the UUP. Trimble's view is that his policies will lead to the IRA's demise but many unionists are sceptical. The election result is a step towards Ian Paisley's DUP becoming the dominant voice among Protestant voters.

xix 4 November 2001: Royal Ulster Constabulary becomes Police Service of Northern Ireland. Sinn Fein refuses to support the changes saying they did not go far enough. The nationalist SDLP does, however, join the policing board and recommends Catholics considering a policing career should join the force.

xx 28 January 2007: Sinn Fein members vote to support policing in Northern Ireland for the first time in the party's history.

xxi 27 March 2007: Devolved government returns to Northern Ireland. After a period of suspension, power sharing returns with Ian Paisley of the DUP 'committed to full participation in government' and Gerry Adams of Sinn Fein heralding 'a new era'.

(Adapted from: BBC News Northern Ireland Timeline
http: //news.bbc.co.uk/1/hi/northern_ireland/4072261.stm
(accessed 12 June 2012))

(d) Northern Ireland Peace Process. Key partnership activities and events

	Perceptions	Actors	Institutional Arrangements
Game management	Covenanting	Selective (de)activation	Creating/implementing the rules of the game
	i; ii; iii	v; vi; vii; xi	xiii; xiv; xvi; xvii; xx; xxi
Network constitution (supra-member management)	Reframing perceptions	Formation of new networks	Changing the rules of the game
	iv; ix	viii; x; xviii	xii; xv; xviii; xix; xx; xxi

Roman numerals refer to chronological events in (c) above.

The positioning of the chronology events within the model should not be taken to imply the Northern Ireland peace process was a sequenced, orderly series of events with a pre-determined or even likely successful outcome. Many events could have – and for periods of time did – led to a breakdown in the process. These 'partnership busters' included: October 1993, IRA bomb blew up a fish shop killing ten people in the Protestant Shankill Road; the Protestant orange order refusing to re-route marches in 1995 and at other times; IRA London docklands bomb February 1996; IRA bomb in Manchester 1996 destroying much of the city centre; various disputes over IRA decommissioning of weapons; suspension of the devolved assembly October 2002 over alleged IRA intelligence gathering; IRA accused of stealing £26m from Northern Ireland Bank in Belfast, December 2004 . . .

Another approach to management of partnerships focuses on the role of individuals and the concept of boundary spanning. Here there is an identification of the roles required to transverse the boundaries of component individuals and organizations in the partnership to ensure inter-organizational collaboration and effective connectivity within the partnership. These roles are considered to be reticulist, interpreter/communicator, coordinator, entrepreneur (Williams 2002, see Table 6.3).

The reticulist role is about the arrangement of the individual elements into a network or partnership and clearly calls for a sophisticated understanding of the partnership's objectives as well as the political and organizational context of the component parts of the network (Williams 2012). Reticulists are those who can bridge interests across the range of participant organizations (Webb 1991). They

Table 6.3 *The boundary spanning roles and associated competencies*

Role	Description	Required competencies
Reticulist	Informational intermediary; manager of relationships	Networking; political sensitivity negotiation
Interpreter/ communicator	Understand and liaise with different interests; importance of trust	Interpersonal; listening; empathising; trust building
Coordinator	Liaison; organiser	Planning; coordinating; administration
Entrepreneur	Initiator; catalyst	Innovation; whole systems thinking; lateral thinking; opportunistic

Source: adapted from Williams (2012)

are important coordinators of information flow. The literature suggests that while such people are strategically placed in an organization they are not usually located at the top of an organization but have ease of access to the top (Challis *et al.* 1988).

The interpreter/communicator role requires the interpretation and communication of interests and rationales behind partners' behaviour and actions and requires continuous time investment in building and sustaining relationships (Williams 2012). It is clear that the 'change fatigue' that may be experienced in some public sector organizations due to continued and disruptive change may make the building and sustaining of relationships challenging. A vital aspect of the interpreter/communicator is trust, which is more complex than it might appear at first: there are various conceptualizations of trust from calculative and rational models to value- or norm-based models (Lane 1998); trust, moreover – or certain conceptions of trust – can be a façade for the exercise of power (Hardy *et al.* 1998). It is also known that in partnership organizations when representatives of particular organizations change trust is difficult to maintain (Williams 2012).

The coordinator role is one which involves organization, planning and managing processes to maintain partnership working. This is a very important role and if underplayed will clearly jeopardize the likelihood of the partnership operating with any degree of efficiency or effectiveness.

As indicated earlier in the chapter, partnerships and other inter-organizational arrangements are set up in the first place because traditional ways of making and implementing policy are difficult in an environment of interdependency and wicked policy problems. It is therefore fair to assume that innovative and different approaches to policy implementation are called for; hence the importance of the entrepreneur role in boundary spanning. Literature on policy entrepreneurs (or public entrepreneurs) focuses on the importance of 'catalysts of change', being 'inventive, energetic and persistent in overcoming barriers to change' (Bryson and

173

Crosby 2005: 156); others stress the importance of a skill set held by individuals – including problem solving, whole systems thinking, risk taking, ability, tenacity and comfort with difference (Roberts and King 1996); a third approach conceptualizes the policy terrain as an arena of unpredictability that requires a conjunction of problems, policy and politics and when this conjunction leads to policy windows opening, then policy entrepreneurs are in place with actions ready to put in place – these policy entrepreneurs have 'excellent antennae, read the windows extremely well and move at the right moment' (Kingdon 1984: 192).

CONCLUSION

The traditional vehicle for public policy delivery and implementation, the bureaucratically organized government department or organization has been considered negatively by some as a barrier to implementation; rather, the focus has been on the value of adaptability, coherence across inter-connected areas, modernization and leadership. Alongside this has been the growth in inter-organizational working necessitated by an increasingly fragmented governance environment (outsourced, 'hollowed out', agencified) as well as the existence and pertinence of cross-cutting issues, all requiring policy coordination between traditional policy and organizational domains. The existence of a multitude of partners, many outwith the confines of governmental organizations, was shown to relate to earlier scholarly concerns focused on policy communities and networks. Some research on the successes and limitations of partnership working was outlined, including factors such as centralization of resourcing and decision-making, the leverage which inter-organizational collaboration can bring in an interdependent environment, the unequal positioning of governmental and non-governmental partners. Political context and democratic accountability were also factors considered. The management and leadership of partnerships were examined, with the application of a strategic model of partnership to the Northern Ireland peace process. An account of boundary spanning activity across partnerships was also outlined.

REFERENCES

Agranoff, R. (2005) 'Managing collaborative performance. Changing the boundaries of the state', *Public Performance and Management Review*, 29, 1: 18–45.

Armbruster, T. (2005) 'Bureaucracy and the Controversy between Liberal Interventionism and Non-Interventionism', in P. Du Gay (ed.) *The Values of Bureaucracy*, Oxford: Oxford University Press.

Bache, I. (2000) 'Government within governance: network steering in Yorkshire and the Humber', *Public Administration*, 78, 3: 575–592.

Barber, M. (2008) *Instruction to Deliver: Tony Blair, public services and the challenge of achieving targets*, London: Methuen.

Bingham, L.B. (2008) 'Legal Frameworks for Collaboration in Governance and Public Management', in L.B. Bingham and R. O'Leary, (eds), *Big Ideas in Collaborative Management*, New York: M.E. Sharpe.

Bovaird, T. and Loffler, E. (2009) *Public Management and Governance*, London: Routledge.

Bovaird, T. and Tizard, J. (2009) 'Partnership Working in the Public Domain', in T. Bovaird and E. Loffler, *Public Management and Governance*, London: Routledge.

Bryson, J.M. and Crosby, B.C. (2005) *Leadership for the Common Good: tackling public problems in a shared power world*, San Francisco, CA: Josey Bass.

Castells, M. (1997) *The Power and Identity*, Oxford: Blackwell.

Challis, L., Fuller, S., Henwood, M., Klein, R., Plowden, W. and Webb, A. (1988) *Joint Approaches to Social Policy*, Cambridge: Cambridge University Press.

Clarke, M. and Stewart, J. (1997) *Handling the Wicked Issues – A Challenge for Government*, University of Birmingham School of Public Policy Discussion Paper.

Currie, G., Boyett, I. and Suhomlinova, O. (2005) 'Transformational leadership within secondary schools in England – a panacea for organisational ills?' *Public Administration*, 82, 2: 265–296.

Dowding, K. (1995) 'Model or metaphor? A critical review of the policy network approach', *Political Studies* XLIII: 136–158.

Du Gay, P. (2005) 'Bureaucracy and Liberty. State, Authority and Freedom', in P. Du Gay, (ed.) *The Values of Bureaucracy*, Oxford: Oxford University Press.

Du Gay, P. (2011) 'Problems of Involvement in "Post Bureaucratic" Public Management', in S.R. Clegg, M. Harris and H. Hopfl (eds) *Managing Modernity. The End of Bureaucracy?* Oxford: Oxford University Press.

Fainstein, S. (1994) *The City Builders: politics, property and planning in London and New York*, Oxford: Basil Blackwell.

Fenwick, J., Miller, K. Johnston and McTavish, D. (2012) 'Co-governance or meta-bureaucracy: perspectives of local governance "partnerships" in England and Scotland', *Policy and Politics*, 40, 3: 405–422.

Ferlie, E., Fitzgerald, L., McGivern, G., Dopson, S. and Bennet, C. (2011) 'Public policy networks and "wicked problems": a nascent solution?' *Public Administration*, 89, 2: 307–324.

Hamel, G. (2000) *Leading the Revolution*, Boston, MA: Harvard Business School Press.

Hardy, C., Phillips, N. and Lawrence, T. (1998) 'Distinguishing Trust and Power in Inter-Organisational Relations: Forms and Facades of Trust', in C. Lane and R. Bachman (eds) *Trust Within and Between Organisations*, Oxford: Oxford University Press.

Hartley, J. (2011) 'Editorial, special issue: public leadership', *Public Money & Management*, 31, 5: 303–304.

175

Hartley, J. and Allison, M. (2000) 'The role of leadership in the modernisation and improvement of public services', *Public Money & Management*, 20, 2: 35–40.

Hill, M. and Hupe, P. (2009) *Implementing Public Policy*, London: Sage Publishing.

Hulst, R. and van Montfort, A. (eds) (2007) *Inter Municipal Co-operation in Europe*, Dordrecht: Springer.

Hulst, R. and van Montfort, A. (2012) 'Institutional features of inter-municipal cooperation: cooperative arrangements and their national contexts', *Public Policy and Administration*, 27, 2: 121–144.

Jessop, B. (1994) 'Post Fordism and the state', in A. Amin (ed.) *Post Fordism. A reader*, Oxford: Blackwell.

Jordan, A.G. and Richardson, J.J. (1987) *British Politics and the Policy Process: an arena approach*, London: Allen and Unwin.

Kickert, W.J.M. (1997) 'Public governance in the Netherlands: an alternative to Anglo-American "managerialism"', *Public Administration*, 75, 2: 731–752.

Kingdon, J.W. (1984) *Agendas, Alternatives and Public Policies*, Boston, MA: Little, Brown.

Klijn, E.H. and Koppenjan, J.F.M. (2000) 'Politicians and interactive decision-making: institutional spoilsports or playmakers', *Public Administration*, 78, 2: 365–387.

Klijn, E.H. and Skelcher, C. (2007) 'Democracy and governance networks: compatible or not?' *Public Administration*, 85, 3: 587–608.

Klijn, E.H. and Teismann, G.R. (1997) 'Strategies and Games in Networks', in W.J.M. Kickert, E.H. Klijn and J.F.M. Koopenjan (eds) *Managing Complex Networks: Strategies for the Public Sector?* London: Sage.

Koppell, J. (2003) *The Politics of Quasi Government: hybrid organisations and the dynamics of bureaucratic control*, Cambridge: Cambridge University Press.

Koppenjan, J.F.M. and Klijn, E.H. (2004) *Managing Uncertainties in Networks*, London: Routledge.

Lane, C. (1998) 'Introduction: theories and issues in the study of trust', in C. Lane and R. Bachman (eds) *Trust Within and Between Organisations*, Oxford: Oxford University Press.

Loffler, E. (2009) 'Public Governance in a Network Society' in T. Bovaird and E. Loffler (eds) *Public Management and Governance*, 2nd edition, London: Routledge

McGuire, M. and Agranoff, R. (2011) 'The limitations of public management networks', *Public Administration*, 89, 2: 265–284.

McTavish, D. and Mackie, R. (2003) 'Joint Future initiative in Scotland: development and early implementation experience of an integrated care policy', *Public Policy and Administration*, 18, 3: 39–56.

Marsh, D. and Rhodes, R. (eds) (1992) *Policy Networks in British Government*, Oxford: Oxford University Press.

Meier, K.J. and O'Toole, L.J. (2001) 'Managerial strategies and behaviour in networks: A model with evidence from US public education', *Journal of Public Administration Research and Theory*, 11, 3: 271–294.

176

Moran, M. (2010) 'Policy Making in an Interdependent World', in C. Hay, (ed.) *New Directions in Political Science*, London: Palgrave Macmillan.

Morrell, K. and Hartley, J. (2006) 'A model of political leadership', *Human Relations*, 59, 4: 483–454.

O'Toole, L. and Meier, K. (2003) 'Public management and educational performance: the impact of managerial networking', *Public Administration Review*, 63, 6: 689–699.

O'Toole, L. and Meier, K. (2004) 'Desperately seeking Selznick: co-optation and the dark side of public management in networks', *Public Management Review*, 64, 4: 681–693.

OECD (2001) *Public Sector Leadership in the Twenty-First Century*, Paris: OECD.

Pollitt, C., Bathgate, K., Caulfield, J., Smullen, A. and Talbot, C. (2001) 'Agency fever? Analysis of an international policy fashion', *Journal of Comparative Policy Analysis: Research and Practice*, 3, 3: 271–90.

Provan, K. and Milward, H. (1995) 'A preliminary theory of inter-organisational network effectiveness: a comprehensive study of four community health systems', *Administrative Science Quarterly*, 40, 1: 1–33.

Radin, B.A., Agranoff, R., Bowman, A.O.M. (1996) *New Governance for Rural Americans: creating intergovernmental partnerships*, Lawrence, KS: University Press of Kansas.

Rhodes, R.A.W. (1997) *Understanding Governance. Policy Networks, Governance, Reflexivity and Accountability*, Buckingham: Open University Press.

Richards, S. (2000) 'Why Labour ministers rage against Whitehall', *New Statesman*, 129, 4489: 21–22.

Rittel, H. and Weber, M. (1973) 'Dilemmas in a general theory of planning', *Policy Sciences*, 4, 2: 155–169.

Roberts, N.C. and King, P.J. (1996) *Transforming Public Policy: dynamics of policy entrepreneurship and innovation*, San Francisco, CA: Josey Bass.

Rodriguez, C., Langley, A., Beland, F. and Denis, J.L. (2007) 'Governance, power and mandated collaboration in an inter-organisational network', *Administration and Society*, 39, 2: 150–193.

Selznick, P. (1949) *TVA and the Grass Roots: a study of politics and organisation*, Berkeley, CA: University of California Press.

Shoop, T. (2004) 'Unheeded advice', *Government Executive*, 36, 9: 70

Skelcher, C. (2005) 'Public private partnerships and hybridity', in E. Ferlie, L.E. Lynn and C. Pollitt (eds) *Oxford Handbook of Public Management*, Oxford: Oxford University Press.

Skelcher, C., Mather, M. and Smith, M. (2005) 'The public governance of collaborative space: discourse, design and democracy', *Public Administration*, 83, 3: 573–596.

Smith, M.J. (1993) *Pressure, Power and Policy: state autonomy and policy networks in Britain and the United States*, New York: Harvester Wheatsheaf.

Sørensen, E. (2002) 'Democratic theory and network governance', *Administration Theory and Praxis*, 24, 4: 693–720.

Sullivan, H. and Skelcher, C. (2002) *Working across Boundaries: collaboration in public services*, Basingstoke: Palgrave Macmillan.

't Hart, P. (2011) 'Evaluating public leadership: towards an assessment framework', *Public Money & Management* 31, 5: 323–330.

Walti, S., Kubler, D. and Papadopoulos, Y. (2004) 'How democratic is "governance"? Lessons from Swiss drug policy', *Governance*, 17, 1: 83–113.

Webb, A. (1991) 'Co-ordination: a problem in public sector management', *Policy and Politics*, 19, 4: 229–241.

Weber, M. (1947) *The Theory of Social and Economic Organisation*, Glencoe, IL: Free Press.

Weir, S. and Hall, W. (1994) *Ego-Trip: Extra Governmental Organisations in the UK and Their Accountability*, London: Charter 88.

Williams, P. (2002) 'The competent boundary spanner', *Public Administration*, 80, 1: 103–124.

Williams, P. (2012) *Collaboration in Public Policy and Practice*, Bristol: Policy Press.

Wilson, D. (2004)' New patterns of central–local relations', in G. Stoker and D. Wilson (eds) *British Local Government into the Twenty First Century*, Basingstoke: Palgrave Macmillan.

Chapter 7

Professionals, users, consumers and markets

LEARNING OBJECTIVES

■ To be able to distinguish the features of professional, user, consumer, market led approaches to public policy and service delivery
■ To develop a conceptually grounded appreciation of the above approaches and the dynamics within contemporary approaches to policy and service delivery like co-production

KEY POINTS IN THIS CHAPTER

■ The domination of professional-led public services in the key growth period from 1940s–1980s
■ Key perspectives on professionalism and professional power in public services
■ Why and how market and other approaches have evolved
■ How users, co-producers and co-production is placed in the production and delivery of public services

INTRODUCTION

This chapter highlights the professional-led model of service delivery which accompanied the substantial growth in public sector funded services after 1945. This was underpinned by a trustee model of professional activity which has subsequently been challenged and/or modified. The chapter also tracks and critically analyzes the growth of market mechanisms in public service delivery. The various notions and concepts of 'client', 'user', 'consumer' and 'customer' are identified and assessed. Finally, co-production is defined and the important issues surrounding such initiatives outlined.

PROFESSIONALS, POLICY AND SERVICE DELIVERY

Professionals and professional power have long been considered an important analytical lens when discussing the implementation of policy and the delivery of public services (Mosher 1978; Wilding 1982; Massey 1993). Professionals have power in policy making especially in areas like health care, education and the law, but in other areas too (see Boxes 7.1, 7.2). Professionals and their representative bodies also have the power to define needs and problems (Wilding 1982).

The growth of the public sector – and in particular the growth of services labelled as welfare services (in the UK and western Europe the 'welfare state') – from the 1940s to around the 1980s has been seen as part of a 'professional society' (Perkin 1989), 'the golden age for welfare professionals' (Foster and Wilding 2000). The focus was on the recipient of public service as a client: '. . . it is widely acknowledged that the relationship between post war welfare services and their

---

BOX 7.1   BRITISH RAILWAYS 1947–1995.
CONTROLLED BY PROFESSIONALS?

Successive governments left railway policy to the managers who ran the system and saw railway modernization essentially in engineering terms that followed technically complex and prestigious 'grand projects' over more incremental and technically feasible but mundane improvements . . . the outcome can hardly have been intended by architects of post-war railway nationalization, since it neither followed an economic logic of investment in projects that concentrated in those parts of the rail system which yielded the bulk of passenger fares nor the political logic of rewarding key electorally favoured areas at the expense of economic efficiency. That engineering view of modernity which came to prevail as the default system led to a concentration of investment in longer distance inter-city lines rather than commuter lines around London that carried larger traffic volumes and on which passenger spends could have been greatly increased by technically feasible options such as investment in lighter electric trains, more station platforms . . .

Source: Margetts et al. *(2010: 155)*

---

users was one characterised by clientism' (Sullivan 1994: 118). Such a technocratic system of politics and public policy with reliance on professional experts has been widely observed in the USA, Western Europe and Australia (Mosher 1978, Sherwood 1997).

It is argued much of this reliance on professionals has been predicated on a trust model: governments set budgets at various levels, but then professionals and professional organizations are given considerable autonomy and trusted to allocate and spend resources in an accountable way, ensuring quality of provision and by and large equitable provision (Le Grand 2010). This somewhat simplistic view – set out as such to highlight an argument – can help explain continuing professional autonomy better in some public sector areas (e.g. health care) than in others (e.g. childcare or education); of course whether this 'trust' afforded to some professionals in the public sector has more to do with professional power than trust is a moot point.

The other end of the spectrum – a model of 'distrust' (ibid) – indicates professional capture of a range of public services and areas of service provision (Enthoven 2007). In this view it is believed that professionals are motivated by self-interest and not especially worthy of trust (at least without it being earned). Much public choice theory is based on the self-interest motivation of bureaucrats and professionals (Olson 1971). The varying perspectives on the role of professionals in public services are highlighted in Box 7.2.

If trust and distrust are the stereotypically polarized analytical frames underpinning the role of professionals in policy implementation and service delivery, there has been little mention of 'trusteeship'. Professionals can be viewed as holding considerable expertise and in this capacity can represent and act on behalf of their clients or service users. According to Pitkin, 'people do behave differently, reach decisions differently when they are acting on behalf of others. And we have certain expectations of someone who acts for us that we would not have if he were entirely on his own' (Pitkin 1967: 118). Aligned with this notion of trusteeship is the view that an underlying aim of public policy should be the system's capacity to help citizens develop preferences and that professional input to public policy and its implementation must retain some obligation to future citizens who will carry consequences of current decisions (Fountain 2001).

However, there can be no doubt that the professional-led model of policy and service delivery has been under stress since the 1980s. The underlying factors include the growth of managerialism and performance management occasioned by the objectives of increasing efficiency and cutting spending, accompanied by targets and league tables where performance is identified across a number of organizations within a sector. Much of this is reflected in changing ratios of professional to administrative or managerial staff – and to this extent representing a diminution (or at least a sharing) of professional control and presence, most notable in health care (in the UK's NHS) and social care sectors (Ackroyd *et al.* 2007). A range of

181

BOX 7.2   PROFESSIONALISM IN PUBLIC SERVICE

Professionalism has clear links to motivation. Sometimes the motivational point can be put in terms of vocation – that those in public service have a vocation to serve the public. In doing so they are guided by professional values which emphasise service. Professionalism also has a link to knowledge in that the administrator or the provider of service in the public sector has access to knowledge which may not be widely shared and indeed in the case of law or medicine may be esoteric. There is a need therefore to ensure that this knowledge which can be used to meet social needs e.g. in law, medicine, education, is to be used for the public good rather than primarily for private benefit.

(Plant 2003: 562).

Another of the groups I encountered in government – one that generally comprised seasoned politicians or long term civil servants – had a ready explanation for the difficulties afflicting policy implementation and reform. For them, self-interest was all. Everyone, both in and out of government (except perhaps themselves) was a knave. If a policy was failing, that was because it did not serve the self-interest of the people delivering that policy. New policies stalled and good practice did not spread, partly because they involved change: change that was uncomfortable thus violating self-interest and making it unpopular with everyone concerned. But, even more importantly change always generated losers: people both in and out of government, whose self-interest was adversely affected. Those out of government shouted at the top of their voices – often very loud ones – and regularly drowned any feeble expressions of support for the change from any gainers . . . reform was obstructed by what we might call the three Ds of policy obfuscation: delay, diversion and distraction.

(Le Grand 2010: 60)

new audit practices and bodies outwith the traditional professional, peer-controlled audit and inspection has proliferated (especially in the UK); although some of these bodies have subsequently been abolished (e.g. the Audit Commission in England), the framework is essentially in place albeit with mixed impact (Power 1997, Clarke 2009a). But any notion of policy and its implementation being an arena where the professions have been subordinated and are somewhat less privileged in the managerial environment of measurement, inspection and targets would be somewhat misleading and over simplistic. First, it has been noted that many features of the NPM (focus on outcomes, measures and use of an evidence base) have indeed been used to professionalise hitherto semi-professional occupations in areas of personal and social care and some occupations allied to health care and medicine (Noordegraaf 2007).

Second, there remains a persistence and resilience of professional power in policy and service delivery. Research has indicated that the role and power of professional control of activities and practices vary across sectors. A study across three sectors found that in health care in particular, the attempt to managerialize clinical audit has been unsuccessful, with clinicians able to impose their own definition of quality and control the use of data: 'active clinical audit represents a return to the basic professional values of self-regulation and performance review by peers' (Fitzgerald and Ferlie 2000: 735). Similar examples of professionals maintaining control are found in social care (where professions are generally less powerful than in health care), and even in housing (which contained the least powerful professional groupings) where managerial reforms were used by housing professionals to strengthen their position against other powerful professional groups like architects and surveyors (see Ackroyd et al. 2007).

Third, there is strong evidence of professionals resisting implementation of policies that threaten to change existing practices. A former UK prime minister famously said: 'You try getting change in the public services. I bear the scars on my back after two years in government.' (Blair 1999) There are numerous examples from other countries ranging from Switzerland to the Netherlands to Canada and beyond (White 1996, Friedson 2001, Emery and Giauque 2003, Duyvendak et al. 2006). However it would be misleading to characterize such 'negativity' or reluctance as symptomatic of professional exclusion from policy change and implementation. Research undertaken in the Netherlands, using the concept of policy alienation along dimensions of strategic powerlessness, tactical powerlessness, societal meaninglessness and client meaninglessness, indicates that change in willingness of implementing professionals is largely dependent on the perceived added value of the policy for society and their clients rather than their own perceived influence at strategic level. The study shows that resistance is unlikely to come because professionals lack influence in shaping policy at national or organizational levels; resistance is more likely where policies are not seen as meaningful for society or the professionals' clients (Tummers 2011).

Yet despite the persistence of professional power in the implementation and management of policy, it is a somewhat dynamic, shaky and pressurized environment where professionals operate. This is particularly so when examining the relationship between professionals and service users – in an era when (at the risk of over generalizing) there is less automatic acceptance of the view that 'professionals know best'. Research undertaken in the UK 2003–2005 indicated varying levels of readiness of service users and service professionals to challenge/be

183

challenged: health staff were ready for challenge but not as much as users were to challenge; social care staff were more ready for challenge than users were to challenge them; police staff were not ready for challenge, but users were ready to challenge (Clarke 2009b). There is also an awareness that 'users and consumers' once evoked in public services bring the possibility of unpredictability and unmanageability for professionals (Gabriel and Lang 1995). It is often at the delivery level, at the front line where the activities and behaviour of front-line staff – 'street level bureaucrats' (Lipsky 1980) – are important in determining the role and power of professionals in policy implementation. Such front line staff often inhabit a pressurized and conflicted environment:

> People often enter public employment with at least some commitment to service. Yet the very nature of this work prevents them from coming close to the ideal conception of their jobs . . . large caseloads and inadequate resources combine with uncertainties of method and the unpredictability of clients to defeat their aspirations as service workers.
>
> (Lipsky 1980: xii)

Lipsky goes on to suggest that street-level bureaucrats live in a 'corrupted world of service' and they develop techniques, conceptions of their work and clients to salvage 'service and decision-making values'. More intensification and attempts at command and control from the top increase the pressures further, for there is little control over either resources to do the job or predictability about client needs. However, within this compromised, conflicted and pressurized world of the street-level bureaucrat lie some very important issues for the implementation of public policy and the delivery of public services.

Street-level professionals are gate-keepers of many public services; they hold varying often significant degrees of discretion and deal extensively with members of the public i.e. service users. It is not overstatement to say that such professionals can have an impact on individuals' life chances and communities' enrichment. The discretion that they hold and require to undertake their job may be used in a benign manner; however, as Lipsky noted, discretion may be used that involves 'favouritism, stereotyping and routinizing'. Street-level bureaucrats' perceptions of their clients are often determined by whether these clients are deemed worthy – which may have adverse consequences for some (Maynard-Moody and Musheno 2003). Lipsky himself noted how teachers paid special attention to able pupils, which was in part motivated by a positive quest to gain professional satisfaction but also a negative tactic to avoid students with learning difficulties. In a tragic and now well-documented child protection failure in the UK ('Baby P'), several of Lipsky's coping practices at key junctures including 'rubber stamping', relying on assertions of other professionals (see Lipsky 1980: 130–131) without proper assessment of the information, had a devastating impact. In fact this particular case – and preceding

184

child protection failures in the same geographical area, which apparently had led to the introduction of robust preventive and protective and other 'control' mechanisms – highlights the importance of analyzing street-level professional activity (that is what actually happens at the front line delivery level) in the implementation of policy (Marinetto 2011).

MARKETS

As discussed in Chapter 2, the post 1945 'policy activism' in many countries and, in particular, the increased provision of public services was confronted by a sustained slowdown of economic growth triggered by the sharp rise in world oil prices after 1977. It has been estimated that compared with the previous ten-year period, 1973–1981 saw a significant reduction in the average increase of world trade from 9 to 3 per cent (Kreiger 1986). Of particular importance was the impact of this on the public sector: the expanding role of the state, especially in the 'non-market sector', was seen by some as largely responsible for economic decline (particularly in Britain) as the 'wealth consumed' by the public sector crowded out investment in the 'wealth-creating' private sector (see e.g. Bacon and Eltis 1978). A medium to long-term consequence has been the acceptance by governments of limits to its controllable size (Le Grand 1991). Allied to this, the growth of consumerism with its inevitable impact on delivery of public services (Taylor-Gooby and Lawson 1993), a non-deferential, if not suspicious, view of professionals (Clarke 2004) and a loss of legitimacy for paternalistic welfare principles (Jessop 1999), led to the paradigm for the management and implementation of policy for public service provision altering from one based on a state-centric, hierarchically controlled and professionally driven perspective to one based on users (and giving users choice), consumers and markets.

In this latter paradigm, markets are viewed positively. It is claimed they increase responsiveness to the needs of service users and improve efficiency and that new (often market-based private) providers will increase competition and drive up standards (Taylor-Gooby *et al.* 2004). The language of choice is also a proxy for individual empowerment: 'ordinary consumers are getting a taste for greater power and control in their lives' (Milburn 2007). Choice is also seen as an important aspect of the personalization of services 'as a process by which services are tailored to the needs and preferences of citizens' (Prime Ministers Strategy Unit 2007: 34).

The key intellectual framework to analyze management and implementation of public services thereby is voice, choice, exit (Hirschman 1970). For choice of service provider or professional to have force, it will require the ability of the user to exit, that is to cease engagement with the current service provider or professional. Voice refers to the ability to exert influence or effect change through making views known to existing providers either on an individual or collective basis. Although voice (which may not require an alternative provider of service) may be conceptually

185

different from choice (which does require an alternative provider), there is an assumption that choice is rather fundamental, a view that 'choice gives power to voice' (Le Grand 2006: 2).

However the extent to which the market-choice assumptions are always appropriate in the management of public services is questionable on various grounds. First, while a privileging of consumer or user is based on an assumption that they can and will use exit, in the private sector, firms often supply services to retain customers and customer satisfaction at just above the level required to prevent exit. This would not be considered appropriate – at least openly – in a wide range of public services; also in the private sector where competition does exist, firms often adopt practices to lock in customers or create exit barriers. For example, it is not always easy for customers to change banks or energy supplier. Again, this type of activity may not be acceptable in public service provision. Second, the use of voice to improve service delivery may, especially in an environment of resource constraint, lead to demands on the service exceeding supply (Fountain 2001), the result of which may lead to quite different policies and practices on the ground to those which appear in the glare of public policy announcements due to the activities of front line providers, the street-level bureaucrats:

> discretion in processing large amounts of work with inadequate resources means that street level bureaucrats must develop short cuts and simplifications to cope with the press of responsibilities. The coping mechanisms of street level bureaucrats . . . often are unsanctioned by managers of their agencies . . . lower level participants develop coping mechanisms contrary to an agency's policy but actually basic to its survival.
>
> (Lipsky 1980: 18–19)

The actual practice of voice in a customer-oriented business also raises doubts about its straightforward applicability in public service management. Generally a customer must express dissatisfaction (voice) to get improvement: a retail business may exchange a worn item if required by a customer, but those not making such requests will receive a standard level of service; yet public services have an obligation to provide services equitably (Fountain 2001). Finally, behind the choice, voice, exit framework is an assumed direct relationship between monopoly (public sector) provision and lack of drive to improve quality for the user; this bypasses much empirical research in the USA and Europe on public service motivation and the desire of public servants to serve (Fountain et al. 1993).

There are often other key aspects of a functioning market not met in the management of public services. An easy configuration of users of service, suppliers of service and user choice in most cases does not exist, and the attempts to create such are often the motivation behind policy making. In the UK, for example, in

186

social care – where the use of choice and private provision is furthest advanced with 10–15 years' development of private residential care devolved and the use of personal budgets, it is still unclear how users can make choices between predominantly private providers of residential care or between social care providers for at-home help (Greener 2008). In schools education, the picture is mixed. Since most primary schools are relatively small, most people in urban areas will have a number of schools to choose from and some (albeit crude) criteria upon which choice can be made (e.g. inspection reports, pre-selection visits, etc.). However, with secondary education where schools are larger, there is a tendency for location and catchment area to be more of a determining factor thereby circumscribing choice.

Health is also complex. In the case of the UK, there is choice via a private market (i.e. outwith the NHS) predominantly for patients receiving private facilities and quicker access. But users in this private market may find the same supplier (doctor) providing treatment privately as well as in the NHS. Conversely, in parts of the UK some professional clinical services have been contracted to private providers (e.g. some orthopaedic services and some cosmetic, reconstructive and clinical work), so NHS users may receive (within the NHS) treatment from private providers. Finally, reform in the NHS in England will see consortia of general practitioners act as the major commissioner of health care from a diversity of providers (NHS and other) making it difficult to see how users are meant to make choices in the NHS.

The more general point to be made is that the use of market and quasi-market mechanisms has been a key trajectory in service provision now for over two decades. This is highly accentuated in the UK but also evident in other European, Scandinavian and Australasian countries to a greater or lesser extent. 'User pays' approaches are also likely to continue and intensify which is clearly the approach used in US higher education and more recently in parts of the UK. It is also likely to develop and/or intensify in other service areas (see e.g. Bain 2002). But not all services will lend themselves to such approaches. For example in some services, benefits may be primarily communal in nature, where the obvious primacy of political and policy objectives results in the focus being social justice and equity rather than user benefit or choice (Van der Hart 1991; Laing 2003). This is illustrated below:

Social Benefit Dominant _____ Private Benefit Dominant

Customs and Revenue> Criminal justice> Education> Health care> Transport> Public housing

Figure 7.1
Spectrum of public services

187

USERS

The idea of giving consumers choice according to their individual needs and preferences has, as indicated, been strongly conjoined with market-based approaches to the management of public services. In the UK, Michael Young – the founder of the Consumers Association – saw organized consumers as a 'third force' in society alongside labour and capital (Gabriel and Laing 2006). Such a construction of consumerism could, it is argued, be used to combat 'consumer detriment' – defined as poor people getting fewer or poor quality goods and services than richer ones – across both public and private sectors (Caplovitz 1963; Williams 1977).

There are clearly benefits and advantages in prioritizing and focusing on the user in many areas of service delivery. Disabled people and disability advocacy groups have argued for direct cash payments to enable the individual to purchase their own support rather than directly provided services (Glasby and Littlechild 2006). An important link has also been made between individuals' ability to exercise free choice and citizenship rights, the argument being that without this autonomy, citizenship is compromised (Lister 1997). Research on frail, older people has shown that poor mental health is likely to be linked with constrained decision-making capacities rather than physical abilities (Boyle 2005). Other research on older people and younger disabled people indicates that the ability to choose is a desired outcome in terms of care delivery (Vernon and Qureshi 2000) and also important in mediating the relationship between givers and receivers of care.

There are, however, difficulties with the extensive use of user–consumer approaches to managing public service delivery. Clearly a focus on the individual, personalised approach can lead to adverse consequences – characterized at its most extreme as infinite needs and finite means to address these needs. This can be seen in areas of education through parental choice where 'in over-subscribed schools, the satisfaction of one person's choice necessarily denies that of another' (Education and Skills Select Committee 2005: 31). There are also instances of individuals' use of direct payment for domiciliary care leading to people in need being in competition with each other for the use of care assistants in scarce supply (Scourfield 2007). Such situations are likely to intensify as many governments (e.g. in the UK) move towards greater personalization of services in an era of financial constraint.

It is also the case that a user–consumer approach may not be appropriate for many who require public services: varying levels of ability, social capital, cognitive capacities, may make choice a very difficult process:

> knowledgeable, informed, active consumers may not be a reality in many cases; in a broader context this managerialization of the self, with service users taking on more responsibilities previously undertaken by the state, may be problematic. One wonders where this leaves sections of society that have neither the desire nor the ability to be entrepreneurial and who cannot be self-sufficient.
>
> (Scourfield 2007: 119)

188

In fact, research on how public service users perceive and behave towards these services shows a somewhat differentiated pattern. Clients in professionalized services (medicine and law) have generally become more active and consumer oriented, moving away from traditional service recipients (Laing *et al.* 2009); other research indicates that few who use public services see themselves as consumers but rather as patients, service users or simply members of the public (Clarke 2009c; Simmons and Birchall 2009).

There is also the possibility that the prioritizing of consumers–users in public services may raise expectations that cannot be fulfilled, leading to negative reactions. In addition, the over-emphasis on individual entitlements and rights may be socially divisive, operate against social cohesion and solidarity and undermine legitimacy in the institutions that manage and provide a wide range of public services. For example, as Needham (2003: 33) argues:

> Consumerism may be fostering privatised and resentful citizen–consumers whose expectations of government can never be met. It presents government and the state as a realm utterly detached from the individual, rather than a realm that the individual is a part of and active participant in.

Newdick (2008: 108) also argues that:

> The danger of these approaches is that they undermine a sense of solidarity and social cohesion. In the EU e.g. market citizenship may have developed to engage individuals with a personal benefit of free market values. But a policy of promoting citizen self-interest will not necessarily generate a sense of allegiance. At the national level too if consumerism comes to dominate the concept of social welfare rights, it will not be surprising if patients felt diluted concern for the institutions that provided their care, or for the welfare of their fellow citizens . . . consumer orientation directs attention away from the political context. The bright light that is made to shine upon the consumer casts a gloomy shadow upon the citizen and the broader consequences of personal choice remain undisclosed in those very same shadows. This attitude and solidarity do not go well together . . .

USERS AS CO-PRODUCERS

Co-production as a concept can be thought of as positioned somewhere between the opposite ends of a spectrum: at one end of the spectrum would be the professionally driven, producer-led notion of public services; at the other a consumer-, customer- and choice-based perspective. Co-production has been defined as 'the involvement of citizens, clients, consumers, volunteers and/or community organizations in producing public services as well as consuming or otherwise benefiting from them' (Alford 1998).

189

Co-production can be defined from the very basic minimalist activities of individuals in service delivery, such as recycling household waste, completion of tax returns, the taking of medicine prescribed by a medical practitioner or some forms of neighbourhood or community involvement; to the more sophisticated maximalist approaches involving the complementing, supplementing or replacing professionals' activities. A maximalist definition of co-production has been offered: 'Co-production means delivering services in an equal and reciprocal relationship between professionals, people using services, their families and their neighbours. Where activities are co-produced in this way, both services and neighbourhoods become far more effective agents of change' (Boyle 2009).

Co-production can take place at the 'softer' but nonetheless important end of service delivery including public involvement in formulating strategies, community appraisals, designing and monitoring of services. Implicit in the UK's Best Value quality inspection and improvement framework is the requirement for option appraisal and public consultation. Co-produced initiatives also take place in the operational delivery of services in areas ranging from criminal justice to health care (see Box 7.3); in some instances these are transformational in terms of relationships between professionals and service users.

BOX 7.3 SOME CO-PRODUCTION INITIATIVES

Case A

Co-production approaches are emerging in the UK in both the public and voluntary sectors, even in the justice system. Preston in Lancashire has been developing a UK youth jury approach. In 2009, the NACRO Centre for Restorative Justice /Preston Peer Panels won the justice team award for tackling youth crime. The project started in September 2007 and already more than 80 cases have been successfully concluded, affecting some 250 victims. The team has now extended the project within the Street Law programme which offers training to young people as a part of their contract, allowing them to become peer panel members and addressing areas of concern in their own lives. Adult versions of this approach are also beginning in the UK with the Community Justice Panel in Chard.

Source: Boyle and Harris, NESTA, 2009: 13

Case B

Co-production ranges across programmes that are aimed specifically at prevention, such as the Nurse–Family Partnerships, which support first

---

time mothers and children in low income families by partnering them with registered nurses until the child is two, with a core purpose of coaching them into a sense of capacity and encouraging them to support each other. Co-production also includes programmes that give responsibility back to service users, like KeyRing, which supports people with learning difficulties to live in their own homes by embedding them in mutually supportive local networks.

Sources: Boyle and Harris, NESTA, 2009: 13–14; www.nursefamilypartnership.org; www.keyring.org (accessed 19 June 2012)

Case C

The Expert Patient Scheme, where patients with long term health conditions teach others about the experience, has so far involved 50,000 people. [There are] also programmes to provide for mutual support such as the Shared Lives scheme that pair up disabled people and those with long term problems with families. Shared Lives has done this now for 30 years in 130 schemes across the UK, in such a way that caring becomes a joint activity between the people and the families they live with.

Sources: Boyle and Harris, NESTA, 2009: 14; www.expertpatient.org (accessed 20 June 2012)

Case D

Co-production is about mobilizing the huge untapped resources that people represent, in and around schools or surgeries, but also prisons, probation centres, housing estates and social work. What they all have in common is this shift in attitude to the users of service. This is how Dr Abby Letcher describes the impact on mainstream practices that the Community Exchange had on her own health centre outside Philadelphia:

> It is a fairly radical change, and it does challenge people's ethical and professional sense. But it has transformed the way we practice medicine. It has stopped us seeing our patients in terms of us and them, as if we were just service providers to people who are classed as 'needy'. We are no longer looking at them as bundles of need, but recognising that they can contribute, and when you see people light up when you ask them to do so, it changes your relationship with them. The culture has changed. The relationships are different, deeper and more therapeutic than they are in the usual doctor's office.
>
> *Source: Boyle and Harris, NESTA, 2009: 14–15*

The potential benefits of co-production appear to be significant in terms of improving trust and co-operation between professionals and users, significantly improving outcomes and increasing social capital. According to Leadbeater, these benefits include:

> more personalised solutions, in which the user takes responsibility for providing part of the service, should enable society to create better collective solutions with a less coercive intrusive state, a lower tax burden, a more responsible and engaged citizenry and stronger capacity within civil society to find and devise solutions to problems without intervention.
>
> (Leadbeater 2004: 88).

There also appear to be benefits in terms of cost reduction. For example the Expert Patient programme (Box 7.3) indicated reduced visits to GPs and A&E by 7 and 16 per cent respectively, resulting in substantial cost savings (Boyle and Harris 2009: 20). However, such headline figures may tempt hard-pressed public services to shunt costs indiscriminately from current arrangements to users themselves via co-production initiatives in cases where this would not be appropriate. Co-production arguably gives greater prominence to the front line professionals – street-level bureaucrats – whose behaviour is shaped by organizational constraints, pressures and resulting coping mechanisms; it is argued that this can encourage a lack of sympathy with interests of service users (Ellis 2007); others, however, have argued that in an environment of governance, street-level bureaucrats are as likely to be 'policy entrepreneurs', navigating their way around complex governance and partnership structures in the interests of their clients (Goss 2001; Durose 2011).

CONCLUSION

The professional 'producer' led approach to the implementation of key aspects of public policy (i.e. the growth of public and welfare services) was premised on a notion of professional trust: professionals were given considerable discretion over delivery of services but also over key resourcing decisions. This model has been pressurized since the 1980s, though professional power – right down to 'street level' – is still of importance. The producer dominant view of public services has been challenged over the last thirty or so years, with the use of markets, consumerism and user focus considered appropriate in an environment where spending and fiscal pressure has led to questions about the limits of state growth, and socio-cultural changes have expanded citizen and customer expectations. The universal appropriateness of consumer and market accentuated approaches was seen to be questionable. Co-production, where services are jointly designed, produced and used, was seen to have various dimensions. Co-production claims benefits in terms of service outcomes and social capital formation and may even enhance or intensify the role of front-line professionals; however, given that the protagonists of co-production claim cost benefits, there is also a danger of such initiatives being used primarily to shunt cost from the public sector, with only secondary consideration given to other benefits.

REFERENCES

Ackroyd, S., Kirkpatrick, I. and Walker, R.M. (2007) 'Public management reform in the UK and its consequences for professional organisations: a comparative analysis', *Public Administration*, 85, 1: 9–26.

Alford, J. (1998) 'A public management road less travelled: clients as co-producers of public services', *Australian Journal of Public Administration*, 57, 4: 128–137.

Bacon, R. and Eltis, W. (1978) *Britain's Economic Problem: too few producers*, London: MacMillan.

Bain, G. (2002) *The Future of the Fire Service: reducing risk saving lives*, Report of the Independent Review of the Fire Service, London: HMSO.

Blair, T. (1999) Speech to the British Venture Capitalists Association, London.

Boyle, D. and Harris, M. (2009) *The Challenges of Co-production. How Equal Partnership Between Professionals and the Public are Crucial to Improving Public Services*, London: NESTA and New Economics Foundation.

Boyle, G. (2005) 'The role of autonomy in explaining mental ill health and depression among older people in long term care settings', *Ageing and Society*, 25, 5: 731–748.

Caplovitz, D. (1963) *The Poor Pay More*, New York: The Free Press of Glencoe.

Clarke, J. (2004) *Changing Welfare, Changing Welfare States*, London: Sage.

Clarke, J. (2009a) 'Scrutiny, Inspection and Audit in the Public Sector', in T. Bovaird and E. Loffler (eds) *Public Management and Governance*, London: Routledge.

Clarke, J. (2009b) Beyond citizens and consumers? Politics and public service reform, *Journal of Public Administration and Policy*, 2,2: 33–44.

Clarke, J. (2009c) 'The People's Police? Citizens, Consumers and Communities', in R. Simmons, M. Powell and I. Greener (eds) *The consumer in public services: choice, values and difference*, Bristol: Policy Press.

Durose, C. (2011) 'Revisiting Lipsky: front line work in UK local governance', *Political Studies*, 59, 4: 978–995.

Duyvendak, J.W., Knijn, T. and Kremer, M. (eds) (2006) *Policy, People and the New Professional: de-professionalization and the new professionalism in care and welfare*, Amsterdam: Amsterdam University Press.

Education and Skills Select Committee (2005) *Secondary Education*, London: HMSO.

193

Ellis, K. (2007) 'Direct payments and social work practice: the significance of "street level bureaucracy" in determining eligibility', *British Journal of Social Work*, 37, 3: 405–422.

Emery, Y. and Giauque, D. (2003) 'Emergence of contradictory injunctions in Swiss NPM projects', *International Journal of Public Sector Management*, 16, 6: 468–481.

Enthoven, A. (2007) 'Afterword: An American Perspective', in J. Le Grand, (ed.) *The Other Invisible Hand: delivering public services through choice and competition*, Princeton, NJ: Princeton University Press.

Fitzgerald, L. and Ferlie, E. (2000) 'Professionals: back to the future', *Human Relations*, 53, 5: 713–739.

Foster, P. and Wilding, P. (2000) 'Whither welfare professionalism?' *Social Policy and Administration*, 34, 2: 143–159.

Fountain, J. (2001) 'Paradoxes of public sector customer service', *Governance*, 14, 1: 55–73.

Fountain, J., Kaboolian, L. and Kelman, S. (1993) *Service to the Citizen: the use of 800 numbers in government, in customer service excellence: using information technologies to improve service delivery in government*, Cambridge, MA: John F. Kennedy School of Government.

Friedson, E. (2001) *Professionalism: the third logic*, Cambridge: Cambridge University Press.

Gabriel, Y. and Lang, T. (1995) *The Unmanageable Consumer*, London: Sage.

Gabriel, Y. and Lang, T. (2006) *The Unmanageable Consumer*, 2nd edition, London: Sage.

Glasby, J. and Littlechild, R. (2006) 'An Overview of the Implementation and Development of Direct Payments', in J. Leece and J. Burnet, (eds) *Developments in Direct Payments*, Bristol: The Policy Press.

Goss, S. (2001) *Making Local Governance Work: networks, relationships and the management of change*, Basingstoke: Palgrave Macmillan.

Greener, I. (2008) 'Markets in the public sector: when do they work and what to do when they don't?' *Policy and Politics*, 36, 1: 93–108.

Hirschman, A.O. (1970) *Exit, voice and loyalty: responses to decline in firms, organisations and states*, Cambridge, MA: Harvard University Press

Jessop, R. (1999) 'The changing governance of welfare: recent trends in its primary functions, scale and mode of co-ordination', *Social Policy and Administration*, 33, 4: 348–359.

Kreiger, J. (1986) *Reagan, Thatcher and the Politics of Decline*, Cambridge: Polity Press.

Laing, A. (2003) 'Marketing in the public sector: towards a typology of public services', *Marketing Theory*, 3, 4: 427–445.

Laing, A., Hogg, G., Newholm, T. and Keeling, D. (2009) 'Differentiating Consumers in Professional Services: Information Empowerment and the Emergence of the

Fragmented Consumer', in R. Simmons, M. Powell and I. Greener (eds) *The Consumer in Public Services: choice, values and difference*, Bristol: Policy Press.

Leadbeater, C. (2004) *Personalisation Through Participation: a new script for public services*, London: Demos.

Le Grand, J. (1991) 'The theory of government failure', *British Journal of Political Science*, 21, 4: 423–442.

Le Grand, J. (2006) 'Choice and competition in public services', *Research in Public Policy*, Summer: 2.

Le Grand, J. (2010) 'Knights and knaves return: public service motivation and the delivery of public services', *International Public Management Journal*, 13, 1: 56–71.

Lipsky, M. (1980) *Street Level Bureaucracy: dilemmas of individuals in public services*, New York: Russell Sage Foundation.

Lister, R. (1997) *Citizenship: feminist perspectives*, Basingstoke: MacMillan.

Margetts, H., 6, P., Hood, C. (eds) (2010) *Paradoxes of Modernisation*, Oxford: Oxford University Press.

Marinetto, M. (2011) 'A Lipskian analysis of child protection failures from Victoria Climbié to "Baby P"', *Public Administration*, 89, 3: 1164–1181.

Massey, A. (1993) *Managing the Public Sector: a comparative analysis of the United Kingdom and United States*, Aldershot: Edward Elgar.

Maynard-Moody, S. and Musheno, M. (2003) *Cops, Teachers, Counsellors: stories from the front line of public services*, Ann Arbor, MI: University of Michigan Press.

Milburn, A. (2007) *A 2020 Vision for Public Services*, speech at London School of Economics, May 2007.

Mosher, F. (1978) 'Professions in public service', *Public Administration Review*, March–April: 144–150.

Needham, C. (2003) *Citizens and Consumers: New Labour's market place democracy*, London: Catalyst.

Newdick, C. (2008) 'Preserving social citizenship in health care markets: there may be trouble ahead', *McGill Journal of Law and Health*, 2: 94–108.

Noordegraaf, M. (2007) 'From "pure" to "hybrid" professionalism: present day professionalism in ambiguous public domains', *Administration and Society*, 39, 6: 761–785.

Olson, M. (1971) *The Logic of Collective Action*, New York: Shocken Books.

Perkin, H. (1989) *The Rise of Professional Society*, London: Routledge.

Pitkin, H. (1967) *The Concept of Representation*, Berkeley, CA: University of California Press.

Plant, R. (2003) 'A public service ethic and political accountability', *Parliamentary Affairs*, 56: 562.

Power, M. (1997) *The Audit Society. Rituals of Verification*, Oxford: Oxford University Press.

195

Prime Minister's Strategy Unit (2007) *Building on Progress: public service policy review,* London: HMSO.

Scourfield, P. (2007) 'Social care and the modern citizen: client, consumer, service user, manager and entrepreneur', *British Journal of Social Work,* 37, 1: 107–122.

Sherwood, F. (1997) 'Responding to the decline in public sector professionalism', *Public Administration Review,* 57, 3: 211–217.

Simmons, R. and Birchall, J. (2009) 'The Public Service Consumer as Member', in R. Simmons, M. Powell and I. Greener (eds) *The Consumer in Public Services: choice, values and difference,* Bristol: Policy Press.

Sullivan, M. (1994) *Modern Social Policy,* Hemel Hempstead: Harvester Wheatsheaf.

Taylor-Gooby, P. and Lawson, R. (eds) (1993) *Markets and Managers,* Buckingham: Open University Press.

Taylor-Gooby, P., Larsen, T. and Kananen, J. (2004) 'Market means and welfare ends: the UK welfare state experiment', *Journal of Social Policy,* 33, 4: 53–92.

Tummers, L. (2011) 'Exploring the willingness of public professionals to implement new policies: a policy alienation framework', *International Review of Administrative Sciences,* 77, 3: 555–581.

Van der Hart, H.W.C. (1991) 'Government organisations and their customers in the Netherlands: strategy, tactics and operations', *European Journal of Marketing,* 24, 7: 31–42.

Vernon, A. and Qureshi, H. (2000) 'Community care and independence: self-sufficiency or empowerment?' *Critical Social Policy,* 20, 2: 255–276.

White, D. (1996) 'A balancing act: mental health policy making in Quebec', *International Journal of Law and Psychiatry,* 19, 3–4: 289–307.

Wilding, P. (1982) *Professional Power and Social Welfare,* London: Routledge and Kegan Paul.

Williams, F. (ed.) (1977) *Why the Poor Pay More,* London: Macmillan.

Chapter 8

Case study: partnerships and practices

LEARNING OBJECTIVES

■ To delineate difficulties and challenges of working across traditional local government and health boundaries as evidenced in the case
■ To be able to apply interrelated policy cycles (Figure 1.5) to the policy process outlined in the case i.e. partnership working in Community Health Partnerships

KEY POINTS IN THIS CHAPTER

■ The broad policy aims being addressed through Community Health Partnerships
■ An outline of the different types of relationship observed in the partnership
■ A range of issues in cross sectoral, organizational, professional and other boundaries are highlighted in the case

INTRODUCTION

Chapter 7 indicated in some detail the differences in managing service delivery when viewed through the policy prisms of users, consumers and markets. Although some of these terms are coupled and/or interchangeable, the 'traditional' professional or producer-led view has seen public services as those run dominantly by professionals who control resources, define and deliver the needs and requirements of users, that is 'patients', 'pupils' and their parents, 'students', 'residents' etc. Perceived or real inefficiencies, insensitivities to individual needs, a greater focus on differentiated requirements of public service users and of course stress on public financing have led to an accentuation of market mechanisms, choice of provider and consumerist approaches to significant swathes of public service management. Individual citizen engagement with this has also been described in Chapter 7, ranging from passive (as recipients of service determined and provided by others), to the chooser/consumer, through to active involvement in the co-production of services. A broader categorization of engagement can be employed: 'adversarial', through community and collective action for desired ends; electoral and legislative approaches through political parties or issue-related activity; deliberative engagement and dialogue to achieve social or community consensus (see Cooper *et al.* 2006). As also noted previously, partnerships and networks are often intended to bring coordination to public service delivery.

A constant theme in the literature and research is the extent to which partnership and networks arrangements are emergent, self-organizing (Rhodes 1997; Bardach 2001) or top-down with budgets, targets or other control mechanisms in place (Osborne and Plastrik 2000). The resulting relationships within a partnership can be considered as a taxonomy:

Table 8.1 *Taxonomy of types of relationships*

Category	Type of relationship	Definition
Coordination	Dialogue	Strategy development
	Joint planning	Information exchange
Integration	Joint working	Collaboration
	Joint venture	Some joint working and planning
Increased closeness and mutual involvement	Strategic alliance	Long-term joint planning
	Union	Formal administrative unification
	Merger	Creation of new structure with a single new identity

Source: adapted from 6 (2004)

Partnerships: some reflections

An issue of some relevance to the case study is partnership and network operation across professional boundaries (see Chapter 7). Such partnerships, in relation to healthcare, have been defined as: 'A grouping of individuals, organizations and agencies organized on a non-hierarchical basis around common issues and concerns' (World Health Organization 1998); and as: 'Linked groups of health professionals and organizations working in a coordinated way that is not constrained by existing organizational or professional boundaries to ensure equitable provision of high quality clinical care' (Baker and Lorimer 2000).

However – and of pertinence to the case – research on Community Health Partnerships,

> revealed a strong professional identity in the health and social care context and showed that it is an issue that individuals held and continue to hold dear to their heart and would defend if under threat. The partnership vision, in contrast, lacked clarity, although there was a broad understanding of the potential of partnership to effectively improve health and wellbeing. Therefore under these circumstances individuals' sense of occupation has been heightened due to perceived attempts to erode their professional identity and modifications to their sense of 'self' have not been challenged by a strong partnership ethos. In some circumstances, individuals may seek to maintain professional boundaries and thus jeopardise full integration of services.
>
> (Pate *et al.* 2010: 211)

A range of other issues should also be considered: first, working in partnership or collaboration across sectoral, organizational or other boundaries. While much has been (justifiably) written about the rigidities of traditional boundary (sometimes referred to as 'silo') working, these boundaries may exist for good reasons – organizational division of labour, professional training development and regulation. Second, performance regimes are usually equipped to handle vertical organization management and coordination (Christensen and Laegreid 2007), but there is often a contemporary focus on a common ethic or cohesive culture with public agencies, especially those in partnership arrangements, attempting to create a single distinctive ethos (Shergold 2005). Finally, with particular relevance to the case, the evaluation of networks and partnerships should be considered. The traditionally accepted evaluative framework of Provan and Milward (2001) examines this at various levels including the community/individual level, the partnership itself and the organizational participants. At the most basic individual/community level, evaluation should be based on the extent to which individuals' and communities' needs are met in terms of outputs and outcomes and the sense in which these needs would not have been met without the partnership's existence. At the network or partnership level, the evaluation is about the sustainability of the partnership: indicators like stability in terms of partnership members, range of services provided, how the partners work together and the efficiency and effectiveness of administrative and managerial structures. At the organization participant level, evaluation will assess the extent to which participant organizations' interests are met in terms of cost, accessing resources and gaining credibility and legitimacy in the broader partnership. A fourth evaluative criterion could be added: partnerships are rarely

199 ◼

democratically elected bodies, though constituent participants may be; hence the 'democratic performance' of the partnership is worth evaluation.

CASE STUDY: COMMUNITY HEALTH PARTNERSHIPS (CHPs)

The following is an extract from the Auditor General for Scotland's Review of Community Health Partnerships (Audit Scotland 2011):

> There have been a number of approaches to improve joint working between health and social care and a focus on partnership working across the public sector as a whole since devolution [in 1999]. However, the different attempts have had varied success. Approaches to partnership working have often been incremental which has led to the current position where there is a complex and uncoordinated set of partnership arrangements across Scotland. In 1999, GP-led Local Health Care Cooperatives (LHCCs) were established across Scotland to bring health and social care practitioners together to deliver services. LHCCs were still in place when the Scottish Executive introduced the Joint Future Agenda in 2000. This encouraged a more formal approach to joint planning and resourcing between health and social care. In 2001, the Scottish Executive set up a Joint Future Unit (JFU) to support local NHS board and council partnerships to progress joint working. The JFU provided detailed guidance and tailored support to local partnerships to establish governance and operational arrangements for the joint management and resourcing of services. By 2003, each council area had its own Joint Future Partnership Group which was responsible for the oversight of joining up health and social care services for their local population.
>
> The Scottish Executive used the Local Government in Scotland Act 2003 to establish community planning on a statutory basis. The role of community planning is to bring together public sector and other organizations to develop a coordinated approach to identifying and solving local problems, improving services and sharing resources. Community Planning Partnerships (CPPs) were established as the key over-arching partnership and were expected to help coordinate other initiatives and partnerships and, where necessary, rationalize these. CPPs are not statutory bodies.
>
> Councils have a statutory duty to coordinate community planning in their areas and report annually on overall progress in improving services and outcomes for local people. NHS boards and a number of other public sector bodies have a statutory duty to participate in community planning and provide information to the council on their contribution to enable the council to prepare its annual Single Outcome Agreement (SOA) report. In 2008, Scottish ministers gave CPPs the lead role in tackling health inequalities. An important

200

part of community planning is to engage with local communities so they can contribute to how services are planned and to support them to contribute to their own well-being. This is also an important feature of health policy in Scotland.

Around the same time that community planning was introduced on a statutory basis, major changes in the NHS were also being planned separately under the NHS Reform (Scotland) Act 2004. Since 2000, the NHS has been moving towards integrated management of acute and primary care services. The 2004 Act abolished separate acute and primary care trusts and NHS boards were required to manage both primary and acute health services under a single system. As part of the Act, the Scottish Executive also introduced CHPs as committees or subcommittees of NHS boards. CHPs replaced the previous LHCCs and were to bridge the gap between primary and secondary healthcare, and between health and social care. CHPs were also expected to coordinate the planning and provision of primary and community health services in their area. There are a number of key legislation and policy developments that have been instrumental in supporting partnership working in the public sector and, more specifically, joined-up working between health and social care in Scotland. The 2004 statutory guidance set CHPs a challenging agenda. The guidance required them to focus on nine broad priorities to move care from hospital settings to communities where appropriate, and for the integration of health and social care.

Since CHPs have been in place, community planning and, more specifically, health and social care policy, have continued to develop and the expectations of what CHPs should do have become wider and more complex. However, the Scottish Government has not updated the 2004 statutory guidance for CHPs to reflect these changes although it has committed to do this after we publish our report. The role and responsibilities of each of the CHPs in Scotland vary and in many areas they have evolved in response to changes in policy, the economic climate and other local circumstances.

Governance arrangements for joint working are generally weak. Guidance on good governance for joint services recommends putting in place formal partnership agreements which detail joint financial and other resource arrangements. However, we found that NHS boards and councils do not always have agreements in place covering services which the council has delegated to the CHP. Where agreements are in place, these do not always cover all financial and other joint resourcing arrangements between partners. This is a potential risk to NHS boards and councils in case of dispute at a later date or in the event of relationships deteriorating.

Governance arrangements for integrated CHPs vary but are generally more complex because they need to take account of different lines of accountability and the existing corporate governance arrangements of both partners. There are increased risks that there is a lack of transparency in how decisions are taken, people are making decisions out with their levels of delegated authority and that decision-making is slow.

Internal auditors carried out a review of financial management and budgetary control and a review of procurement at the previous Glasgow City integrated CHPs. Internal auditors also reviewed the governance arrangements for Western Isles integrated CHP. In all cases, auditors found weaknesses in joint governance arrangements such as a lack of clarity on financial management processes including budgetary control, and evidence of decisions being taken out with the authority of the integrated CHPs. NHS Western Isles has since reported that work is under way to address the issues identified in the internal audit report. However, NHS Greater Glasgow and Clyde disagreed with the findings of its internal auditors. NHS board and council partners in some areas cited the complexity and risks in relation to integrated structures as key factors in their decision to set up a health-only CHP. NHS Greater Glasgow and Clyde had a vision of developing integrated CHP arrangements with its council partners in each area. Glasgow City Council was one of the first councils to sign up to the approach and together the board and the council set up five integrated CHPs within Glasgow. However, problems from the outset have led to the dissolution of the integrated arrangements.

In 2009/10, £13 billion in total was spent on health and social work but CHPs have little influence over how this is used. Scottish public sector spending on health and social work increased in real terms from £11 billion in 2005/06 to £13 billion in 2009/10, accounting for approximately 37 per cent of the total Scottish Government budget in 2009/10. The NHS in Scotland spent a total of £10 billion in 2009/10, which is equivalent to £1,873 per head of population but this varied across the country from £1,541 in NHS Forth Valley to £2,602 in NHS Western Isles. Only a relatively small part of this total NHS budget is devolved to CHPs.

Social work expenditure in Scotland was around £3 billion in 2009/10, which is equivalent to £544 per head of population but this varied significantly among councils. Older people's services accounted for 45 per cent of Scotland's social work expenditure (£1.3 billion). CHPs have limited responsibility for managing social care budgets. The amount of NHS money that CHPs manage is increasing each year. In 2009/10, CHPs managed approximately £2.9 billion of NHS expenditure compared to approximately £875 million in 2005/06. This is not a complete picture because a number of CHPs were unable to provide details of their overall NHS budgets or expenditure for one or more years since 2005/06. In 2009/10, 18 CHPs reported overspends against their NHS budgets compared to 12 in 2008/09. At the time of our fieldwork, 11 CHPs projected an overspend on their 2010/11 NHS devolved budget. This indicates pressure on NHS budgets devolved to CHPs or weaknesses in financial control. Few councils have delegated responsibility for social care services to CHPs.

There is significant variation in councils' approaches to delegating social care services and budgets to CHPs. Although there were 11 integrated CHPs, only East Renfrewshire's integrated CHP had full delegated responsibility from the council for all social care services and budgets in 2009/10. A number of other councils delegated specific social care services to a further 21 CHPs in 2009/10 but only 14 of these CHPs had the delegated budget responsibility for the services. This means that seven CHPs were responsible for the day-to-day service provision of council social care services but councils retained control over service budgets. Of those CHPs with delegated budget responsibility for services and which provided information on budgets and actual expenditure in 2009/10, only one CHP reported a minor budget overspend.

There are some significant, long-standing and complex issues in Scotland which no partner can tackle on its own and which need action across the whole system. CHPs are not always able to demonstrate their specific contribution to improving the health of local people or shifting the balance of care to community settings. However, we looked at their performance against a range of indicators to which we would expect CHPs to contribute through changes to services, for example, long-term conditions and services for older people.

Progress in moving services from hospital to the community and joining up frontline health and social care services is slow despite this being a key Scottish Government priority since 2000 and significant support and investment being made to drive this forward. CHPs were expected to contribute significantly to the 'shifting the balance of care' agenda. The Shifting the Balance of Care Improvement Framework was introduced in 2009. It identifies eight broad areas for work that will support progress in this area; and 48 impact changes for monitoring improvement. However, the framework has limitations; for example, some work areas and impact measures are intangible, such as 'enhancing carers' capacity'. Others give a misleading picture of the direction of travel if considered in isolation; for example, improved care in the community could result in the average inpatient bed days increasing because only patients with severe illness reach hospital.

All CHPs have worked with NHS boards, councils and other health and social care providers to set up local initiatives focused on supporting older people and those with long-term conditions such as COPD, asthma, diabetes and angina. There is no evidence of a significant shift in the balance of care, although this may be because of a lack of information on community activity and data systems not keeping up with changes in the way that services are delivered. But there is evidence of learning through piloting different approaches and, where these have been successful, rolling the approach out to a larger number of people. Similarly, there is evidence of CHPs learning from different approaches in other areas, both in Scotland and other parts of the UK.

(Adapted and abridged from Review of Community Health
Partnerships (2011), Audit Scotland)

SCOTTISH GOVERNMENT RESPONSE TO THE REVIEW

The Health Secretary today set out the Scottish Government's plan to integrate adult health and social care. The move aims to improve the quality and consistency of care and put an end to the 'cost shunting' between the NHS and local authorities . . . [the Minister] confirmed the government had decided not to create a new statutory organization separate from the NHS and local authorities which could create further barriers to integration. Instead legislation will be introduced to Parliament and will herald a radical reform of Community Health Partnerships. Key elements of the system will be:

Community Health Partnerships will be replaced by Health and Social Care Partnerships which will be the joint responsibility of the NHS and local authority, and will work in partnership with the third and independent sectors.

Partnerships will be accountable to Ministers, leaders of local authorities and the public for delivering new nationally agreed outcomes . . . these will include measures such as reducing delayed discharges, reducing unplanned admissions to hospitals and increasing the number of older people who live in their own home rather than a care home or hospital.

NHS Boards and local authorities will be required to produce integrated budgets – to bring to an end the 'cost shunting' that currently exists.

A smaller proportion of resources will be directed towards institutional care and more invested in community provision.

(Source: Scottish Government News Release Integration of Health
Care, 12/12/2011 (www.scotland.gov.uk/news /releases/
2011/12/12111418 (accessed 19 July 2012))

Some statements on the response:

[These measures] lay the foundation for an integrated approach by local authorities and health boards. The measures will be set in legislation, will require the reformed community health partnerships under a single accountable officer to use integrated budgets to deliver specified outcomes. The accountable minister will be the cabinet secretary for health, wellbeing and cities. (Chair of the expert group on future options for social care, Sir John Arbuthnott)

(Scottish Government 2011 Supportive quotes for integration of
adult health and social care. www.scotland.gov.uk/resources/
dec/924/0123935.pdf (accessed 21 July 2012))

I welcome the cabinet secretary's strong focus on improving outcomes, her commitment to dealing with aspects of the current system that need improvement and the emphasis placed on the importance of clinical and professional leadership.

> (Scotland's chief medical officer, Sir Harry Burns. Scottish Government 2011 Supportive quotes for integration of adult health and social care. www.scotland.gov.uk/resources/dec/ 924/0123935.pdf (accessed 21 July 2012))

I am convinced that staff will be much more able to organize services that best meet the needs of the people they are caring for if the artificial barriers between health and social care are broken down . . . in Highland we have been planning for the last year to move to a lead agency model where we can create single management, budgets, and governance across the whole range of services . . . in my opinion, integration of budgets, management and governance is the bottom line if we are going to deliver the quality of services we know the public want in these difficult times.

> (NHS Highland Chair Garry Coutts. Scottish Government 2011 Supportive quotes for integration of adult health and social care. www.scotland.gov.uk/resources/dec/924/0123935.pdf (accessed 21 July 2012))

Plans to integrate Scotland's health and social care services by 2014 must learn lessons from similar efforts elsewhere in the world. Professor Alison Petch of the Institute for Research and Innovation in Social Services: 'We're not talking about integrated structures but integrated care around the person who needs it. Integration is only a means to an end – it is not about people working together nicely but about whether it delivers better outcomes at the end of the day for people that organizations are seeking to support. The reason it keeps cropping up is that there are some issues that seem enduringly difficult to get right. Professor Petch pointed to the example of Sweden for evidence of the limitations of organizational reform alone: 'in one geographical area they developed a comprehensive model with one organising body and one provider . . . the structural integration alone didn't deliver what people hoped for. It didn't on its own lead to improved care coordination on the front line – issues of tribalism and all the difficult things we know about partnership working can get in the way'. Professor Petch also suggested that repeated references in Scotland to the experience of integration in Northern Ireland needed to be treated with caution: 'Northern Ireland is often presented as an example of a really integrated structure of health and social care but let me disabuse you as the research seems to show it doesn't work too well at all. Health in Northern Ireland appears to continue to dominate the agenda, despite the joined up structure – the hegemony of health and the focus of resources on acute care and health targets lead the way, rather than broader social care concerns. There is little development of important agendas such as personalization and children's services, and very little attention paid to more creative opportunities that integration might offer.'

(British Association of Social Workers 20/3/2012, Scottish health and social care integration must heed lessons from abroad. www.basw.co.uk/news/scottish-health-and-social-care-integration-must-heed-lessons-from-abroad/ (accessed 21 July 2012))

QUESTIONS

1   What are or will be the key difficulties of partnership working across traditional local government and health boundaries? Include consideration of: professional roles and responsibilities; similarities and differences in local government and health care organizational objectives; co-production of services; leadership of partnership initiatives.

2   Do the Scottish Government response to the 2011 'Review of Community Health Partnerships' and the other responses listed indicate that the new Health and Social Care Partnerships in Scotland will be successful?

3   Use the interrelated policy cycles, explained in Figure 1.5, to discuss the policy process of CHPs.

REFERENCES

6, P. (2004) 'Joined up government in the western world in comparative perspective: a preliminary literature review and exploration', *Journal of Public Administration Theory and Research*, 14, 1: 103–138.

Audit Scotland (2011) *Review of Community Health Partnerships*. Edinburgh.

Baker, C.D. and Lorimer, A.R. (2000) 'Cardiology: the development of a managerial clinical network', *British Medical Journal*, Nov 4; 321 (7269): 1152–1153.

Bardach, E. (2001) 'Developmental dynamics: inter-agency collaboration as an emergent phenomenon', *Journal of Public Administration Research and Theory*, 11, 2: 149–164.

Christensen, T. and Laegreid, P. (2007) 'The whole of government approach to public sector reform', *Public Administration Review*, 67, 6: 1059–1066.

Cooper, T.L., Bryer, T.A. and Meek, J.W. (2006) 'Citizen centred collaborative public management', *Public Administration Review*, 66, special issue 1: 76–88.

Osborne, D. and Plastrik (2000) *The Re-inventor's Field book: tools for transforming your government – practical guidelines, lessons and resources for revitalising schools, public services and government agencies at all levels,* San Francisco, CA: Josey Bass.

Pate, J., Fischbacher, M. and MacKinnon, J. (2010) 'Health improvement: countervailing pillars of partnership and profession', *Journal of Health Organisation and Management,* 24, 2: 200–217.

Provan, K. and Milward, H. (2001) 'Do networks really work? A framework for evaluating public sector organisational networks', *Public Administration Review,* 61, 4: 414–423.

Rhodes, R.A.W. (1997) *Understanding Governance: policy networks, governance, reflexivity and accountability,* Buckingham: Open University Press.

Shergold, P. (2005) 'Regeneration: new structures, new leaders, new traditions', *Australian Journal of Public Administration,* 64, 2: 3–6.

World Health Organization (1998) *Health Promotion Glossary,* Geneva.

Chapter 9

Public policy and accountability

INTRODUCTION

Too many corporate managers, auditors and analysts are participating in a game of nods and winks . . . I fear that we are witnessing an erosion in the quality of earnings, and therefore, the quality of financial reporting. Managing

208

may be giving way to manipulation; integrity may be losing out to illusion
. . . How many half-truths, and how much accounting sleight-of-hand, will it
take to tarnish that faith?

(Arthur Levitt 1998)

The aforementioned quote is an extract from a speech entitled 'The Numbers
Game' by Arthur Levitt, former Chairman of the US Security and Exchange
Commission, in 1998 to the New York University Centre for Law and Business.
The speech was made during the then emerging Enron scandal. Enron was one of
America's largest public utility companies in terms of service provision – providing
energy, gas and electricity to thousands of US citizens – and revenue, estimated
into the billions of US dollars (Committee on Governmental Affairs US Senate
2002). The company was eventually declared bankrupt in 2001. The failure of
Enron is often described as an auditing and accounting failure (ibid). This is in part
due to the accounting practices of Enron and the acquiescence of its auditors,
Arthur Andersen. Arthur Andersen, in the wake of the scandal, faced criminal
charges and it too was made defunct. A report by the Committee of Governmental
Affairs US Senate (2002) has also described failures of oversight:

> Despite the magnitude of Enron's implosion and the apparent pervasiveness
> of its fraudulent conduct, virtually no one in the multi-layered system of
> controls devised to protect the public detected Enron's problems, or, if they
> did, they did nothing to correct them or alert investors. Not one of the
> watchdogs was there to prevent or warn of the impending disaster.

The case of the bankruptcy of Enron is much more than a financial, service provision
and corporate failure. Employees of Enron, Arthur Andersen, subsidiary companies
and companies linked to Enron and Arthur Andersen; employees' families;
corporate investors; ordinary citizens as service users and those who had their
pensions linked to the profitability of these companies faced financial ruin and
worse bankruptcy itself (ibid). The case is more than an accounting failure; it is a
case of ethical bankruptcy. It was intentional, fraudulent and illegal practices for
personal gain with a disregard for the broader public interest. You may agree that
the speech could have been delivered today in the wake of the current financial
crisis and the emerging unethical poor governance practices within the banking
sector, which rippled into a global crisis affecting millions of people.

This chapter is not necessarily about financial accounting and auditing, but
rather principles of accountability in public policy, specifically government.
Although the aforementioned case concerns the private sector, as repeatedly stated
in this book, there is an integration of various sectors in the economy with
government as the authoritative decision maker having the power and authority to
make public policy. As discussed in previous chapters, public policy involves the

209 ■

distribution and redistribution of resources in society, and regulation to prevent unlawful and corrupt practices. Government formulates public policy to regulate itself as well as other sectors of the economy (see Chapter 5). The criticism of government concerning the current financial crisis is its earlier deregulation (or at least 'light touch' regulation) of the banking sector in the 1980s and 1990s, which many have argued has resulted in corrupt practices within the banking sector. Some have argued for more regulation of the banking sector to protect the public and others have argued that over-regulation will stifle market activity and economic growth. Government in financial, economic and consumer policies often has to mediate these various competing interests for the greater public good. In a discussion of accountability there are related concepts of regulation, rules, responsibility, codes of practice, transparency, corruption, good governance, ethics, etc. This chapter will therefore first provide a conceptual discussion of accountability and related concepts. The chapter will draw upon Anglo-Saxon democracies, but reference will be made to other countries. Second, the chapter will outline, within a public policy and government context, accountability as: political and legislative controls; constituency relations; managerial processes; judicial and quasi-judicial reviews; and market accountability. The chapter will also discuss accountability when public policy is a success or failure. Finally, as a conclusion, the chapter will discuss the role of government with philosophical arguments of accountability, public service ethos and good governance in society.

ACCOUNTABILITY: A CONCEPTUAL DISCUSSION

There are a number of perspectives and definitions of accountability as applied within a public policy context. Simply, accountability can be defined as the responsible actor or an organization representing a body of actors, which has the regulatory or ethical obligation to answer, report, explain and/or justify actions and practices undertaken by another actor or body of actors. Lawton and Rose (1991: 23) categorize accountability in terms of political, managerial, legal, consumer and professional typologies. Most forms of accountability, in both the public and private sectors, invariably follow these typologies of accountability, which can be overlapping. For example, most organizations include professionals who follow professional rules and regulations; organizations adhere to legal and regulatory requirements; there are invariably a number of managerial accountability systems such as performance management mechanisms and, whether public or private, organizations have to account to users, in some form or another, for the service they provide. A case in point would be, for example, local government, which consists of a number of professional skilled employees (e.g. accountants who follow generally accepted accounting principles); there is legal and regulatory accountability (e.g. the statutory obligation to provide annual financial statements); the employees are held accountable by management (e.g. through annual performance reviews); and the local authority is accountable to the community as to the level of service provision and performance of the organization (e.g. the UK Comprehensive Performance Assessments). This of course could be true of both public and private organizations, but the difference is the typology of political accountability. While in public, private and voluntary organizations there are many accountability mechanisms that are standard operating procedures such as audits, annual financial reports, performance reports according to various indices (see Chapter 10), human resource reports, etc., it is the political environment that provides a different dimension to accountability of government.

Politics adds a dimension to the accountability of government in that politicians have to account to the electorate for public policies in formulation and implementation, particularly with regard to public service delivery. As we have discussed, the linear relationship of politicians formulating policies, expecting civil and public servants to deliver upon policy objectives and report through an organizational hierarchy for the performance of the policy does not, in the real world, necessarily hold true. The assumption is that accountability within government adheres to a Weberian bureaucracy with hierarchical structures and clear chains of command from official to senior official, senior official to minister, minister to Parliament and from Parliament to the people (McGarvey 2001; Miller, et al. 2010). This is also referred to as official accountability (see Massey and Pyper 2005). As discussed in Chapter 3, there are political–administrative relations and with the introduction of NPM reforms of the public sector there has been a challenge to the hierarchical chain of command with increasingly managerialist forms of accountability (Miller et al. 2010).

Thus, the very concept of accountability has become a contested one, particularly in relation to official accountability, suggesting that there is a need for an alternative perspective, based on the concept of accountability 'layers' (Miller et al. 2010). The first level is basic answerability or, in Marshall's (1986) terms, 'explanatory accountability'. Explanatory accountability involves the political leadership providing full disclosure of a problem which has occurred within his or her policy portfolio and/or government agency for which s/he is responsible (ibid). In the Westminster model, the explanation is usually to Parliament (ibid). Second is 'amendatory accountability' where systems, processes and/or policies which have caused problems in the first instance are changed (Miller et al. 2010). The third and strongest layer of accountability is 'redress' where a proven error which caused difficulties for service users involves the exposure of actors to sanctions in cases of serious error (Miller et al. 2010). The latter may involve the discipline and/or resignation of an actor and in some cases compensation such as financial and/or public apology.

In addition to the aforementioned typologies of accountability there can also be ethical accountability, where an employee within an organization feels that others within the organization are not acting in the public interest. These employees often

211

feel compelled to 'whistle-blow' and report on organizational practices which do not strictly adhere to the rules and regulations, or ethical behaviour. Perhaps a famous or infamous example of modern whistle-blowing in a government context is the release of sensitive, redacted security and diplomatic information by Bradley Manning, a US soldier, to WikiLeaks. In the private sector too there are whistle-blowers, as some have argued of Sherron Watkins in the Enron case. Yet caution should be exercised: what may be considered unethical by an actor may be ethical for another, as ethics are a social construction. A distinction should be made between professional, legal and regulatory accountability and that of ethical account-ability – although these are interrelated concepts. An actor may feel compelled ethically to report others who have not complied with rules and regulations. For example, an accountant discovers endemic fraudulent behaviour in an organization, which seeks to conceal the fraud, and the accountant proceeds to inform the relevant authorities. Furthermore, in the absence or presence of rules and regulations an actor may decide that practices by others are not in the public or customer interest, and whistle-blowers following their own internal ethical or moral compass. For example, a social worker feels that the quality and duty of care are not being provided to vulnerable clients, given the reduction in staff due to austerity measures. Consequently the increase in case workload for social workers becomes unmanageable, increasing the risk for vulnerable groups and the social worker reports the concerns to the media or an organization that regulates the service.

Accountability in the public sector can be an inward sense of values by public servants to serve the public according to professional standards – a public service ethos – and also to an external mode of operation in the direction of the political realm (see Mulgan 2000; Miller *et al.* 2010). Thus, accountability is 'to account' to some authority for one's actions (Jones 1992: 73). Accountability is therefore external since it requires account to be given to some person or body; it involves an exchange in that there is a quest for information, answers and/or rectification; it implies rights of authority in that those who are calling for account are asserting superior authority over those who are being held to account, including the right to impose sanctions (Mulgan 2000: 555). Elcock (1991: 162) discusses account-ability in terms of the 'upwards, outwards and downwards' directional model. Similarly, McGarvey (2001) argues for a multi-faceted approach to understanding the concept of accountability in terms of traditional, professional, managerialist, democratic, governance, regulatory and rational choice perspectives. The dimen-sions of accountability include: a sense of individual responsibility or concern for the public interest (inward and professional accountability); checks and balances to control actions of state actors (regulatory accountability); the pursuit of citizens' needs or wishes (responsiveness and consumerist accountability); and a dialogue with citizens on which democracies depend (political and democratic accountability) (see Mulgan 2000; Miller *et al.* 2010). Similarly, Stone (1995) argues that there are five conceptions of accountability in many democracies:

- parliamentary control through the traditional understanding of accountability in the Westminster model and the doctrine of ministerial responsibility;
- managerialism, which has gained prominence after the introduction of NPM mechanisms and processes of performance management regimes;
- judicial or quasi-judicial review such as a commission of inquiries;
- constituency relations with a duality of accountability: bureaucrats accounting to political representatives through an upward process in a hierarchical structure to Parliament and then ultimately to the public, and downwards directly to the public; and
- market accountability with a 'customer' focus to users of public services in efforts to make bureaucrats more responsive through NPM-type initiatives such as Citizen Charters.

We shall discuss these conceptions and dimensions of accountability in the following sections of this chapter and in Chapter 10.

ACCOUNTABILITY AS POLITICAL RESPONSIBILITY

At this juncture it is useful to discuss the related concepts of accountability and responsibility. Accountability is not responsibility. Responsibility involves a duty, whether due to professional and/or ethical values, and thus involves a sense of morality of what is right and wrong – within a government context – what is in the public interest (see Gregory 2003). Invariably, when discussing accountability within a political and governance context, there is a discussion of the relationship between politicians and civil servants. As discussed in Chapter 3, the conventional understanding of the political–administrative interface, within the Westminster system, is that of a public service bargain. The political leadership – the minister – is vicariously responsible for the acts of civil servants within his or her department, taking both blame and credit for civil servants' actions (Marshall 1986). Civil servants remain anonymous and their personal failures and poor performance are accounted for by the minister (ibid). Yet, this convention gives rise to a contradiction. There is an understanding that in the policy-making process there is a need for closed and private decision-making between the minister, senior civil servants and advisers (Marshall 1986; Judge 1993). The minister is the ultimate authoritative decision maker and, since all decisions are taken in the name of the minister and the government of the day, there is no need for civil servants to be identified with decisions – they remain anonymous (ibid). The political–administrative interface is predicated on the idea that policy is formulated by the political leadership and implemented by the civil service administration – the political–administrative dichotomy. As previously discussed, this dichotomous relationship does not necessarily hold true in reality. Nonetheless, the dichotomous political–administrative relationship is manifest in the convention of ministerial

213 ■

responsibility in the Westminster parliamentary model. The minister is accountable to Parliament and thereby the public. The public or 'the people' are represented in Parliament by members of parliament (MPs) and therefore ministerial accountability is de facto to the public (Pyper 1996) – accountability as constituency relations through an upward process. In terms of ministerial/political accountability there are four forms of responsibility:

- Informatory responsibility – it is the obligation of the minister to inform Parliament of the performance and operation of the department or executive agency in his or her portfolio (Venter 1999). The minister has a duty to provide Parliament with a full disclosure of information and not knowingly mislead Parliament (Marshall 1986; Judge 1993; Pyper 1996; Venter 1999).
- Explanatory responsibility – the minister has to defend, to Parliament, policy decisions s/he has taken and if there is a problem has an informatory responsibility to explain to Parliament the causes, consequences and outcomes of the policy and actions related to the implementation of the policy (Pyper 1996; Venter 1999).
- Amendatory responsibility – the minister acknowledges to Parliament an error relevant to the department or executive agency and provides, in good faith, amendments and remedial action which would be undertaken in order to prevent further or future errors (Marshall 1986; Pyper 1996; Venter 1999). In cases of serious misconduct or criminal behaviour by minister and/or civil servant the amendatory or remedial action could take the form of disciplinary procedures and criminal prosecution (Venter 1999).
- Resignatory responsibility – this is probably the more contentious form of ministerial accountability where a minister is required to resign for policy failures that emanate from his or her department. However, this form of accountability is rare (ibid). Pyper (1991) in a survey of ministerial resignations identified four reasons for resignations: electoral defeat; personal grounds; does not agree with the government/Cabinet/Prime Minister's policy and therefore cannot take collective responsibility in defending the policy; and grounds of individual responsibility where the minister has made an error of judgement.

The idea of vicarious responsibility by ministers and accountability to Parliament has been consistently upheld in contemporary British polity. For example, the Scott Report of 1996, which was a judicial inquiry into the sale of military equipment by British companies to Iraq during the 1980s, upheld the view that ministers have to fully disclose information to Parliament and not knowingly mislead Parliament in their informatory, explanatory and amendatory responsibility. The Westminster model of accountability is evident in most Commonwealth countries usually involving, in some form or another, answerability, an exchange of information, efforts to correct errors and sanctions. Through a historical legacy of colonial administration, this model has been exported to many countries. Stone (1995), for example, argues that in the Westminster system ministerial responsibility has become the dominant principle by which the administration is held accountable. Although, depending on the political architecture of a country, there may be nuances and differences in the manner and mechanisms of accountability. For example, in the US, those employed in federal government are accountable to the President as part of the political executive, which is separate from the legislature, i.e. Congress, which is in turn accountable to the public.

There are a number of mechanisms and processes through which accountability can take place. In the Westminster system MPs may use informal processes such as personal letters and verbal communication with ministers requesting some form of information, explanation, etc. and hold the minister to account; there are Parliamentary Questions sessions where ministers have to answer to Parliament; parliamentary debates; standing committees; the Public Accounts Committee; and departmentally based select committees (see Pyper 1996).

In the UK there is also a Committee on Standards in Public Life which was established in 1994 to deal with concerns about unethical conduct among MPs, including accepting financial incentives for tabling Parliamentary questions, and issues over procedures for appointment to public bodies (Committee on Standards in Public Life 2012). The Committee is an independent advisory body to the UK government, and advises government on ethical standards across the whole of public life in the UK; it also monitors, reports and makes recommendations on issues relating to standards in public life (ibid). The Committee promotes and holds those in public office to account according to seven principles, commonly known as the Lord Nolan (former Chairman of the Committee) Principles:

- Selflessness – holders of public office should act solely in terms of the public interest. They should not do so in order to gain financial or other material benefits for themselves, their family, or their friends.
- Integrity – holders of public office should not place themselves under any financial or other obligation to outside individuals or organizations that might seek to influence them in the performance of their official duties.
- Objectivity – in carrying out public business, including making public appointments, awarding contracts, or recommending individuals for rewards and benefits, holders of public office should make choices on merit.
- Accountability – holders of public office are accountable for their decisions and actions to the public and must submit themselves to whatever scrutiny is appropriate to their office.
- Openness – holders of public office should be as open as possible about all the decisions and actions that they take. They should give reasons for their decisions and restrict information only when the wider public interest clearly demands.

- Honesty – holders of public office have a duty to declare any private interests relating to their public duties and to take steps to resolve any conflicts arising in a way that protects the public interest.
- Leadership – holders of public office should promote and support these principles by leadership and example (ibid).

These principles are consistent with the Weberian notion of bureaucracy and embody a public service ethos – the ideation of personal sacrifice for the greater good of society. We shall return to this issue in the latter section of this chapter.

ACCOUNTABILITY AS MANAGERIALISM

Accountability is a matter of political and organizational assurances to prevent the abuse of power and corruption (Gregory 2003). Often the goal of accountability through various mechanisms and processes is the ineluctable quest for control over government to prevent poor policy decisions, actions and outcomes (ibid). Although the positive intended outcome of accountability processes is to prevent poor governance and corruption, the negative outcome can be red tape. As Gregory (2003) argues, public agencies in democracies are subject to a plethora of externally imposed institutional and statutory mechanisms, which create regulatory frameworks that bind bureaucracies and tend to make public sector organizations risk-averse, conservative and compliant with regulation (ibid). As discussed earlier, Amann (2006) argues that the civil servant's role has become more complex with the demands for leadership, innovation and entrepreneurship within a political– administrative environment that necessitates accountability with consequent bureaucracy and red tape. The result is that civil servants are caught in a conundrum of the 'innovation narrative', which is underpinned by NPM demands for efficiency and managerialism, and the 'accountability narrative', which is underpinned by a traditional public service bargain (ibid).

Hood and Lodge (2006: 186–187; Hood and Scott 2000) argue that NPM and managerialism have changed the nature of the public service bargain. Through political accountability, politicians want to report results, invariably successes, to constituents. Thus, to demonstrate results, managerial accountability is employed with a combination of market accountability with more 'customer' focus to users of public services, and performance management regimes. The idea is to ensure that bureaucrats are more responsive to users of services (downward account-ability) and report results and policy delivery to political masters (upward accountability). Ironically managerial regimes have had unintended outcomes with civil servants becoming defensive about performance rather than being innovative – the exact opposite of what managerial regimes are designed to achieve (ibid). Arguably there is a fault line within the public service bargain of ensuring the 'innovation narrative' while preserving the 'accountability narrative'. Indeed, if

216

bureaucrats do take the initiative by circumventing red tape to deliver more responsive services, regulation and the accountability narrative may become more explicit (Hood and Scott 2000). Another unintended outcome of NPM public sector reforms has created a fragmentation of accountabilities with services being contracted out to the private and voluntary sectors, internal markets being introduced and quangos and non-departmental bodies also being involved in service delivery, etc. (Miller *et al.* 2010). Yet, when things go wrong, invariably it is the political and administrative realm of government that is held accountable (see Box 9.1). The impact of managerial accountability and mechanisms of performance management with unintended outcomes of game playing will be discussed in greater detail in the following chapter of this book. Nevertheless, managerialism has become a feature of accountability in government to ensure downward and upward directionality of accountability.

BOX 9.1   POLITICAL ACCOUNTABILITY FOR PRIVATE SECTOR FAILURE

The following is an extract from an article which appeared in a newspaper, the *Independent*, authored by Steve Richards, in the wake of the failure of G4S, a private company, contracted by government to deliver security for the Olympic Games in London in 2012.

The deeply embedded assumption that a slick, efficient, agile, selfless private sector delivers high-quality services for the public is being challenged once more in darkly comic circumstances. Those inadvertent egalitarians from the security firm G4S have failed to recruit enough security officers, so it seems anyone will be able to wander in to watch the 100 metres final. Or at least that would have been the case if the public sector had not come to the rescue in the form of the army. What an emblematic story of changing times. From the late 1970s until 2008, the fashionable orthodoxy insisted that the public sector alone was the problem. Advocates of the orthodoxy took a knock or two when the banking crisis cast light on parts of the pampered, sheltered and partially corrupt financial sector. Now we get a glimpse of incompetence and greed in another part of the private sector. As light is shed wider and deeper, we keep our fingers crossed that the public sector can rescue the Olympics from chaos.

The pattern is familiar but has been obscured until the arrival of this accessibly vivid example, an Olympic Games staged in a city paranoid about security without many security officers. For decades, private companies were hired on lucrative contracts for projects that the state could never allow to fail. If the companies delivered what was required, they earned a fortune. If they failed, the taxpayer found the money to meet the losses and those responsible for the cock-up often moved on to new highly paid jobs. The lesson should have been learnt when Labour's disastrous Public Private Partnership for the London Underground collapsed, as this was another highly accessible example of lawyers, accountants and private companies making a fortune and failing to deliver. The Underground could never close, so all involved knew that in the event of failure, the Government or the Mayor of London would be forced to intervene. Boris Johnson described the arrangement at the time as 'a colossal waste of money'.

He was right, but that has not stopped his colleagues in Government looking to contract out to the private sector at every available opportunity ... G4S already runs prisons and some of the police operations that are being increasingly contracted out to private companies. The welfare-to-work contract secured by another company, much hailed by gullible ministers when the deal was announced as an example of efficiency and effectiveness, is already under critical scrutiny.

A fortnight ago, I argued that we are living through a slow British revolution partly as a result of the financial crisis and the exposure of reckless, unaccountable leadership from the City. The era of light regulation that allowed some bankers without much obvious talent to make a fortune is over. Now, slowly, the assumption held from Thatcher to Blair to Cameron that the delivery of public services should lie with the private sector is being overturned, too.

As is always the case in British revolutions, the change is being driven by startling events and not by political leadership. The Coalition still burns with an ideological zeal formed in the 1980s, the Conservative wing at one with Orange Book Liberal Democrats in their indiscriminate hunger for a smaller state and their undying faith in the private sector. At the top of both parties, there are crusading advocates of an outdated vision that places too much faith in the likes of G4S and not enough in the potential dependability of a more efficient and accountable public sector ... Instead of focusing on the arduously unglamorous task of making the public sector more efficient and adaptable, ministers, like their New Labour predecessors, prefer still the deceptive swagger of the incompetent entrepreneur. The gullibility is more extraordinary now we finally get to know more about these supposed geniuses. Senior bankers earning millions stutter hesitantly when questioned by unthreatening MPs on select committees, incapable of articulating a case. Nick Buckles from G4S was so thrown by the Home Affairs Committee that he lapsed into a debate about whether the few security guards he had managed to hire spoke 'fluent English', claiming not to know what such a term might mean. One of the great revelations since Britain's slow revolution began in 2008 is how many unimpressive mediocrities had risen in the unquestioning, unaccountable darkness that, until recently, acted as a protective layer for parts of the private sector.

But in the end look who is ultimately held to account. The Home Secretary, Theresa May, was called to the Commons twice this week to answer questions about what went wrong. She will be back in September. A government can outsource but it will still be held responsible, quite rightly, for the delivery of public services. So political survival should motivate ministers in future to draw up much tighter deals with companies and to focus more on improving the public sector rather than expensively bypassing it. The voters have had enough of these abuses and yet, trapped by the past, some ministers show an ideological inclination to be abused for a little longer.

*Source: www.independent.co.uk/opinion/commentators/
steve-richards/steve-richards-time-to-explode-the-myth-that-the-
private-sector-is-always-better-7956887.html (accessed July 2012)*

ACCOUNTABILITY AS JUDICIAL AND QUASI-JUDICIAL REVIEWS

In most democracies there is a separation of powers between the executive arm of government, legislature and judiciary (e.g. the US), or at least the independence of the judiciary is assured. This independence is pivotal in holding government to account and maintaining a check and balance of governmental power. Citizens therefore have the right to challenge government policy and actions in court using available statute and common law. As discussed in Chapter 3, the European Court of Justice is also becoming a domain where citizens can assert their rights and hold government accountable.

Judicial reviews use court proceedings in deciding whether the correct legal basis has been used in reaching a decision (Howlett and Ramesh 2003; The Public

Law Project 2006). In the UK a decision by government or public official(s) can be challenged as unlawful if: the official does not have power to make that decision or is using the power they have for an improper purpose; the decision is considered irrational; the procedure followed by the official was unfair or biased; the decision was taken in breach of the Human Rights Act; or the decision breaches European law (ibid). For example, the UK uses judicial reviews about decisions concerning immigration cases since the Immigration and Asylum Act 1999 provides for appeals against decisions; and the exercise of powers by public authorities including a minister and officials (The Home Office 2001). The judicial review in cases of immigration decisions does not assess the merits of the decision, but rules upon its lawfulness (ibid). Thus, there are limits on the authority of the Court in the judicial review (ibid). The Court's involvement in judicial review is the consideration of decisions that are illegal, irrational or subject to procedural impropriety (ibid).

In addition to judicial reviews, in many countries there also exists an office of the ombudsman (or ombudsperson) as a quasi-judicial mechanism of accountability. Here too individual complaints can be voiced by citizens seeking redress due to an error by government and/or public officials. The ombudsman's origins can be traced to the Swedish efforts of accountability from 1809, but its contemporary form spread from Scandinavian countries in the 1960s (Cheng 1968; Gregory and Giddings 2000; Reif 2004). By the 1990s at least ninety countries had adopted the institution as a mechanism of holding government accountable and ensuring good governance (Gregory and Giddings 2000). According to Cheng (1968) the institution of the ombudsman is flexible and therefore adaptable to different political and administrative contexts. Its transferability to many democracies is that: the institution of the ombudsman is provided for by a country's constitution or by the action of a legislature; it is headed by an independent, high-profile official who is responsible to the legislature and public; it receives complaints from aggrieved persons against government agencies and/or actors; it has the power to investigate, recommend remedial action and issue reports for public record; and it is relatively more expeditious than judicial reviews and court proceedings (Reif 2004). In Scotland, for example, the Public Services Ombudsman, in addition to publishing findings in the form of a decision letter and report, can and does issue commentaries so that lessons can be learned for improvements in public service delivery (Scottish Public Services Ombudsman 2012). A further attraction of the institution is that the ombudsman promotes good governance as Danet's (1978) evaluation of the role of the ombudsman concludes that it serves as a symbol of the possibility of justice for ordinary people, and inspires members of the civil service and government agencies to maintain a high level of public service and commitment to a public service ethos. For further reading of the institution of the ombudsman as applied in various countries and a description of case studies refer to Reif (2004) and Gregory and Giddings (2000).

220

Government itself may respond to an identified error and wrongdoing, usually after a public outcry, and decide that it is in the broader public interest to establish a commission of inquiry. Government may take the view that there is a systemic failure and the redress should be a policy learning process to prevent future errors. Thus, the inquiry is beyond an individual aggrieved citizen but is wider in scope. Commissions of inquiry are usually quasi-judicial with investigatory powers and report recommendations to address and prevent failures. Inquiries are held for one of the two main reasons: they enable information to be gathered and views canvassed for policy making; or they are held to investigate and discover information about some past event (e.g. the UK Chilcot Inquiry into the Iraq War) (see O'Donnell 1996). For example, in the UK the Lord Justice Leveson Inquiry was established to investigate the culture, practices and ethics of the media with a particular emphasis on the relationship of the press with the public, police and politicians. Under the UK's Inquiries Act of 2005 the Inquiry has the power to summon witnesses, giving evidence under oath and in public, and with the final report to make recommendations on the future of press regulation and governance consistent with maintaining freedom of the press and ensuring the highest ethical and professional standards for the public interest (Leveson Inquiry 2012).

EXTRA-PARLIAMENTARY ACCOUNTABILITY

The preceding discussion focused on accountability within government whether downward (constituency, managerialism and marketization) or upward (political and judicial) in directionality. Yet, there is arguably a horizontal dimension of accountability: accountability outwith the parliamentary and judicial control. Extra-parliamentary accountability could emanate from civil society actors such as pressure groups and the media. We have discussed policy communities and networks that are involved in the policy-making process but these actors can also play a role in holding government accountable. Examples would be Human Rights Watch, Amnesty International, Oxfam, etc. which, as part of the policy process, may report on the outcomes of public policy and seek to lobby government and/or mobilize action to address a perceived policy failure. The media too plays a role in holding government accountable. The most famous example of accountability is that of the Watergate Scandal with investigative journalists from the Washington Post exposing the corrupt and unethical behaviour of the Nixon administration forcing President Nixon to resign. In contemporary public policy the increasing use of social media cannot be ignored. Social media presents a significant and immediate accountability of government policies and action mobilizing civil society actors on a large scale within a short period of time, for example, the use of social media in mobilizing opposition to the UK's forestry policy (see Box 5.5) and in the Middle East and North Africa region resulting in the fall of autocratic regimes.

Increasingly many extra-parliamentary actors are using government regulation itself to gain information about public policy outputs and outcomes. For example, many countries have adopted some form of access to government information such as the UK Freedom of Information Act 2000 (see Holsen 2007; Holsen and Pasquier 2010). Transparency is a dimension of accountability as it allows for the examination of the inner workings of government and provides for the ability to examine government performance (Hall 2010). These regulatory mechanisms are efforts to ensure transparency and openness of government. It also ensures accountability in terms of responsiveness to constituents. Yet, despite all the dimensions and regulations relating to accountability to ensure good governance, effective public policy and service delivery, government action may result in unintended and negative outcomes.

ACCOUNTABILITY: POLICY SUCCESS AND FAILURE

When things go wrong we hold government to account. Often government and public agencies are involved in high-risk operations and environments from national security to the protection of children and vulnerable adults, law enforcement and emergency services, etc. In these high-risk environments when things go wrong, they go horribly wrong. For example, the successive intelligence failures leading to the terrorist attacks in the US on 9/11 led to a tragic loss of life on a large scale. Even at local government level, the failure to protect vulnerable children (e.g. in the UK the cases of Baby P and Victoria Climbié) has led also to a tragic loss of life. Within a public policy context, government action may have negative, unintended outcomes. Policy actors, particularly the media, will invariably define these negative outcomes as failures or even a crisis. These may be actual or perceived events. For example, as described in Chapter 11, the foot-and-mouth crisis was a failure in agricultural policy and maladministration; or as in the case of the financial crisis it is perceived to be failure of financial services and banking regulatory policy. State actors and politicians ameliorate failures because of electoral liabilities and/or potential sanctions and redress.

When government action has the intended, positive policy outcomes, government, state actors, and politicians often herald successes. Their hope is that constituents and the target service recipients perceive the benefits of the policy. State actors and politicians invariably highlight the benefits of the policy for career advancement and electoral advantage, respectively. For example, President Barack Obama sought to capitalize on the death of Osama Bin Laden at the hands of US forces in his 2012 Presidential election campaign. Career officials such as Efraim Haley, the deputy chief of Mossad, played a pivotal role in the Middle East polity and were rewarded for perceived success by the Israeli government with successive high-ranking bureaucratic positions (Halevy 2006).

The inherent assumption in policy success and failure is causality. Yet, it is difficult to determine whether a particular action by government caused a success or failure in outcome. Whether a policy is a success or failure involves a judgement about events and actions (Bovens and 't Hart 1996; Howlett and Ramesh 2003). Judgements are linked to factors such as how the policy problem was framed in the agenda-setting process, the conceptualizations of policy options when making policy, the expectations by policy actors, time, and policy evaluation (Howlett and Ramesh 2003). The evaluation of policy can be undertaken by many policy actors such as government agencies (e.g. National Audit Office), policy analysts, research centres, inquiries, judicial reviews, academics, think tanks, media, consultants, private and voluntary sector organizations, supra-national bodies, political opposition parties. The information derived from a policy evaluation process may provide for policy learning and in a feedback loop inform problem identification, decision-making, options and more effective implementation. We encourage you to read, Davies *et al.* (2000) *What Works: Evidence-based policy and practice in public services*, as further reading to understand when policy evaluation and evidence is used to inform public policy, or indeed even change policy.

Yet, policy evaluation does not necessarily take place in a systematic manner – hence the question mark in the integrated policy process model (see Chapter 1). According to Dye (2002) and Anderson (1997) there are a number of reasons, inter alia, for the lack of evaluation in public policy:

- There may be an uncertainty in policy goals as a result of the policy-making process. The policy-making process may have resulted in diffuse and ambiguous goals given the diversity of policy actors, whether as an advocacy coalition or policy network or community, involved in the formulation of the policy. Thus, evaluating whether a policy has been a success or failure is difficult to determine if the goal is opaque. There may also be a reluctance to evaluate the policy since it may reopen conflicting interests that were seemingly satisfied (satificing) during the policy-making process.
- There is a difficulty in determining causality as policy involves societal changes over a lengthy period of time. For example, the effects of introducing an educational programme for children may be difficult to determine, given extraneous variables (e.g. parental and peer influences) that happen as a matter of course over time.
- Policies involve a substantial investment in terms of time, financial and human resources. A negative evaluation of a policy may be viewed as a waste of resources and becomes a sunk cost and political liability for government.
- In democracies there are electoral cycles and the time and attention span of politicians are limited to the next election. Politicians in an effort to get re-elected are not necessarily interested in longitudinal studies, rather in quick results to demonstrate policy successes.

223

- Policy evaluation requires resources such as time, money and human capacity, which, in a resource-constrained environment, may distract from investing in other policy areas.
- There may be limits to capturing and collecting data for policy evaluation. Although, in an age of computerization this is not an insurmountable task, human cognitive abilities and reluctance to share data present problems in evaluation.
- Government agencies and state actors may have strong vested interests in proving the value of policies and demonstrating the positive effects of policy. Bureau-shaping behaviour and career advancement can be incentives to evaluate the outcomes of policy positively. Bureaucrats may also resist evaluation as perceived problems with a policy may require change. In bureaucracies there may be organizational inertia, conservativism and resistance to change.

Even when there are policy failures or negative outcomes, government can explain the findings of the evaluation as:

- The effects of the policy are long ranging and cannot be adequately measured.
- The effects of the policy are diffuse and subtle and cannot be measured by crude statistical analysis.
- The evaluation is incomplete or did not include the appropriate and valid measures.
- The fact that the policy did not have the desired effect demonstrates inadequate resourcing, and indeed more resources are needed.
- There may be biases in the evaluation or government may even question the credibility of non-state evaluators (Dye 2002).

Hogwood and Gunn (1984) nevertheless argue, as do we, that policy evaluation in a normative sense should be part of the policy process. The evaluation of policy, whether as a success or failure, is essential for policy learning and integral to the policy process itself. Policy actors ought to learn of poor and good practices in order to identify problems, develop options and effectively formulate and implement policy.

ACCOUNTABILITY AS PUBLIC SERVICE ETHOS

There have been efforts and mechanisms to ensure good governance, prevention of corruption and effective public policy formulation and implementation. The aforementioned discussion outlined various dimensions, mechanisms and pro-cesses. Governments can introduce as much regulation as they wish – they have the authority to do so – but good governance and serving the public interest depends on inward accountability. A discussion of accountability cannot be complete without the mention of internal accountability – ethical and moral conduct. Indeed if there is too much regulation then government is accused of being a regulatory or 'nanny' state; too little and government is considered ineffective or 'regulation light'. As discussed previously, governments often have to balance and mediate interests, particularly when it comes to introducing regulation. Governments act as guardians and custodians of public trust in regulating other sectors of the economy and itself as an actor in the policy process. Yet, regulation can only go so far and a pervasive question is 'who guards the guardians?' Thus, beyond regulation, accountability very much depends on public officials having internal accountability and a sense of serving the public and doing so according to ethical conduct.

Ethical norms derive from moral traditions, which are enduring, systematic and widely held belief systems of thought about right and wrong that are in turn normative, cultural and/or religious in formulation (Lewis 2008). Ethics involve: (1) universal principles and duties of good conduct; and (2) proper effects on others, the community and society (ibid). Thus, serving the public involves making policies and delivering upon them for the best possible outcomes for society – ensuring public good. It requires public officials and bureaucrats to set aside their own personal interests for the greater good of society. This is essentially the principle of the Weberian bureaucracy and Platonian ideation of personal sacrifice for public office. For example, O'Toole (1993: 3) defined public service ethos as:

> the setting aside of personal interests . . . working altruistically for the public good . . . it is about working with others, collegially and anonymously, to promote that public good . . . it is about integrity in dealing with the many and diverse problems which need solving if the public good is to be promoted.

Thus, we as a society expect and entrust government – which has the power and authority to make public policy, enact and enforce laws, extract resources in the form of taxation, and has been given a mandate to do so in a democratic state – to uphold the laws in a just manner. We do not expect government to engage in corruption, deceit, discrimination, fraud, injustice, maladministration and waste (see Caiden 1991).

The public service ethos is an internal accountability. It is a professional responsibility of public officials as a duty to serve the public and act in the public interest. The UK Civil Service Code and Lord Nolan Principles, for example, entrench this sense of duty and professional accountability. Public service ethos in some sense is downward accountability in terms of constituency relations. It is also predicated on trust: as constituents and the electorate we have given government a mandate to govern. It becomes a socio-political contract: having given government this mandate they are custodians of our public trust. The various afore-mentioned dimensions and mechanisms of accountability are designed to ensure an adherence to the public service ethos and trust in government. For example, performance management systems, which will be discussed in the next chapter, provide information about what government does, transparency of government actions and create a consciousness of whether government can be trusted (see Bouckaert and Van der Walle 2003). Trust in government underpins legitimacy and thus accountability mechanisms and processes are important for good governance and democratic principles (Barberis 2003). Indeed, President Woodrow Wilson (1887), in his seminal paper on public administration, discussed the 'greater principles' of public service. The public service ethos is a pivotal element in ensuring that above political, judicial and quasi-judicial, managerial, etc. accountabilities, service to others is a fundamental value and a greater principle.

CONCLUSION

We began this chapter with an outline of poor governance and corruption in a specific case. We argue that, whether in the public, private or voluntary sectors, accountability is essential to ensure good governance and actions within the broader public interest. In a public policy and government context accountability is essential as government has the power and authority to make policy, enact laws and take actions that affect society. As such, there are a number of dimensions and mechanisms of accountability that are employed as checks and balances of this power and authority. The dimensions of political, managerial, professional and judicial accountabilities – upwards and downwards – to constituents have been discussed. Moreover, these dimensions and mechanisms of accountability ensure trust in government, which in turn underpins legitimacy of government. Indeed without legitimacy – motivation that induces persons to obey given commands regardless of whether these commands are addressed to them personally or in the language of rules, laws and regulations (Weber 1968) – it will be difficult for a government to govern. As history has shown, whether an autocratic regime, corrupt government or private sector organization, those who do not serve the greater good of society invariably suffer from a lack of trust and legitimacy and in time are assigned to the dustbin of history.

REFERENCES

Amann, R. (2006) 'The circumlocution office: a snapshot of civil service reform,' *The Political Quarterly*, 77, 3: 334–359.

Anderson, J. (1997) *Public Policymaking*, 3rd edition, Boston, MA: Houghton Mifflin Company.

Barberis, P. (2003) 'Civil Society, Virtue, Trust: implications for the public service ethos in the age of modernity', in T. A. Butcher (ed.), *Modernizing Civil Services*, Cheltenham: Edward Elgar: 185–200.

Bouckaert, G. and Van der Walle, S. (2003) 'Comparing measures of citizen trust and user satisfaction as indicators of "good governance": difficulties in linking trust and satisfaction indicators', *International Review for Administrative Sciences*, 69, 3: 329–343.

Bovens, M. and 't Hart, P. (1996) *Understanding Policy Fiascoes*, New Brunswick, NJ: Transaction Press.

Caiden, G. (1991) 'What really is public maladministration?' *Public Administration Review*, 51, 6: 486–493.

Cheng, H.Y. (1968) 'The emergence and spread of the ombudsman institution', *The Annals of the American Academy of Political and Social Science*, 377, 1: 20–30

Committee on Governmental Affairs US Senate (2002) *Financial Oversight of Enron: the SEC and private-sector watchdogs*, www.gpo.gov/fdsys/pkg/CPRT-107SPRT 82147/html/CPRT-107SPRT82147.htm. (Accessed August 2012.)

Committee on Standards in Public Life (2012) www.public-standards.org.uk/. (Accessed August 2012.)

Danet, B. (1978) 'Toward a method to evaluate ombudsman role', *Administration & Society*, 10, 3: 335–70.

Davies, H.T.O, Nutley, S.M. and Smith, P.C. (2000) *What Works? Evidence-Based Policy and Practice in Public Services*, Bristol: The Policy Press.

Dye, T. (2002). *Understanding Public Policy*, 10th edition, Upper Saddle River, NJ: Prentice Hall.

Elcock, Howard (1991) *Change and Decay? Public Administration in the 1990s*, Harlow: Longman.

Gregory, R. (2003) 'Accountability in Modern Government', in B. G. Peters and J. Pierre (eds) *Handbook of Public Administration*, London: Sage Publishing.

Gregory, R. and Giddings, P. (eds) (2000) *Righting wrongs: the ombudsman in six continents*, Amsterdam: IOS Press.

Halevy, E. (2006) *Man in the Shadows: inside the Middle East Crisis with the man who led Mossad*, London: Weidenfeld & Nicolson.

Hall, J.L. (2010) 'Transparency and Accountability in Economic Development Efforts: causes and consequences', in T. Brandsen and M. Holzer (eds) *Future of Governance*, National Center for Public Performance, EGPA and ASPA, Newark, NJ: 169–185.

Hogwood, B. and Gunn, L. (1984). *Policy Analysis for the Real World*, Oxford: Oxford University Press.

Holsen, S. (2007) 'Freedom of information in the UK, US, and Canada', *Government Insight*, www.arma.org/bookstore/files/Holsen.pdf. (Accessed September 2012.)

Holsen, S. and Pasquier, M. (2010) 'The Swiss Federal Law on Transparency: much ado about nothing?', in T. Brandsen and M. Holzer (eds) *Future of Governance*, National Center for Public Performance, EGPA and ASPA, Newark, NJ: 151–167.

Hood, C. and Lodge, M. (2006) *The Politics of Public Sector Bargains: reward, competency, loyalty – and blame*, Oxford: Oxford University Press.

227

Hood, C. and Scott, C. (2000) *Regulating Government in a 'Managerial' Age towards a Cross-National Perspective*, www.lse.ac.uk/researchAndExpertise/units/CARR/pdf/DPs/Disspaper1.pdf. (Accessed August 2012.)

Howlett, M. and Ramesh, M. (2003). *Studying Public Policy: policy cycles and subsystems*, Oxford: Oxford University Press.

Jones, G.W. (1992) 'The Search for Local Accountability', in S. Leach (ed.) *Strengthening Local Government in the 1990s*, London: Longman.

Judge, D. (1993) *The Parliamentary State*, London: Sage Publishing.

Lawton, A. and Rose, A. (1991) *Organisation and Management in the Public Sector*, London: Pitman.

Leveson Inquiry (2012) www.levesoninquiry.org.uk/. (Accessed December 2012.)

Levitt, A. (1998) 'The Numbers Game', www.sec.gov/news/speech/speecharchive/1998/spch220.txt. (Accessed August 2012.)

Lewis, C. (2008) 'Ethical Norms in Public Service: a framework for analysis', in L. M. Huberts (ed.), *Ethics and Integrity of Governance: perspectives across frontiers*, Cheltenham: Edward Elgar: 44–64.

McGarvey, N. (2001) 'Accountability in public administration: a multi-perspective framework of analysis', *Public Policy and Administration*, 16, 2: 17–28.

Marshall, G. (1986) *Constitutional Conventions: the rules and forms of political accountability*, Oxford: Clarendon

Massey, A. and Pyper, R. (2005) *Public Management and Modernisation in Britain*, Basingstoke: Palgrave Macmillan.

Miller, K. Johnston, McTavish, D. and Pyper, R. (2010) 'Changing Modes of Official Accountability in the UK', in T. Brandsen and M. Holzer (eds) *Future of Governance*, National Center for Public Performance, EGPA and ASPA, Newark, NJ: 187–206.

Mulgan, R. (2000) 'Accountability: an ever-expanding concept?' *Public Administration*, 78, 3: 555–573.

O'Donnell, A. (1996) 'Legal and Quasi-Legal Accountability', in R. Pyper (ed.) *Aspects of Accountability in the British System of Government*, Wirral: Tudor Business: 82–118.

O'Toole, B. (1993) 'The loss of purity: the corruption of public service in Britain', *Public Policy and Administration*, 8, 2: 1–6.

Pyper, R. (1991) *The Evolving Civil Service*, Harlow: Longman

Pyper, R. (ed.) (1996) *Aspects of Accountability in the British System of Government*, Wirral: Tudor Business.

Reif, L.C. (2004) *The Ombudsman, Good Governance and the International Human Rights System*, Leiden, Netherlands: Martinus Nijhoff.

Scottish Public Service Ombudsman (2012) *Scottish Public Services Ombudsman*, www.spso.org.uk/. (Accessed July 2012.)

Stone, B. (1995) 'Administrative accountability in the "Westminster" democracies: towards a new conceptual framework', *Governance*, 8, 4: 505–526.

The Home Office (2001) *Immigration Directorates' Instructions,* www.ukba.homeoffice.gov.uk/sitecontent/documents/policyandlaw/IDIs/idischapter27/section1/section1.pdf?view=Binary. (Accessed July 2012.)

The Public Law Project (2006) 'How Can Public Law Help Me?' www.publiclawproject.org.uk/downloads/HowPubLawHelpMe.pdf. (Accessed August 2012.)

Venter, A. (1999) 'The Ethics of Ministerial Accountability to Parliament', in J.S. Wessels and J.C. Pauw (eds) *Reflective Public Administration: views from the south,* Oxford: Oxford University Press.

Weber, M. (1968) *Economy and Society. An Outline of Interpretative Sociology.* Translated Günther Roth and Clause Wittich (eds), New York: Bedminster Press.

Wilson, W. (1887) 'The study of administration', *American Political Science Quarterly,* 2, 2: 197–222.

Chapter 10

Public policy and performance management

LEARNING OBJECTIVES

- To understand the differences in various aspects of performance: outputs, outcomes, rational and other approaches
- To recognize the complexities and different contexts of performance management
- To critically appreciate the use of performance management as an accountability tool – and some of the difficulties thereof

KEY POINTS IN THIS CHAPTER

- The scale and scope of performance management in government is extensive
- Performance measures can be used in such a way that they do not measure what is intended or required
- There can be difficulties using performance management to hold people accountable for outcomes – individual performance may not be directly linked to outcome

INTRODUCTION

This chapter will analyze a key aspect of public policy and accountability: performance. It will commence by viewing performance management as a rational process, underpinned by notions of modernization, about governments aiming to improve and evaluate what public sector bodies do. Although performance

 230

management has a historical context, interest has accelerated from the last two decades of the twentieth century, internationally but to a greater or lesser extent in specific countries. The chapter introduces and defines a range of performance measurement concepts ranging from inputs to outcomes, and outlines the complexity involved at organizational, governmental and policy sector levels. The chapter then examines the three broad aims of performance management: research into what works; managerial control; and accountability.

PERFORMANCE MANAGEMENT PERCEIVED AS A RATIONAL PROCESS

Performance management is presented as a rational process, often used to justify what government and the public sector do and how governments and various agents within the public sector are accountable for actions and results. This can be presented as a rationality posed against the presumed (or otherwise) dysfunctionalities of politics (Wildavsky 1975), often elevated by an accompaniment of quantitative measures to sustain 'rational' decision-making – a belief it must be said with sustenance and power in modern political culture (Rose 1991).

Behind this image of rationality, of course, there are various definitions of 'rationality', ranging from a bureaucratic rationality (e.g. what to measure), technocratic rationality, institutional and contextual rationalities (often only understood within a particular organizational setting) (see Townley 2008). Performance management is often viewed by governments within a modernization, rational business process and improvement paradigm. The following statement from the UK Cabinet Office in 2006 could have resonance in many governmental activities from the 1990s to the present: 'The government's approach seeks to create "self-improving systems" which combine government and citizen pressure for improvement . . . to improve capability and capacity . . . It is a "self-improving system" because incentives for continuous improvement and innovation are embedded within it' (Cabinet Office 2006).

The rational process approach's philosophical underpinnings were outlined by a highly respected professional body's working party report on professional monitoring in public services:

> Performance management (PM) was introduced across government in an attempt to measure the process and outcomes of the public services, and as a goad to efficiency and effectiveness . . . such monitoring can take place at the level of the entire programme, an organisation delivering a service, or an individual. The rise of PM was linked to the increased capacity to record aspects of the public services which has been brought about by developments in information technology . . .
>
> (Royal Statistical Society 2003)

Within this rationalistic frame of reference, the broad aims and purposes of performance management seem straightforward. It is about government and public sector bodies setting objectives to give a statement of what is being attempted; delivering services and using performance management to improve these; evaluating what does and what does not work; and using incentives and improvement measures to address success on the one hand and under-performance and failure on the other (Treasury 2004).

SCOPE OF PERFORMANCE MANAGEMENT IN GOVERNMENT

Performance management – the use of targets for management control in business – has an historical depth reflected in business and management history literature (see Wren 1994). Management practices in various parts of the public sector were certainly not devoid of concern for efficiency and the measurement of activity, input and output control (for the Civil Service see Fry 1969; 1999; local government, Wilson and Game 1998 and subsequent editions; health care, Eckstein 1958; Webster 1988; 1996; state-run industries, Foreman-Peck and Milward 1994; Milward 1997).

The work of FW Taylor and others in analyzing control, efficiency, measurement and 'scientific management' is well known in terms of business and particularly manufacturing organizations; what is less well known is that 'Taylorism' also addressed the public sector (Taylor 1916). At governmental and international governmental levels there is much evidence of the use of measurement and rankings, from the late nineteenth and early twentieth centuries, in assessing naval capacity, measuring crime levels and of course munitions and other military production during the twentieth-century world wars (see Blau 1955; Jowett and Rothwell 1988; Hood 2007). It has also been shown that in the UK, central government allocated a proportion of funding to local school boards on the basis of pupils' achievements in numeracy and literacy (Rhodes 1981). Research has also shown that historically there has been a concern for efficiency and measurement at the individual public sector organization level. For example, a study of the departmental archives of Glasgow Corporation in the early- to mid-1950s, show some departments with detailed analysis of supervision and management costs and in some instances detailed comparison with similar measures in similar departments in other local authorities (McTavish 2005). Nonetheless, the widespread use of performance measures and indicators snowballed and became widespread from the 1980s and 1990s, expanding sharply with the election of New Labour in 1997. Performance measurement has had a reach that is international: New Zealand used service outputs in the late 1980s; the US introduced the Government Performance and Results Act 1993. But it has been shown that the United Kingdom – especially England – has been almost 'exceptional' (Hood 2007), standing out from comparative country studies in its focus on performance measurement (Pollitt 2006a).

The scale and scope of performance management can be almost overwhelming. Much of the remainder of this chapter will explore various aspects of performance measurement and management. Research on performance measures used in the OECD, gives an indication of scale and scope. These can include measures relating to human resource management (e.g. recruitment and retention measures), the facilitation of learning and change management, compliance with regulatory and legislative requirements; input measures (for financial and other resources); output and – to a much lesser extent – outcome measures; measurement of the achievement of policy goals; measures on resource usage, both efficiency and effectiveness (OECD 2007).

The scope of performance measurement should be viewed dynamically across time. In the early 1980s and 1990s, the public sector context was coloured by reducing deficits coupled with an ideological view of rolling back the state. Consequently a key objective of performance measurement was increasing efficiency and spending cuts (Jackson 2009). This objective changed from the mid-1990s to one pitched at increasing national competitiveness, thereby prioritizing performance measurement around outcomes and quality (Pollitt and Bouckaert 2011). From the middle of the twenty-first century's first decade to the present and beyond, fiscal cutbacks and consolidation once again prioritize efficiency; and in some countries and locations, co-production and localism along with individually centred service delivery may turn towards a collaborative focus on performance measures. Finally, in terms of the scope of performance management, it is important to distinguish the different uses and users. Much is known – or at least much has been written – about the scope and use of performance in terms of management. Boyne and others have shown the centrality of management as a means to public service improvement – which is hardly surprising given that the thrust of NPM and managerialism has often been about the adoption of generic approaches to management into public sector domains (Lynn *et al.* 2001; Boyne 2003). Others have indicated that much less is written and known about the use and scope of performance measurement and management for the 'public triad' of ministers/elected representatives/citizens who, it is argued, are qualitatively different (at least in democracies) from other stakeholders including users, consumers, customers, employees and professionals (see Pollitt 2006a).

TERMINOLOGY AND COMPLEXITIES OF PERFORMANCE MEASUREMENT

An important way to conceptualize performance can be through a typology of performance measurement, with indicators, and which includes a definitional outline of inputs, outputs and outcomes. A simple typology could include:

■ Inputs – human, physical and other resources used in the organization's activities. Could include employees, money, land and equipment.

■ Outputs – what the inputs are used to produce or provide. Could include number of students taught, number of welfare claimants processed, number of discharged patients.

■ Outcomes – usually there is a distinction between outputs and outcomes. Outcomes are changes in conditions or attitudes, not what the organization did itself (which may be an output) but a consequence of what the organization did. There is a distinction between intermediate outcomes and end outcomes.

■ Intermediate outcomes – interim achievements expected to lead to end outcomes, for example, increased skill levels or new knowledge, number of recovered patients.

■ End outcomes – the end results. May include increased school grades, increased health and well-being.

(Adapted from Bouckaert and van Dooren 2009)

In reality it is more complex than the typology indicates for several reasons. First, final outcomes can be influenced by environmental factors over which the organization has little impact (e.g. wider socio-economic or cultural trends, policies from other governments). Second, inputs and outputs in public policy are often best thought of in process or systems terms. In this view the policy and wider political and administrative environment is viewed as an open system transforming or converting inputs into outputs: the outputs of other systems (or sub-systems) are inputs into the political system, and outputs of the political system in turn influence the environment (Easton 1965). Third, it is recognized that different types of organization – or more accurately, certain activities within these organizations – have different levels of observability and therefore different levels of ease of identification and measurement of process, outputs and outcomes (Wilson 1989). Some organizations have both outputs and outcomes observable, for example, garbage collection and passport issuing. Others have observable outcomes but less precision on outputs and processes: a police crime prevention and reduction strategy in an area can result in fewer crimes being committed and a safer neighbourhood created (an outcome), but outputs (more arrests, less crime in the area) may not be easily visible from the processes and actions, which might include more police patrols, more selective targeting of crime, more intelligence gathering, use of community policing methods etc. Other organizations have observable outputs but less observable or defined outcomes. For instance, higher student contact hours with academic staff can be seen and measured; it is less easy to see or know if this leads to improvement in educational learning. Yet other organizations may find both output and outcome difficult to observe. For example security-related intelligence gathering may be difficult to define using a combination of formal (investigating specific databases) and informal (e.g. intercepting and interpreting conversations or meetings) methods and activities with results frequently difficult to identify, measure or relate to organizational activities – success for instance could be 'no activity' (i.e. no major security breaches or incidents).

This typology raises complex issues of differential degrees of observability and measurability of outputs and outcomes. It is claimed by some authors, with a considerable degree of evidence, that the linkage between public service activities and outcomes is ignored and what is more verifiable in fact becomes more privileged, for instance intermediate outcomes like exam results or waiting times; and where outputs are also problematic, the focus is then on inputs (e.g. costs) (Power 1997).

Perhaps the most significant aspect of performance in the public sector is its complexity. This is captured by van Dooren et al. (2010), when outlining the different levels and inter-linkages between three levels of performance: these are defined as the macro, meso and micro levels. Macro refers to performance at governmental level (from local to national to supra-national bodies such as the EU and the UN), micro to the individual organization and meso, which often straddles the other two, to a policy sector or the performance of governing a chain of events or networks (van Dooren et al. 2010: 25). The following gives a flavour of performance complexity in such an environment.

At the macro level, much public policy and service delivery is framed within multi-level governance. That is to say, policy may be influenced by supra-national bodies (such as the EU Convention on Human Rights or the UN Beijing Declaration on Women's Rights) whose guidelines and regulations may be incorporated into national policy and legislation. Policies and initiatives cascaded in this way from the supra-national to the national may be done tightly and prescriptively leaving relatively little room for performance discretion (e.g. application of the EU's Common Agricultural Policy); or it may be done more loosely giving scope for performance variation (e.g. the general use of the EU's 'open method of coordination') where national governments are given latitude for interpreting and implementing a range of policies. Within national jurisdictions there can be unitary, federal or devolved governmental arrangements; in the latter two, national government at the centre may shift certain areas of responsibility to states or provinces or devolved assemblies with or without appropriate resource – this can affect performance in certain policy areas; indeed in some areas there is evidence that policy performance can be enhanced by use of multi-level governance leverage, for example, in the arena of equality (Fyfe et al. 2009; Miller 2012). The central–local government environment can also have implications for performance. Where the balance between central (national) government and local government is skewed in favour of the former, local performance can be more easily impacted by central action: in fact recent research on English and Welsh local authorities indicates that increased resourcing levered through central action, is a more significant factor in performance improvement than scrutiny measures (Lockwood and Porcelli 2011).

At the micro level, performance may be complicated by organizations being involved in different policy sectors. A social services organization will be involved with health care policy (for various groups including children, the elderly, drug abusers etc.), the criminal justice sector (for certain categories of offender), the education sector (for at-risk children). Regulatory organizations, in addition to involvement with their own client group/sector, may also have relationships with other countries' parallel regulatory bodies – banking and financial regulation being a topical example. Organizations in security and intelligence may have to liaise and perform with equivalent bodies in other countries.

At the meso level, policy sectors may overlap or intersect, again adding to the complex picture of performance. In building or extending an airport, the transport policy sector will be pre-eminent (and there will be sub-policy sectors with an interest too, road, rail and air), but environmental policy will also be important. Public sector response to infectious disease may involve a policy chain including civil aviation policy (restricting or controlling international air travel), public health policy (screening and immunization programmes), policy and justice (controlling public events or criminal proceedings if laws have been violated). Defining and attributing performance in such situations can be very challenging.

PURPOSE OF PERFORMANCE MANAGEMENT

The purpose of performance management in the public sector has been summarized by the Royal Statistical Society:

> Three broad aims of public sector performance data can be identified: to establish 'what works' in promoting stated objectives of the public services; to identify the functional competence of individual practitioners or organisations; and public accountability by ministers for their stewardship of public services. These can be viewed respectively as the research, managerial and democratic roles of performance data . . .
>
> (Royal Statistical Society 2003)

This presents an interesting way of assessing the purposes and broad aims of performance management: research into what works; managerial control; accountability.

PERFORMANCE AS RESEARCH INTO WHAT WORKS

Intelligence-led approaches to performance can be thought of as an attempt to gain greater understanding and knowledge about how an organization system or programme works. Such an approach may be used by managers or others to diagnose problems or trends in the organization's activities or outputs and should be thought of as quite distinct from target-based control systems (Hood 2007). For example, a police authority may wish to interrogate its crime and arrest statistics: are there more crimes committed and arrests made during and after major football matches than 'normally'? Are the numbers similar or dissimilar to crime and arrests at all crowd-based events where alcohol consumption is significant? Such diagnostic work should in fact precede the allocation of appropriate police resource and the creation of targets such as crime reduction levels at major crowd-based events. It has been claimed that considerable reform and improvement in New York's police was driven by monthly comparisons and learning between police force areas. Intelligence-led approaches to performance management can be used as a powerful instrument of learning, adapting practices to what is actually occurring on the ground or is seen as working best. There is case-based research on such effects (Moynihan 2008).

A number of writers have indicated that, in many areas of public sector activity, a series of 'soft' performance measures (many of which can actually be headed 'intelligence led' or learning based) are very significant steps in managing performance. Political decision makers often base decisions not on formal performance reporting systems but on intelligence gained by networking and verbalizing with senior officials (Pollitt 2006b). Some have also recognized that only the knowledge and intelligence of specific organizations and institutions can make performance information and management meaningful (Bussman 1996; Radin 2000; Walker 2001). Others have gone further and added that the entire exercise (of performance measurement and management) could be self-defeating if there is a narrow focus on targets and measurement without the intelligence and knowledge seeking approach – since top-down, target-based approaches frustrate critical self-examination and lead to over justifying and defending current practices, as well as a reluctance to recognize that improvement or change is required (Perrin 1998).

PERFORMANCE MANAGEMENT AS MANAGEMENT CONTROL: COMPLEXITIES, CONTEXT AND GAMING

A key function of performance management has been a control tool or instrument used by managers and others to achieve certain levels of activity or output in the organization. Performance-based pay for managers in public sector organizations can be targeted to the achievement of goals that have been set for the organization. For example, university managers may have performance-based pay related to the recruitment of international students if that is an organizational goal or target; senior civil servants may have an element of their pay related to the targeted achievement of the number of women employed in certain grades in their department.

There is a range of international examples of performance management driving managerial control and improvement in public organizations. UK governments have claimed that improvements in service delivery have to a large extent been attributable to performance management at organizational and governmental levels, especially heralded in the attainment of educational qualifications (Cabinet Office 2006). Similarly, other countries have seen a link between management control, performance management and improvement. In Belgium, direct managerial intervention via performance budgeting has led to a decrease in waiting times between unemployment date and benefit disbursement (Baeck and van Neyen 2003 cited in van Dooren *et al.* 2010); in Slovenia and the Baltic states police activity has been improved through active use of performance management (Verheijen and Dobroylyubova 2007; Vitezic 2007). There is, however, research in the UK that indicates in some instances improvements can be better attributed to increased finance inputs rather than active direction or steering via performance management and targeting (Lockwood and Porcelli 2011).

But the use of performance management as a managerial control instrument must be viewed in a cautionary, nuanced way with an appreciation of the effects, some unintended and/or unforeseen. Social scientists have recognized for some time that when members of an organization know they are being observed (or measured or judged) this in itself affects how people act: in other words the existence of such 'observations' is not neutral in its impact. Known as the 'Hawthorne Effect' this was first discovered by researchers at Harvard University studying the relationship between productivity and work environment at the Hawthorne works plant of Western Electric. The original aim was to determine whether changes in lighting conditions (and later other variables) had an impact on productivity. The findings indicated in fact that productivity increases were due to attention from the research process rather than the lighting and other variables. More recent analyses of the original data in 2009 indicated that original results may have been overstated and that other factors played a role with the effect originally described being 'weak at best' (*Economist* 2009: 80); it has also been claimed that the variance in productivity could be accounted for by the weekly work cycle or seasonal temperatures (Levitt and List 2011). This, of course, is not to say that the existence of performance management as a controlling or steering force has no Hawthorne-like impact on behaviour, simply that the effect cannot be over-determined. Perhaps we can go no further than to say that the existence of performance management may have some impact on the culture of the organization in turn impacting on behaviour: perhaps it keeps people aware and 'on their toes', and can be an instrument if things go wrong or deviate from an acceptable pattern (see e.g. Pollitt 2006b).

There is also research and literature that indicates the actual work of managers does not in fact sit easily with many of the key concerns of performance management. Mintzberg's important empirical research in the 1970s indicated the key concerns of managers were focused around some key factors: managers processed large, open-ended workloads under tight time pressures; managerial activities were short-term in duration and highly fragmented; communications were action driven, informal and strongly influenced by verbal communication; involvement in the execution of work was limited but managers did initiate many decisions. These activities were clustered into roles around interpersonal contact, information processing and decision-making (Mintzberg 1973). This is not to suggest that such a study – considered seminal in the management literature – indicates little concern for performance management, but simply that much managerial activity is not thus focused. More recent managerial and leadership studies, far from concentrating on performance management, tend to focus on the 'softer' inter personal aspects of management (e.g. Huczynski 1994; van Wart 2003). Some significant authors have also indicated that performance management and measurement-based approaches have generally not resulted in achieving their aims and have inhibited the development of a key aspect of managerial activity, the development and implementation of strategy (Mintzberg 1994). And of course in the public sector context such approaches cannot always capture the public manager's job at the political and regulatory interface (Wilson 1989). Nevertheless, performance management regimes have been introduced in the public sector and there is a range of complex and complicating issues to be considered.

The first issue surrounds questions of what is measured, why some areas of activity and/or some organizations are targeted more than others for performance management activity. Van Dooren *et al.* (2010) offer a reasonably comprehensive explanatory framework for addressing this issue. Performance management may be prioritized by organizations or governments when a specific problem or problem area has come to light. The UK Passport Agency experienced problems issuing passports timeously in 2008 and subsequently introduced target waiting times between submission of application and passport issue. If an organization is structured in such a way that a small number of identifiable activities comprise a large proportion of the budget then it will be a candidate for performance management. For instance, a university with a significant proportion of income emanating from undergraduate and continuing undergraduate students may choose a performance management regime focusing on targeting student recruitment, retention and throughput. Visibility and salience of issues may be a driver for performance management. Abuse of members of parliaments' and other politicians' expense claims – although financially not particularly significant – has immediate media and public exposure and high issue salience; systems and performance management regimes may be installed to address disquiet in this area. Feasibility, ease of measurement and cost are important factors. If a range of activities or processes can be easily measured then performance management is more likely to appear there than in areas of greater difficulty: 'what is measured is what gets done'. Quality assurance systems are particular cases in point in this regard (see Power

239

1997). Cost of measurement and complexity involved in installing a performance management regime may be a significant factor – in some cases the cost may exceed the potential benefits, so would be difficult to justify.

The 'balanced scorecard' (Kaplan and Norton 1992; 1996; 2000) attempts to capture complexity across the organization with a range of measures often including softer areas like learning and innovation. This has been adapted for and widely applied in the public sector (Donaldson *et al.* 2008), so clearly the diversity of the public sector environment has not been a barrier to adoption; but the use of tools such as the balanced scorecard has been criticized for not capturing the complexity of 'public value', so as an alternative, a public value scorecard has been proposed, based on the public value chain, measuring how well organizations are performing against declared social mission (Moore 2003). Finally, van Dooren *et al.* (2010) indicate that the introduction and use of performance management may in fact be predetermined e.g. within the EU the Lisbon criteria amount to a series of international performance management reporting obligations.

The second issue is to analyze a range of considerations regarding the context and barriers to using performance information affecting the credibility of the information and data source upon which performance measurement and management are based. Some governments have established independent budget offices and economic policy units to eliminate the fear (perceived or otherwise) of political or other contamination of key data and information. For example, the powerful Netherlands Bureau for Economic Policy Analysis carries much authority across the political divide because its analysis is seen as politically neutral and credible (de Vries *et al.* 2010); similar comments can be made about Sweden's Office of Fiscal Policy (Fiscal Policy Council); the UK has more recently established an Office of Budget Responsibility (OBR) and although it is yet too soon to determine whether this will move in the Dutch or Swedish direction, it is less likely: unlike the Netherlands, the OBR's capacity is not available to the opposition party; it is less well resourced with staff mainly seconded from the UK Treasury.

Managers and decision makers in an organization will inevitably match information against their own pre-existing paradigm of actuality based on knowledge and experience (Weiss and Bucuvalas 1980). For example, university staff, seeing information of significantly higher exam pass or fail rates or other such information, will check this against views of student performance based on a previous knowledge base and founded on experience, discussion and judgement of others, knowledge of alterations in student recruitment, etc. and form a judgement on the information accordingly.

An important contextual factor in the effective use of performance information is based on the extent to which the conditions exist for maximizing and rationalizing in the organization. Simon's model of rationalizing/satisficing is significant here (Simon 1976 – see also van Dooren *et al.* 2010). As discussed in Chapter 1, rational decision-making is based on a range of premises including knowledge of the

240

environment, all information, knowledge of all courses of action and the ability and capacity to compute all this and make the relevant choice and then implement. On the ground, such a criteria set often does not exist, so the option taken is to satisfice, that is take courses of action which are good enough but not necessarily the most rational–optimal. So the actuality of satisficing provides the context for using performance information and introducing and implementing performance management: despite the aims to maximize the rational and optimal aspect of performance management, this much has been known about organizational life for some time. Furthermore, research on individual decision-making suggests that self-reported maximizers–optimizers are more likely than satisficers to exhibit poor decision-making, less behavioural coping, greater degrees of decision avoidance (Schwartz *et al.* 2002; Parker *et al.* 2007). To extend this research to the arena of organizational performance would raise interesting research questions like: are attempts to maximize/optimize performance measurement regimes leading to poor decision-making? Do satisficing strategies (somewhat counter-intuitively) lead to better performance management in the organization?

Cultural values and norms can be considered as a contextual factor. Various typologies of culture – aspects of which are assigned or attributed to specific countries – have been researched and formulated. For example, Bendix (1974) has outlined entrepreneurial and by contrast bureaucratic cultures; Sartori (1969) rationalist and pragmatic cultures; Hofstede's (2001) work has focused on five dimensions including power distance, collectivism–individualism, masculinity–femininity, uncertainty avoidance, long-term orientation–short-term orientation. As van Dooren *et al.* (2010) indicate, performance systems will operate differently dependent on the culture: individualistic cultures may adopt, more easily than others, performance related pay and other such incentives; fatalistic cultures (see Hood 2000) will adopt ritualistic systems; egalitarian cultures will have greater difficulty with performance systems and measures that prioritize individual above group; hierarchical cultures will see performance running through the organization with a strong regulatory tone. There is also evidence that heavily target-based performance systems, typified by many NPM regimes, can operate in a gendered way, often to the detriment of women (McTavish and Miller 2009).

The third major issue to consider surrounds the various (mis)interpretations, distortions and gaming which often accompany performance measurement and management regimes. Various situations can be considered here. An increase in observations or activity over a time period may not be an actual increase on the ground but simply more measurement. For instance, the increase in the number of rape cases reported may be due to an increase in reporting (due to more sympathetic and supportive policing, greater confidence in charging and conviction of offenders) rather than an increase in rape per se. Or conversely, under-reporting may occur if there is evidence (real or perceived) that inadequate protection or anonymity is provided for witnesses.

Over-representation may also be used as an attempt to 'artificially' inflate an activity or incidence of an event. For example a university wishing to provide evidence that large numbers of its staff are research active may inflate 'real' numbers by encouraging the appearance of multiple authorship of publications – the assumption being that all names on the publication are active in the research process that produced the publication; such action would be ethically if not legally dubious and would presumably be resisted by the 'actual' researchers named on the publication.

If incentive structures are based on measured output, this can lead to over-supply. This has been documented for certain health care products in Europe where reimbursement is based on measured output from producers (Dawson and Street 2000). At certain times, this has undoubtedly been the case with agri-cultural produce support in Europe under the EU's Common Agricultural Policy and indeed elsewhere. Another consequence of performance measurement can be 'cream skimming' where service providers and producers will address the easy hits: this may frustrate – certainly sub-optimize – public policy goals. For example, schools may use various proxy measures for selection (if they can), if they are measured by positioning on league tables or exam performance; health care providers may target high-throughput, low-cost patients or clinical procedures; job placement contractors will select easier-to-place candidates, that is those more likely to find employment.

Measurement can also be manipulated or misinterpreted if inappropriate aggregation and/or disaggregation are used. Figures from the Scottish Govern-ment indicate planned expenditure for colleges and universities, via funding to the arm's-length body the Scottish Funding Council, increasing by 4 per cent from 2011/2012 to 2014/2015, from £1470.9m to £1532.4m. However, disaggrega-tion of the figures shows an increase to higher education (mainly delivered in uni-versities) of c.14 per cent (from £926.2m to £1061.7m) but a decrease in further education funding (mainly delivered in colleges) of c.13 per cent (from £544.7m to £470.7m) (THES 2011; www.scotland.gov.uk/resource/doc/358356/0121130. pdf (accessed 29 April 2013)).

There is a range of gaming effects surrounding measurement and targeting. A measurement and target-setting culture and regime may see much gaming activity ranging from the setting of relatively undemanding targets to threshold effects where pressure is put on those performing above target to deteriorate towards target (Bird *et al.* 2005), to ratchet effects where next year's targets are based on this or last year's performance, leading managers not to exceed targets where perhaps they could (Litwack 2003). Performance targets can also lead to short-term behaviour, which may ignore the long term. For example many targets in health care will be to deal with people in the system (waiting times, treatment times, reduction in infections, mortality etc.), whereas long-term benefits for a nation's health may accrue from expenditures, actions and performance targets on prevention and health education. Such short-term/long-term dichotomies, either not captured or perhaps even exacerbated by performance system, can be found in business sectors too. For example, in banking where short-term targets and rewards for key agents within the system led to the growth of non-transparent products with little regard for the long-term health or resilience of the banking sector, let alone the economy as a whole. Another case can be illustrated in the oil exploration and production industry in Box 10.1.

Finally, the sheer complexity of current practice in the public sector raises issues for performance management. Two instances will illustrate. First, it is especially, but not exclusively, the case in the public sector that there can be multiple meanings due to the complex interplay of professional and managerial activity, changes in practice over time (which often a performance systems lags). Without an interrogation of the measurement, the numbers in a complex system may be meaningless, as Box 10.2 and the Enron case study in Chapter 9 indicate.

Second, a substantial amount of public services are delivered collaboratively within partnerships and networks. This can of course pose challenges for performance management in determining where responsibility for performance lies. It is particularly difficult holding one organization to account for results produced collaboratively, especially when in many instances budget lines and accountabilities are retained by individual organizations for their separate input to the partnership effort. This can have an adverse effect on the partnership (Denhardt and Aristigueta 2008). Every successful partnership has willing parents, but performance failures often indicate very little acceptance of responsibility. In the UK several high-profile failures in the protection of at-risk children have revealed failures in the lead authority (local authority childcare services or social work departments) to manage performance, but equally significant failures in other bodies within the formal child protection arena (e.g. police, health care workers, doctors) coupled with a major failure in the over-arching partnership body itself (in these cases the local Safeguarding Children Board) to interrogate and manage performance of front-line staff and others (Marinetto 2011).

PERFORMANCE AND ACCOUNTABILITY

Hood (1991) outlines different types of accountability related to the dimensions of concern in the public realm. There is a concern for the production of goods and services, the efficiency and effectiveness of matching public sector inputs to public service outputs. An additional concern is the method and process by which government and public sector organizations operate with key conceptual concerns such as honesty, transparency, equity etc. Finally there is an interest about resilience and dependability, the ability to respond to crises. These are ways in which the public in general can keep account of governments' and public sector organizations' activities.

BOX 10.1   SHELL'S OIL AND GAS RESERVES

The Anglo–Dutch oil company Shell announced in 2004 that its estimates of proven reserves had been too high. Reserves that had been stated in the books had to be reduced by 20 per cent to comply with criteria of the US Security and Exchange Commission (SEC); the consequences were serious with senior executives forced to resign. An important factor was the performance management system operated by Shell, where bonuses were linked to the size of reserves: the greater the reserves the higher the bonuses.

A proven reserve is ambiguous with no clear definition. The SEC says that a reserve is proven if a field could be 'economically and legally extracted or produced at the time of the reserve determination'. This leaves considerable scope for interpretation. A proven reserve is not open to question but is hard to quantify – only when fields are actually exploited does a clearer picture emerge. The consequences for performance management are clear. Quantification leaves considerable scope to be exploited by professionals when reporting the performance. Roel Murris (Shell's ex-head of exploration) said 'if you demand success from those who work for you, this is what you get, especially if a financial or career bonus is attached'. In these circumstances there is equilibrium: management is satisfied with the impression that its objectives are being achieved; the professionals are satisfied by not having to put up with management interference or even by being rewarded. And perverse information has taken root in the organization.

The chances of this occurring are particularly high if an organization has too few checks and balances; strong incentives exist for blocking any information that might disturb a peaceful equilibrium or prompt discussion about the performance measurement system. Shell's external auditor, Anton Barendrecht, warned in successive annual reports that the reliability of the reserves was strained by the link with bonuses. Dutch investigative journalists received confirmation from many sources that the Shell country managers put Barendrecht in his place on several occasions, being told to 'keep off the bonuses'. Meanwhile many in Shell were under the impression that all was well in the organization.

Source: adapted from De Bruijn (2007: 45)

BOX 10.2 HOSPITAL MORTALITY RATE

Many countries publish hospital mortality rates, i.e. the number of patients who die in hospital. The meaning of such figures is extremely difficult to interpret without further information. For example:

- Mortality rates in rural Scotland are higher than in England. The main reason is that patients have a longer journey to hospital and therefore arrive in a poorer condition.
- Low mortality rates may result from shorter hospitalization periods, because patients are discharged to die at home and so do not count in the figures.
- The nature of many treatments (e.g. oncology) has changed, so that the norm is now for treatment in hospital, thereafter the patient returning home, reporting later for another session – so an uninterrupted stay in hospital is rather unusual. If a patient dies this may be likely to occur at home; only if he/she dies in hospital would the figure appear.
- As medical knowledge advances, patients once deemed untreatable are now admitted. Mortality rates may thereby be affected.
- Some hospitals collaborate with hospices to offer terminal care; collaboration of this kind will impact on hospital mortality rates.

Source: adapted from De Bruijn (2007: 74)

There has undoubtedly been a shift in the emphasis of accountability from the 'traditional' concerns of legality (to ensure legal requirements are met, that there is accountability for the expenditures, which legislatures vote, etc.) to a concern about accountability for outputs (Kettl 2002). In general terms, the former may be characterized by a hierarchical bureaucracy with a legally and/or constitutionally enshrined separation of power with checks and balances, with key agents in the system typified by the budget-maximising civil servant who is focused on legal compliance and financial control (Chan and Xiao 2009). The latter is particularly cost focused, operating with strategic business units, key agents in the system defined in terms such as 'public entrepreneurs' concerned with customer/user satisfaction and orientation and the achievement of outcomes to meet their needs. For example, UK government's departmental business plans (the name is a giveaway!) are clearly authored with this output–delivery language in mind; the assumption being that departments and ultimately government itself will be held accountable for outputs and expenditure.

However, it must be noted, despite the proclaimed focus on outcomes, these are rarely used as the key tool of accountability. The distinction between output and outcomes has been mentioned above, with outcomes seen as impacts or consequences of outputs (but with the difficulty sometimes of showing a causal relationship to outputs). Performance measurement and accountability therefore often concentrate on outputs such as examination results in education, reductions in waiting times or numbers of surgical procedures in health, rather than outcomes such as the contribution of a more highly educated population to business and economic performance or increases in the health and well-being of the population. Although there is a relationship between the outputs and outcomes in these cases, it is complex, not always causal and may include other variables. Therefore outputs rather than outcomes are often the focal point of accountability. And it can also be shown that, where the relationship between organizational or institutional activities and outputs is also problematic, inputs (e.g. costs) and how these are used become the focus of accountability (Power 1997).

There are two other aspects of accountability and performance management to be considered. First, the relationship and alignment between principals and agents; second, the political and wider democratic context of accountability. Traditional notions of principal–agent relationships, where principals are elected politicians who hold agents (civil servants, departmental heads etc.) to account, are deceptively simple and have been recognized as such by public administration scholars. Principal–agent relationships are easier to conceptualize where agents can perform particular functions easily controlled by the principal (Donahue 1989). In the NPM and post-NPM environments of agencification, contractual relationships, partnerships and networks, such clarity of configuration between principals and agents may be difficult to obtain. Conceptually, this has been addressed through attempts to redefine government's (i.e. the principal's) role as 'steering' the strategic policy and direction, leaving the 'rowing' and delivery to semi-autonomous, independently managed and managerially empowered entities (e.g. Osborne and Gaebler 1992). Implicit in this steering/rowing divide is that those steering (ultimately the principal) will be able to judge and hold accountable those who have been managerially empowered to deliver public policy outputs and services, underwritten by a performance management regime. Performance management can also be used as an important tool of policy and programme evaluation, ultimately of (potential) use to principals in holding agents to account (McDavid and Hawthorn 2006).

While such accountability of agents to principals may be conceptually neat, there are in reality complexities. Literature on regulation indicates the difficulty of designing effective monitoring systems, necessary for this conception of accountability; there can be difficulties developing systems that can give principals the appropriate information on client performance without information overloading, often a consequence of game-playing (Kettl 1993; Sinclair 1995; Power 1997).

246

Measures and mechanisms for accountability may actually be negotiated between agents and principals; this may be sensible to take into account professional, technocratic or operational knowledge, much of which is likely to reside with the agents; or it may be an attempt by agents to 'persuade' principals of the appropriate accountability measures to adopt that will favour the agent, for example, to magnify weighting given to specific factors favourable to the agent in a composite criteria league table of university performance. The prevalence of multi-organizational partnership and collaborative environments can often lead to difficulties in identifying who the principals and agents are, let alone addressing the problems and issues in managing these delivery instruments of vital public services (Koppenjan and Klijn 2004).

So perhaps more fundamentally the reality is that the NPM and post-NPM world has increased complexity of relationships between principals and agents. A response to this from governments has been to give greater policy presence and visibility to audit bodies. There is no doubt that audit bodies have grown in significance and the key question is whether accountability to citizens and the electorate has been supplemented (or indeed displaced – see Power 1997) by managerial conceptions of accountability, downplaying wider policy–societal concerns about programme objectives etc., thereby circumventing this form of accountability. Literature and research have tended to support this view, noting in particular that such bodies have directed their activity, reporting to funders 'in the public interest', but often ignoring any accountability responsibilities to representatives of the public (see Bowerman et al. 2002).

Second, the political context of accountability is vitally important in terms of how the 'ultimate' accountability to principals, elected politicians and citizens, relates to performance. The extant literature and research tend to show that elected representatives' use of performance measurement and management for accountability purposes is, at best, patchy. Comparative work on Australia, Sweden, Netherlands and Canada indicate little linkage between performance budgeting and improved accountability in legislatures (Sterck 2007). Other studies at a local government level have shown similar results (Ter Bogt 2004). Research also shows that performance information and reports are quite disjointed in terms of what interests politicians, information overload on politicians' time, the questionable relationship between interest in performance reports and political careers – much political activity being focused on inputs to the public policy and management process (e.g. legislative inputs, resourcing and funding priorities) with performance and outcomes of secondary concern (Sterck 2007; Bouckaert and Halligan 2008; Bourdeaux 2008). Other evaluative studies (in US, UK, Finland) have shown very minimal use of performance information by legislatures (e.g. see Pollitt 2006b). The OECD has made the following observation: 'The growing popularity of performance measurement around the budget and reporting process . . . often creates flows of superfluous information that nobody in fact uses' (OECD 2003).

247

Citizen accountability is clearly an important dimension in a democratic polity, particularly so in the context of the co-production of public services. There is research and an emerging literature on co-production that addresses the extent to which co-production may enhance accountability to individual citizens, communities and neighbourhoods. Comprehensive evaluation is dependent on the extent to which governments accelerate co-production as a means of delivering public services and the extent to which this enhances (or not) citizen accountability through service performance. The UK and other governments intend to embark on this path (see *Commission on 2020 Public Services* 2011). Citizens holding service delivery performance to account will be based on personal experience but also on mediated information (from the press, television and other media). The short case in Box 10.3 on 'health reporting' shows how the presentation and mediation of information can give an incorrect impression thereby giving a poor information and evidence base which will ultimately compromise the worth of accountability.

Added to this, research on public satisfaction in health and education fails to show a direct relationship between evidenced improvements and public satisfaction, with members of the public basing perceptions on factors other than measures showing performance improvement (see Flynn 2007); public expectation of service level has also been shown as significant when considering and measuring satisfaction (see James 2011).

PERFORMANCE MANAGEMENT AND ACCOUNTABILITY: UNCLEAR BOUNDARIES

In addition to the issues discussed in this chapter previously, there are two broad areas where boundaries are unclear in terms of what the performance management regime's purpose is. The first of these is where there are differing perceptions and views on the regime in question. The second is where the performance arena is under-knowledged or under-theorized.

Medical audit provides an example of the first. This can be seen as a professionally, clinically driven instrument based on peer review, learning and dissemination of best practice. It may also be seen as a tool to cost-evaluate medical procedures and interventions with strong managerial intent to control. These approaches may or may not be compatible or complementary; but they are different and each perspective is outlined:

> Medical audit was never intended as a public accountability device . . . its status has been a heuristic tool to improve practice.
>
> (Power 1997: 109)

> Audit activities must differentiate . . . between a management tool whose prime purpose is control and cost, and medical audit which is a professional

BOX 10.3 HEALTH REPORTING

[to undertake research for a publication in the journal *Public Understanding of Science*] we needed a representative, unbiased sample of news stories, so we bought every one of the top 10 bestselling UK newspapers every day for one week . . . we pulled out every story with any kind of health claim which could be interpreted by a reader as health advice, then the evidence for every claim was checked, through a searchable archive of academic papers, the evidence for each claim was graded using two standard systems for categorising the strength of evidence. We worked with the Scottish Intercollegiate Guidelines Network and the World Cancer Research Fund scale widely used for ease of use and rigour. Here's what we found: 111 health claims were made in UK newspapers over one week. The vast majority of these claims were only supported by evidence categorized as 'insufficient'. After that, 10 per cent were 'possible', 12 per cent were probable and in only 15 per cent was the evidence 'convincing'. Fewer low quality claims were made in broadsheet newspapers but there wasn't much in it . . . this is a worrying finding. It seems that the majority of health claims made, in a large representative sample of UK national newspapers, are supported only by the weakest possible forms of evidence. People who work in public health bend over backwards to disseminate evidence-based information to the public. I wonder if they should also focus on documenting and addressing the harm done by journalists. And for the people who have denied there is a problem here: the onus is now on you to produce evidence justifying your dismissiveness.

Source: adapted from Ben Goldacre, 'How far should we trust health reporting', Guardian, 18 June 2011, p. 48.

task with a prime purpose of education . . . any organised medical audit activity must acknowledge this distinction.

(Richards 1991: 153)

The NHS could save up to £500m a year by carrying out fewer ineffective and inefficient procedures . . . a single approach to defining these low value treatments could help reduce duplication of effort and ensure consistency across the country . . . the types identified include tonsillectomy, those with a close benefit and risk balance . . . potentially cosmetic procedures.

(Audit Commission 2011)

International performance ratings provide an example of an area which is under-theorized. Lack of knowledge leads to a very tenuous relationship between performance and accountability. A study of the World Bank Institute world governance indicators (WGI) indicates there is no normative definition of what constitutes good or bad governance in a country's ratings – they simply reflect traditions existing within the country, and a compilation of ratings from a variety of sources to give a single indicator without any definition of norms used; the norms may differ from year to year and from country to country. Furthermore, the study indicates that lack of knowledge and theoretical underpinning can lead to hidden bias in the ratings system: the examples highlighted include the negative ratings (e.g. 'unfriendly to markets') given to labour rights and environmental protection; yet other studies give high ratings to countries with such regulations; and also the higher relative weightings given to business risk ratings than to evidence gained from individual citizens. The study states:

> While the most popular indicators are very useful in gaining a first idea of how experts perceive a country's quality of governance, too little attention is paid to indicators' limitations. The more users rely on the same indicators the more they become 'generally accepted internationally' which spreads their use further.
>
> (Arndt and Oman 2008: 25)

Such indicators are used for foreign aid allocation decisions and also play a large part informing media representation of country governance. However, for the reasons outlined their utility in linking performance to accountability is somewhat limited. But to end more positively, the study also noted that (more recently) there have appeared very specific indicators – rather than 'catch-all' governance indicators – with the potential that such specificity and definition will, at least in theory, be able to engage with notions of institutional and agency accountability (Arndt and Oman 2008).

CONCLUSION

This chapter indicated the considerable scale and scope of performance management targeted at organizational functions and processes, measurement of inputs, outputs and outcomes. Some of the complexities of these were outlined: the diversity of factors affecting outputs and outcomes; the differing levels of salience and observability of public sector activity; multi-levels of organization, government and policy sectors interacting in the performance management outcome.

The purposes and broad aims of performance management were outlined. First, an analysis of performance as an attempt to understand more fully how the organizational system actually works, including soft and intelligence-led approaches.

250

Second, its role in enabling management control. Here, a range of factors were considered including cultural issues, contamination of performance data and various distortions arising from 'gaming' activity (ranging from 'cream skimming' to ratchet and threshold effects to inappropriate aggregation), extent and degree of measurability, rival interpretations and perspectives on the performance being managed. Third, performance management and accountability were considered. The difficulty of using outcomes as an accountability device was noted, leading to the more common linkage of accountability to outputs (or even inputs). The traditional accountability of agents to principals was shown to be subject to considerable complexities in the governance terrain of partnerships and professional technocratic environments where agents may hold considerably more power than principals. The interest and locus of principals to oversee accountability for performance was shown to be patchy as were practices of accountability to the wider citizenry. Finally, there was brief consideration of some unclear performance and accountability boundaries where there exist different perceptions of the purpose of the performance management regime in question, and where the performance management arena was under-knowledged.

REFERENCES

Arndt, C. and Oman, C. (2008) *Politics of Governance Ratings,* Maastricht: Maastricht Graduate School of Governance Working Paper MgSoG/2008/WP003.

Audit Commission Health Briefing (April 2011) *Reducing Spending in Low Clinical Value Treatments,* London: Audit Commission.

Baeck, K. and Van Neyen, S. (2003) 'Risicobeheer bij de Rijksdienst voor Arbeidsvoorziening', *VTOM,* 8, 3: 26–35.

Bendix, R. (1974) *Work and Authority in Industry,* Berkeley, CA: University of California Press.

Bird, S.M., Cox, D. and Farewell, V.T. (2005) 'Performance indicators: good bad and ugly', *Journal of the Royal Statistical Society,* Series A, 168, 1: 1–27.

Blau, P.M. (1955) *The Dynamics of Bureaucracy,* Chicago, IL: Chicago University Press.

Bouckaert, G. and Halligan, J. (2008) *Managing Performance: international comparisons,* London: Sage.

Bouckaert, G. and van Dooren, W. (2009) 'Performance Measurement and Management in Public Sector Organisations', in T. Bovaird and E. Loffler (eds) *Public Management and Governance,* London: Routledge.

Bourdeaux, J. (2008) 'Integrating performance information into legislative budget processes', *Public Performance and Management Review,* 31, 4: 547–569.

Bowerman, M., Francis, G., Ball, A. and Fry, J. (2002) 'The evolution of benchmarking in UK local authorities', *Benchmarking: An International Journal,* 9, 5: 429–449.

Boyne, G. (2003) 'What is public service improvement?' *Public Administration*, 81, 2: 211–217.

Bussman, W. (1996) 'Democracy and evaluation's contribution to legislation, empowerment and information: some findings from Swiss experience', *Evaluation*, 2, 3: 307–319.

Cabinet Office Prime Minister's Strategy Unit (2006) *The UK Government's Approach to Public Service Reform*, London.

Chan, J.L. and Xiao, X. (2009) 'Financial Management in Public Sector Organizations', in T. Bovaird and E. Loffler (eds) *Public Management and Governance*, London: Routledge.

Commission on 2020 Public Services (2011) Final Report: 2020 Public Services Trust.

Dawson, D. and Street, A. (2000) 'Comparing NHS hospital unit costs', *Public Money & Management*, 20, 4: 58–62.

De Bruijn, J.A. (2007) *Managing Performance in the Public Sector*, London: Routledge.

Denhardt, K. and Aristigueta, M. (2008) 'Performance Management Systems: providing accountability and challenging collaboration', in W. Van Dooren and S. Van de Walle (eds) *Performance Innovation in the Public Sector: how it is used*, Basingstoke: Palgrave Macmillan.

De Vries, A., Halffman, W. and Hoppe, R. (2010) 'Policy Workers Tinkering with Uncertainty: Dutch econometric policy advice in action', in H. Colebatch, R. Hoppe and M. Noordegraff (eds) *Working for Policy*, Amsterdam: Amsterdam University Press.

Donahue, J. (1989) *The Privatization Decision*, New York: Basic Books.

Donaldson, C., Bate, A., Mitton, C., Peacock, S. and Rutta, D. (2008) 'Priority Setting in the Public Sector: turning economics into a management process', in J. Hartley, C. Donaldson, C. Skelcher and M. Wallace (eds) (2008) *Managing to Improve Public Services*, Cambridge: Cambridge University Press.

Easton, D. (1965) *A Systems Analysis of Political Life*, New York: Wiley.

Eckstein, H. (1958) *The English Health Care Service*, Cambridge, MA: Harvard University Press.

Economist (2009) www.economist.com/businessfinance/displaystory.Cfm?story_id=13788427. (Accessed 19 February 2012.)

Flynn, N. (2007) *Public Sector Management*, London: Sage.

Foreman-Peck, J. and Milward, R. (1994) *Public and Private Ownership of British Industry 1920–1990*, Oxford: Clarendon.

Fry, G. (1969) *Statesmen in Disguise*, London: MacMillan.

Fry, G. (1999) 'More than counting manhole covers: the evolution of the British tradition of public administration', *Public Administration*, 77, 3: 527–540.

Fyfe, G., Miller, K. Johnston and McTavish, D. (2009) '"Muddling through", in a devolved polity: implementation of equal opportunities policy in Scotland', *Policy Studies*, 30, 2: 203–219.

Goldacre, B. 'How far should we trust health reporting', *Guardian*, 18 June 2011, p. 48.

Hofstede, G. (2001) *Culture's Consequences: comparing values, behaviours, institutions and organizations across nations*, Thousand Oaks, CA: Sage.

Hood, C. (1991) 'A public management for all seasons', *Public Administration*, 69: 3–19.

Hood, C. (2000) *The Art of the State. Culture, Rhetoric and Public Management*, Oxford: Oxford University Press.

Hood, C. (2007) 'Public service management by numbers: Why does it vary? Where has it come from? What are the gaps and puzzles?' *Public Money & Management*, 27, 2: 95–102.

Huczynski, A.A. (1994) *Management Gurus. What Makes Them and How to Become One*, London: Routledge.

Jackson, P.M. (2009) 'The Size and Scope of the Public Sector', in T. Bovaird and E. Loffler (eds) *Public Management and Governance*, London: Routledge.

James, O. (2011) 'Citizens' expectations of public service performance: evidence from observation and experimentation in local government', *Public Administration*, 89, 4: 1419–1435.

Jowett, P. and Rothwell, M. (1988) *Performance Indicators in the Public Sector*, London: MacMillan.

Kaplan, R.S. and Norton, D.R. (1992) 'The balanced scorecard: measures that drive performance', *Harvard Business Review*, 70: 71–79.

Kaplan, R.S. and Norton, D.R. (1996) *The Balanced Scorecard and Translating Strategy Into Action*, Boston, MA: Harvard Business School Press.

Kaplan, R.S. and Norton, D.R. (2000) *The Strategy Focused Organization – How Balanced Scorecard Companies Thrive in the New Business Environment*, Boston, MA: Harvard Business School Press.

Kettl, D.F. (1993) *Sharing Power: public governance and private markets*, Washington, DC: Brookings Institution.

Kettl, D.F. (2002) *The Transformation of Governance*, Baltimore, MD: John Hopkins University Press.

Koppenjan, J.F.M. and Klijn, E.H. (2004) *Managing Uncertainties in Networks: a network approach to problem solving and decision-making*, London: Routledge.

Levitt, S.D. and List, J.A. (2011) 'Was there really a Hawthorne effect at the Hawthorne plant? An analysis of the original illumination experiments', *American Economic Journal: Applied Economics*, 3, 1: 224–238.

Litwack, J.M. (2003) 'Co-ordination, incentives and the ratchet effect', *The Bell Journal of Economics*, 24, 2: 271–285.

Lockwood, B. and Porcelli, F. (2011) *Incentive Schemes for Local Government: theory and evidence from comprehensive assessment performance in England*, University of Warwick Research Paper. www2.warwick.ac.uk/fac/soc/economics/staff/academic/lockwood. (Accessed 15 March 2012.)

Lynn, L., Heinrich, C. and Hill, C. (2001) *Improving Governance: a new logic for empirical research*, Washington DC: Georgetown University Press.

McDavid, J.C. and Hawthorn, L.R.L. (2006) *Programme Evaluation and Performance Measurement: an introduction to practice*, Thousand Oaks, CA: Sage.

McTavish, D. (2005) *Business and Public Management in the UK 1900–2003*, Aldershot: Ashgate.

McTavish, D. and Miller, K. Johnston (2009) 'Gender balance in leadership? reform and modernization in the UK further education sector', *Educational Management Administration and Leadership*, 37, 4: 350–365.

Marinetto, M. (2011) 'A Lipskian analysis of childhood protection failures from Victoria Climbié to "Baby P": a street level re-evaluation of joined up governance', *Public Administration*, 89, 3: 1164–1181.

Miller, K. Johnston (2012) 'Representative bureaucracy and multi-level governance in the EU: a research agenda', *Geo-Politics, History and International Relations*, 4, 1: 50–70.

Milward, R. (1997) 'The 1940s nationalisation in Britain: means to an end or means of production?' *Economic History Review*, L, 2: 209–234.

Mintzberg, H. (1973) *The Nature of Managerial Work*, New York: Harper Collins.

Mintzberg, H. (1994) *The Rise and Fall of Strategic Planning*, New York: The Free Press.

Moore, M.H. (2003) 'The Public Value Scorecard: a rejoinder and an alternative', in R. Kaplan (ed.) *Review of Strategic Performance Measurement and Management in Non Profit Organizations*, HCNO Working Paper Series, May.

Moynihan, D.P. (2008) *The Dynamics of Performance Management: constructing information and reform*, Washington DC: Georgetown University Press.

OECD (2003) 'Public sector modernization', *OECD Observer*, October: 1–8.

OECD (2007) *Measuring Government Activity*, Paris: OECD.

Osborne, D. and Gaebler, T. (1992) *Reinventing Government*, Reading, MA: Addison Wesley.

Parker, A.M., de Bruijn, W.B. and Fischhoff, B. (2007) 'Maximisers versus satisficers: decision-making styles, competence and outcomes', *Judgement and Decision-Making*, 2, 6: 342–350.

Perrin, B. (1998) 'Effective use and mis-use of performance management', *American Journal of Evaluation*, 19, 3: 367–379.

Pollitt, C. (2006a) 'Performance management in practice: a comparative study of executive agencies', *Journal of Public Administration Theory and Research*, 6, 1: 25–44.

Pollitt, C. (2006b) 'Performance information for democracy. The missing link?' *Evaluation*, 12, 1: 38–55.

Pollitt, C. and Bouckaert, G. (2011) *Public Management Reform. A Comparative Analysis: new public management, governance and the Weberian state*, Oxford: Oxford University Press.

Power, M. (1997) *The Audit Society. Rituals of Verification,* Oxford: Oxford University Press.

Radin, B. (2000) 'The government's performance and results act and the tradition of federal financial reform: square pegs in round holes', *Journal of Public Administration Research and Theory,* 10, 1: 111–135.

Rhodes, G. (1981) *Inspectorates in British Central Government,* London: Allen and Unwin.

Richards, C. (1991) Untitled, *British Medical Journal,* 302: 153–155.

Rose, N. (1991) 'Governing by numbers: figuring out democracy', *Accounting, Organizations and Society,* 16, 7: 673–692.

Royal Statistical Society (2003) *Performance Indicators: good, bad and ugly,* London.

Sartori, G. (1969) 'Politics ideology and belief systems', *American Political Science Review,* 63: 398–411.

Schwartz, B., Ward, A., Monterosso, J., Lyubomirsky, S., White, K. and Lehman, D.R. (2002) 'Maximising versus satisficing: happiness is a matter of choice', *Journal of Personality and Social Psychology,* 83: 1178–1197.

Simon, H.A. (1976) *Administrative Behaviour: a study of decision-making processes in administrative organizations,* New York: Free Press.

Sinclair, A. (1995) 'The chameleon of accountability: forms and discourses', *Accounting Organization and Society,* 20, 2/3: 219–237.

Sterck, M. (2007) 'The impact of performance budgeting on the role of the legislature: A four country study', *International Review of Administrative Sciences,* 73: 189–203.

Sterck, M., van Dooren, W. and Bouckaert, G. (2006) *Performance Measurement for Sub-National Service Delivery. Report for OECD,* Leuven: Public Management Institute, Katholieka Universiteit.

Taylor, F.W. (1916) 'Government efficiency', *Bulletin of the Taylor Society,* December: 7–13.

Ter Bogt, H.J. (2004) 'Politicians in search of performance information? Survey research on Dutch aldermen's use of performance information', *Financial Accountability and Management,* 20: 221–252.

Townley, B. (2008) *Reason's Neglect: rationality and organising,* Oxford: Oxford University Press.

Treasury (2004) *The UK Government's Public Service Agreement Framework,* London: HMSO.

Van Dooren, W. Bouckaert, G. and Halligan, J. (2010) *Performance Management in the Public Sector,* London: Routledge.

Van Wart, M. (2003) 'Public sector leadership theory: an assessment', *Public Administration Review,* 63: 214–228.

Verheijen, T. and Dobrolyubova, Y. (2007) 'Performance management in the Baltic States and Russia: success against the odds?' *International Review of Administrative Sciences,* 73: 205–215.

Vitezic, N. (2007) 'Beneficial effects of public sector performance Management', *UPRAVA: mednarodna znanstevena revija za teorijo in prakso*, 5: 7–27.

Walker, R. (2001) 'Great Expectations: can social science evaluate New Labour's policies?' *Evaluation*, 7, 3: 305–330.

Webster, C. (1988) *The Health Service Since the War Volume 1. The Problems of Health Care*, London: HMSO.

Webster, C. (1996) *The Health Service Since the War Volume 2. Government and Health Care*, London: HMSO.

Weiss, C.H. and Bucuvalis, M.J. (1980) 'Truth tests and utility tests: decision makers' frames of reference for social science research', *American Sociological Review*, 45: 302–313.

Wildavsky, A. (1975) *Budgeting: a comparative theory of budgetary processes*, Boston, MA: Little Brown.

Wilson, J.Q. (1989) *Bureaucracy: what government agencies do and why they do it*, New York: Basic Books.

Wilson, D. and Game, C. (1988) (and subsequent editions) *Local Government in the UK*, London: MacMillan.

Wren, D.A. (1994) *The Evolution of Management Thought*, New York and London: Wiley.

Chapter 11

Case study: public policy and the UK foot-and-mouth epidemic 2001[1]

INTRODUCTION

The foot-and-mouth disease (FMD) crisis began on 20 February 2001 when the first case was officially confirmed in an abattoir in Brentwood, Essex. The crisis effectively ended almost one year later on 15 January 2002 when the United Kingdom was officially declared disease-free. Across this timeline, 2,030 UK farms were infected with the virus and 10,157 farms had livestock destroyed in an effort to control the spread of the disease. A significant amount of political and economic damage can also be attributed to the epidemic between these two dates. The first post war cancellation of a general election, the removal of a Minister, the reorganization of a Whitehall ministry, a ban on UK farm exports, a crisis response costing £3 billion, and the decimation of many rural businesses all followed the confirmation of that first infection in February 2001.

The initial operational crisis response was controlled entirely by the Ministry of Agriculture, Fisheries and Food (MAFF), and the State Veterinary Service (SVS), led respectively by Nick Brown, the Agriculture Minister and Jim Scudamore, the Chief Veterinary Officer (CVO). The Ministry of Agriculture and the SVS have been heavily criticized for an initial crisis management response that increased the scale of the epidemic. One independent lesson-learning inquiry into FMD, for example, stated that the first month of the crisis, characterized by MAFF's failings, constituted: '31 days during which a serious veterinary problem became a national disaster'. These early problems provide an important insight into the operations and politics of the FMD response.

The principal disease control measure was a 24-hour cull policy, which demanded that all infected livestock be slaughtered within one day of diagnosis. However, the 24-hour policy was not implemented effectively, particularly during the initial stages of the epidemic. According to a number of epidemiologists from the FMD scientific advisory team, 'if achieved from the start of the epidemic, meeting the 24-hour cull policy would have reduced the total epidemic size by more than 40 per cent up to 16 July'.

Problems in implementation were compounded by communication breakdowns between the SVS in the field, MAFF's regional centres and its headquarters in Whitehall. This meant that:

> Those at the top responsible for major decisions were not provided with timely, accurate and relevant information about what was happening on the ground . . . For the first two months of the outbreak – including the absolutely critical first two or three weeks – there was a serious deficiency in the reliability and completeness of the information available to those in charge.

These initial weaknesses changed the political climate surrounding the operational response. Solidarity gave way to an atmosphere of fault-finding and blaming, particularly within the media, which continued throughout the acute stages of the crisis. Support for MAFF and the SVS deteriorated rapidly and conflicts emerged between the Ministry and other departments.

It has been argued that the eventual control of the disease must be considered to be something of a pyrrhic victory – given the sheer number of healthy livestock that were culled in order to rectify the crisis response's early failures. The last FMD epidemic in the UK occurred between 1967 and 1968, resulting in 2,364 infections and the culling of 433,987 animals. In contrast, the 2001 epidemic, despite infecting fewer farms, led to 6,456,000 animals being culled. The pre-emptive slaughter of healthy livestock, while effective at stopping FMD transmission, intensified the antagonistic political climate surrounding the crisis response by invigorating a public debate about the appropriateness of culling.

On 27 March, the Government requested permission from the EU to use vaccines in Cumbria and Devon, which were the main areas of infection. Over the next four weeks, the vaccination versus 'stamping out' debate intensified further. Reports in the media suggested that the Prime Minister, worried about negative public opinion, which might sway votes or even postpone the upcoming general election (scheduled to coincide with local elections on 3 May), favoured the use of vaccination. This position, according to the National Farmers' Union (NFU) and certain sections of the media, had more to do with cleaning up television screens ahead of a general election than disease control. However, 'stamping out' remained the core response policy because the Agriculture Minister could not generate enough consent among the farming community, veterinarians, the food industry and consumers to implement a vaccination programme effectively.

DAMAGE TO TOURISM SECTOR

In March, it also became apparent that the disease control policies had focused entirely on the needs of the farming industry without considering the damage that was being done to the tourism sector. Vivid images of slaughter and disposal and misperceptions about the risks that FMD posed to humans combined to create an apocalyptic picture of Britain's countryside. As the tourism slump became evident, the Prime Minister led a media campaign in conjunction with the Department of Environment Transport and the Regions (DETR) to assure tourists – particularly Americans – that the countryside was 'open for business – and for pleasure'. This public relations offensive was designed, according to the Environment Minister, to counter 'the grossly esoteric treatment of our country' in overseas media which was 'scurrilous and mischievous in its inaccuracy, which is gross'. The confusion between MAFF's early message that the 'countryside was closed' and the DETR's 'open for business and pleasure' campaign became a widely used parable among critics of the government who argued that departmentalism had beset the crisis response.

After the general election, MAFF and the DETR were merged into the Department for Food and Rural Affairs (DEFRA). Nick Brown was removed from his post, replaced by Margaret Beckett and demoted out of the Cabinet to the position of Minister of Work within the Department of Work and Pensions. During August 2001, a series of independent inquiries into the crisis were announced. Dr Iain Anderson was appointed by the Prime Minister to chair a 'lessons to be learned' inquiry into the overall handling of the crisis. This inquiry published its report in July 2002. The Policy Commission on the Future of Farming and Food published a report in January 2002 that advocated a shift towards sustainable, environmental farming practices which would be less focused on product outputs and more focused on an integrated, transparent food chain. The Commission was appointed and endorsed by the Prime Minister and its findings underpinned DEFRA's first farming policy strategy. The National Audit Office investigated the crisis response in relation to 'value for money' principles, with particular attention being given to the high level of compensation given to farmers, which the Public Accounts Committee later criticized extensively. Finally, the Royal Society carried out two separate inquiries in England and Scotland on the scientific aspects of each response.

POLICY AND ACCOUNTABILITY

It is important to realize that the crisis management thus represented by the foot-and-mouth epidemic does not exist in a vacuum. A crisis like this does not 'simply' require a 'scientific' reaction from the state. What is often required is an understanding of the players/actors in the system, the multiple accountabilities required to be factored into the implementation of policy. What may be required is an ability to resolve conflict, to understand and negotiate complex power relationships over a multiplicity of actors and to respond to significant internal and external pressures. There were four such pressures of significance during the foot-and-mouth crisis:

- political pressure in terms of a pending general election and public opinion, and the government's sensitivity to this;
- pressure group activity particularly that exercised by the NFU;
- international pressure including the EU;
- political–bureaucratic factors within government itself.

POLITICAL PRESSURE: GENERAL ELECTION AND GOVERNMENT SENSITIVITY TO PUBLIC OPINION

In the heat of a crisis, public opinion in a democracy remains a potent force. Political strategists often have to respond speculatively to what they perceive to be the mainstream of public opinion. A crisis can be defined as bad publicity and in addition the foot-and-mouth crisis appeared very close to a general election. The government reacted to the epidemic by initiating an overzealous cull policy to eradicate the crisis and then consciously manipulated the crisis agenda to strengthen the legitimacy of the cull policy and dampen pre-election criticism.

The countryside lobby and farming community represent a strong and articulate force that saw a strengthening of influence prior to the 2001 general election as government attempted to appease disgruntled rural voters. Opinion polls showed a bleak picture for New Labour in the countryside and, although rural seats accounted for only 10 per cent of the national electorate, combined with semi-rural seats they accounted for 24 per cent.

An excessive cull policy was accompanied by the Prime Minister taking a 'hands-on' role to resolve the crisis after the delay of the general election date. A contiguous cull policy (i.e. slaughtering beasts on farms next to confirmed cases) with the help of the military led to substantial slaughter. For example, in comparison with the 1967 outbreak where 2,364 confirmed cases led to a slaughter of 433,987 beasts, 2001 claimed in excess of 3.5m with less than 2,000 farms infected. As well as livestock losses being high, expenditure and compensation payments were significant and the policy was continually questioned scientifically, socially and economically.

A highly effective piece of political agenda management during the epidemic was the delay of the general election – the first post war postponement of national polling. The Prime Minister was influenced by the feelings of rural communities but also by polling of the wider electorate's adverse reaction to holding an election in the middle of a crisis. The government did not wish to appear to be putting their party or personal interests before the countryside. They wished to show politics would not distract from crisis management.

The contiguous slaughter policy, effective in terms of political timescale and showing the government had a grip on policy, did though have an impact on public opinion. The sight of burning pyres and the concerns expressed by bodies such as the Country Landowners Association and Soil Association led the government, through MAFF, to dampen down the appearance of overkill through use of statistics. A major cause of concern was that during the heightened culling stage, when regional vets clinically confirmed a case of foot-and-mouth in a farm, the contiguous cull would be initiated on premises in a 3km zone. Confirmed outbreaks that later proved negative under laboratory testing, however, were still being recorded by MAFF as confirmed infections. Government then resorted to reclassification of infected premises which had the effect of under-reporting. This allowed the government to highlight a daily reduction in outbreaks and declare the epidemic under control – if a farm was slaughtered on suspicion or as a contiguous cull then it is not listed as a confirmed outbreak but rather detailed separately and less publicly. This resulted in the slaughter rate rising as the official number of infected cases was falling.

PRESSURE GROUP ACTIVITY: NATIONAL FARMERS' UNION

The NFU has enjoyed a close symbiotic relationship with MAFF almost resembling the exclusive 'iron triangle' relationships cultivated between congressional

Committees and American interest groups. The NFU can be considered as an 'insider' group or as a policy community. The Ministry has historically followed a deliberate policy of giving the NFU a privileged, quasi-monopoly role in agricultural representation. This central policy position and close relationship between union and ministry led to the belief expressed in some areas of the media that MAFF's primary function is best defined as the political wing of the NFU. The suggestion that MAFF is a political tool of the one union is too simplistic. It tends to ignore the pluralistic pressures that ministries must take into account when formulating and implementing policy. However, by choosing one key interest group and by mutually advocating common beliefs and policy both union and ministry have been able to achieve their sectional goals together.

The key policy role for most large interest groups, such as the NFU, is played during the implementation phase of policy execution and outcome fulfilment. During the foot-and-mouth epidemic the NFU established significant input in all stages of policy because of the crucial nature of their implementation role. The strength of the NFU during the epidemic was their perceived ability to engender policy delivery through its 60,000 membership. Their position to influence policy was strengthened by the government's need to have agricultural co-operation, not just acquiescence, as a prerequisite component in the eradication and control policy.

During the early stages of the epidemic the NFU reinforced MAFF's initial cull and control policies and the early signs indicated that the NFU would buttress MAFF decisions by reassuring its members of the need for co-operation and compliance to measures. Early press releases, drafted during the pre-epidemic stage of the crisis, are indicative signs of the closer-than-usual relationship described above between the NFU and the MAFF bureaucracy. The NFU was quick to declare that they 'fully support all the measures which have been speedily put in place by MAFF' and that they were 'in constant contact with MAFF and will support them in any action they take'. The draconian measures were not ideal but they were essential, the NFU assured members. As the crisis intensified and consensus between the national and regional layers of the NFU started to strain, the NFU tone began to shift on both levels and pressure politics ensued within the union, and also in their interactions with MAFF and Downing Street.

THE 2001 EPIDEMIC: WAS THE GOVERNMENT LISTENING?

During February and March it was clear to regional NFU members and local veterinary officers that MAFF's initial 24-hour cull policy was not being implemented effectively. During talks with MAFF the President of the NFU, Ben Gill, was under considerable pressure from farms near 'breaking point' because of the 'intolerable' delay in slaughter and disposal. Mr Gill revealed after the talks that 'We left the Minister in no doubt that there is a need for the whole process to be speeded up'. It appears, however, that MAFF were not initially prepared to listen to the NFU's claims that the cull policy was not being implemented effectively enough to control the disease.

On 29 March Mr Gill met with the Prime Minister in an attempt to expose the full extent of the Ministry's failed 24-hour response. This led the Prime Minister to give a robust commitment that the problem would be resolved and that resources would no longer be a problem. It is interesting to note that, while the concerns of the NFU were disregarded by MAFF, the Prime Minister, concerned about a crisis affecting public opinion near an election, was more prepared to listen. That day the Prime Minister visited Cumbria and was met by angry protestors demonstrating over a lack of slaughter and disposal resources. Later, the Prime Minister repeated his resource commitment, proclaiming that it was necessary to 'massively gear up to the scale of the challenge that we have and make sure there is absolutely nothing, no piece of little bureaucracy, no obstacle, that stands in the way of getting the job done'. The failure of MAFF to listen and react to the concerns raised chiefly by the NFU about the 24-hour cull policy led to Jim Scudamore being removed from primary control of the epidemic and being replaced by Downing Street officials.

This period represents the beginning of the end of the crisis consensus within the NFU that would eventually weaken the union's power when they tried to oppose vaccination. The 3km policy prompted over 1,000 members of the NFU's Carlisle branch to publicly denounce the decision; The National Sheep Association condemned the policy as 'killing for killing's sake'; and one pressure group, Farmers For Action, declared 'all-out war' with the government. It was clear from this early stage that some members of the NFU felt their leadership were being forced to market unpalatable decisions that were not always going to be in their best interest. From this point on the NFU could not guarantee the full support of its membership for policy implementation or co-operation.

The need to appease farmers that were being asked to assist implementation of a slaughter policy was critical. The announcement of compensation was symbolic; it showed farmers that 'The Prime Minister and the Government have understood the severity of the plight of British farmers' and conveyed a message of co-operation. Compensation, however, would require a lot more than the £152 million available from the EU. An additional compensation package was clearly required to keep farmers 'on board' in relation to the eradication policy. The NFU seized on this factor to press for high rates of compensation that in turn angered many other sectors affected by the epidemic. As the compensation rose, it is possible to argue that farmers were, at times, rewarded for their assistance in the implementation of a difficult policy. The generous compensation rates provided initially to farmers were testimony to the government's need to appease farmers.

It is interesting to note that the NFU's hegemony over policy consultation developed into a source of frustration for some farmers as smaller unions, such as the Small and Family Farming Alliance, complained of hitting 'the proverbial brick wall' when trying to communicate with MAFF and the government. Many farmers remain unhappy at the NFU's dominant representative role. One farmer told the media why he left the NFU and joined the National Sheep Association during the crisis:

> The NFU has been irritating the hell out of me. They put forward the views of the 20 per cent of big farmers who get 80 per cent of the subsidies, not family farms under 200 acres which form the majority in Cumbria.

THE VACCINATION STRATEGY

On 9 April the Prime Minister, through Ben Gill, reiterated the government's commitment to slaughtering on infected and surrounding farms. The NFU policy committee and leadership suddenly found itself in the position of having to defend its policy to its own membership and also to a government being pushed by internal and external pressures to remove FMD from the public diet. In an effort to delay the vaccination decision the NFU drafted fifty-two detailed questions about the impact of a vaccination strategy. This action was an attempt to manipulate the agenda. It was hoped that the questions would act as a delay, and as the number of official cases declined so would the case for vaccination. The NFU argued that the purpose of the questions was to 'concentrate the thinking in government' but, as one member of the Agriculture Committee noted, it managed to kick the vaccination issue into the tall grass for a period and delay a difficult decision.

INTERNATIONAL PRESSURES

Internal pressures were not the only factors to affect the government's crisis response. Two major external influences also prejudiced the crisis decision-making processes. First, the impact that the epidemic would have on international tourism was a factor initially ignored by the government, but it soon imposed itself on the agenda as the economic downturn, allied to increased stakeholder anger, became a serious issue to the Treasury and Downing Street. Second, the EU today regulates and controls more agricultural policy areas than the UK. The machinations of the various supra-national institutions and their reaction to wider trade bans also constituted a pervasive influence, legally and politically, over the crisis response. These two pressures do not solely explain the crisis response in its entirety, but rather provided additional spurs that reinforced the policy decisions to slaughter excessively and to consciously manage public perception.

An underpinning factor of the crisis strategy was the need to declare the UK countryside 'open for business'. It soon became apparent that the tourism industry was suffering without receiving the same level of public interest and policy consideration as agriculture. Economically, the tourism trade was a greater concern to both treasury and government. For example, the tourism industry pre-epidemic employed around 1.85 million, while agriculture employed around 429,000.

In total, 25.3 million overseas visitors came to Britain in 2000. Of these, 4 million were North Americans, constituting Britain's largest source of tourist revenue with nearly a fifth of all foreign visitors. As most developed countries imposed import bans on many UK products, there was clear evidence of international misconceptions, paranoia and ignorance about the nature of FMD. CNN, for example, informed the US public during one report that holidaymakers that had booked a trip to the UK could have their money returned without penalties. The report continued that BSE had already killed 100 people in Europe, and America had not had one single death. The report then informed viewers about the epidemic and how large parts of the UK were off limits. Throughout the report, the implication was clear . . . stay at home. The US Department of Agriculture (USDA) declaring 'war' on foot-and-mouth could not have helped these misconceptions. Richard Dunkle, of the USDA Animal and Plant Inspection Service, issued advice to travellers as part of the campaign to keep foot-and-mouth out of North America.

In the year 2000, overseas visitors spent around £12.76 billion, which was an increase of 2 per cent from 1999. The English Tourism Council (ETC) estimated that spending by overseas visitors in the countryside amounted to £12 billion in revenue and supported around 380,000 jobs. Figures compiled by the British Tourist Authority (BTA) show that overseas visitors in March were down by 30 per cent from the 1.8 million recorded the previous year. During April there was a decline of around 20–25 per cent in England and a larger decline in Wales. The ETC stated that around a fifth of bookings were lost and advance bookings were down by a third. In Scotland, the Financial Times estimated the tourism trade was losing around £10 million a week and the Wales Tourist Board stated that enquiry and booking levels had fallen by 25 per cent on the normal level.

THE CRISIS RESPONSE

The initial crisis response, by focusing exclusively on slaughter and control, failed to promote a wider perspective, compounding the poor international perception of the crisis. Around 80 per cent of the country was not affected by outbreaks and only a small percentage of the national herd was being slaughtered. The disease was not initially put in a national context and this did not help the tourism industry. As the tourism slump became apparent, the emphasis changed and the Prime Minister led the campaign to assure tourists that 'there is absolutely no reason why

265 ■

you shouldn't come, if you're an American tourist come and visit the UK and visit as you always have and you'll find the things you want to do are still there' and that 'the best way to help the countryside recover from the effects of foot-and-mouth on tourism is for people to visit the countryside. Be careful, yes but visit, yes. The countryside is open for business – and for pleasure'.

One spokesman for the BTA praised the government's role in curbing the disease but argued that they had fallen short in providing adequate funding for the tourist industry. The government's strategy for helping the tourism trade had been heavily criticized, especially in the face of generous farming subsidy and compensation. Unlike the farming community, the tourism sector could not be compensated and was instead provided with extra funding for tourist boards; a loosening of inland revenue and customs and excise payment enforcement, improved credit continuation, rate relief, deferred payment of business rates and changes to rate valuations and appeals were also announced. The central aim of the government was to attempt to promote the countryside, not to financially support it.

THE EUROPEAN DIMENSION

The disease-free status of the EU, and its implication for external trade, represents a pervasive influence over the UK's crisis response. Since 1991, the EU has maintained disease-free status, without the use of vaccination. Compulsory general vaccination of livestock ceased in 1992. A foot-and-mouth eradication policy was delineated in Directive 85/511/EEC, which permitted general vaccination. This was subsequently amended, in order to prohibit vaccination, by Directive 90/423/EEC. The impetus for the policy change was provided by the EC who argued in favour of a non-vaccination policy. The change from vaccination to slaughter and control was also viewed as a success by the UK government, who had championed the slaughter policy in the EU and helped the Commission successfully persuade other member states to abandon vaccination as a control measure, primarily to protect their own disease-free status. The new directive delineated the withdrawal of general vaccination to be accompanied with a new 'policy of total slaughter and destruction'. This meant that EU law advocated a clear policy of killing infected herds and initiating strict control procedures.

Prior to the Parliament's resolution the UK government, reacting to multiple domestic pressures, engaged in a policy U-turn and requested that the Commission examine the circumstances under which vaccination might take place. Directive 90/423/EEC permits the use of emergency vaccination in certain defined circumstances. The union's Scientific Committee on Animal Health and Animal Welfare endorsed the use of an emergency vaccination strategy in 1999 provided determining parameters permitted. The Scientific Committee provided a list of ten criteria that should be met before a member state embarks on emergency vaccination. Adherence to these criteria should have led to a decision to vaccinate within the UK. This meant that the Standing Veterinary Committee and the Commission could not legally or technically object to the use of emergency vaccination. Commission Decision 2001/257/EEC subsequently permitted the application of emergency vaccination in the UK, within certain restrictive conditions. An important issue was the manner in which vaccination was perceived internationally, particularly in the US where the use of vaccination of any kind is wrongly equated with widespread evidence of the disease. Recourse to any kind of vaccination would inevitably affect the international trade for many member states and this was a primary concern of the Commission throughout the height of the epidemic. The inability of the EU to effectively establish specific regional-only trade restrictions with external states compounded the vaccination problem. If third countries were discriminating against the EU over slaughter then it was perceived they would also discriminate if non-suppressive vaccination were introduced. Indeed some importers of EU meat had insisted on total eradication before trade would recommence.

The final serious policy pressure worth consideration was the export ban, imposed on the UK from February. The ban was constantly reviewed and then extended by the Standing Veterinary Committee because the government was unable to stop outbreaks occurring over a sustained period. In France, the Netherlands and Northern Ireland the ban was lifted, however, it remained in place for mainland Britain. Exporting cattle, pigs and sheep to the EU in 2000, was worth a relatively small £310 million, representing a decline of over 39 per cent from 1999. Macro-economically the export ban was certainly not disastrous but during this intensive crisis the ban took on a symbolic meaning. It was a sign that foot-and-mouth was still there regardless of what the government stated. It was a rallying point for interest groups such as the NFU to coalesce around, and it was a serious variable on public opinion sympathetic to the farming community. Although the actual intra-community trade was not substantial the ban still represented a symbolic external pressure imposed by Europe.

POLITICS WITHIN GOVERNMENT BUREAUCRACY

A reaction to a large-scale crisis will involve conflict and compromise over a multiplicity of governmental layers. The correct structural mix, however, also requires to be complemented with an effective decision-making process. This means that a decentralized crisis reaction will be severely influenced by a state's political system and culture as they provide the contextual underpinning for structure and decision-making. The very fact that responses require multi-layer provision from various areas of government courts fragmentation. The UK's crisis institutions in this case were divided. The quasi-dissection of the country by devolution has exacerbated the need for clear crisis coordination, particularly when considered against the gradual shifting of the constitution pre-devolution, which has tended to fragment governance in the UK and 'hollow out' central government. Within this newly devolved fabric, any crisis response will have an increased susceptibility to fall victim to paralysis through bureau–political conflict or operational fragmentation.

Modernization had been the cornerstone of most New Labour pledges since they came to power. It is then, perhaps, unsurprising that most New Labour politicians and advisers had something of a non-partisan contempt or disillusion when referring to MAFF. If New Labour was to be believed, MAAF represented almost the last outpost of civil service non-conformity and bureaucratic arrogance. Labour's inability to modernize the department was clearly a source of concern within Downing Street.

Crisis situations profoundly challenge bureaucratic structure and norms, however, MAFF had had enough practice, having responded to BSE and swine fever outbreaks in recent years preceding the foot-and-mouth crisis. This experience of reacting to disease outbreaks was another factor that encouraged an inherently departmental response. It contributed to MAFF's initial self-installation as the core authority in charge of the crisis. The problem was, however, that the department's previous crisis handling, particularly of BSE, was never going to be taught as a crisis manager's parable. The Ministry's stubbornness to listen to non-Whitehall expertise, its resource parsimony, its reliance on outdated information and its departmentally exclusive attitude were all factors that led to conflict in the crisis response. The Phillips Report, post-BSE, specifically emphasized the benefits of seeking out and using external expert advice within government. The lessons of previous MAFF failures were well documented but were not learned.

A perfect example of this 'painful', insular culture was exemplified by MAFF's reluctance to accept epidemiological assistance offered by numerous scientific centres of excellence, including Imperial College in London and Edinburgh University. These scientists were able to predict the future spread of the disease, providing a basis for policy making. Instead of following the disease using the MAFF's traditional 'paper and pencil' approach, epidemiological modelling projected the spread and intensity of the disease, allowing decision makers to plan make quickly. Initially, MAFF delayed providing the College with the data it required because the information was sensitive. It was at this meeting that the Prime Minister's Chief Scientific Adviser, David King, decided to impose himself on the situation and brief the Prime Minister. Professor King was 'surprised' that despite MAFF's dominant position, Ministry officials only 'contributed minimally' to the discussion yet they were taking the policy decisions in an unacceptably exclusive manner. 'I had to engage myself immediately. In other words there was no longer any question in my own mind as to whether, as Chief Scientific Adviser, I should impose myself on the situation. At that point I immediately knew.' Professor Anderson, the leader of the Imperial College epidemiological team was not quite as diplomatic in his opinion of the Ministry's representation during the meeting:

> The subsequent discussions were interesting because on one side there was the Chief Scientist saying 'we must act, we must do something' and on the other side there was almost a feeling – this was a personal impression – of hopelessness within MAFF, saying that 'logistically we can't do this we haven't got the resources'. The professor admitted being 'dumbstruck'. I thought that's not the issue.

The failure of MAFF to listen to outside scientific expertise, combined with their refusal to listen to farming stakeholders, led to an overhaul of the foot-and-mouth response structure. Authority for decision-making transferred to the Prime Minister's office, to be advised by a scientific team chaired by David King. This early episode of bureau politics did have a positive effect on the overall aggregate effectiveness of the crisis response. The attempt by MAFF to 'wish things better' using a style born out of departmentalism resulted in an improved crisis response because it forced Downing Street to take over the crisis handling. Cross departmental co-operation and an influx of scientific advice was established through the Cabinet Office Briefing Room (COBRA) meetings. The first decision taken by COBRA was to implement the contiguous cull policy. Decision-making was centralized with ultimate authority and the Prime Minister enforced a 'joined-up' response authoritatively.

Most criticism during this crisis was directed towards the centralized Whitehall bureaucracy. Centralized decision-making was not the problem. It was, rather, that the centralization was done poorly. MAFF's bureaucratic malaise meant that decisions were taken wrongly or not at all. This resulted in implementation on grounds that were inadequate, incoherent and under-resourced. The foot-and-mouth epidemic did expose structural weaknesses in government, however, an epidemic of this scale would have challenged any governmental structure. The scale of implementing the control and eradication policies alone has far exceeded the logistical demands of the Gulf War, for example. Examining the main actors in the slaughter policy highlights the multiplicity of actors involved. At a local level, local authorities were statutorily required to respond alongside the police. Private contractors assisted the Army in slaughter and disposal after the SVS diagnosed the disease with the assistance of MAFF scientists at Pirbright Laboratory. MAFF also had to provide trained slaughtermen and livestock valuers to determine compensation. The Chief Vet is in charge of the SVS throughout the UK (except Northern Ireland) but devolved authorities provide the administrative support for vets in Scotland and Wales. The lack of veterinary officers and administrative staff also forced the government to recruit from European states and external government departments, deepening the degree of incoherency. Slaughter housing

269

and meat hygiene falls under the remit of the Food Standards Agency. It is important to note that these agencies are only those concerned with slaughter and control. Looking at other areas, such as the 'open for business' or animal welfare policies, exposes a similar wealth of organizations such as the RSPCA and The National Trust.

There was clear evidence of horizontal fragmentation of action and purpose between central and local government. For example, the closure of footpaths is a local government competence. When the number of outbreaks grew, many local authorities closed footpaths, using large blanket bans. The government's Environment Minister, Michael Meacher, had to request an explanation from each authority as to why they had closed footpaths and why they had not reopened those closed without reason. The panicked blanket bans were proving counterproductive to the 'open for business' message, highlighting a lack of communication between centre and region. The local authorities were never informed of the overarching policy goals and this created a clear division between the purpose of the locality, focusing on eradication and control, and the centre, focusing on multiple policy objectives. Local Authority Trading Standards Officers were also required to administer livestock movement. During April, MAFF attempted to introduce a new movement scheme that would ease welfare concerns among farmers. The scheme was to be introduced on Monday 23 April and farmers were well notified, but when the day came a majority of local authorities had received no details from MAFF relating to the scheme administration. Ultimately, the delay slowed the movement of animals to abattoirs and caused distress among farmers who had expected to be able to move their livestock. Communication breakdowns were also evident horizontally between the regional MAFF centres and the central crisis centres. Farmers complained of being unable to contact crisis centres and if they did get through being told by MAFF officials that they 'were not in a position to advise' on various policy areas. The Devon NFU Chairman, David Hill, said that it was important to look at the quality of communication in the regions. He said that MAFF may have been given praise at national level, but at local level enquiries went unanswered: 'members were phoning to say they could not get anyone to answer simple questions, such as, could they walk their cows along the road to a field,' said Mr Hill. A lack of communication between MAFF and farmers added to a feeling of isolation and uncertainty in the country. This led to scare stories and rural myths developing that affected the level of actor acquiescence to difficult policies.

The eventual improvement in central government decision-making impacted on the overall crisis structure. Twelve regional operations directors were created to assist implementation, the army involvement was significantly improved and additional resources were used to free up the SVS so they could focus on veterinary, not logistic, issues. The average disposal time in early March was around two to three days, after the change in the central decision-making structure the 24-hour deadline was met in 75 per cent of cases. The regional directors coordinated disposal alongside the army. At a central level, a Joint Coordination Centre (JCC) was established to maintain an accurate picture of the operational progress in the field and to relay instructions from the daily COBRA meetings to the regional Local Disease Control Centres and other functional branches. In summary, the improved decision-making ameliorated but did not eradicate levels of horizontal and vertical fragmentation through improved communication and cross-governmental collaboration. The EU's Animal Health Office inspectorate noted during an inspection in April that 'the organisation and operation of the FMD eradication programme has improved significantly' because 'responsibilities are assigned to specific Ministers and executive bodies in a planned, coordinated manner. Major policy decisions are taken at the highest level'. The group concluded that the changes made, combined with the increased resources, allowed a much more effective operational campaign.

The foot-and-mouth epidemic represented the first major crisis that required a coordinated response from all the devolved institutions of the UK. All the institutions pragmatically followed the national policy direction set in London. The various executives, however, continually repeated their willingness to only implement programmes that would be appropriate for their region. A key strength of any devolved policy is its ability to 'fit' with a decentralized environment for maximum effectiveness and local acceptance. As a consequence, policies applied to England – such as the additional standstill period imposed after the vaccination strategy – were not implemented in Scotland. A regional slant on policy was achieved by devolved administrations amending implementation routes and by relaying regional considerations to the central policy forums in London. In this way, cull policies in Scotland and Northern Ireland proceeded efficiently and effectively with the desired effect. This efficiency created its own problems in Scotland because the culling in Cumbria, from where the disease had spread northward, was running well behind schedule. Without eradication happening consistently there was an increased chance of Scottish farms becoming reinfected. Jim Walker, the leader of the Scottish branch of the NFU, pressed hard to make sure that Cumbria moved at speed and felt it was 'not good enough that one part of the country can make this thing work and other parts of the country can't'. Scotland's cull policy was significantly regionalized. More resources were directed towards firebreak culling in sheep to contain the disease in the Borders than the overall contiguous cull policy. This ultimately allowed more cattle to be saved; retrospective contiguous culling for all livestock was not required because there was an effective firebreak stopping transmission.

In Wales, the coalition executive was forced to change disposal methodology numerous times in order to appease strong local concerns. The Welsh executive

271

quickly learned the value of public consultation and inclusive decision-making before establishing large-scale disposal sites as recommended by Whitehall. One large landfill site in Trecatti generated such strong local concern that a Welsh Education Minister, Huw Lewis, resigned because of the 'disgusting' manner in which the Agriculture Minister, Carwyn Jones, took the decision. Mr Lewis's resignation was one sign of the intense public concern over disposal in Wales that caused division in the coalition. When the contiguous culls started, two large disposal sites had to be abandoned after local protests. In Powys, local protests disrupted disposal plans when MAFF scientists found pollution in a nearby borehole ten days after the site became operational. Shipments to the site were suspended and an inquiry was launched to investigate the claims. Carcasses had to be moved to a new site within the burial pit to reduce the level of contamination. Glynn Powell, deputy president of the Farmers' Union of Wales said 'I welcome this action but it is one that has been forced on MAFF, they have been compelled to act. This went ahead in the face of widespread opposition'. Before the find, the site was blockaded by around 200 hundred local protestors worried about the long-term effect of pollution. The blockade only ended after one protestor drove a stolen excavator through the demonstration, injuring a policeman. The Powys site was only being used after local councillors blocked the use of a nearby site in Penhesgyn. Another policy U-turn was witnessed in Anglesey after farmers legally challenged the use of a pyre site that was polluting a nearby stream. The site was to be used to dispose of 40,000 sheep but only 10,000 were destroyed and the remaining number had to be moved.

Despite the fragmentation caused by increased stakeholder responsiveness regionally, the Welsh Assembly's proactive crisis response may have helped consolidate its constitutional position. By taking difficult implementation decisions, such as the prioritization of mass slaughter in Anglesey and Powys, the Assembly's administration proved it could represent the national interest. The process, according to one think tank, 'developed a sense that Cardiff is increasingly replacing London as the main location of political accountability for Wales'.

QUESTIONS

1   Outline the different actors in the foot-and-mouth crisis. To whom are each of these accountable?
2   How important a part was played by elected politicians in responding to the crisis?
3   Does the experience of MAFF show that 'traditional government bureaucracies' are neither flexible nor directly accountable enough to the elected government to implement policy in a crisis?
4   Identify the main insider and outsider groups. Account for the relative importance of these.

5   Explain how the multi-level governance environment (from Europe and elsewhere to UK national government, to devolved governments within the UK and to local government) impacted on responses to addressing the crisis.
6   How would you evaluate whether the government's performance during the Food and Mouth crisis was a success or failure?

NOTES

1   This chapter is based on original research undertaken by Dr Alastair Stark, University of Queensland, Australia. Some of the research has been published: McConnell and Stark 2002a; 2002b.

REFERENCES

McConnell, A. and Stark, A. (2002a) 'Bureaucratic failure and the UK's lack of preparedness for foot and mouth disease', *Public Policy and Administration*, 14, 4: 39–54.
McConnell, A. and Stark, A. (2002b) 'Foot and mouth 2001: the politics of crisis management', *Parliamentary Affairs*, 55, 4: 664–681.

Conclusion

In the introduction to this book, the question is asked, why study public policy? Public policy results from governments' actions, and it's a matter of contention what the scale and scope of government should be. A former US President (Ronald Reagan) famously said that government was not part of the solution but indeed the problem behind America's real or perceived feelings of decline and malaise. Debates can be seen in many countries that reflect quite different ideas about how large government and state action should be, ranging from a rather minimalist view of state and government action to ideas of significant state action to empower individuals or communities and deliver a broad range of services. Broadly speaking, in the twenty-first century, those differing perspectives are labelled respectively 'right' (conservative) and 'left' (social democratic or socialist).

Yet despite differences in political programmes or ideologies most countries will have a wide range and scope of public policy initiatives, ultimately the result of government action, affecting most citizens at most stages in their lives. Registration at birth is compulsory in most countries, though public policy differs from country to country how this is done, for example, from an almost automatic, technologically driven system in Finland to a traditional, manually inputted system in Britain: somewhat ironic given Britain's drive for modernization in most areas of government service provision (Pollitt 2011). The population's education is a result of public policy whether this is provided privately in state schools (and pre-school) or in state-funded or private colleges and universities. Public policy will be evident even in privately provided provision: e.g. at a minimum there will be inspection or regulatory frameworks as a result of public policy. The same can be said of health care and many more activities which impact on people through their lives.

We have also indicated throughout the book that public policy has a rather broad definition, including policy made in the public's name by government, but also that it is often influenced, implemented and managed by public and private, state and non-state actors; it is about what governments do (not always the same as what they intend to do) and choose not to do. Failure of the government's tax authority to pursue underpayment of tax, may have a strong rational justification (e.g. using scarce resources to pursue fraud may result in higher collection rates), but the failure or inaction nonetheless is a policy action.

It also makes sense to study public policy in the context of state power. The authorizing environment for public policy – giving it legitimacy or not – is significant. As the introduction made clear, authoritarian forms of government will enact public policy, perhaps 'for the good of the public' if benevolent, or for the interests of the regime itself. This is still public policy (affecting the public) but the authorizing environment is rather narrow – the regime itself, parts thereof or perhaps favoured ethno-religious groups as found within some Middle Eastern societies, either currently or in the recent past. Even democratically elected governments, especially in fractured societies, may find their authorizing environment limited or constrained if it's felt by some communities that they are excluded from areas of public policy, resources and other benefits available to others, for example, in the past, elements of the predominantly Catholic nationalist community in Northern Ireland; native, first nation or aboriginal populations in the USA, Canada or Australia. In such environments, government actions to extend and legitimize the authorizing environment and make the scope of public policy more inclusive may involve conflict resolution strategies, as the case of the Northern Ireland peace process, set out in Chapter 6, indicates. The seemingly intractable problems in the Middle East, as observed through relationships between Israelis and Palestinians, have at times progressed through conflict resolution processes, but (at the time of writing) little sustainable progress is apparent.

A related question to 'why study public policy?' is 'who should study public policy?' The interdisciplinary nature of public policy was previously outlined, and those with a variety of scholarly backgrounds have significant contributions to make. The importance of economics, which studies resource allocation, is recognized in the investigation of public policy. So too history, for it is well recognized that the historical path along which institutions of government have travelled will be a determinant factor in how these institutions handle and frame, manage and implement policy (known as path dependency) (e.g. Greener 2005; Pollitt 2008). Law and jurisprudence is a significant disciplinary area especially in the context of supra-national authorities which, in a multi-level governance environment, may have jurisdiction over the traditional authors of public policy i.e. the national legislatures. More recently there has been a focus on the role played by behaviourally based disciplines, founded on the grounds that many areas of public policy require assumptions to be made about how people behave (e.g. how people will respond to financial incentives to save for retirement); indeed some areas of public policy may require behavioural change (e.g. changes in lifestyle or diet to combat obesity). Behavioural psychologists, sociologists or economists all research factors that may influence behaviour such as: the extent to which we are influenced by who communicates information; which incentives shape behaviour most; emotional associations; the propensity of people to go for default or pre-set options. Proponents of such approaches claim that public policy issues can be successfully addressed thereby in crime and antisocial behaviour, as well as prosocial behaviour like voting and volunteering, healthy and prosperous lifestyles (Dolan *et al.* 2009).

After justifying the importance of studying public policy and outlining the key disciplinary inputs impacting study, the book gave a contemporary account of the policy process and a detailed analysis of the domain and agents of public policy: where public policy is made, how it is made and by whom. We have built from, developed and advanced the idea of policy cycles, used conventionally to analyze policy in a cyclical fashion involving problem identification, decision-making, options review and appraisal, implementation, review or evaluation. However we have conceptualized the idea of interrelated policy cycles recognizing the dynamic and interactive nature of cycles within a real policy world of globalization and interdependence, with governance encompassing a variety of political systems and a range of state and non-state actors, external and internal stakeholders some of whom are under-represented in making and managing public policy. Figure 1.5 (Interrelated policy cycles), outlined in Chapter 1, illustrates this (see page 45).

The book has recognized three overarching themes of public policy: the policy capacity of governments to address increasingly complex problems; the success and limitations of modernization, reform and NPM initiatives, which have captured public policy thinking and practice over the past twenty to thirty years; and the requirement for good governance to deliver positive policy outcomes in an interdependent globalized world. Some concluding comments will be made on each of these themes and some illustration given of the applicability of the interrelated policy cycles approach. However, as will be clear to those who have read the book, it should be recognized that this is not a prescriptive model so is not used as such; rather, it gives an explanatory account of the complex and interrelated nature of public policy.

The policy capacity of governments is seen as particularly challenging. As the book has made clear, the public policy domain is diverse and non-localized (that is, as seen from Figure 1.5, interrelated policy cycles with a strong focus on the external environment). We know that the traditionally recognizable actors and spaces of policy – politicians and bureaucrats operating in the machinery of government – now encompass an understanding that, while these actors have different roles, there are overlaps; that policy input from the bureaucracy occurs not only at senior levels; that various bureaucratic and organizational interests, ranging from those that can be categorized as self-serving to those that display a public service ethos and those focused on managerial efficiency can have an impact on policy; that the locus of policy now includes the marketplace and the world of contracts and compliance. Clearly this can be seen in the internal environment outlined in the interrelated cycles figure; so too the focus on managerial efficiency and contracts, which may bring their own evaluation frameworks also shown on the figure.

The 'hollowing out of the state' and the existence of supra-national governmental bodies (such as some institutions of the EU) would appear to constrain individual governments' policy capacity, as would truly global policy issues and problems, such as, for example, the banking and financial crisis. Likewise, the outsourcing and migration of many state activities laterally to semi-state bodies (such as executive agencies or other arm's length bodies) or contractually to private organizations could be seen to limit state policy capacity. However, in each of these three arenas we have shown that loss of capacity is over simplistic. First, in supra-national governance environments, by pooling sovereignty the nation state may have influence in an internationally integrated world it could not have on its own; and indeed there are cases where EU influence can be used to uplift the state's policy capacity by giving leverage to nation state governments' policy objectives, which may be more in tune with EU objectives than those of key players within the nation state – the example of the German and Dutch transport policy sectors was outlined in the book. This is a clear illustration of external and internal environments interacting in policy. Second, many of the major global issues that seem intractable at national and other levels are often the result of nation states' political decisions, not uncontrollable global forces: the decision not to introduce controls on US mortgage corporations played a significant part in the 2008 global financial crisis (i.e. a chosen option in terms of our interrelated cycles). Third, the creation of lateral bodies may be justified on the grounds that it leaves the operation and management of essential activities (such as the running of prisons or the funding of education) to organizations with specific managerial accountability for doing so, leaving strategic and policy to core government, thereby enhancing policy capacity at the centre; or it may be about the state buying in strategic capacity (like IT systems) from external experts or organizations. On the other hand, too much outsourcing may over time lead to the loss of state capacity, for example, in many areas of health care where the state may have a near monopoly of provision, for instance in the UK.

The policy capacity of governments may seem to be limited by the operation or design of the political system. Two contrasting examples can be used. The US system can at times appear gridlocked, especially when the president is from a different party to the majority party in either or both Houses of Congress: this was witnessed at key points in President Obama's first administration, the result being gridlock and/or the passage of over-compromised diluted legislation. One can apply decision-making and options cycles here: e.g. the decision by the executive to remove the 'public option' proposal from the health care bill, thereby focusing on existing insurance-driven providers. It has of course been argued that the US constitution was designed to prevent one branch of government gaining too much power at the expense of others – the result may be a strong separation of power,

277

or policy gridlock in some instances. A second example is the Scottish Parliament, created as a devolved institution within the UK. Enacted by the passage of the Scotland Act 1997, the proportional electoral system was designed to make it very difficult for one party – specifically the Scottish National Party (SNP), with its aim of independence – to gain an overall majority in the Parliament, in effect making coalition or minority governments likely and a mandate for independence unlikely: in a sense, a design gridlock. However, the SNP had a significant increase in its vote at the 2011 Scottish election, giving the party an overall majority in the parliament. Two very different examples, but each show that gridlock as a limitation on policy capacity, may well be better explained by political design than capacity limitation – whether or not the design achieves its objectives.

Marketization, reform and managerial initiatives have clearly taken hold of public policy and management in the last three decades as outlined throughout the book. The use of markets, consumerism, choice, managerial processes including internal and external audit and inspection are all evident internationally, though there is a clear variation from country to country. Such approaches may be the most efficient and effective way to run some areas of public policy or public service provision, but may run up against other issues. For example a focus on individual and user rights, giving people choice in areas of service provision can be a meaningful articulation of what it means to be a citizen; but in some environments (e.g. resource constraint), individual choice may be at the expense of others either more in need or less able to articulate or pressurize for choice – so individualistic approaches may run counter to policies based on social cohesion. This can also be seen with the use of markets. Used for service provision (in effect the implementation and delivery of public policy) there may be areas where the conditions for effective market operations do not exist: competitive and alternative providers may not be in place (often only one service provider is feasible); symmetrical information may not exist for all providers, purchasers or users (users either cannot or do not wish to access information, for example, on their medical needs, some purchasers and providers may have a monopoly of information, kept commercially confidential and not available to others etc.); opportunities to exit the market may not exist. Turning to managerialism and, in particular, performance management, it was seen that while much of this had a rationalistic basis, much practice highlighted issues and consequences which could have negative impacts on public policy, ranging from game playing within target regimes and difficulties linking managerial performance to policy outcomes; while some performance had greater salience than others. The interrelated policy cycles approach can be illustrated and applied using the example of health care reform in part of the UK (England – Health and Social Care Act 2012). Health care reform in England was, according to the UK government, premised on medium- to long-term changes in the external environment (demographic changes with resource implications, projected increase in the scope, cost and use of drugs and other medical treatments).

In the internal environment, within the UK government, the policy issue has been problematized as an urgent need for reform of the NHS around a cluster of needs (efficiency, choice, resourcing). Decisional processes and cycles were set out in terms of consultative and legislative proposals, which were modified (the main modification being to maintain overall responsibility for NHS directly with the Secretary of State) after lobbying within the coalition government. Options too can be considered part of the policy process. The reform includes the creation of a commissioning, market-choice system with groups of general practitioners commissioning services from a variety of health care providers on behalf of their patients who are able to be given a range of choices. However, ideal market conditions do not exist: in many areas the NHS is the monopoly provider and there are asymmetries of information. So to make the reform a viable option, the proposal is to create such conditions, for example, by incentivizing (or forcing) groups of general practitioners to form purchasing consortia; enabling the creation of a diversity of providers (NHS, private sector and others) to make a market. Whether this is the policy system choosing from alternative options or attempting to create conditions for a favoured option is of course a moot point. It remains to be seen over time how implementation will proceed, though previous NHS reforms have indicated interactions and negotiations between powerful interests (e.g. some medical professional interests) and actual intended actions and policy proposals. The future will also tell whether evaluation occurs and whether shocks in the external environment (e.g. a change in government) and internal environment (e.g. further resource restraint) cause further interactions and disruptions in the cycles.

However, at overall government level it can be argued that failure to recognize the importance of some key aspects of public management and managerialism can be responsible for the compromising of public policy. An academic commentator has argued that the activities of public management 'which means the arduous task of defining goals and then planning, strategizing and budgeting towards them' did not take place when the US stimulus legislation (valued at $900 billion) was put in place in 2009 to combat fears of post-financial crash depression; the result – and continuing trend since then – has been a lack of consideration of real policy priorities and how to resource, achieve and evaluate and 'a continuing resort to short run measures – temporary tax cuts, temporary spending programmes, repeated quantitative easing – that have done almost nothing to restructure the economy. Keynesian stimulus policies have become the substitute for strategy, planning and implementation' (Sachs 2012). This analysis could be viewed as a problematization of the policy issue as fear of the external environment (an ensuing world recession fuelled by international financial markets losing confidence). This then led to a very messy and conflicted internal political process with 'pork barrel' compromises required to get the stimulus package through Congress. And the above direct quote from Sachs implies (in his view) that options and evaluation cycles were either cursorily addressed at best or largely ignored.

In addressing the third overarching theme of public policy, we return to the definition of public policy outlined in the introduction: an intended course of action made by government, which has power and/or authority to make a decision among competing interests, with the purpose of achieving an outcome beneficial for society. In an interrelated, interdependent, globalized world, good governance is required. Several key aspects of governance and the governance environment are significant. First, multi-level governance environments and institutions, and particularly at the supra-national level, are often portrayed and perceived as being distant from the citizen, either in terms of geography or complexity. The EU is no exception to this negative picture. However, in the area of environmental policy – international in nature and by definition impacting everyone – the EU provides an example of how an organization founded and grounded in inter-governmentalism and supra-nationalism can provide a governance setting for ambitious policy aims and outcomes. The increasing power of environmental interests throughout Europe from the 1990s and the EU's response through harmonization encouraged the EU to adopt strict environmental legislation, consequently taken on to the world stage. The EU has been a leading supporter of every major international environmental treaty since 1989; its world leadership role is greatly facilitated by the removal of a major nation state – the USA – from policy leadership in this area (Keleman 2010). Interrelated policy cycles can provide explanatory frameworks here: the interaction between environmental politics in many European countries can be considered an external factor interacting with the internal governmental mechanisms of the EU to get environmental issues problematized at EU level; external factors and stakeholders in the USA have not had a similar impact on the US government, which has not seen the environment as a significant policy issue, and in fact has at the time of writing decided not to act as a major policy player in this sphere. Second, at both national and international levels, partnership working is firmly embedded in governance structures. The arguments have been well rehearsed: partnerships enable participants (when working with others) to gain more control over their environment and can allow for various configurations in the network or partnerships, giving strategic strength in centralization in some areas, but enabling de-centralization and innovation in others. Partnerships may run against inclusiveness if they provide a platform for the most advantaged, since inevitably these will gain a response from various actors and agents in the governance chain. Yet as part of the governance environment, partnerships if carefully constructed can bring those into governance who may otherwise be excluded from more hierarchical or 'traditional' arrangements and structures, thereby increasing inclusivity. However, for partnerships to be positive instruments of governance, care must be taken at the micro-management level to ensure key roles are filled and competently carried out by partnership members. Third, there is a broader aspect to inclusion in the governance of public policy and management. At state and interstate level, where there is a tradition of fractured or excluded communities and where a political willingness to change exists, game setting and game changing strategies can be used to move the governance paradigm to involve a wider range of actors and agents, a more inclusive approach to governance and policy making. This had some success, highlighted in the book, in Northern Ireland, but not (for example) in relationships between Israel and its Palestinian neighbours. At the level of individual organizations, there is a link between who is represented or 'included' in the organization and the outcome of policy as was indicated in the case study in Chapter 4, the key implication being that exclusion or under-representation of key groups and their interests from institutions of public governance will lead to an impoverishment of public policy.

Finally, the quest for good governance in public policy must surely resonate at the level of individuals and communities. Processes like co-production, co-governance between citizens and the state, if they are to be at all meaningful in the governance and delivery of public policy, must be grounded in high levels of social capital and individual and community confidence. The key argument here is that the governance system is much more likely to respond if pressured effectively from ground level. The following narrative illustrates this.

Barack Obama, when a community organizer, arranged for a group of women to meet Chicago's mayor, Harold Washington, to press for improved conditions in their run-down community; Obama apparently was frustrated when, instead of pressing the mayor to attend a community rally, they were star-struck by the photo opportunities with the mayor and his entourage. According to a recent commentator:

> Obama was well aware that it was only by making demands that the powerless could further their interests – the lesson now is that [if people and communities] want to be taken seriously they will have to stop behaving like star-struck children – there is plenty of evidence of this [from Obama's first Presidency] – after years of claiming that his view on gay marriage was evolving, it miraculously matured five months before an election as support from gay and lesbian voters and young people appeared to be softening. A month later he halted the deportation of thousands of young undocumented immigrants, mainly Hispanics, with an executive order. He could have done either one at any time. He did them when he did because he faced two well organised communities who held his feet to the fire.
>
> (Younge 2012)

The reach for good governance is an appropriate conclusion for this book. The making and managing of public policy is only fit for purpose if it is engaged with the real world and can address the following questions:

- How does the external environment impact on public policy? This ranges from global forces and trends to the activities of multiple layers and levels of government.
- How do agents, organizations and institutions in the internal environment interact with the external world?
- How are policy problems identified and problematized . . . realizing that these are often contested?
- How and why are decisions taken, or not taken?
- Are policy options considered and are policies evaluated?
- How is policy implemented and managed, and in a governance environment by whom?

This book has shown that while these questions are fundamental, many of them are not discrete. Many of the subject and problem areas and underlying processes interact with each other within a framework of interrelated policy cycles.

REFERENCES

Dolan, P., Hallsworth, M., Halpern, D. and Vlaev, I. (2009) *Mindspace. Influencing Behaviour through Public Policy*, London: Institute for Government and Cabinet Office.

Greener, I. (2005) 'State of the art – the potential of path dependence in political studies', *Politics*, 25, 1: 62–72.

Keleman, R.D. (2010) 'Globalising European Union environmental policy', *Journal of European Public Policy*, 17, 3: 335–349.

Pollitt, C. (2008) *Time, Policy, Management: governing with the past*, Oxford: Oxford University Press.

Pollitt, C. (2011) 'Mainstreaming technological change in the study of public management', *Public Policy and Administration*, 26, 4: 377–397.

Sachs, J. (2012) 'The election', *New York Review of Books*, 20 October 2012.

Younge, G. (2012) 'After Obama's re-election, liberals need to drop the blind devotion', *Guardian*, 9 November.

Index